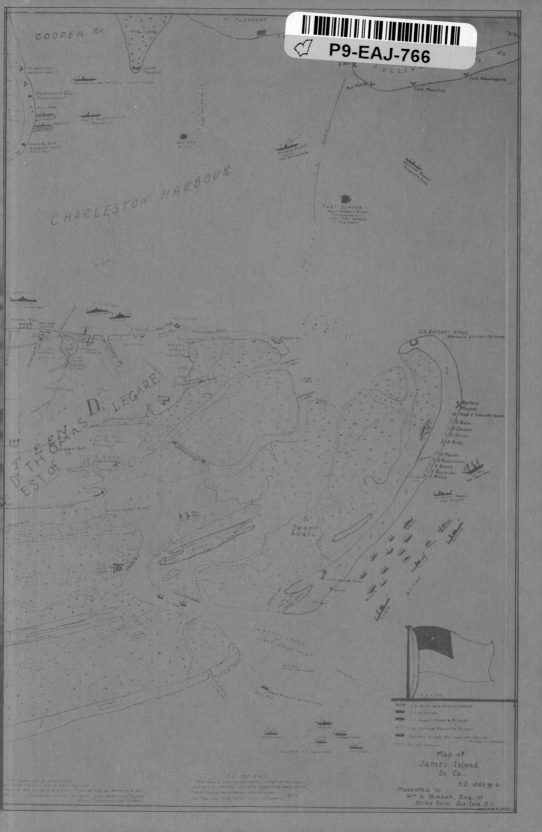

Map of
James Island
So. Ca.

A.D. 1863 & 4

Presented to
Wm. G. Hinson, Esq. of
Stiles' Point, Jas. Isld. S.C.

The SIEGE *of* CHARLESTON

E. MILBY BURTON, Director of the Charleston Museum and Chairman of the Charleston Historical Commission, himself has a distinguished naval record as a Commander USNR (Ret) and as the recipient of the Silver Star, earned in the Normandy-Brittany campaign. The author of two books, *South Carolina Silversmiths* and *Charleston Furniture,* he has also written articles for numerous journals, including the *William and Mary Quarterly* and the *Scientific Monthly.* He edited Sprunt and Chamberlain's *South Carolina Bird Life* and wrote the supplement for the revised edition. Listed in *American Men of Science,* he is also an honorary member of the Academia de San Romualdo, Spain.

FORT SUMTER AFTER THE FIRST MAJOR BOMBARDMENT

Painting by Leutz, Courtesy of the Charleston Museum

E. MILBY BURTON

The SIEGE of CHARLESTON
1861-1865

University of South Carolina Press
Columbia, South Carolina

Copyright © 1970 by the University of South Carolina Press
Published in Columbia, S.C., by the UNIVERSITY OF SOUTH CAROLINA PRESS, 1970

International Standard Book Number: 0–87249–125–0
Library of Congress Catalog Card Number: 70–120584

Manufactured in the UNITED STATES OF AMERICA *by*
KINGSPORT PRESS, INC., KINGSPORT, TENN.

Designed by ROBERT L. NANCE

Dedicated to My Father-in-Law
CHARLES COTESWORTH PINCKNEY
Captain, Confederate States Army
One of the Heroic Defenders of Charleston

ACKNOWLEDGMENTS

IN THE writing of this work I have had the assistance of many people, and I cannot regard it as complete until I have expressed to them in some manner my deep sense of gratitude. In no instance, at any place, or under any circumstances have I not been treated with the utmost courtesy—which all goes to prove that people are nice.

High on the list of those who were helpful are Miss Virginia Rugheimer and Mrs. Minnie Pringle Haigh of the Charleston Library Society. Looking back over the years spent in research, I must have been a sore trial to them, but never once did they lose their equanimity or lady-like behavior. They were always most helpful in every way possible, and to them I shall always be indebted.

Mrs. T. Granville Prior of the South Carolina Historical Society not only placed any material that I requested at my disposal, but made pertinent suggestions as to where I might find additional, and to me unknown, material of interest.

Mr. E. L. Inabinett and his entire staff at the South Caroliniana Library were always most cooperative. They, too, went out of their way to make available to me diaries, letters, and other material that I was unaware existed.

The Director of Naval History, Rear Admiral E. M. Eller, U.S.N. (Ret.), and the Assistant Director, Captain Kent Loomis, U.S.N. (Ret.), were not only cooperative in giving information requested, but always, in some manner, added some pertinent facts that were helpful.

The late Dr. J. Harold Easterby, former Director of the South Carolina Archives Department, gave freely of the store of knowledge that he carried in his head. Rarely did he consult a book or manuscript other than to tell me where to look in it. Mr. Francis M. Hutson, also of the Archives Department, always went out of his way to be helpful.

I also wish to thank Dr. James Heslin of the New-York Historical Society and Dr. Edouard A. Stackpole of the Marine Historical Association at Mystic, Conn., for giving me permission to quote from their publications; Dr. Harald R. Manakee of the Maryland Historical Society, for sending me a photograph of Winan's torpedo boat; and Mr. Nicholas Biddle Wainwright for letting me go through the files of the Philadelphia newspapers located in the Pennsylvania Historical Society.

To Mr. Caldwell Delaney of Mobile, Alabama, one of the foremost authorities on the *Hunley*, I am most grateful. Over the years we had a great deal of correspondence on this somewhat enigmatic submarine, and I am somewhat aghast to find that it was thirty years ago when I first started writing to Mr. Harold Sniffen of the Mariners Museum at Newport News, Va., on this same subject.

The monumental work *South Carolina Goes to War*, by the late Dr. Charles Cauthen, former head of the Department of History at Wofford College, was a constant source of reference. Dr. Cauthen and I corresponded at length on some of the debatable questions that arose in the first chapter of my book. I only wish I could thank him and let him know how much I appreciate his help.

To Mrs. Lila Hawes of the Georgia Historical Society; Mr. M. V. Brewington, formerly of the Peabody Museum in Salem, Mass., but now of the Kendall Whaling Museum; the Archivist of the Public Record Office in Belfast, North Ireland; Dr. Philip Ludenberg, Curator of Naval History at the Smithsonian Institute, as well as the librarians at Lansing, Michigan, and Providence, Rhode Island, I wish to express my deepest appreciation for their help.

To Mr. Arthur M. Wilcox and Mr. Warren Ripley, two dyed-in-the-wool Civil War buffs, I shall always be indebted for their constructive criticism. Mr. Emmett Robinson was helpful in many ways.

My lifelong friend, the Honorable L. Mendel Rivers, Congressman from the First District, and chairman of the Committee on Armed Services, U.S. House of Representatives, I wish to thank for expediting information requested from the Armed Services.

Mrs. Caroline Martin Borowsky typed most of the first draft of this work. How she deciphered my handwriting will always be an enigma to me, but, notwithstanding, she did an excellent job. To her I wish to express my deepest appreciation.

Finally, I shall ever be indebted to Mr. and Mrs. John G. Leland, for encouragement when my spirits were low, for their constructive criticism, and above all for their sound advice. Mrs. Leland typed the final draft of this work. They were wonderful.

Undoubtedly I have overlooked the names of some who were helpful. If your name does not appear, I wish to express my apologies. It was not a deliberate oversight.

To all of these wonderful people: *Thank you!*

E. Milby Burton
Charleston, South Carolina

CONTENTS

Introduction / xiii

1 THE UNION IS DISSOLVED / *1*

2 WAR / *66*

3 THE NAVY IN ACTION / *120*

4 MORRIS ISLAND / *151*

5 SUMTER BOMBARDED / *183*

6 THE BLOCKADE: Torpedoes and the Submarine / *211*

7 THE CITY BESIEGED / *251*

8 THE THIRD GREAT BOMBARDMENT OF SUMTER / *296*

9 A CITY OF ASHES / *304*

Bibliography / 327

Notes / 339

Index / 363

ILLUSTRATIONS

(*Frontispiece*)

FORT SUMTER AFTER THE FIRST BOMBARDMENT

(*Following page 172*)

OCCUPATION OF CASTLE PINCKNEY
FORT JOHNSON
FIRING ON THE *STAR OF THE WEST*
BOMBARDMENT OF PORT ROYAL
THE RAMMING OF THE UNION GUNBOAT *MERCEDITA*
CAPTAIN WIGG ACTING AS A HUMAN FLAGPOLE
THE IRONCLAD *KEOKUK*
INTERIOR OF FORT SUMTER AFTER FIRST GREAT BOMBARD-
    MENT
THE MAGAZINE OF FORT MOULTRIE
GUNBOATS IN CHARLESTON HARBOR—1863
THE BOAT ATTACK ON FORT SUMTER

(*Following page 204*)

UNION BATTERIES ON BLACK ISLAND
BOMBARDMENT OF THE CITY OF CHARLESTON
FORT SUMTER AFTER SECOND GREAT BOMBARDMENT
GUNS ON WHITE POINT GARDENS
SUBMARINE *HUNLEY*
THE TORPEDO-RAM *DAVID*
FLAG OVER FORT SUMTER
INTERIOR OF FORT SUMTER AFTER THIRD GREAT BOMBARD-
    MENT
PART OF THE CITY BURNED IN THE FIRE OF DECEMBER, 1861
NORTHEASTERN RAILROAD STATION AFTER THE EXPLOSION

INTRODUCTION

THE SIEGE of Charleston—and it was a siege even though the back door was open—probably differs from any other in history because so many kinds of warfare were involved. Hostilities started off with fort against fort. At least 13 modes of warfare were employed thereafter:

(1)   Sinking of ships to block the mouth of the harbor, thereby preventing, at least in theory, any vessel from entering or leaving the port.

(2)   Ships fighting ships.

(3)   A powerful fleet pitting its strength against forts and batteries.

(4)   Amphibious assaults preceded by devastating gunfire from the fleet just prior to the assault.

(5)   Ferocious hand-to-hand combat.

(6)   Large concentration of siege artillery to reduce a fortification.

(7)   Indiscriminate firing into the city by long-range guns to break the morale of its inhabitants.

(8)   Hurling "Greek fire" into the city to burn it to ashes.

(9)   Torpedo-boat attack against a powerful fleet.

(10)   The first successful submarine attack in history.

(11)   Large mine fields placed at the entrance of the harbor, thereby preventing a fleet from entering.

(12)   Heavily gunned men-of-war ascending rivers and battling with field artillery—not the usual concept of a warship.

(13)   Huge lights (Drummond) used to illuminate fortification at night.

Some of these methods were novel; others were older than organized war. The combinations of them may have been unique.

The length of the siege (587 days) is also remarkable. Few sieges have lasted longer. The hideous cacophony of gunfire continued for weeks on end. By night as well as by day silence was a rarity both welcome and suspect.

Citizen and soldier showed gallantry and fortitude enough to satisfy any chronicler, and the story of the defense of "the Cradle of the Secession" needs no embellishment. As symbols of the Confederacy, Charleston and Fort Sumter had to be defended at any cost. General Robert E. Lee, writing Major General Pemberton, then in command of the area, admonished him that Charleston must be held under all circumstances and if necessary fought "street by street and house by house." There might be complete obliteration, but there was to be no surrender.

As one Union officer put it after the city was evacuated, "And thus, after a siege which will rank among the most famous in history, Charleston becomes ours."

This work is an attempt to give, in some detail, the principal events from the Ordinance of Secession, passed on December 20, 1860, to the city's evacuation on February 17, 1865. It must not be assumed that no military action took place between the principal events. Quite the contrary, some type of skirmish, feint, or bombardment was going on almost every day, especially after November 7, 1861, when Admiral Du Pont gained control of Port Royal and Hilton Head Island. This gave the Union Army of some 13,000 men, backed by a powerful fleet, an excellent staging area to make raids, of which there were so many that the recitation of them would soon become boring. Furthermore, I have tried to confine myself to events in the general vicinity of Charleston, although Union forces were continually threatening the Charleston and Savannah Railroad above Beaufort, South Carolina. If they had been successful in cutting off the railroad, the Confederate forces would have had difficulty rushing reinforcements to various places along the coast when an attack threatened.

The political aspects of the events leading up to the war have been ignored. Much has been written on this subject, and doubtless as much more remains to be written. The only time politics is mentioned in the present study is when it has a direct bearing on one of the officers involved—usually in connection with his being removed from command.

My effort throughout has been to present the facts as objectively as I could after 100 years, during which Charleston has aged handsomely. It is hard not to be sentimental about Charleston, but my purpose has not been to defend again this beautiful city, whose charms are now the only defense she needs.

No doubt there was cowardice and folly on both sides, but there was also courage, courage tested and intensified by circumstances that were often as ferocious as any that men have ever faced. The impulse to salute the officers and men of both Confederate and Union forces is not a gesture of escape into the past. On the contrary, what remains not only fascinating but also soberly instructive in the story is the way it emphasizes the special quality of America's Civil War, that quality that caused Bismarck's officers to study it so intensively. For it was to the United States what World War I was to Europe, the last of the old wars and the first of the new. It involved and jeopardized the lives of civilians, of women, children, and old men, in the necessarily indiscriminate fashion that makes modern warfare so disgusting. But it also put some individuals under a fierce magnifying glass and gave them the opportunity that a different kind of war had offered men for millennia, the opportunity to have their loyalty, their bravery, their strength, and their gentleness splendidly displayed without egotism.

The men engaged in the siege of Charleston epitomized the best of American manhood. No attempt has been made to reconstruct incidents or conversations between individuals unless fully documented. History cannot be changed; it can only be clarified.

The SIEGE of CHARLESTON

1

The Union Is Dissolved

1

"THE UNION NOW SUBSISTING BETWEEN SOUTH CAROLINA AND other States, under the name of the 'United States of America' is hereby dissolved." Those 22 words were to affect the lives of millions living and the destinies of many yet unborn. The Union is dissolved. South Carolina no longer admits to being a part of the United States.

The Convention of the People of South Carolina had moved from the state capital at Columbia to Charleston because of smallpox. On December 20, 1860, it met in St. Andrew's Hall with 169 delegates ready to cast a vote that would split the union of 1787 and at the same time bring unity of force to the Republic.

The Ordinance of Secession had been drafted by the state's leaders. The Convention heard it read in polite silence. There was debate, quiet and orderly. Then the delegates voted, in alphabetical order. John H. Adams of Richland District was the first to cast his ballot on the question that was to put to physical test the United States Constitution. Henry C. Young of Laurens District made the break unanimous by joining the others in voting "yea."

When the result was announced to the citizens crowding Broad Street outside, a mighty shout notified those farther away. The news spread rapidly through the city, penetrating luxurious drawing rooms, echoing through offices on Lawyer's Row, even causing German merchants to close their shops and join in the celebration. Cannon roared. Flags of every description save one —the Stars and Stripes—hung from balconies, flew from poles, or were draped from windows. Grog shops and taverns overflowed. From the windows of the Charleston *Mercury* were tossed hastily printed sheets which read, "The Union Is Dissolved." There was bedlam in Charleston's usually quiet streets.

Though unanimous, the voice vote was not legally binding, and the delegates met again at 6:30 P.M. in St. Andrew's Hall, formed a solemn procession, and marched to the South Carolina Institute Hall. The seating capacity of Institute Hall was greater than that of St. Andrew's Hall, and the delegates felt that as many people as possible should witness the signing of so important a document as the Ordinance.

More than 3,000 persons were in the Institute Hall to cheer the delegates as they entered. Governor Francis W. Pickens and the members of both houses of the General Assembly were present. The Convention was called to order, and the Reverend John Bachman, the great naturalist, gave the opening prayer, asking divine blessing on the new Declaration of Independence. The Ordinance of Secession was spread on a table and the delegates, in alphabetical order by election districts, signed their names. Then the president of the Convention, David F. Jamison, rose before a hushed audience to proclaim that the state of South Carolina was "an Independent Commonwealth." [1]

The crowds flowed into the streets in an outburst of ecstasy. Bonfires were lighted, and Roman candles and rockets flashed into the night. Their glare was reflected in the gilded ball on top of St. Michael's and silhouetted St. Philip's spire. Church bells rang continuously; many private residences and places of business were brilliantly lighted. The "Liberty Pole" at Hayne and Meeting streets was illuminated with lanterns, whose flickering light cast shadows against the tall pillars of the Charleston Hotel, where celebrations were in full force. The state's military companies formed. Private citizens followed bands playing the "Marseillaise" in impromptu parades which marched to the homes of the most prominent citizens and moved on only when their demands for speeches were met. Above the sound of marching feet and shouting crowds church bells pealed and cannon thundered.[2]

Dawn came, and still the excitement continued. A large crowd serenaded Governor Pickens and then moved to the residence of Mayor Charles Macbeth. Two days later, the mayor had to issue a proclamation forbidding the shooting of fireworks within the city, except in time of public rejoicing, under penalty of a fine of ten dollars for each offense. However, only complete exhaustion of the celebrants brought quiet once again to the city.[3]

Meanwhile, the telegraph had carried news of South Carolina's secession to other parts of the United States. In Augusta, Georgia, the Washington Artillery fired a 100-gun salute as the sound of bells resounded from that inland city's churches. In Columbia, South Carolina's capital, the news was received with "every demonstration of joy." In Mobile, Alabama, the city was illuminated and the "wildest enthusiasm prevailed among all classes." Baltimore at first received the announcement quietly, with no demonstrations. The newspapers recorded it as "an historic fact, with special interest." In Philadelphia the stock market remained steady.[4]

In New York and Boston, however, most of the leading newspapers printed vitriolic editorials and launched vituperative attacks on the action of South Carolina. Washington, D.C., in spite of the fact that secession had long been seen as inevitable, was thrown into a frenzy of confusion.

It must not be assumed that the members of the South Carolina Convention were hot-headed young men. They were men of maturity and judgment, from every walk of life and stratum of

society in the state. Many were outstanding leaders in their pro-
fessions and vocations. They reflected the feelings of the vast
majority of the white citizens of South Carolina—a sentiment of
independence and a determination to secede at any cost. Few, if
any, foresaw that the outcome would be war and its tragic after-
math. The politicians thundered, but it is doubtful that they
really meant all they said.[5]

The news gathered momentum and penetrated every village,
city, and town in South Carolina. Military companies were
formed rapidly, and the most popular toast was "Damnation to
the Yankees." Moreover, if the South Carolinians were eager for
warlike action, there were businessmen from the North who saw
no reason not to make some money out of it. Captain A. H. Colt,
agent for Colt Revolvers, manufactured in Hartford, Connecticut,
was staying at the Charleston Hotel, from the portico of which
the events of December 20 were visible. He gave out information
concerning his company's famous weapon and took orders for
delivery. An agent for the Maynard Arms Company, a Massachusetts firm, set up headquarters in the Mills House. With so few
arms owned in the state, and with military companies being
formed almost every hour, the two did a profitable business.[6]

2

With cheers and exhilaration South Carolina became a free
and independent nation—with the exception of approximately 15
acres of strategically important land.

Dominating the sea approaches to Charleston harbor and the
harbor and city itself were three federally occupied fortifications
—Fort Moultrie, on Sullivan's Island at the northeast side of the
harbor entrance; Fort Sumter, on a sand bar almost in the center
of the lower harbor; and "Castle" Pinckney, only three quarters
of a mile from the city on a low-lying island. These fortifications
were supplied by an arsenal within the city proper.

Fort Moultrie was a post-Revolutionary War brick fort of no

great strength; it had been built for the sole purpose of protecting the harbor from an invasion from the sea. Because its military importance was limited, it had been permitted to fall into a state of near ruin. The walls were badly cracked, and sand, blown from the beach, was piled high in drifts along the southwestern wall facing the channel. The guns, which were set in barbettes (on a platform protected only from the sea side), were vulnerable, and the fort was almost indefensible from the land side. Numerous buildings and high sand dunes could cover an attacking force from the mainland.

Fort Moultrie's walls were dominated by the guns of Fort Sumter, about a mile away across the open channel. Fort Sumter was the strong point of the harbor defenses, standing as it did in the center of the passageway to the sea. It commanded all ship channels and could provide fire power against the entire shoreline of the harbor at its back, as well as against the whole city of Charleston.[7] Work on the fort, begun in 1829, had progressed slowly, and 31 years later was far from finished. However, its walls were 60 feet high, and the pentagonally shaped structure covered about two and a half acres of a sand spit that was almost completely under water at high tide. The fort had been designed for two tiers of guns in casemates and one in barbette, but few of the guns had been properly mounted and much work remained to be done before the fort could be considered ready to withstand a prolonged siege. No garrison was maintained in it, and it stood tall and empty above the water, a monument to the reluctance of the national Congress to spend money on the military.

Farther up the harbor, at the southern tip of a marshy island about three-fourths of a mile east of Charleston's wealthy downtown residential area, stood Castle Pinckney. This was a small brick fort begun in 1808, with one tier of casemates to house its guns. Its garrison consisted of one officer, an ordnance sergeant, and some laborers who were repairing the fort.[8]

On the western side of the city, overlooking the marshes of the Ashley River, was the Federal Arsenal, which contained a large quantity of military materiel belonging to the United States government. This unit was commanded by a military storekeeper with a staff of several men.

Over these four military posts—Fort Moultrie, Fort Sumter, Castle Pinckney, and the Arsenal—the American flag floated defiantly as the South Carolinians in Charleston went about the business of divorcing their state from the Union.

On November 15, 1860, Major Robert Anderson, U.S.A., had been ordered to report to Fort Moultrie for duty to relieve Brevet Colonel J. L. Gardner. Formerly, Fort Moultrie had been a post sought after by army officers because the cordial relations between its officers and the people of Charleston made it a socially desirable assignment.[9]

Major Anderson's assignment to Moultrie, however, was not because of the social joys of the area. The tension that had been building up within South Carolina and the events that were leading up to the Ordinance of Secession had made the army look for a special officer for Fort Moultrie. It was hoped that Major Anderson would alleviate some of the tension. Militarily, he had an outstanding record, having fought in the Black Hawk, Seminole, and Mexican wars. He was wounded in the latter and had been twice brevetted (promoted) for gallantry in action.

More important, however, he was from Kentucky, and his wife was from Georgia. Only recently he had owned slaves and property in Georgia, and it was known that his sympathies were largely with the South. This combination of military talent and social acceptability made him an altogether admirable choice; if anyone could keep relations smooth, he might. His father had taken part in the defense of Fort Moultrie (Fort Sullivan) during the Revolutionary War, and Anderson had served a previous tour at Moultrie. Consequently, he had a special interest in Charleston.

Upon his arrival, Anderson found discipline lax. Old Colonel Gardner had not bothered with the details of maintaining an army post and had had even less liking for political matters. Major Anderson immediately found himself in a difficult situation. He was in charge of three fortifications and an arsenal, had been assigned the unenviable task of avoiding aggression, and yet was obligated to repel any efforts to capture the forts.[10]

His first action was to inspect the fortifications. This was followed by a report to Colonel Cooper, Adjutant General of the United States Army (later to become Adjutant General of the Confederate Army), in which he strongly recommended that Castle Pinckney be made secure from attack. Since Castle Pinckney's guns commanded the city, Anderson reasoned that the Charlestonians would not venture to attack Fort Moultrie. He wrote: "Fort Sumter and Castle Pinckney must be garrisoned immediately if the government determines to keep command of the harbor." In the same letter Anderson stated that he realized his position was politico-military rather than strictly military and asked for specific instructions from the government. Aware of the delicacy of his position, he wrote: "I need not say how anxious I am—indeed determined, so far as honor will permit—to avoid collision with the citizens of South Carolina." [11]

The word "honor" was to play an important part in Major Anderson's future negotiations with the South Carolina authorities. The Adjutant General replied to him: "If attacked, you are of course expected to defend the trust committed to you to the best of your ability." Early in December, accompanied by Colonel Benjamin Huger, U.S.A., Anderson met with the mayor of Charleston and several prominent citizens. He came away from that meeting with the feeling that within two weeks South Carolina would be out of the Union. He was correct.[12]

The Assistant Adjutant General, Major Don Carlos Buell, was sent down from Washington to inspect the fortifications. On December 11 Buell gave Anderson the following verbal instructions: "You are to hold possession of the forts in this harbor and, if attacked, you are to defend yourself to the last extremity. The smallness of your force will not permit you, perhaps, to occupy more than one of the three forts . . . and you may put your command into either of them which you may deem most proper to increase its power of resistance." There was no ambiguity in this order, and since it came from the assistant adjutant general, who had been sent to Charleston specifically to examine the situation there and direct Major Anderson as to how to proceed, there was no reason that it should not be carried out. Anderson was used to carrying out orders to the letter.[13]

Ten days later, however, when President Buchanan heard of Buell's verbal orders to Anderson, he disapproved of the clause stating that the forts should be defended "to the last extremity." He instructed the Secretary of War to write Major Anderson as follows: "It is neither expected nor desired that you should expose your own life, or that of your men, in a hopeless conflict in defense of these forts. . . . It will be your duty to yield to necessity and make the best terms in your power." [14]

While these somewhat political decisions were being made, all three fortifications were being prepared for defense as quickly as possible, with laborers under the supervision of Captain J. G. Foster, Corps of Engineers. It was discovered that guns had not been mounted on Fort Sumter because of the decayed condition of the gun carriages, and Major Anderson questioned the advisability of having these guns mounted for fear that they would be turned against Fort Moultrie if Sumter were seized. He also asked Washington for instructions about leveling the sand dunes that dominated Fort Moultrie. He was refused permission for fear such a move might precipitate an armed confrontation with the South Carolinians. Captain Foster suggested that small mines be placed around Fort Moultrie and that the magazine at Fort Sumter be fitted with an electric device that could be detonated from Fort Moultrie in case state troops occupied the fort.

The tension was so great that when forty muskets for use by the Union troops were sent from the Arsenal in the city to Fort Moultrie, such excitement erupted that they were returned in order to avoid an incident.[15]

Anticipating that Major Anderson would move his forces to Fort Sumter, Governor Pickens, on December 18, 1860—two days before the Ordinance of Secession—ordered a guard boat with a detachment of troops to patrol the waters between Moultrie and Sumter. If Anderson did indeed attempt to occupy Sumter, Pickens' men were under orders "to forbid it and, if persevered in, to resist it by force, and then immediately to take Fort Sumter at all hazards." Upon his return to Columbia, the Governor reported his action to the Senate and House. He was assuming considerable responsibility, since he had been elected only recently, November 30, on the seventh ballot.[16]

In the meantime, the state authorities had sent guns to the upper end of Sullivan's Island and had begun the construction of batteries there. Another battery was being set up on Mount Pleasant with provision for two large mortars.[17]

On December 20, South Carolina's secession converted the Federal military units into forces of a foreign nation menacing Charleston. Two days later Major Anderson suggested to Washington in even stronger terms that he be authorized to move his entire force to Fort Sumter, even though he realized that to do this he would have to sacrifice the greater part of his stores. This is probably when Anderson made up his mind to move to Sumter. However, he knew that if the move was to be a succcess not even his company commanders could be informed about it. He made a point of spreading the belief, both among his troops and to persons outside the fort, that he was preparing to make a desperate stand if Moultrie was besieged. Furthermore, he talked freely about evacuating the women and children and moving them to Fort Johnson. This was an old pre-Revolutionary fort across the harbor which was not only unarmed but in ruins.

Captain Foster was requested—not instructed, because he was an engineer and not under Major Anderson's command—to discontinue mounting the guns on Fort Sumter for fear that they would be used against Moultrie. Anderson then ordered Lieutenant Hall, the acting Quartermaster, to procure transportation for the women and children to be taken to Fort Johnson in case of an attack on Moultrie. Aboard the small schooners used for this purpose Anderson placed most of his provisions, ostensibly for Captain Foster's laborers at Fort Sumter.[18]

On the afternoon of December 26, the schooners with the

women and children left the dock at Moultrie under the command of Lieutenant Hall. Not until then did Major Anderson reveal his plan. He instructed Hall to delay unloading his personnel and cargo under the pretext of finding suitable quarters at Fort Johnson. When he heard two guns, Hall was to come at once to Fort Sumter. As soon as the schooners left, Major Anderson instructed Captain Foster—this time Foster took orders from Anderson—to collect all available boats and have them ready between five and six o'clock that afternoon. It was then that he told Foster of his plan. He had chosen that hour because it would be dusk. In the morning he had given orders to the men to pack their knapsacks when they went to their posts and to do it daily as if it were a matter of routine operations.

About sunset Captain and Mrs. Abner Doubleday set out to find Major Anderson to invite him to tea. By this time Mrs. Doubleday was one of the few women left on the post. They found Anderson on the parapet in earnest conversation with a group of his officers. As Doubleday walked up, Anderson greeted him with these words: "I have determined to evacuate this post immediately for the purpose of occupying Fort Sumter. I can allow you 20 minutes to form your company and be in readiness to start."

Doubleday made hasty arrangements for Mrs. Doubleday's safety, put his company into the small boats, and gave the order to row to Fort Sumter. During their transit Captain Foster, Surgeon Crawford, Lieutenant Jefferson C. Davis, and a small detail manned the guns facing Sumter; they had orders to fire on the state guard boat should she attempt to interfere.

As expected, the guard boat appeared and stopped within a hundred yards. When he first saw her approach, Captain Doubleday ordered his men to take off their caps and turn their overcoats so that the military buttons might not be seen. After scrutinizing them as closely as possible in the near darkness, the guard boat turned away, its commander thinking that the boats contained the laborers who daily passed back and forth between Sumter and Moultrie.

When the troops arrived at Fort Sumter, the laborers there were greatly excited. Most of them were Southern sympathizers, but since they were unarmed, they could offer no resistance and were quickly herded back into the fort. The gates were closed and sentinels posted. Meanwhile the rowboats went back to Fort Moultrie and returned with the second company of troops, this time attracting no attention from the guard boat. When the last man from Moultrie was on Sumter, the two guns were fired, signaling recall of the schooners waiting at Fort Johnson with the women, children, and supplies aboard.[19] The captain of one of the schooners, realizing that he had been duped, put up a fight and had to be overcome by force.

Major Anderson was on Fort Sumter with all of his men except one officer (Meade) and a sergeant who were on Castle Pinckney. Captain Foster and Lieutenant Davis had been left at Fort Moultrie with a few men for the purpose of spiking the guns and burning the carriages. Along with the women, children, and laborers, there were nearly four months' rations and a good supply of hospital stores and ammunition at the fort. Early the next morning additional ammunition and supplies were brought over from Moultrie.[20]

Charleston was just beginning to recover from the effects of the celebration that followed passage of the Ordinance of Secession when, on the morning of December 27, dense smoke was seen rising from Fort Moultrie. Mayor Macbeth, believing that the fort had accidentally caught fire, immediately chartered a steamer and ordered two fire companies to go to the aid of Major Anderson, although this was in violation of a city ordinance.

The chartered steamer was getting under way when a man rowed across the harbor from Sullivan's Island with the report that the guns of Fort Moultrie had been spiked, the carriages were burning, and Major Anderson and his entire garrison were established on Fort Sumter. This information was confirmed by the guard boat *Nina*, which sped back to the city with the information.

When the Charlestonians realized the seriousness of the situation, there was widespread dismay. Rumors were numerous. Most people thought that Sumter's guns were trained on the city and that the bombardment would begin momentarily.[21] People climbed church steeples and rooftops with telescopes to satisfy their curiosity and verify the fact that the Federal troops were actually at Sumter. Others went by boat to Sullivan's Island to view the now disarmed Fort Moultrie.[22]

When the initial excitement had passed, officers in the South Carolina militia admitted that Anderson's move was one of "consummate wisdom." More to Anderson's liking, however, was the fact that it met with the "entire approbation" of General Wool, Commanding Officer of the Department of the East and Anderson's Superior Officer.

Although military minds looked on Anderson's action as a smart move, the politicians reacted differently. President Buchanan and his cabinet were horrified, and South Carolina's Governor Pickens and the Secession Convention were stunned by the move.[23]

3

Quickly recovering from his surprise, Governor Pickens sent one of his aides, Colonel J. Johnston Pettigrew, and Major Ellison Capers to Fort Sumter to demand "courteously, but preemptorily" that Major Anderson and his command return to Fort Moultrie. Major Anderson replied equally courteously that he "could not and would not" comply with the governor's request. Colonel Pettigrew then stated that in moving his command to Fort Sumter Anderson had violated an agreement between former Governor William H. Gist and President James Buchanan that no reinforcements be sent to Sumter. Anderson replied that he had not sent reinforcements, but had merely transferred his command from one fort to another, which, as commander of the harbor, he had a right to do. Apparently it was the first he had heard of the unwritten agreement. It was not until Colonel Pettigrew and Major Capers were leaving that Anderson said: "In this controversy between the North and South my sympathies are entirely with the South. These gentlemen [referring to his officers, who were present at the conversation] know it perfectly well." He added that his sense of duty to the United States Army overrode any personal feelings in the matter.[24]

When Colonel Pettigrew returned to the city with Anderson's negative answer, Governor Pickens on orders from the Convention, which had gone into secret session, ordered three companies of South Carolina troops to seize Castle Pinckney. The troops, consisting of detachments from the Washington Light Infantry, the Meagher Guards, and the Carolina Light Infantry, were under command of Colonel Pettigrew.[25] The troops boarded the guard boat *Nina* and set out across the three-quarter mile Cooper River channel toward the marshy island (Shute's Folly) of which Pinckney occupied the southwestern point.

The *Nina* arrived at Castle Pinckney about 4 P.M. The troops expected resistance and thought this would be the first real fight of the impending war. They were deployed and advanced with caution, dashing forward to the walls at the command "Charge." To their chagrin they were met by Lieutenant Meade, the ordnance sergeant and his family, and a party of civilian laborers who were at work repairing the fort. Meade, unable to offer any resistance, could only remonstrate with Colonel Pettigrew. When Pettigrew offered to give him a receipt for the "public property," Meade refused, stating that he did not recognize Governor Pickens' authority. In spite of Meade's refusal to give his parole—since war had not been declared, he did not consider himself a prisoner of war—he was allowed to go to Fort Sumter. When the United States flag was taken down, a flag with a white star on a red ground was hoisted in its place. The flag was borrowed from the *Nina* because no one had thought to bring one on the expedition. In seizing Castle Pinckney, Governor Pickens committed the first overt act of war. This took place before the *Star of the West* was fired on and months before the opening shots on Fort Sumter.[26]

While Castle Pinckney was peacefully changing hands, 225

additional South Carolina troops were being assembled. These were detachments from the Washington, German, Lafayette, and Marion artilleries. Under the command of Lt. Col. Wilmot G. DeSaussure, they marched to the Cooper River wharves to await transportation to Fort Moultrie. When the *Nina* returned from Castle Pinckney, the troops boarded her and another paddle-wheel steamer, the *General Clinch*. These two vessels left Charleston about 7 P.M. for Sullivan's Island. Since it was dark, the troops advanced cautiously towards Fort Moultrie upon debarkation, their advance slowed by rumors that some of Captain Foster's mines had been placed around the fort. When they reached the fort, Col. Charles Allston, another of the governor's aides who accompanied the units, advanced and demanded its surrender. Instead of finding it occupied by Federal troops, he met only an overseer and several laborers.

Because there was no resistance, Allston, DeSaussure, and a few of the state troops quietly marched into the fort, planted the Palmetto flag, and took possession. The rest of the troops remained outside until the following morning before occupying the fort. For more than four years the Palmetto flag continued to fly over Fort Moultrie along with the Confederate one.[27]

The actions of Professor John McCrady of the College of Charleston are indicative of the war fever that was sweeping Charleston. McCrady, an engineering and physics teacher, stowed away on the *Nina* when he learned that the militia companies in which two of his brothers served were to make the assault on the island fort. He went ashore with the soldiers and soon after was commissioned as an engineer and assigned to the work of constructing a battery on Morris Island. He was not missed at the college until the faculty assembled after the Christmas holidays. McCrady's action had immediate results among the students: The entire senior class petitioned the faculty for indefinite leaves of absence and upon approval left the academic world for the infinitely harsher military life. Professor McCrady was commended by General Beauregard for his work on the Morris Island battery and later was in charge of building the fortifications at Savannah, Georgia.[28]

Despite the gravity of the situation, there was one amusing incident. F. C. Humphreys, military storekeeper at the Arsenal, who at various times is referred to as "Captain," accompanied Colonel Allston and his troops to Fort Moultrie. It must have been strange to see a Union officer in the midst of South Carolina state troops taking possession of an abandoned Federal fort. Humphreys wrote a letter to the editor of the *Mercury*, which was published the following morning, stating that he had gone along, through the kindness of Colonel Allston, to deliver a dispatch from the United States secretary of war to the officer in charge of Fort Moultrie. Humphreys must have suspected that by the time he arrived at Fort Moultrie there would be no officer in charge. Nevertheless, if he was bound by duty to deliver a dispatch, he was going to deliver it.[29]

The Arsenal, located on the city's west side at the head of a small marsh creek that afforded access by boat at high tide, had been in something of a state of seizure since November 12, when a detachment consisting of an officer and 20 South Carolina troops had been stationed outside its walls to see that no arms were transferred to the forts in the harbor. The state troops on the outside and the 14 Federal troops inside the 12-acre enclosure were apparently on friendly terms during the period of extreme tension.[30]

Humphreys, a military storekeeper of ordnance, was in charge during this time, with the exception of a short period during which Col. Benjamin Huger, U.S.A., took over command. The Washington authorities thought that the presence of Colonel Huger, a South Carolinian, would appease the feelings of hostility toward Federal troops in the forts and the Arsenal. After a short while, however, Huger returned to Washington and Humphreys again took over.

The Arsenal was an important prize. It had in storage nearly 18,000 muskets, about 3,400 rifles, over 1,000 pistols, and a few

large pieces of ordnance, including five 24-pound field howitzers
—arms enough to equip three divisions.

On December 30, Governor Pickens ordered the Arsenal occupied by state forces, and the Seventeenth Regiment of Infantry
moved in under the command of Col. John Cunningham. Humphreys was allowed to salute his flag before lowering it. He did so
by firing a 32-gun salute, one for each state remaining in the
Union at that time, and he was permitted to take the flag with
him. Since he and his detachment were to occupy their regular
quarters at the Arsenal until instructions could be received from
Washington, Humphreys did not go far. While living in the
Arsenal awaiting these orders, he became alarmed at the careless
manner in which the state troops handled ordnance stores, and he
reported that he expected to be blown up at any moment.[31]

4

Governor Pickens anticipated that it would be only a matter of
time before an attempt would be made to reinforce Major Anderson and his beleaguered garrison at Fort Sumter. On December
31, 1860, therefore, he ordered Major General Schnierle of the
state forces to select a site on Morris Island at which to erect a
battery beyond range of the guns of Sumter. The governor also
wanted Major Stevens and forty cadets of the Citadel Academy to
man the battery and urged that it be constructed as quickly as
possible. His orders were promptly carried out, and a battery
known as Fort Morris was built, consisting of four 24-pound field
howitzers. Its location was such that it dominated the main ship
channel.[32]

The only way to get supplies to Fort Sumter was by water.
Believing that the main channel would be used if an attempt were
made, Pickens ordered Lt. William H. Ryan of the Irish Volunteers and a detail of 20 men from the Fourth Brigade to board the
guard ship *General Clinch* and patrol the bar between 7 P.M. and
daylight. They were to intercept and sink any small boats from

vessels outside the bar which might try to land troops to reinforce Sumter. There was no ambiguity in the governor's order. He admonished Ryan to communicate with the commanders of Fort Moultrie and Morris Island lest he be fired on by mistake.[33] As anticipated, an attempt was made to send aid, in the form of supplies and troops, to Major Anderson. The steamer *Star of the West* was chartered at a cost of $1250 per day. In order to maintain secrecy, she was loaded with supplies and 200 men in New York harbor. Tugs with men and supplies ran alongside her, and the transfer was made on January 5 under cover of night. The ship was on a regular run between New Orleans and New York, and those responsible for sending her thought that if no notice of her departure appeared in the local press, it would naturally be assumed that she had left, as usual, for New Orleans. To further insure secrecy, all communications were cut off between Governor's Island, the point of embarkation, and New York City.

With so many Southern sympathizers in New York, the question of maintaining secrecy was almost ludicrous. On January 7, the *New York Times* came out with the following: "*The Star of the West* is, without doubt already on her way to Charleston. . . . during Saturday night it is believed that some three hundred marines were put on board by a steam tug. . . . they were undoubtedly received on board the steamer, which during the night proceeded to sea." Actually, 200 of the "best-instructed" men, along with a three-month subsistence supply, were placed aboard the ship under the command of 1st Lt. Charles R. Woods of the Ninth Infantry. Upon approaching Charleston harbor, Lieutenant Woods was instructed to place his entire force below deck so that only the ordinary crew could be seen by persons on shore.[34]

On the same day, a telegram was sent from New York to either Governor Pickens or Robert Barnwell Rhett, editor of the Charleston *Mercury*, stating that the *Star of the West* had gone to reinforce Fort Sumter. It was signed, simply, "Jones." The following day two more telegrams arrived stating that the ship was on her way. Actually, the only person kept in secrecy as to her movements was Major Anderson at Fort Sumter.[35]

In order not to arrive prematurely off Charleston, the *Star of the West* stopped about 70 miles from the bar, which should have placed her somewhere off Georgetown, South Carolina, and her crew fished for about three hours. The captain, knowing that she might be fired upon, made arrangements for steering the ship from the lower deck in case the wheelhouse was shot away, and men were stationed below to plug the holes with mattresses should she be hit. Arriving at the harbor entrance about midnight, the pilot brought down from New York found all of the entrance lights extinguished; consequently, the ship groped around in the dark until almost daylight, when the Fort Sumter light was located. At this time the *Star of the West* was discovered by the pilot boat anchored at the entrance of the bar by orders of Governor Pickens. Paying no attention to the pilot boat, she steamed over the bar, at which time she was seen by the guard boat *General Clinch*, which preceded her up the channel, firing rockets to alert the gunners.[36]

In the meantime, the Citadel cadets, under the command of Maj. Peter F. Stevens, were sleeping in the sand dunes. One of the sentries who patrolled the lonely beach, Cadet W. S. Simkins, was only a boy. When he saw a rocket fired from the guard ship, he stopped suddenly and, realizing its significance, woke his companions, who rushed to their guns. There was no confusion, for the cadets were well drilled. As soon as the *Star of the West* was opposite the battery, the guns were aimed, but there was some hesitation on the part of the senior officers. They knew that firing on a ship flying the flag of the United States could precipitate a war.[37] However, Major Stevens quickly gave the order to "commence firing," and the Cadet Captain passed the order "Number One fire." The lanyard of number one gun was pulled by Cadet George Edward Haynesworth from Sumter County, South Carolina. The gun was purposely aimed in front of the ship, and the ball skipped ahead of the vessel. Paying no attention to the shot except to break out a huge garrison flag from her foremast—one was already flying from the peak—the *Star of the West* continued on at undiminished speed. A moment later the second gun fired. This time the ship itself was the target. From then on the firing was general. Major Ripley (later Brigadier General) ordered the guns at Fort Moultrie into action. One, a Columbiad nicknamed "Edith," opened up with a roar, but the shot went wild, for the *Star* was still out of range. Other guns at Moultrie fired, but they soon ceased because their shots were going wild. Meanwhile, firing from the battery on Morris Island continued with precision, but most of the balls passed over the ship. The guns were depressed to shorten their range, and soon the ship was hit near the rudder and in the bow. The shore batteries had found the range, and no help was coming from Fort Sumter. The *Star of the West* turned away and, after scraping bottom several times while recrossing the bar, headed back to New York harbor.[38]

During this incident Major Anderson ran out his guns, but since he had received no notice that reinforcements were being sent—he had read about it in the local newspaper but didn't believe it—he did not open fire for fear of precipitating a general engagement. A dispatch had been sent to him from New York, dated January 5, telling him that the *Star of the West* was being sent with reinforcements and supplies and that if she was fired upon he could use his guns to "silence such fire." The dispatch never reached him. Consequently, with some of his officers urging him to return the fire (Davis) and others imploring him to refrain (Meade), Major Anderson ran out his guns only as a show of force.

The excitement of the soldiers in the fort, as well as their wives, when they saw the *Star* approaching under fire, required the exercise of authority on the part of the officers to keep the men from firing. The wife of one of the soldiers was restrained with difficulty from pulling the lanyard of one of the guns. But this excitement changed to dismay when the *Star* turned away.[39]

Later that day, Anderson wrote to Governor Pickens that he

had not been notified that war had been declared. The "running out" of his guns caused an uneasy moment both at Fort Moultrie and at the battery on Morris Island, although actually the latter was out of range of the Sumter guns.

The sound of the firing created intense excitement in the city. People rushed out of their homes and hurried toward the Battery and the wharves to see what the shooting was about. Several companies of troops were sent to different localities in case they should be needed. The cannonading could be heard for miles around. Families who were awakened by it immediately dispatched their house servants on the fastest horses to ascertain what was going on. To everyone within earshot the sound of the guns meant war.[40]

The following day the *Mercury*, describing the "expulsion" of the *Star of the West*, stated that "yesterday morning was the opening ball of the Revolution. We are proud that our harbor has been so honored." The incident meant war to those in Fort Sumter as well. Capt. J. G. Foster (later to become a major general) wrote in his report: "The firing upon the Star of the West by the batteries on Morris Island opened the war. . . ."

The officers on the *Star of the West* were highly complimentary of the shooting ability of the cadets; they said that the guns were fired rapidly and with a will. One humorist aboard remarked: "The people of Charleston pride themselves upon their hospitality, but it exceeded my expectations. They gave us several balls before we landed." [41]

Thus the first shot fired in the war was from a gun on Morris Island against a vessel loaded with troops and supplies and flying the American flag. Over Fort Morris waved a Palmetto flag presented by the ladies of Hugh E. Vincent's family, owners at that time of most of Morris Island.[42] The South Carolina state flag could be of any color as long as it had a palmetto tree on it. The one that flew over Fort Morris at the time the *Star of the West* was fired on was red; the one flying over Moultrie was white with a green palmetto tree. In order to avoid confusion and to standardize the color, it was decided that the flag have a blue field with a white palmetto tree and crescent superimposed. This was officially adopted on January 28, 1861.[43]

5

Major Anderson must have felt that his failure to defend the *Star of the West* by opening fire on the South Carolina batteries had lost him stature in the eyes of his officers and men. After the incident, he told his command that he proposed to close the port of Charleston and fire on any ship that attempted to enter. That same day he dispatched a note to Governor Pickens asking if the firing on the *Star* had been done without Pickens' sanction; this hope had restrained him from opening up on Moultrie. He stated further that, if he did not receive an answer within a reasonable time, he would fire on any vessel that came within range of his guns. The note was given to Lieutenant Hall, who was rowed over to Charleston in a boat flying a white flag. When Hall arrived at the city, he was surrounded by an excited crowd, who thought he was bringing notice that the city was to be bombarded. Making his way to City Hall, he found Governor Pickens in a meeting. The governor promptly adjourned it to receive him and, after reading the note, asked Hall to wait for his reply. After some delay, the governor gave him his answer, and Hall returned as quickly as possible to deliver it to Major Anderson.

The governor's response must have been a surprise to Anderson. Instead of disavowing the firing on the *Star*, he said that he was perfectly justified in his action because the president of the United States had been officially notified that the sending of any reinforcements to Sumter would be regarded as "an act of hostility." Furthermore, he had placed special agents (the pilot boat) at the bar to warn off any vessel having troops on board to reinforce Sumter and had given orders to all battery commanders not to fire at the vessel, but to fire a warning shot across her bow.[44] As for the closing of the port of Charleston, the governor went on to say "that you must judge of your own responsibilities." Upon consultation with his officers, Anderson found out for the first time that a warning shot had been fired across the bow of the *Star* and had been disregarded. For this reason he decided not to carry out the threat of closing the harbor until he received instructions from Washington.[45]

The governor, realizing that if Sumter could not be secured by peaceful negotiations it would have to be taken by force, the following day ordered certain guns removed from Castle Pinckney and sent to Fort Moultrie "to be put in a newly constructed battery at the east end of Sullivan's Island." To prevent reinforcements from reaching Sumter at night, steps were taken to light the harbor with huge Drummond lights. In addition, the steamers *Aid* and *Marion* were taken into the service of the state as guard ships to assist the *General Clinch* and *Nina* in protecting the harbor.[46]

It was also decided to sink vessels in the main ship channel in order to keep out deep-draft men-of-war. Four old hulks, gifts from the citizens of Savannah, were brought over, loaded with granite being used in the construction of the Custom House, and sunk in the channels. One exception was Maffitt's Channel, which nearly paralleled Sullivan's Island. In case any vessel tried to sneak through this channel to bring supplies to Sumter, a vessel loaded with stone was anchored at the "end" of the channel to be sunk at a moment's notice. Daily it was becoming more difficult for any expedition to bring in troops or supplies to beleaguered Sumter. In spite of the fact that the wind and tide were washing away the superstructures of the sunken vessels, there was sufficient obstruction left to prevent any vessel drawing over 12 or 13 feet from entering. Because of the blocked channel, larger merchant vessels were diverted to Savannah, which seriously reduced the trade coming into Charleston. One humorist remarked that the citizens of Savannah would be happy to present additional hulks to be sunk in the channels.[47]

There was an almost semicircular ring of batteries surrounding Sumter, but it was felt that some sort of battery should be placed between Sumter and the city. Capt. John Hamilton, C.S.N., who had just resigned from the United States Navy, developed an idea for a floating battery. With Maj. J. H. Trapier he presented his idea to the South Carolina Executive Council, which authorized $12,000 for its construction with the understanding that it would be completed in three weeks. Actually the floating battery was nothing more than a huge barge roofed over with iron which was able to contain two 42-pound guns and two 32-pound guns. The weight of the guns and armor was so great that sandbags had to be placed opposite them to keep the barge from capsizing. Since it had no motive power, the floating battery could only be towed into position. There was a great deal of comment both pro and con; critics of the floating battery referred to it as a slaughter pen.[48]

The floating battery was accredited to Captain Hamilton, which apparently disturbed Major Trapier, for he wrote to D. F. Jamison, secretary of war for South Carolina, that the idea was *his* plan and that before submitting it to the Executive Council he had explained it to Captain Hamilton. Trapier wrote that Hamilton had "warmly approved of it and expressed the strongest convictions of its success." Whoever its designer was, it was built in Charleston and was used during the initial bombardment of Fort Sumter. Major Trapier gave its dimensions as 80 by 40 feet and said that it had an eight-foot draft.[49]

Knowing that the garrison at Sumter was desperately in need of fresh meat and vegetables, Governor Pickens, after cutting off their supplies, relented and sent a boat containing meat and vegetables to the fort. Major Anderson was puzzled by the boat's arrival, for he had ordered no supplies. When he realized that it was a gift, he decided with "due thanks to his excellency, respectfully to decline his offer." The garrison was disappointed by Anderson's action, for they had been on a monotonous diet of salt pork and bread, but they returned the food to the boat "without complaint," though with much regret.[50]

In the meantime, the small garrison and the party of workmen were engaged in fortifying Sumter as fast as possible. Fifty-one guns had been placed in position by January 21, and Major Anderson for the first time was beginning to feel secure. State forces under the command of Brig. Gen. John Dunovant were hastily constructing batteries at Fort Johnson and Morris Island. Fort Moultrie was being strengthened, and batteries were being placed on Sullivan's Island. Major Anderson and his officers could see the ring of steel being drawn tighter and tighter around them.[51]

Governor Pickens knew that conditions in Washington were fluid, that there was no fixed policy on the part of the federal government, and he realized that Major Anderson was probably in the most difficult position any American officer had ever found himself; therefore, he decided to attempt to coerce Anderson into surrendering Sumter. He sent former Federal Judge Magrath, now secretary of state for South Carolina, and David F. Jamison, former president of the Convention, now secretary of war for the state, to Fort Sumter with a note to Anderson "to induce the delivery of Fort Sumter to the constituted authorities of the State of South Carolina." Arriving in a small steamer with a white flag tied to its mast, they were met at the wharf by Anderson and escorted to the guardroom, where they handed him the letter from the governor. Anderson knew immediately that his answer would be "No," but he called his officers aside to discuss it; they were unanimous for its rejection. Young Lieutenant Meade brought out the fact that Lieutenant Talbot was on his way to Washington and that they should wait to see what instruction he brought back with him. Major Anderson politely sent his regrets to the gentlemen from South Carolina, saying that he would not surrender the fort, as such a decision was solely up to his government. Magrath, a gifted orator, then gave an impassioned talk; he said that the United States government was almost dissolved, that all was confusion in Washington, and that it was time the garrison looked after its own safety, since South Carolina was going to take Sumter at any cost. When they left with Anderson's polite but negative reply, Captain Doubleday remarked that it was "a grand effort to negotiate us out of the fort." [52]

With such a large number of state troops stationed on Sullivan's Island with money in their pockets and little to do in the evenings, it was only natural that "grog shops" should spring up.[53] They became so popular that Col. Maxcy Gregg, commanding on Sullivan's Island, wrote a note to the Executive Council complaining of "the great evil arising from the sale of liquor . . . thereby demoralizing the troops and causing insubordination amongst them." The governor immediately ordered that martial law be established, not only on Sullivan's Island but on all military stations, and closed up the "grog shops."[54]

Major Anderson was waiting for definitive orders from Washington, which never came. Repeatedly he wrote for specific instructions as to what he should do if the floating battery were anchored near him, or if ships flying the foreign flag entered the harbor. Rarely has a man been left so much on his own to make decisions which could plunge a nation into war. He knew the entire country was looking to him to keep peace. With the responsibility thrown back at him from Washington, the strain was beginning to tell. This was possibly the most flagrant instance of passing the buck in American history.[55]

The presence of the women and children in Fort Sumter presented a serious problem. There was not only the question of what to do with them should the fort be fired upon, but, in addition, the food supply was small. Major Anderson wrote to the governor requesting permission to send the women and children to New York in a ship. The request was approved by the Executive Council, and on February 3 they boarded the *Marion* for Fort Hamilton, New York. As they passed Sumter on the way out of the harbor, the troops "gave repeated cheers as a farewell and displayed much feeling; for they thought it very probable they might not meet them again for a long period, if ever." Major Anderson gave a one-gun salute as they went by. The steamer *Marion* had formerly sailed regularly between New York and Charleston but had been taken over by the state authorities.[56]

Many articles had been overlooked in the hurried departure from Moultrie to Sumter. Already by late January the coal was nearly gone, and the garrison was out of sugar, soap, and candles. Moreover, because the fort was located at the mouth of the harbor and received the full force of winter gales from the ocean, it was often uncomfortably cold. In addition, its 60-foot high walls allowed very little sunshine to enter except at midday. Although the food supply for the garrison was ample for the time being, it was monotonous.[57]

State forces continued the work of building new batteries and strengthening those already erected. Anderson made an almost daily report to Washington of the activities taking place around him. Expecting to give the order to take Sumter momentarily, Governor Pickens on February 6 directed Brigadier General Dunovant to have the commanding officers of each post and battery in the harbor put them in full preparation for an attack with a sufficient amount of ammunition for a 48-hour bombardment. The following day the governor received a telegram from John Tyler of Virginia, former president of the United States, which read as follows: "Can my voice reach you? If so do not attack Fort Sumter. You know my sincerity. The Virginia Delegates here earnestly united." C. G. Memminger and William Porcher Miles, delegates from South Carolina attending the Convention of Southern States in Montgomery, Alabama, were advising the governor to be cautious in ordering an attack on Sumter. On February 9 the governor received a telegram from Montgomery informing him that a constitution for a Provisional Government of States had been unanimously adopted. At the same time Miles wired that "all of the hottest Southern men advise against the immediate attack upon Sumter." A few moments later the governor received word that Jefferson Davis and Alexander Stephens had been unanimously elected president and vice-president. With this he must have realized that the authority to fire on Sumter had been taken out of his hands. Three days later he received formal notification from Montgomery that the Confederate government was taking under its charge the questions and difficulties now existing between them and the government of the United States relating to the occupation of forts, arsenals, navy yards, and other public establishments.[58]

Apparently the initiative was to be left to the Confederate

government. But Governor Pickens had different ideas. He called a meeting of the Executive Council at which he announced that he considered that he "still had the right to attack Fort Sumter, in case of any invasion," and that preparations should go on as before. On February 18 the governor sent a telegram back to Montgomery, saying that he desired to open fire on Sumter at the close of the week. The next day he called a council of war with his officers, and one of the resolutions dealt with the matter of carrying Sumter by assault and the best method of doing so. It appeared that the governor was going ahead regardless of the Confederate government. Fearful of what might result from such action, Jefferson Davis wrote Governor Pickens that he hoped Pickens would "be able to prevent the issue of peace or war for the Confederate States from being decided by any other than the authorities constituted to conduct our international relations." Davis was imploring Governor Pickens not to start a war and to let the issue be settled by peaceful negotiations.[59]

A dawn on Washington's birthday, the guns of Castle Pinckney boomed out a 13-gun salute in honor of the great patriot. Major Anderson ordered a salute fired at noon. Each side was convinced that, if Washington had been living, he would have supported their cause.[60]

As there was some criticism among the state officers about the removal of a battery, Maj. W. H. C. Whiting, a competent engineer, was sent by Jefferson Davis to examine the batteries in the area and to make recommendations. Whiting arrived at the end of February and after a two-day inspection reported that he was not satisfied with their present state and did not think it advisable to attack Sumter. This must have been something of a shock to the governor. If he ordered an attack on Sumter and it failed, he would be the scapegoat not only of the Confederacy, but of the United States as well. Nevertheless, the governor was adamant. A few days later he wrote Davis: "We would desire to be informed if when thoroughly prepared to take the fort, shall we do so? Or shall we wait your order, and shall we demand the surrender or will that demand be made by you?" He signed off impatiently with this request: "An answer to this telegraph is desired." He received an answer signed by L. P. Walker, secretary of war for the Confederacy: "This Government assumes the control of the military operations at Charleston and will make demand of the fort when fully advised. An officer goes tonight to take charge." Pickens could no longer, singlehandedly, give orders for an attack on Sumter; it was up to the entire Confederacy to make the decision. Jefferson Davis realized that, if the attack was a failure, it would not only demoralize the people, but in the eyes of the world would make the Confederacy look "reckless and precipitate." Walker's answer was accompanied by a directive stating that President Davis assumed control of all military operations in South Carolina. Pickens was no longer head of an independent state; he was just another governor.[61]

The officer "to take charge" was Brig. Gen. P. G. T. Beauregard, a native of Louisiana and an 1838 graduate of West Point. With his engineer officers, he made an inspection and realized that the batteries were far from ready for either a bombardment of Sumter or repulsion of a relieving force. Beauregard, who was noted for his diplomacy, wrote to Secretary of War Walker: "Everyone here seems to be gradually becoming aware through my cautious representations, that we are not yet prepared for this contest." This must have been a jolt to those who were demanding an immediate attack on Sumter.[62]

Since the occupation of Sumter, the Confederate artillery, either for training purposes or for ascertaining the range, had been firing their guns, sometimes loaded, but mostly with blanks. One morning, Major Stevens was training his command by having them fire blank charges. Suddenly, without warning, a ball was seen coming out of the muzzle of one of the guns and speeding toward Sumter. It landed on the wharf. Major Stevens had no idea how the shot had gotten in the gun. Major Anderson had every reason to assume that hostilities had begun. The Sumter guns were readied and "one and all desired to fight it out as soon as possible." Major Stevens got into a small boat with a flag of truce and was rowed quickly to Sumter to explain that it was a mistake, that war had not been declared, and to apologize to Major Anderson. What had occurred was that a member of Major Stevens' company, E. Lindsley Halsey, had become bored and had slipped a ball in one cannon just to see what would happen.[63]

On March 11, Major Anderson and his garrison read in the morning newspaper that upon good authority they were to be evacuated, but their elation at this news evaporated when no telegraphic instructions were received from Washington. Two days later they knew that the rumor was true and that it would be only a few days before they were on their way. The headlines in the morning paper read: "THE EVACUATION OF FORT SUMTER DETERMINED ON. ANDERSON TO GO TO FORT MONROE."

Captain Foster wrote to General Totten in Washington: "The pacific news . . . seems to have created a pleasant feeling in those around us if we may judge by the quantity of powder they burned here today. About one hundred and fifty guns in all were fired, but not with regularity." [64]

The Confederate forces were also elated at the news of the evacuation and enthusiastically fired their cannon. They were not worried about how much powder was consumed, because they believed that it would not be needed any longer. Even work on the batteries surrounding Sumter was discontinued. With the evacuation of Fort Sumter expected daily, Secretary of War Walker wrote to General Beauregard telling him to put little credence in rumors of an amicable adjustment and not to slacken his energies in strengthening the ring of fortifications surrounding Sumter.[65]

The one thing Anderson feared more than anything was an amphibious assault on Sumter. With a force of less than 80 men, only one-tenth the strength needed to fully garrison the fort, he knew that if the assault was made from all sides simultaneously he would have little chance of repelling it. The weak point of the fort was the gorge facing Morris Island, about 1400 yards away, and the logical point of attack. Realizing this, Captain Foster had the wharf thoroughly mined and reinforced the main gate with a solid wall three feet thick. A small passageway just wide enough for a single man to pass was left open. Two guns were mounted on either side of the gate, while an eight-inch howitzer loaded with canister was mounted so that it could sweep the entire wharf. In addition, piles of stone loaded with a heavy charge of powder were placed along the walkway. These could be detonated from within the fort. Another ingenious device was a barrel of stone containing a canister of powder placed along the parapet. This, when rolled over, could be exploded when it hit the ground by means of a long lanyard. To impress the Confederate forces, a barrel was exploded with a huge detonation, churning up the water some distance from the fort just as a vessel was passing by. The effect of the explosion was duly reported to the higher Confederate authorities.[66]

Gustavus V. Fox, formerly an officer in the United States Navy and a strong advocate of reinforcing Sumter at any cost, arrived in Charleston on March 21. He immediately looked up his old friend Capt. Henry J. Hartstene, C.S.N., who took him to Governor Pickens. The governor was naturally suspicious of Fox's motives, but Fox reassured him that his mission was peaceful and that he had come only to ascertain the amount of provisions on hand and the condition of the garrison. The governor gave him permission to visit Sumter, but he ordered Captain Hartstene to accompany him and watch him closely. Fox's arrival must have been a great surprise to Major Anderson. Fox made almost no mention of his plan of reinforcing Sumter and mainly questioned Anderson about how long he could hold out even on short rations. Fox spent only a few minutes alone with Anderson, during which time Captain Hartstene talked with the officers, who, he reported, were "indignant at the neglect of their government." When Hartstene returned, General Beauregard asked him whether he had kept his eyes on Fox. He replied, "All but a short period of time when he was with Anderson." General Beauregard replied, "I fear that we shall have occasion to regret that short period." Except for Fox's visit, Major Anderson was left completely in the dark about what was going on in Washington or what his fate was to be, aside from what he read in the newspapers. Simon Cameron, the new secretary of war under Lincoln, was even less communicative than his predecessor, which meant that Anderson, marooned on Sumter, received no instructions. Despite poor food and miserable living conditions, the morale of the garrison remained high. They were still able to get newspapers and some mail, and they realized that they were the most talked-of group in the country. By this time the coal supply was exhausted, and in order to keep warm they were using a temporary building for fuel.[67]

Though isolated in Sumter, Anderson and his officers were aware that someone with a sound knowledge of engineering and artillery had taken over in Charleston. They knew that General Beauregard had assumed command, and through glasses they could clearly see the changes being made in the construction of the batteries and the guns being moved to new positions. The ring of steel was gradually tightening around them.[68]

It was felt certain that if Sumter were relieved, it would occur at night. Four huge Drummond lights arrived to illuminate any relieving vessels, but, to General Beauregard's disappointment, no operators were sent with them. However, the well-known Professor Lewis R. Gibbes, of the College of Charleston, offered to instruct personnel in their operation. These lights, together with fire barges and fire rafts, would make the harbor as bright as day.[69]

Military companies were organized all over the state. Hundreds of men eager for service had to be turned down. General Beauregard received an additional 64 recruits from Baltimore. Unable to return home, they were billeted in Castle Pinckney with three officers assigned to duty with them and were subsequently sworn into the regular Confederate service.[70]

When it was thought that Major Anderson and his garrison would be evacuated, a marked relaxation developed in the feeling toward them on the part of the Confederate forces. One of the governor's aides, Lt. Col. A. R. Chisolm, sent to Sumter on an official errand, lingered to chat with some of the officers. During the conversation one of them jokingly remarked that it had been a long time since he had enjoyed a good cigar. Chisolm said that he would see if he could do something about it. Obtaining General Beauregard's permission, on his next trip he brought not only cigars but several cases of claret. Major Anderson alone did not appreciate the gifts; he immediately wrote Beauregard saying, "Orders have been given which will prevent the recurrence of such an irregularity." [71]

Still thinking that the evacuation was an assured fact, General Beauregard wrote to Major Anderson: "Having been informed that Mr. Lamon, the authorized agent of the President of the United States, advised Governor Pickens, after his interview with you at Fort Sumter, that yourself and command would be transferred to another post in a few days, and understanding that you are under the impression I intend under all circumstances to require of you a formal surrender or capitulation, I hasten to disabuse you, and to inform you that our countries not being at war, and wishing as far as it lies in my power to avoid the latter calamity, no such condition will be expected of you, unless brought about as the natural result of hostilities." It was a diplomatic and courteous note, more like a communication to an old friend than one to a potential enemy. In a letter to the secretary of war, General Beauregard said of Anderson: "In my opinion, a most gallant officer, incapable of any act that might tarnish his reputation as a soldier." [72]

On March 29, General Beauregard received orders instructing him to allow no further communications between Washington and Fort Sumter unless they were first submitted to him. Major Anderson was even further cut off. [73] Shortly afterward, Beauregard received further instructions from the secretary of war. These advised him not only to cut off Anderson's mail delivery but to prevent his receipt of any further supplies. "The fort must be completely isolated." [74]

Daily expecting to be evacuated and with his food supply nearly exhausted, Anderson requested Captain Foster to discharge his laborers. Most of the important work had been done, and Anderson saw no reason for keeping them in the fort; he wrote a letter to Governor Pickens requesting their removal. Fewer people to feed would mean more for the garrison; on April 1 the last barrel of flour had been issued to the cooks. Secretary of War Walker, realizing Major Anderson's dilemma, and knowing that he was short of food, refused to give permission for the removal of the laborers unless the entire garrison was evacuated. Writing to Washington, Major Anderson stated that he had told Fox that he could hold out on short rations until April 10, but since he had received no instructions, he had not curtailed the garrison's food. Again no reply was received from Washington. On April 3, Anderson again wrote to Washington that his bread would last only four or five days. Again no reply.

6

On March 29, finally, Lincoln had sent a note to the secretary of war: "I desire that an expedition, to move by sea, be got ready to sail as early as the 6th of April next." Sumter was to be reinforced. Amid much confusion and a reasonable amount of secrecy, the expedition was readied in New York. Secretary of War Cameron placed it under the command of Captain Gustavus W. Fox, who was instructed to enter Charleston harbor and, if opposed, to report the fact to the senior naval officer present, who was to "use his entire force to open a passage, when you will, if possible, effect an entrance and place both troops and supplies in Fort Sumter." There was no ambiguity in this order, though it seems strange that Fox was to report the fact that he was "opposed" to the senior naval officer present, who would be equally aware of that fact. Fox was first to attempt to send in a boatload of provisions on arrival, and, if no resistance was offered, to do no more. However, if he was halted or fired upon, he was to try to force a passage and supply Sumter not only with provisions but also with troops.[75]

Early in April, Major Anderson received his first orders from Secretary of War Cameron. The Lincoln government had been in

office for a month and during that time had left Anderson igno-
rant of what was going on or how he was to conduct negotiations
with Governor Pickens. The orders he received indicated that an
expedition was being sent to him before April 15, as Captain Fox
had informed the secretary of war that Anderson could hold out
that long without great inconvenience. Anderson had told Fox
that he could hold out until April 10 if he went on short rations, but, since he had received no instructions, he had kept the
garrison on their usual rations, which meant that they did not
have enough food to hold out until that date. The secretary of war
went on to say that, if the flag was still flying over Sumter, the
expedition "will attempt to provision you, and, in case the effort is
resisted, will endeavor to re-inforce you." He stated further: "you
will therefore hold out, if possible, till the arrival of the expedition." But he continued by saying that "whenever, if at all, in
your judgment to save yourself and command, a capitulation
becomes a necessity, you are authorized to make it." [76]

Major Anderson was "deeply affected" by this communiqué,
for he realized that the Confederate forces would allow neither
supplies nor reinforcements to be landed. During the months he
had been confined in the fort, he had accepted humiliation to his
flag and to himself. He had hoped that peace would be maintained and the possession of Sumter settled by peaceful negotiations. Now all was changed; war was inevitable. Anderson replied to the secretary of war that the order had come to him as a
surprise, for he was assured that his command would be evacuated, by peaceful means. He feared that the expedition would be
disastrous to all concerned and that the loss of life would be heavy.
Furthermore, since the garrison was out of oil, it was impossible
to light a lantern, and the ships attempting to enter at night
would have to rely on other marks. He ended his letter by saying:
"We shall strive to do our duty, though I frankly say that my
heart is not in the war which I see is to be thus commenced. That
God will still avert it, and cause us to resort to pacific measures to
maintain our rights, is my ardent prayer." This letter never

reached Washington; it was seized by Confederate authorities and read by General Beauregard.[77]

The government in Washington did not want to be accused of duplicity, nor did it want another *Star of the West* incident; therefore, Washington decided to notify Governor Pickens officially that supplies would be sent to Fort Sumter. On April 8, Robert L. Chew, a clerk from the State Department, and Bvt. Capt. Theodore Talbot—the latter had been sent to Washington by Anderson and promoted while there—arrived in Charleston to deliver the message. Talbot immediately called on the governor to inform him of the nature of the instructions and asked if he would see Chew at his earliest convenience. Acquiescing, the governor said that he would see him at once. Upon arrival, Chew read the message that supplies would be sent to Sumter. The governor told him that, since South Carolina was now a part of the Confederate government and General Beauregard was in charge of all military operations around Charleston, he would like to have him present. When Beauregard appeared, the governor read the message to him. Along with Anderson, Beauregard and Pickens knew that this meant war. Talbot asked Beauregard if he could return to Sumter, but permission was refused because all communications had been cut off from the fort except those necessary to convey an order for its evacuation. Chew and Talbot left for Washington that night. The governor and General Beauregard received this message two days before the expedition to relieve Sumter sailed from New York.[78]

In the meantime, all was confusion in Washington; one expedition was being fitted out to relieve Fort Pickens and another to reinforce Fort Sumter. Both were to have been secret, but, because there were so many Southern sympathizers not only in New York, where the expeditions were being readied, but also in Washington, it was impossible to keep them secret. On April 6, the day Talbot and Chew left Washington for Charleston, a telegram was received in Charleston which read: "Positively determined not to withdraw Anderson. Supplies go immediately, supported by a naval force under Stringham if their landing is resisted." It was signed, simply, "A FRIEND." As both the governor and General Beauregard were on a tour of inspection, it was opened by former judge A. G. Magrath. Not knowing who "A FRIEND" might be, Magrath telegraphed Washington to find out his name. It turned out to be James E. Harvey, a native South Carolinian, now a newspaper correspondent living in Washington, whose information was absolutely correct. Therefore, when Chew arrived with the official notification from Washington, it was no news to the governor, merely a confirmation of what he already knew.[79]

All during this time the batteries were systematically firing their guns in order to determine the exact range of Sumter. This, of course, gave the officers on Sumter an opportunity to know what to expect when hostilities began; in addition, it enabled them to make an accurate estimate of the size and number of guns in each battery. During the course of fire practice from the two ten-inch mortars located at Mt. Pleasant, one shell burst so close to Sumter that it brought forth a protest from Major Anderson. In a letter to General Beauregard, he wrote that the shell had exploded so near that it was dangerous to the occupants of the fort. He continued: "I have never regarded myself as being in a hostile attitude towards the inhabitants of South Carolina." He ended by saying: "I most earnestly hope that nothing will ever occur to alter, in the least, the high regard and esteem I have for so many years entertained for you. I am, dear general, yours, very truly, ROBERT ANDERSON, Major, U.S. Army, Commanding." [80]

This letter was written on April 6. The next day General Beauregard replied that he had given orders to the commander of the mortar battery to fire his guns in other directions when practicing. He closed with these words: "Let me assure you, Major, that nothing shall be wanting on my part to preserve the friendly relations and impressions which have existed between us for so many years." [81]

Exactly a week later, Anderson was forced to capitulate to his friend General Beauregard. With the relief expedition on its way, both sides prepared for war.

7

The knowledge that a relief expedition was on its way from New York kept the Fort Sumter garrison looking seaward for the first mast to show over the horizon. Despite their original anticipation of being evacuated to a less warlike area with the pleasures of good food and feminine companionship, when Major Anderson told them of the plan to fight it out inside Sumter, the troops reacted with enthusiasm.[82]

Though Anderson's heart was not in the task, he made every effort to put the encircled fort in condition for battle. A traverse was built to guard the south gate against fire from Cummings Point, a hospital was prepared to care for the wounded, and ammunition was moved to areas convenient to the guns.[83]

Around the periphery of the harbor, General Beauregard was pushing his troops into last-minute preparations for the fight. When a powerful nine-inch Dahlgren gun arrived, orders were given for it to be placed in attack position at once, regardless of its condition. The much-discussed floating battery, which had shown signs of being slightly unseaworthy, was towed to Cove Inlet between Sullivan's Island and Mount Pleasant. There, to strengthen the attack from the northeast, the battery was beached at high tide and made into a fixed unit. To add to the danger from that side of the harbor, the Confederates erected a new battery on Sullivan's Island, using a residence to conceal the construction. When the battery was completed, the house between it and Sumter was blown up, revealing the battery. The officers at Sumter realized that the new battery made the barbette guns useless, since their exposed positions made it suicidal to attempt to man them.[84]

While Confederate batteries were being established, troops were arriving from all over South Carolina. The newcomers were rushed to Morris Island to defend that side of the harbor mouth from the amphibious assault which General Beauregard felt sure would be made when the relief fleet arrived. He estimated that this Federal attack would be made by at least 2,600 troops, and he planned to oppose them from the dunes of the sandy beach.[85]

The situation began to look desperate for the small garrison at Sumter. Lieutenant Meade, finding the supply of cartridge bags limited, set out to remedy the situation by cutting up extra blankets and any extra clothing he could find. On the same day, the supply of bread ran out. The garrison was forced to eat rice that had become mixed with broken glass from window panes shattered by the guns fired in practice for the expected attack.[86]

At night the harbor was patrolled by eight Confederate guard boats, some painted black for camouflage and all charged with preventing supplies from reaching Sumter. Detachments of cavalry were landed on both Sullivan's and Morris islands to act as beach patrols and to alert the troops in case of beach-front landing attempts. The inevitable clash was approaching.[87]

On April 10, President Jefferson Davis and his cabinet realized that negotiations were no longer possible. Davis instructed Secretary of War Walker to order Beauregard to make a last demand on Anderson for the evacuation of Fort Sumter: "You will at once demand its evacuation and if this is refused proceed, in such manner as you may determine, to reduce it." General Beauregard postponed the demand until the following day, and only after making sure that his batteries were in readiness did he initiate the move that was to result in open war.

About 3:45 P.M. on April 11, a sentry on Fort Sumter announced to the officer of the day, Lt. Jefferson Davis (no relation to the Confederate leader), that a small boat bearing a white flag was approaching. Lieutenant Davis met the boat at the dock and found that it contained three of Beauregard's aides, Col. James Chesnut, Jr., Lt. Col. A. R. Chisolm, and Capt. Stephen D. Lee. They were escorted to the guardroom, where they greeted Major Anderson and handed him a dispatch from General Beauregard. This demand read:

The Government of the Confederate States has hitherto forborne from any hostile demonstration against Fort Sumter in the hope that the Government of the United States, with a view to the amicable adjustment of all questions between the two governments, and to avert the calamities of war, would voluntarily evacuate it. . . . I am ordered by the Government of the Confederate States to demand the evacuation of Fort Sumter . . . . all proper facilities will be afforded for the removal of yourself and your command, together with company arms and property, and all private property, to any post in the United States which you may select. The flag which you have upheld so long and with so much fortitude, under the most trying circumstances, may be saluted by you on taking it down.[88]

As Surgeon Crawford, one of Anderson's officers, put it so aptly: "Was ever such terms granted to a band of starving men?" [89]

Major Anderson immediately summoned every officer on Sumter into another room and read the dispatch. To a man they voted to refuse the demand, and Major Anderson composed his reply:

I have the honor to acknowledge the receipt of your communication demanding the evacuation of this fort, and to say, in reply thereto, that it is a demand with which I regret that my sense of honor, and my obligations to my government, prevent my compliance. Thanking you for the fair, manly and courteous terms proposed, and for the high compliment paid me, I am, General, very respectfully, your obedient servant, ROBERT ANDERSON, Major, First Artillery, Commanding.[90]

While his sympathies may have been with the South, Major Anderson's sense of honor required that he carry out his instructions and defend the fort. The aides were handed the reply, and Anderson walked with them to the dock, where he asked if Beauregard's batteries would open fire without further notice. Colonel Chesnut replied: "I think not, no, I can say to you that he will not without further notice." To which Anderson replied: "I shall await the first shot, and if you do not batter us to pieces, we shall be starved out in a few days."

Expressing surprise at the reference to being "starved out," Colonel Chesnut asked if he might report this to Beauregard. Although he confirmed the meager state of his food supplies, Anderson refused to put it into the form of a report.[91]

The party arrived in the city a little after 5 P.M. and delivered the reply to Beauregard, reporting Anderson's verbal statement as well. The refusal to evacuate, along with the "starved out" comment, was sent by telegraph to Secretary of War Walker in Montgomery with a request for instructions. Walker's telegraphic reply was prompt and to the point: "If Major Anderson will state the time at which, as indicated by him, he will evacuate, and agree that in the meatime he will not use his guns against us unless ours should be employed against Fort Sumter, you are authorized thus to avoid the effusion of blood." Walker's reply stated that, if these terms were refused, Beauregard was to fire on his friend Major Anderson and to reduce the fort.[92]

Both sides watched the sea for the first sight of the relief fleet. The Confederates, expecting its arrival hourly, towed fire barges into position in the channel, where they were anchored, ready to be set on fire should the fleet appear by night. These and the Drummond lights would illuminate incoming ships or landing craft, making them excellent targets for the shore batteries.[93]

Major Anderson gave orders that the exposed barbette guns not be used and directed his troops to fire only the ones in the lower casements. He realized that the newly unmasked battery on Sullivan's Island and the floating battery would sweep the top of the fort with a hail of shot, making it impossible for the gunners to man the guns. Had there been a full complement of men to garrison the fort, instead of only one-tenth of such a force, it is possible that he might have ordered the guns manned, but Anderson was anxious to keep casualties at a minimum. This solicitude for his men greatly reduced the firing power of his fort, because the heaviest and most effective guns were on the barbette.[94]

Ashore, the new nine-inch Dahlgren gun had been mounted on Sullivan's Island and a rifled 12-pound gun, which had arrived from Liverpool as a gift from Charles K. Prioleau, was in place. The Confederates could count on 27 guns of varying size and

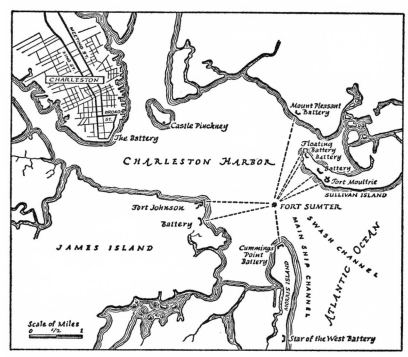

POSITION OF CONFEDERATE BATTERIES DURING THE INITIAL
BOMBARDMENT OF FORT SUMTER, APRIL 12–13, 1861

caliber and 16 ten-inch mortars located at strategic points about
the harbor.[95] The only thing lacking was the order to "commence
firing." And that was not long in coming.

Shortly before 1 A.M., Friday, April 12, 1861, a boat bearing a
white flag approached Sumter. It halted at a sentry's challenge,
then moved up to the wharf. In it were the three aides who had
brought the evacuation demand, accompanied by Roger Pryor of
Virginia, one of Beauregard's newly commissioned aides. Since
Virginia had not joined the Confederacy, Pryor remained in the
boat while the three aides presented Major Anderson with another communication from Beauregard which stated that he had
received the message relative to being "starved out" and stipulated: "If you will state the time which you will evacuate Fort
Sumter, and agree in the meantime that you will not use your

guns against us unless ours shall be employed against Fort Sumter, we will abstain from opening fire upon you." [96]

After reading the demand, Anderson brought out all of his officers for consultation. Asked how long the men could hold out, Surgeon Crawford replied that they could last about five days, the last three without food. After much delay, Major Anderson replied that he would evacuate Sumter by noon, April 15, "Should I not receive prior to that time controlling instructions from my Government or additional supplies." [97]

Colonel Chesnut commented that there were too many "ifs" in the note. He then sat down and began to write the following reply, which he handed to Anderson: "Sir: By authority of Brigadier General Beauregard, commanding the Provisional Forces of the Confederate States, we have the honor to notify you that he will open fire of his batteries on Fort Sumter in one hour from this time." It was then 3:20 A.M. Major Anderson accompanied the Confederate officers to the wharf and cordially shook hands with them. By way of farewell he told them: "If we never meet in this world again, God grant that we may in the next. . . ." [98]

As the boat disappeared into the darkness surrounding the fort, Anderson and his officers roused the sleeping troops. Ordering them to remain where they were, Anderson told them the bombardment was about to begin. He then ordered the huge garrison flag raised over the fort, where it was to fly for the next 34 hours. [99]

Colonel Chesnut and his party were rowed directly to Fort Johnson, where they reported to Capt. George S. James, who commanded one of the batteries there. Colonel Chesnut ordered James to open fire at 4:30 A.M. with one of his ten-inch mortars; the high-arching mortar shell was to be the signal. It was to be war.

8

The deep-throated roar of the mortar, its shell making a beautiful parabolic curve and bursting precisely over Sumter, alerted those who were awake and awakened those who were asleep. When this was followed by another shell from the same battery, all within hearing distance knew that the conflict had begun. Anticipating that the bombardment might start before daylight, General Beauregard had issued General Order Number 14: "In case an alarm is given the mortar batteries will open at any rate on the firing of a shell from Fort Johnson." [100]

The morning of April 12 dawned dark and cloudy, with sunrise at 5:37 A.M. and a heavy mist covering the harbor. The mortars, primed and loaded, could be fired by the jerk of a lanyard. When the shells from the Fort Johnson mortars were seen, the guns on Sullivan's Island quickly opened up, followed in a few minutes by those on Cummings Point. By 5 A.M. Sumter was receiving the concentrated fire of the 43 guns and mortars that nearly ringed it. [101] The little garrison could do nothing but crouch down in the casemates away from the fragments. The guns in the lower casemate had no rear sights. Deep within the fort daylight penetrated only when the sun was well up, and there was no oil or candles by which to sight the guns.

Knowing that the order to fire might come at any moment, Lt. Col. R. S. Ripley, in command of the artillery on Sullivan's Island —which included the mortar battery on Mt. Pleasant—had placed his gunners under arms at 9:30 P.M. on the evening of April 11 and had his furnaces heated. Consequently, when the shells went up from Fort Johnson, his batteries were quickly brought into action. Mortar Battery One was the first to fire from Sullivan's Island; it was followed quickly by Mortar Battery Two and by the Enfilading Battery. Because the sky was overcast and sunrise was still over an hour away, the direct fire of the guns was slow, but after dawn the fire was quickened. Meanwhile, the mortars were pounding away, casting their shells high in the air with the fuses timed so that they would burst in Sumter. From a pyrotechnic point of view it was magnificent, but the men crouching in the casemates probably thought otherwise. [102]

On Morris Island there was a delay in getting the mortars and guns into action. Brig. Gen. James Simons, thinking the order to open the bombardment would come earlier that night, had kept his troops under arms until 8 P.M. When heavy rain began to fall, he allowed them to return to their camp a few hundred yards away. They were sleeping when the mortars were fired from Fort Johnson. Capt. Gadsden King's Trapier Battery, with its three ten-inch mortars, was the first to go into action, but these guns were soon followed by the three mortars of the Cummings Point Battery under the command of Capt. G. B. Cuthbert. These, in turn, were followed by Maj. P. F. Stevens' much talked about Iron Battery, consisting of three eight-inch Columbiads.[103]

Among the gunners in the Iron Battery was Edmund Ruffin of Virginia, who had come to take part in the excitement. He had been made an honorary member of the Palmetto Guard, which was attached to the Iron Battery and along with the others he hurried to the guns at the sound of the firing. The commanding officer, Captain Cuthbert, gave him the honor of firing "the first shell from Columbiad No. 1" of the Iron Battery. Ruffin's aim was true; the shell "burst directly upon the parapet of the south-west angle of the fort." [104] After getting off the first round, the Iron Battery continued to fire at 15-minute intervals throughout the day. As the light increased, every available gun joined in with the mortars. For two and a half hours the rain of metal descended uninterruptedly on Sumter with no response from the fort. This was both a disappointment and a surprise; many wondered if Anderson would surrender without a fight.

In Sumter, reveille was sounded as usual at 6 A.M., although the bursting of the shells would have made it almost impossible for anyone not to have been awake. The roll was called as usual, under the bomb-proofs instead of on the parade ground, and the garrison was given a breakfast of fat pork and water.[105]

When there was enough light in the lower casemate, which was surrounded by 60-foot walls, Major Anderson ordered his guns into action, dividing them into three details under the commands of Captain Doubleday, Lt. Jefferson Davis, and Surgeon Crawford; the latter had requested to be allowed to take an active part in the defense. Just before seven o'clock Captain Double-

day's 32-pound gun began firing. The ball bounced off the slant-
ing iron roof of the Iron Battery. The sound of the shot coming
from the fort caused great excitement. It was almost a relief to the
Confederate gunners, who had felt ashamed of firing on a man
who refused to fire back; they stepped up the rate of fire with
enthusiasm.[106] The guns under Captain Doubleday concentrated
their fire on the Iron Battery on Cummings Point; those of Lieutenant Davis took on the Fort Johnson mortar batteries; and
Crawford fought with the Floating Battery. Unfortunately for
Anderson, all of his heavy guns, primed and loaded, were located
on the barbette high overhead; in spite of accurate shooting, his
32- and 42-pound guns at a range of almost a mile were doing
very little damage. As it turned out, Anderson's order not to use
the guns on the barbette was sound, for, with the concentrated
fire of the guns of the Enfilading Battery sweeping it with shells,
no one could have manned it for any length of time. Surgeon
Crawford, seeing that he was having little effect on the Floating
Battery, got permission to shift his fire to Fort Moultrie. But
Moultrie's guns, heavily protected with sandbags and bales of
cotton, were also undamaged by the light guns of Sumter. No
casualties occurred, and the gunners in Moultrie came to regard
the contest as a game. Every time a bale of cotton was knocked
over by one of the shells, someone would exclaim, "Cotton is
going down," and when a direct hit occurred on the bake oven,
scattering loaves of bread in every direction, one man cried out,
"Foodstuff is going up." Meanwhile, the laborers in Sumter
pitched in with a will. Some carried powder and shot to the
gunners; others sewed up cartridge bags.[107] At first the aim of the
Confederate gunners was too high. As the firing progressed,
however, it became more effective. In the fort, pieces of masonry
flew in every direction, shells ricocheted, and the mortars dropped
ten-inch projectiles timed to burst after impact. However, the
gunners in the lower casemate were protected from the direct fire
from without, as well as from the fragments of shells and masonry within the fort.

The battle had a large and enthusiastic audience. Anticipating that the order for the bombardment would be given the previous day, spectators had crowded the high battery, the wharves, and every vantage point in the city. As the night wore on and the rain began, the crowds gradually dispersed and returned to their homes, although a few remained throughout the night. However, with the roar of the mortars from Fort Johnson everybody within hearing distance hurried out of bed, and soon a stream of people converged on the battery, the wharves, and the houses overlooking the harbor. Although the spectacle was awesome, with its portent of heavy casualties, it held their gaze in a hypnotic way.[108] The crowd was quiet and orderly. Not only the windows but the houses themselves were shaken by the vibrations of the heavy guns.

The waiting crowd breathed an almost audible sigh of relief when a dispatch arrived about 9:30 A.M. stating that so far no casualties had occurred at Fort Moultrie. The Floating Battery had sustained no casualties either and was still functioning, though it had been hit 11 times. News was also brought that the Iron Battery was heavily damaging the south and southwest walls of the fort. More important still, the small 12-pound-gun was not only shooting with the accuracy of a rifle, but doing a great deal of damage by the deep penetration of its shells. Because there was only a limited supply of ammunition, it was fired sparingly. The Enfilading Battery on Sullivan's Island directed a devastating fire at the guns on the parapet. Later in the morning, the guns on Sumter opened up on Moultrie, and it was literally fort against fort. During a period of an hour 42 shots were fired by one against 46 from the other.[109]

The fact that the light guns were doing no effective damage to Moultrie was too much for the discipline of Pvt. John Carmody. Knowing that the heavy guns on the barbette were aimed, loaded, and primed, he sneaked away from his command and ascended the circular stairway. On reaching the barbette, he fired every gun that was aimed at Moultrie. As Sergeant Chester said later, "The contest was merely Carmody against the Confederate States." Unable to reload the guns by himself, he was forced to return to the lower casemate, proud and unbeaten. Following Carmody's example, two other members of the garrison slipped away, mounted the parapet, and fired the ten-inch Columbiad at the Iron Battery. Their aim was a little high. Had they hit directly, the ten-inch shell, weighing 128 pounds, would probably have penetrated the armor. Though exposed to deadly fire, they managed to reload the gun, but they were unable to get the carriage into gear, a job requiring six men. But they decided to take another shot at the Iron Battery anyway. They depressed the gun slightly and let go. Their aim was straight, but the shell hit under the battery, throwing sand all over it. The gun recoiled, jumped off its carriage, and dismounted a howitzer next to it. The two men —veteran sergeants—were fortunate not to have been killed by the recoiling gun or by the enemy shells sweeping the parapet.[110]

Although they were almost out of food and physically exhausted, the garrison, as well as the laborers, worked the guns with enthusiasm. Surgeon Crawford was expecting some of the men to collapse at any moment.

The firing from the surrounding batteries continued, and its effect began to show on the parapet and the upper part of the barracks. The Confederates' aim was improving; shells that had been skimming over the parapet now hit the barracks, while the mortar shells buried themselves in the parade ground before exploding and shook the fort violently when they did explode, sending splinters of brick and cement flying in every direction. Colonel Ripley on Sullivan's Island had kept his furnaces going since the previous evening and now decided that it was time to let Major Anderson have a sample of "hot shot." The barracks on Sumter were supposed to be fireproof, but when put to the test, proved not to be. When the "hot shot" cracked through the roof, the building ignited. The first time it caught fire, it was extinguished with water from the cistern. During the day it burst into flame twice more. The last time, the men partially extinguished the fire by destroying three iron cisterns over the quarters and dumping their contents on the flames.[111]

The garrison at Sumter had started out with 700 rounds of

ammunition, but no fuses. By midday, the rapid rate of firing had so reduced the supply that Major Anderson ordered that only six guns be used. There were only six needles in the fort, and powder bags could not be made fast enough to keep up with the guns.[112]

In the meantime, the relief expedition under Captain Fox was standing by. The *Baltic* arrived off the bar at 3 A.M. and found only the *Harriett Lane* in position. Just about the time Fort Sumter opened fire, the *Pawnee* showed up. All day the men in Sumter could see the three vessels anchored off the bar, and they expected them to stand in and send reinforcements momentarily. But the day dragged on, and nothing of the sort occurred. To let the vessels know that he was waiting for them, Major Anderson ordered his garrison flag dipped as a signal. Just as he gave the order, a bursting shell cut the halyards and the flag stuck at half mast.[113] There was no letup from the fire of the surrounding batteries, which continued to rain iron on the fort all afternoon. The lack of cartridge bags and the fact that only six guns were being used made the fire from Sumter relatively slow. About 7 P.M., probably because the men were unable to aim the guns in the darkness, the fire from Sumter ceased. Shortly afterward the general fire from the Confederate batteries also stopped. The clouds, which had been threatening all day, now released a heavy rain. Everyone hastened for shelter. The mortars kept up a steady fire on the fort at 15-minute intervals during the entire night. To insure that the fleet would be detected if it made any attempt to aid Anderson during the night, the fire barges anchored in the inner channels were ignited, casting an eerie glow over the forts and harbor.[114]

That night Lieutenant Meade and some of his men, with their six needles, sewed powder bags while mortar shells burst over the fort with regularity. At midnight Major Anderson told them to try to get some sleep.[115]

Saturday, April 13, 1861, was a clear day, and the visibility was excellent. It was now apparent that Sumter had received heavy damage. The concentrated fire from Morris Island had left its mark on the south and southwest side, and the facade facing

Sullivan's Island was severely scarred. The parapet was a wreck; many of the guns were dismounted, and among those missing were the ten-inch Columbiad that had been fired against orders and the eight-inch howitzer that had been knocked off by the recoil of the Columbiad. Though they could not see the interior of the fort, the Confederate authorities knew from the accuracy of their mortars that it must have been a ruin.

After reveille the garrison had its usual breakfast of fatback and water. One Charleston wit remarked that the Confederate gunners were giving them, in addition to their meager fare, "hot rolls for breakfast." During the night, in spite of the high wind, heavy rain, and strong seas the garrison had been watching for small boats bringing supplies from the vessels anchored off the bar. They could still see the ships lying off the bar and did not know the reason for their inactivity; the members of the garrison heaped curses on the crews. Even the Confederate gunners, knowing that Major Anderson's situation was becoming critical, began to feel sympathy for him and to express contempt for the "timorous inaction" of the fleet.[116]

With practice, fire from the Confederate batteries became more accurate and more effective. That from Fort Sumter, with its light guns throwing solid shot, was doing almost no damage to the batteries. The Sullivan's Island guns soon got the range, and for a time a lively battle went on, with the Sullivan's Island guns knocking large fragments out of the parapet.

Having had good results with his "hot shot" the day before, Colonel Ripley repeated the attack with effectiveness. Shortly after 8 A.M. a loud shout went up from the Confederate gunners at the sight of dense smoke, pierced by flames, rising from the barracks. The smoke, blown by a high wind, almost completely covered the parapet. Realizing that Anderson was in serious trouble, they increased their rate of fire, so that at times shells could be seen exploding in clusters over the smoking fort.[117]

The fire in the barracks spread to the hospital and finally to the magazine, which contained 300 barrels of powder. If ignited, the powder would blow the fort and the garrison to bits. Every available man went to work moving the powder to safety, which in itself was a hazardous operation. Because of the haste in which the powder bags had been filled in the darkness the previous night, the floor was covered with loose powder that was liable to ignite at any moment. More than 100 barrels of powder were carried inside the casemates and covered with wet blankets. When the men could no longer stay in the magazine because of the heat, orders were given to close the door, bank it with dirt, dig a trench in front of it, and fill it with water in the hope that it would keep out the flames. Realizing that the powder in the casemates might explode at any moment in spite of the blankets, Major Anderson ordered it thrown overboard; only five barrels and the stack of cartridges already made up were retained. With the powder so drastically reduced, only one gun could be fired every ten minutes.[118]

By 11 A.M. the smoke and flames had become so intense that it was almost impossible to remain in the fort. Men were lying on the ground with handkerchiefs over their mouths gasping for air. Others, in spite of the danger of shell fire, crowded into casemates trying to breathe. From a distance the fort looked like an erupting volcano. Confederate Major Whiting (later to become a major general), watching the scene from Morris Island, was moved almost to tears at the thought that Anderson and the garrison might all be suffocated.[119]

Every time a gun was fired from the fort, the Confederate gunners both on Sullivan's and Morris islands manned the parapets and cheered the garrison for their courage.

Suddenly the fort was shaken by an explosion so violent that it shook the wharves in Charleston. A plume of smoke rose high in the air. More explosions followed, showering the interior of the fort with blazing timbers and fragments of brick. By this time everyone watching was sure that no one could survive. The people in the city were intensely excited and expressed sympathy for the garrison.[120]

The Confederate gunners expected to see a white flag appear any minute. Still the fight continued, and occasionally a gun was fired from Sumter, followed by cheers from the gunners manning the Confederate batteries.[121]

More "hot shot" was poured into the fort. Still there was no white flag. Within the fort the gunners, red-eyed, coughing, and almost suffocating from the heat and smoke, were still manning their guns. With cartridge bags nearly exhausted, they resorted to using socks. One of the sergeants said later, "We fired away several dozen pair of woolen socks belonging to Major Anderson." [122]

About 1 P.M. the flag staff toppled, bringing down with it the huge garrison flag that had been flying defiantly the entire time. It had already been struck by nine shells. The shot which caused it to fall is thought to have been fired by Lt. William Preston. When the flag fell, Lieutenant Hall raced into the parade ground to pick it up. The heat was so intense that his hair was badly singed and his eyebrows completely burned off. His gold epaulets became so hot that he had to rip them off. Hall, Peter Hart—one of Anderson's former sergeants turned carpenter—Lieutenant Snyder, and a laborer named Davey found a long spar, attached the flag to it, and raised it about twenty minutes later, while shells burst all around, to the cheers of the garrison. It appeared again, this time on the eastern rampart, to announce that resistance had not ended. When the flag had gone down, the fire from the Confederate batteries had ceased almost entirely, but it was reopened with increased vigor when the flag reappeared.[123]

9

When the flag went down, Brig. Gen. James Simons, in command of the forces on Morris Island, sent Colonel Wigfall to Sumter to inquire if Anderson would surrender to General Beauregard. Wigfall and Gourdin Young were rowed across to the fort in a small boat. The Morris Island batteries, who could see the boat, suspended firing. The other batteries could not see the boat and continued their shelling. As the boat approached the smoking fort, Wigfall attached a white flag to the end of his sword.

Unable to land on the wharf because the main gate was ablaze, he was forced to crawl in an open embrasure, where he was met by Pvt. John Thompson and another member of the garrison, who at first refused to admit him. After a few words on Wigfall's part, they allowed him to crawl through the embrasure into the smoking fort.[124] Lieutenant Snyder came up to see what was going on, and Wigfall identified himself and asked for Major Anderson. While Snyder was looking for the major, Wigfall ran into Lt. Jefferson Davis and shouted at him above the din, "Your flag is down and you are not firing your guns, let us quit. General Beauregard desires to stop this." "No, Sir," answered Davis, "our flag is not down. Step out here and you will see it waving over the ramparts." Wigfall then said, "Let us stop this firing," and, handing him his sword with the white flag attached to it, said, "Will you hoist this?" Davis' reply was negative: "It is for you to stop it." Finally, one of the soldiers standing nearby put it out one of the embrasures. A solid shot from Moultrie caused the soldier to jump back, shouting, "They don't respect the flag—they are firing on it!" [125] Wigfall remarked that he, too, had been fired on while crossing over from Morris Island. Neither Davis nor Wigfall had the authority to wave a flag of truce; Major Anderson was the only one who could make such a decision. As he came up, Wigfall turned to him and said, "Major Anderson, I am Colonel Wigfall. You have defended your flag nobly, sir. It's madness to persevere in useless resistance. General Beauregard wishes to stop this, and to ask upon what terms you will evacuate this work." Anderson, realizing that further resistance was useless, quietly remarked, "I have already stated the terms to General Beauregard. Instead of noon the 15th, I will go now." Wigfall answered, "Then, Major Anderson, I understand that you will evacuate the fort upon the same terms proposed to you by General Beauregard?" "Yes, sir," Anderson replied, "and upon those terms alone." The two discussed the condition of surrender, that Anderson and his garrison be allowed to leave the fort with their arms and all company property. Anderson, in addition, requested permission to salute the flag. Wigfall then left, after again complimenting the major on his heroic resistance. Actually, Wigfall had no authority from General Beauregard to make terms of surrender. He had formerly been a United States senator from Texas, and recently appointed one of Beauregard's aides with the rank of colonel, and he simply took it upon himself to assume the responsibility. It was about 1:30 P.M. when major Anderson gave the order for the garrison flag to be lowered and a hospital sheet hoisted in its place. Sumter had been under continuous bombardment for nearly 34 hours.[126] When Wigfall and Young returned to Morris Island, the troops waded out into waist-deep water and triumphantly carried the two men ashore on their shoulders.

Meanwhile, General Beauregard had dispatched three of his aides from the city to offer assistance to Major Anderson. The three—William Porcher Miles, Roger Pryor of Virginia, and Capt. Stephen D. Lee—were halfway to the fort when they saw the flag again raised. They turned back and had proceeded a short distance, when they saw a white flag flying in its place. Reversing course again, they headed back toward the fort.[127]

When they landed, the three men were conducted to Major Anderson, to whom they delivered General Beauregard's offer of assistance. The major replied, "Present my compliments to General Beauregard, and say to him I thank him for his kindness, but need no assistance." Then Major Anderson asked if they had come directly from General Beauregard. They said that they had. "Why," returned Major Anderson, "Colonel Wigfall has just been here as an aide to and by authority of General Beauregard, and proposed the same terms of evacuation offered on the 11th instant." The aides knew that Wigfall had received no such authority from General Beauregard. They told Anderson that they had just left the general, who was in the city. Wigfall had been on Morris Island for the last two days and during that time had neither seen nor communicated with Beauregard. This was one of the few times Anderson departed from his usual serenity; he was irritated at being placed in such an embarrassing position —the terms of surrender made by Wigfall were null and void. Anderson turned to the three aides and said, "Very well, Gentlemen, you can return to your batteries," and he pointed toward Moultrie. The major then announced that he would immediately hoist his flag, that he regretted taking it down, and that it would not have been lowered if he had known that Wigfall had not come directly from General Beauregard.[128]

The three aides realized there had been a serious misunderstanding. They retired for a conference to the nearest casemate, which happened at the time to house Surgeon Crawford, who was not well and had been taking some medicine for his ailment. Pryor saw a bottle nearby, poured himself a drink, and downed it at a gulp. What he had swallowed, however, was not whiskey, but iodide of potassium. Pryor let out a cry that brought Surgeon Crawford running and told the doctor what had happened. Crawford replied, "If you have taken the amount of that solution that you think you have, you have most likely poisoned yourself." He took Pryor to the improvised dispensary and applied a stomach pump. Captain Doubleday and the other officers questioned "the doctor's right to interpose in a case of this kind"; they felt that, if one of their enemy wanted to come over to Sumter "and poison himself, the Medical Department had no business to interfere with such a laudable intention." The doctor, however, claimed that he was responsible to the United States for the medicine in the hospital and that he "could not permit Pryor to carry any of it away." Pryor had probably furnished Sumter with its first laugh since the bombardment began.[129]

While the stomach pump was being administered, Miles and Lee resumed the parley with Anderson; they tried to convince him of the futility of continuing the fight and assured him that General Beauregard would give the same terms of surrender outlined by Wigfall. They finally persuaded Anderson to put Wigfall's terms in writing and then hurried back to the city to report their conversation with the major.[130] At the wharf the aides were met by hundreds of citizens, and as they marched up the street to Beauregard's headquarters the crowd swelled.[131]

General Beauregard not only agreed to the same terms he had previously offered, but also allowed Anderson to salute the flag "as an honorable Testimony to the gallantry and fortitude with which Major Anderson and his command had defended their post." His aides immediately returned to Sumter and delivered the message into the major's hand. Certain that Anderson would accept the terms, Beauregard sent Fire Chief M. H. Nathans to help extinguish the flames and Surgeon General R. W. Gibbes to offer medical aid.[132]

Major Anderson and the others in the fort showed "the terrible nature of the ordeal from which they had just emerged. Deprived of sleep for many hours, fatigued with their labors at the guns, and prostrated by their battle with an element which waged beyond their control, they look worn, haggard, and ready to drop from sheer exhaustion." Surgeon Crawford noted that "the enthusiasm that had so long inspired them seemed to have gone." That night the garrison slept well.[133]

The fort itself looked exhausted, too; it appeared as if "the hand of the destroying angel had swept ruthlessly by and left not a solitary object to relieve the general desolation." The parapet was a wreck, the parade ground was pitted with shell craters, and the barracks had been gutted by fire; the damage was the result of a total of 3,307 "hot shot" and shells.[134]

Later in the evening the aides returned to the fort to arrange the final conditions of the evacuation. Anderson read Beauregard's outline aloud to his officers and said that he was gratified by its generous terms. Captain Hartstene, C.S.N., who was present, offered to take Lieutenant Synder to confer with the commander of the fleet lying off the bar about evacuating the garrison.[135]

In Charleston, everyone celebrated the victory. Speeches, sometimes slightly incoherent, were made by almost anyone at the slightest provocation.

Sunday was a beautiful, clear day. Even at an early hour the harbor was swarming with boats. Ferrymen were carrying passengers at 50 cents apiece to view the still smouldering fort. The beaches were lined with civilians and troops gazing at it as if fascinated. Church bells pealed, and services commemorated the great but practically bloodless victory. With all the excitement, people almost forgot that it was Sunday. In the afternoon, the Citadel cadets stationed on the Battery gave a dress parade to an admiring audience. The streets were jammed; people had come from a 50-mile radius to see the excitement.[136]

At Sumter, Major Anderson was receiving aides, newspaper correspondents, and politicians and chatting pleasantly with them. Few present realized that he was a man broken by the strain he had endured for the past months. General Beauregard had refrained from going to Sumter, fearful that his presence might embarrass his old friend Anderson. When he met Major Stevens of the Iron Battery, Anderson complimented him on his shooting ability. President Jefferson Davis even sent a telegram to Beauregard: "If occasion offers tender my friendly rememberance to Major Anderson." The major had the pleasant job of delivering mail to the members of the garrison, who had not received any for many days. Brandy was sent over, accepted with thanks, and consumed with relish. Everything possible was done to aid in the departure of the garrison and to make their remaining hours pleasant.[137]

The embarkation was to take place at 11 o'clock; the Confederate steamer *Isabel* was placed at Anderson's disposal to take his garrison to the fleet still anchored off the bar. In reply to a question about the number of guns he would fire in saluting his flag, Anderson answered, "It is one hundred and those are scarcely enough." There was some delay, and it was almost two o'clock before the opening gun boomed out the first of the salutes. The undamaged guns on the barbette were being used. Under the command of Lieutenant Hall, the salutes were fired at measured intervals until the seventeenth, which to some sounded like a double explosion. What happened was that, when Pvt. Daniel Hough inserted a cartridge, there was a premature explosion, which ripped off his right arm, killing him almost instantly, and wounded five others who were nearby. The probable cause was that the barrel had not been thoroughly sponged out after the previous shot; consequently, some of the cartridge bag from the discharge, which was still burning, ignited the new bag. In spite of the tragedy, the guns continued to boom out in cadence, but the salute was reduced from 100 to 50 guns. With each salute the Confederate troops on Morris Island cheered for the gallantry of the garrison. Taking care of the wounded further delayed the embarkation, and the garrison was not ready to leave until four o'clock. With Major Anderson in front, the garrison flag under his arm, the troops fell in under the command of Captain Doubleday and marched down the wharf and on to the *Isabel* to the tune of *Yankee Doodle*. Because of the delay, the *Isabel* had missed the tide and was fast aground; consequently, the garrison could not avoid witnessing the celebration occasioned by their defeat.[138]

When he was boarding the *Isabel*, Captain Doubleday was stopped by a Confederate officer who wanted to know why he had shot a hole in the Moultrie House. Doubleday merely replied that the proprietor had given him a wretched room one night and that he was unable to resist the temptation to get even with him. The officer gave a hearty laugh and said, "You were perfectly right, sir, and I justify the act." [139]

Meanwhile the governor, General Beauregard, Judge Magrath, Roger Pryor, all the politicians, and half of the people of Charleston were milling around in the harbor on anything they could find that floated, waiting to get on Sumter. In spite of the fact that the *Isabel* was stuck fast at the end of the wharf, the decision was made to proceed with the flag-raising and the ensuing celebration. The Confederate flag and the Palmetto flag were raised simultaneously, accompanied by the sound of whistles, bells, the booming of cannons, and the shouts of everyone who could see.[140]

The honor of occupying Sumter for the first night was given to the Palmetto Guard, with Lt. Col. Roswell Ripley as its first commanding officer under Confederate occupancy. With the fort still smouldering and the danger of the magazine exploding, additional fire engines were sent out. The city firemen, with the help of the members of the Palmetto Guard, brought the fire under control, but it was not until the next day that it was finally extinguished.[141]

Early the next morning the *Isabel* finally got under way. As she steamed slowly by Morris Island on her way to the fleet, Anderson received a remarkable acclaim. The Confederate gunners, who had shelled him throughout the bombardment, "lined the beach silent, and with heads uncovered, while Anderson and his command passed before them, and an expression of scorn at the apparent cowardice of the fleet in not even attempting to rescue so gallant an officer and his command." [142]

The men were transferred to the *Baltic*, which, after some delay, crossed the bar and sailed for New York. On board the garrison were enjoying good food for the first time in months, catching up on their sleep, and undoubtedly telling what heroes they had been. When they reached New York they received a hero's welcome, thereby confirming their statements.

Maj. Gen. Samuel Jones, C.S.A., who later succeeded General Beauregard as commander of the defenses of Charleston, said of Anderson: "He was a well trained and tried soldier, and an accomplished gentleman, with a high and scrupulous sense of honor. He acted as might have been expected of such an officer so circumstanced." [143] Anderson lived, fought, and nearly died by his sense of honor.

10

The most frustrated man in the vicinity of Charleston was Captain Gustavus V. Fox. From the bridge of the *Baltic* he could see the entire bombardment, and, though his specific orders were to relieve Sumter, he could do nothing. Because of political chicanery, he found himself off Charleston with no fighting ships to force passage to the fort. Fox had operated through the regular chain of command in outfitting his expedition in New York. The secretary of the navy had assigned to him the men-of-war *Powhatan*, *Pocahontas*, *Pawnee*, and *Harriet Lane* and the transport

Baltic, along with three tugs, which were to run in supplies and troops to Anderson while the men-of-war fought their way in. Unknown to the secretary of war, the secretary of the navy, or Captain Fox, President Lincoln, at the insistence of Secretary of State Seward, had assigned the *Powhatan* to the expedition to relieve Fort Pickens.[144]

The *Baltic* arrived ten miles off Charleston at three o'clock on the morning of April 12. About that time General Beauregard's aides were handing the ultimatum to Major Anderson. The only ship at the rendezvous was the *Harriet Lane*. About 7 A.M. the *Pawnee* came into view over the horizon. Boarding her, Fox asked her skipper, Capt. Stephen C. Rowan, to "stand in for the bar" along with the *Baltic*. Rowan refused; his written orders instructed him to stay ten miles off the bar until the arrival of the *Powhatan*, whose skipper would give him further orders. But the *Powhatan* was miles away somewhere off the Florida coast. Rowan, who did not know that Sumter was being bombarded, told Fox, "I am not going in there to begin Civil War." Fox returned to the *Baltic* and along with the *Harriet Lane* steamed slowly toward the bar. Only when they had gotten closer in did they hear the Confederate batteries firing away at Sumter. Later these two were joined by the *Pawnee*, and when Rowan realized what was going on, he was in favor of blasting his way in and sharing the fate of the garrison. Fox had difficulty dissuading him from doing it and forcing him to anchor. All three were awaiting the arrival of the heavily gunned *Powhatan* and the *Pocahontas*, along with the three tugs. One of the tugs had taken refuge from a heavy storm in Wilmington, North Carolina; another overshot the rendezvous point and ended up in Savannah; the third never left New York.[145]

The three waiting vessels anchored off the bar were being cursed both by the beleaguered garrison and by the Confederate gunners for their apparent cowardice. Actually, had they attempted to "run in," they probably would have been blasted out of the water by the guns on Morris and Sullivan's islands. On the evening of April 13 the *Pocahontas* arrived, just at the time

Anderson was surrendering. It was not until then that Fox learned that the *Powhatan* had been sent on another relief expedition.[146] Fox ended his somewhat bitter report to the secretary of war with the statement "that with the *Powhatan* a reinforcement would have been easy. . . . In justice to itself as well as an acknowledgement of my earnest efforts, I trust the Government has sufficient reasons for putting me in the position they have placed me." [147]

Pvt. Daniel Hough, whose arm had been blown off by the premature explosion during the salute, was given a soldier's burial, with a volley fired over his grave, on Morris Island. The Reverend W. B. Yates came over from the city to read the burial service.[148] George Fielding and Sgt. James Edward Galway, also injured during the salute, were rushed to the hospital in the city. Galway died the next day, while under the care of Dr. J. J. Chisolm, and was buried in St. Lawrence Cemetery. Fielding slowly recovered and six weeks later was given a pass signed by General Beauregard requesting that he be allowed to go through the lines unharmed.[149]

The celebration continued for days after the bombardment was over. William Howard Russell, a correspondent for the London *Times* who arrived in Charleston shortly after Major Anderson's surrender, wrote that the streets of the city "present some such aspect as those of Paris in the last revolution [1848]." Crowds of troops promenaded the streets, restaurants were filled to overflowing, there was reveling in barrooms, and parties took place in private homes.

Second Lieutenant Meade of Virginia, a West Point graduate, had the unique distinction of officially fighting on both sides during the war. He was with Anderson all through the initial bombardment of Fort Sumter. Captain Doubleday was suspicious of him, because he was from the South, but when it was time for him and his detail to work the guns, he gained Doubleday's approbation. Shortly after returning to New York with the garrison on the *Baltic*, Meade resigned from the United States Army and joined with his native state. Three months later he died of disease while stationed at Richmond.

Major Anderson was not wounded during the bombardment, but the strain of bearing alone the responsibility of keeping the peace while his government vacillated back and forth had wrecked him both emotionally and physically. He was really as much a battle casualty as he would have been if he had received a fragment of a shell in his shoulder. Upon his return to New York, where his name had become a household word, he was feted, wined, and dined. In spite of repeated requests, he was unable to write his report about the bombardment of Sumter; he left that to Capt. Gustavus Fox, who wrote in a single sentence Anderson's statement to Secretary of War Cameron. In spite of its brevity, it conveyed Anderson's mixed emotions of pride and failure in having attempted to hold and defend Sumter.

In recognition of his heroic action, Anderson was brevetted brigadier general and sent to Kentucky. It was thought that, as he was a native of that state, with his prestige he could keep it from seceding. On October 27, 1863, he was retired for disability. Just before the end of the war he was brevetted a major general, and he participated in the raising of the American flag at Fort Sumter on April 14, 1865, four years to the day after he had lowered it when he was forced to capitulate.

11

Fort Sumter was in the hands of the Confederate States, but what now? Was there to be war, or would the issue be settled by compromise? If war came, would it be over in 90 days, or would it be of long duration? The politicians with their demagoguery thundered: Armisted Burt of Abbeville District promised to drink all the blood shed in consequence of secession. James H. Hammond expressed amazement that war should have come even after seven states had seceded. Even the vociferous Charleston *Mercury*, after the surrender of Sumter by Anderson, thought that there would be no war. The masses of South Carolinians reading the editorials in the newspapers, as well as listening to the political haranguing to which they had been subjected for months, believed that disunion could be peaceably effected. They were carried away on a wave of popular excitement without realizing the consequences.

There were some, however, who predicted that secession meant war. William H. Gist, who had been governor just before Pickens, forecast that "two battles will end the war and our independence will be acknowledged," but the realistic D. H. Hamilton stated that the people "must be sleeping in fanciful security." [150]

Regardless of what the politicians thought, and probably not caring what they said, General Beauregard planned a series of defenses for Charleston and for the protection of the entire coast. Naturally his first step was to restore Sumter to fighting condition. Most of the batteries on Morris Island had been aimed toward Sumter, and consequently would be of little use in case of a naval attack. The district engineer, Major Whiting, stated that "Fort Sumter could not be taken from Morris Island alone. . . . Let the enemy occupy it entirely." Beauregard concurred, but two years later some of the bloodiest fighting of the war took place on this desolate island. Whiting, however, was correct in his surmise, because even after all of Morris Island had been captured by the Union forces, they were unable to take Sumter.[151]

Governor Pickens, who seemed to think of himself as a military genius, kept harassing Beauregard to erect defenses along the entire coast of South Carolina. Finally Beauregard wrote him on April 18, 1861, that he could not leave the defenses of Charleston, as he considered them "paramount to other points on the coast of this state." [152] He told the governor it was up to him to see about the defenses of Beaufort, Georgetown, and Edisto, if he was so anxious to have them. Three days later, however, Beauregard wrote the secretary of war in Montgomery that when he had removed all of his troops and guns from Morris Island, he would have "some of the latter disposable for other points on the coast of South Carolina or other localities as the Department shall direct."

In other words, Beauregard, not Pickens, was the one who was going to decide where the defenses along the coast were to go.

One of the first to be constructed was a small fortification on Battery Island overlooking the lower part of the Stono River, and named Fort Pickens in honor of the governor. Another small fortification called Fort Palmetto, located on Cole's Island, also overlooked the entrance of Stono Inlet.[153]

Early in May, General Beauregard wrote to J. Townsend on Edisto Island informing him that at the request of General Pickens the guns had been furnished for the two forts on the island overlooking the North and South Edisto rivers. In calling Governor Pickens "General," Beauregard may have had his tongue in his cheek, though actually, by virtue of his office as governor, Pickens was head of the state militia, which at this time was an important position, as almost none of the South Carolina regiment had been sworn into the Confederate service.[154]

Two weeks later, Beauregard submitted to Pickens a plan, along with a list of armaments, "of the works already constructed and to be constructed for the defenses of the South Carolina coast, from North Edisto to Broad River, inclusive." He stated that the two works already completed (Fort Elliott and Fort Schnierle), the location of which had undoubtedly been determined by Pickens for the protection of Beaufort, "when fully and properly armed will answer well against any naval expedition." But he also said that the town would have better protection "if they had been placed elsewhere." Realizing that the coast above Charleston was unprotected, Beauregard ordered his engineer, Capt. F. D. Lee, to select sites for batteries to be located at Bull's Bay, South and North Santee, and Georgetown. He specified that there was to be "one site at each entrance." Beauregard wrote Pickens that the work should be done at once.[155]

But gunfire alone could not keep out a heavily armed fleet. Beauregard, therefore, instructed Col. L. M. Hatch to place obstructions in several of the navigable channels. In the early part of the war, before mines and booms came into use, this was done by driving piles and sinking barges. In theory this was efficient, but because of marine borers, tidal action, and high winds, it was difficult to keep these obstructions intact.[156]

On May 27, 1861, General Beauregard was relieved from duty in the state of South Carolina. He relinquished to Governor Pickens the command of the state volunteer forces and transferred to Col. Richard H. Anderson the command of the Confederate forces in Charleston Harbor and its vicinity.[157]

Three months later, on August 21, 1861, Brig. Gen. Roswell S. Ripley, C.S.A., was assigned to command the department of South Carolina. It was Ripley who had fired the "hot shot" at Sumter which had set the barracks on fire and certainly hastened Anderson's surrender. An able officer, irascible and at times hot-tempered when his superiors did not agree with him, Ripley set out not only to strengthen the fortifications in and around Charleston but to locate new ones. The Confederacy had few arms and many fields of activity, and since an attack on Charleston was not considered imminent, Ripley was not given many guns, which raised his ire. But he prepared his defenses well with the material at his disposal.[158]

Major Ledbetter in Richmond wrote to Major J. H. Trapier, the engineer officer in Charleston, recommending that "the prize ship *A. H. Thompson* be purchased and equipped as a floating battery for Port Royal." Both Major Trapier and General Ripley apparently ignored his recommendation, for no floating battery was placed in Port Royal Sound. They may have thought it impractical to fortify the Sound.[159]

Since few white Southerners would think of soiling their hands with manual labor, the construction of the coastal and harbor defenses was left to slave labor. In the first months of the war the planters seemed to have freely offered the use of their Negroes for this purpose, but by the end of 1861 this was no longer the case.[160] The principal reason for withdrawing the slaves was that the rice had to be harvested during the fall months; consequently, there was a marked slackening in the construction of the defenses. In addition to these problems, there was a shortage of arms and armaments of all types. When the Charleston arsenal was seized in late December, 1860, it contained a quantity of small arms; however, Pickens had given much to other states and had used almost all of the remainder to equip South Carolina troops stationed within the state, as well as those sent to other parts of the Confederacy.[161] When a blockade-runner successfully eluded the blockade squadron, not a difficult accomplishment in the early days of the war, there was always a scramble between the Confederate and state authorities to see who would get the cargo.[162] One runner arrived in Savannah with over 10,000 guns; many others came into Charleston with heavy guns, shoes, blankets, and other war supplies. Without the blockade-runners, it is extremely doubtful if the Confederates could have held out for any appreciable time.

As early as August 2, 1861, Gen. Thomas W. Sherman, U.S.A., was ordered by the assistant secretary of war, with Lincoln's approval, to start recruiting a force in the New England states preparatory to an attack on the southern coast of the Confederate states.[163] This fact was undoubtedly made known to the Confederate authorities, but with the slaves withdrawn to harvest the crops, the malarial season at its height along the coast, and the shortage of heavy guns, work progressed slowly on the defenses.

Word was sent repeatedly to the Confederate authorities that a large expedition was in the making, but they did not know when and where the blow would strike. The Confederate artillerymen standing by their guns did not have long to wait.

2

War

1

TECHNICALLY, THE BATTLE OF PORT ROYAL SHOULD NOT BE included in this study. It took place more than 50 miles from Charleston. It had, however, such a strategic effect upon the siege of that city that it cannot be overlooked or minimized, for it gave the Union forces possession of one of the best harbors on the entire coast. With Port Royal under Union control, blockading vessels could be supplied, repaired, and fueled there. Its capture gave the Union naval forces control of the coast from above Georgetown, South Carolina, to New Smyrna, Florida, with the exception of Charleston, and also provided control of most adjacent inland waterways. In addition, Port Royal was admirably situated to outfit and train the troops used in the siege.[1]

Port Royal Sound and its adjacent islands lie between Charleston and Savannah, and the waterway leads to the town of Beaufort. At that time it was the home of many planters of the surrounding area and had a number of fine houses, many of which still stand.

After his blockade proclamation, Lincoln appointed a "Blockade Strategy Board" to recommend the best way of enforcing the order. Among the many recommendations made was one to seize Port Royal Sound and its nearby island.

Confederate forces were equally aware of the Sound's importance to the Union forces and were making efforts to fortify its entrance against naval attack. But they were faced with two almost insurmountable obstacles: the great distance between the islands on either side of the mouth of the harbor and the acquisi-

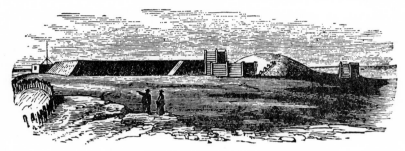

FORT BEAUREGARD

tion of enough heavy guns to repulse an assault. As early as May, 1861, General Beauregard wrote to Governor Pickens: "I am of the opinion that the entrance of the magnificent and important harbor of Port Royal can be effectively protected by two strong works on Bay Point and Hilton Head, on each side of the entrance, and the steel-clad floating battery moored halfway between the two, all armed with the heaviest rifled guns that can be made; but the construction not being practicable at present, I have resorted to local works." Beauregard got neither his "heaviest rifled guns" nor his armored floating battery.[2]

Governor Pickens, overriding Beauregard's objections, ordered the erection of two dirt forts, one on each side of the entrance. The one on Hilton Head Island was called Fort Walker, in honor of the secretary of war; the other, on Bay Point, was named after

General Beauregard. The distance between the two forts was two and five-eighths miles. They were equipped with a motley collection of rebored and small guns.[3]

Fort Walker was built to house seven large guns on its sea face, but since these were never received, thirteen guns of various sizes were mounted in their place. Because they were so close to each other, they prevented the construction of traverses against enfilading fire, and this was the basic weakness of the defense. Two guns that were to command the beach approaches arrived without carriages; they were buried in the sand and aimed in the direction from which it was thought an assaulting party might approach. Once fired, they were absolutely useless. Essentially the same thing applied to the guns in Fort Beauregard across the bay.[4]

Three months after the beginning of construction, a recommendation was made to the secretary of war that the captured schooner *A. H. Thompson* be purchased and used as a floating battery. Again the lack of suitable heavy guns was mentioned. No notice was taken of either communication, which made Beauregard doubt whether the entrance could be adequately defended, an opinion apparently shared by his engineers. At the time of the battle of Port Royal, Beauregard was in Virginia.[5]

As early as mid-September, 1861, President Lincoln was urging Gideon Welles, his secretary of the navy, to prepare an expedition against Port Royal. Prodded by the president, the secretary immediately began to gather the most formidable armada ever assembled under the American flag. In theory, this expedition was to have been kept secret, but the news leaked out and was picked up by newspaper correspondents. In early October, William Howard Russell wrote about "the new expedition which I have been hearing for some time is about to sail to Port Royal . . . in order to reduce the works erected at the entrance of the Sound, to secure a base of operations against Charleston, and cut in upon the communication between that place and Savannah . . . the Yankee invasion, which surely must succeed, as the Naval force will be overwhelming."[6]

The naval forces, consisting of 15 men-of-war, carrying about 148 guns of all caliber, with some as large as 11 inches, were under the command of Flag Officer Samuel Francis Du Pont. The army contingent, consisting of 12,653 troops, was under the immediate command of Brig. Gen. Thomas W. Sherman.[7]

The first group of the expedition sailed from New York harbor on October 17, arriving two days later at Hampton Roads, Virginia, where another large fleet was waiting. For the next ten days ships loaded with troops and supplies continued to arrive; finally, on October 29, they set out, but there were so many that it was nightfall before all were in proper position. The 36 transports, containing nearly 13,000 troops were formed in three columns, preceded by the 44-gun flagship *Wabash*, which was surrounded by 14 men-of-war. As one of the naval officers remarked, "It looked like an emigration." The invasion fleet was a heterogeneous group, consisting of everything from a full-fledged man-of-war to a New York ferryboat. The 51 vessels, sailing in three columns, stretched out for a distance of six miles.[8]

That night, most of the ships managed to hold their positions, but by the next morning the wind had increased in intensity and almost all of them were out of place. The weather continued to grow worse, and the ships rolled and pitched violently. Some of the smaller vessels could not take it. One was forced to hoist a signal of distress, and two tugs returned to Hampton Roads. All during the day the wind became stronger, and the waves reached mountainous heights. In order to save the smaller vessels from disaster, it was decided to run close to Cape Hatteras, which in itself made navigation extremely dangerous. Throughout the night great anxiety prevailed; one of the vessels signaled "ship ashore" and another fired several rockets, indicating that she, too, was in serious trouble. With the seas so high, however, nothing could be done even if a ship was in distress. But the armada continued on, hoping for the best, every vessel on her own. Daylight revealed that 20 ships had disappeared during the night, and all the next day vessels were dispatched from the convoy to look for the missing ones. The sea had grown calmer and the wind had fallen, but what the convoy had gone through was only a prelude to what was about to happen. On November 1, the wind reached gale force, threatening destruction of the entire fleet and abandonment of the expedition. The next morning only one sail could be seen from the bridge of the flagship *Wabash*. It appeared to be a major disaster.[9]

Once separated from the convoy, each captain had opened the sealed orders he had received upon departure. Consequently, vessels straggled into Port Royal for the next two days. Only a few ships were lost. The *Isaac P. Smith* finally made port with only one gun; she had been forced to jettison her main battery of eight eight-inch guns to aid a sinking ship.

Waiting to meet the "overwhelming" Union fleet was Tatnall's "mosquito fleet," consisting of three small river steamers and a tug, each armed with two 32-pound guns (smooth-bore). Commodore Josiah Tatnall had resigned from the United States Navy to go with his native Georgia and was known to almost every officer in the fleet as a resolute and courageous officer. On November 4, several gunboats anchored in Port Royal Sound out of range of the guns of the forts. About sunset, Tatnall's "mosquito fleet" sallied out and fired at them at long range. Immediately the gunboats weighed anchors and got under way, ready for the fight. Realizing that if he continued on course, the gap between the opposing fleets would be closed to such an extent that the 11-inch bow guns of the approaching gunboats could be brought to bear, Tatnall made an abrupt turn and headed for the protection of Skull Creek.

Early the next morning he tried the same maneuver; again the gunboats gave chase, and this time they came into the range of the forts, who immediately opened fire. A lucky hit from one of the gunboats blew up a caisson in Fort Beauregard. The only damage to the pursuing gunboats was to some of their rigging, but they did get an idea of the number of guns in the fort and their range.[10]

Flag Officer Du Pont's plan of attack was for his heavy ships to steam up the Sound equidistant from both forts and to return their fire at a point about two and a half miles up the Sound. They were then to turn to port, steam slowly by Fort Walker, and pound the fort with their heavy starboard broadsides. When they reached the lower extremity of the Sound, they were to turn and again engage Fort Walker, this time with their port broadsides.[11]

Du Pont planned to attack the forts on November 5, since all of his fighting ships and most of his transports had arrived safely. However, when he was about to run up the signal to begin, his flagship *Wabash*, drawing 22½ feet, grounded while passing over Fishing Rip Shoals. By the time the *Wabash* was freed, Du Pont felt that it was too late to make the attack and postponed it to the next morning. The following day a gale blew, and the attack was again postponed.

November 7 was clear; a dead calm covered Port Royal Sound. The day was ideal for accurate shooting from ships, and Du Pont hoisted his signal. His plan was to attack Fort Walker first, though some of his officers felt that the weaker fort (Beauregard) should be attacked first. As this was strictly a navy show, the army being merely spectators, the navy personnel felt that they should set an example, and everyone put forth his best effort. On board the ships the drums beat to quarters and the men stood by their guns. Slowly and majestically, with the 44-gun *Wabash* leading the way, and with 14 men-of-war astern, the columns steamed up the Sound equidistant from either fort.[12]

Suddenly the morning quiet was shattered by a roar from a gun from Fort Walker; this was followed by a large shell screeching over the *Wabash*. A moment later the ten-inch bow gun on the *Wabash* shot at one of the "mosquito fleet." Following Du Pont's plan, the ships deployed into two parallel columns. The left column—the *Wabash* and heavily gunned men-of-war— swung to port, making an ellipse between the two forts. The right column, consisting of six gunboats, was to make sure that Tatnall's "mosquito fleet" could neither get to the transports anchored out of range of the forts nor sink any disabled vessel. After the "mosquito fleet" was immobilized, the gunboats were then to join in the major engagement by enfilading the forts. The larger ships were slowly steaming in ellipses which were alternately taking them away from the forts, then bringing them nearer. This, in conjunction with their forward movement, made it difficult for the gunners in the forts to adjust their range. But it enabled the fleet to bring to bear about 50 heavy guns each time it came within range of either fort. After making the turn in the center of the Sound, the column started down, bucking the flood tide. They approached slowly, with the *Wabash* in the lead. She received the attention of the gunners in Fort Walker and was hit repeatedly. Nevertheless, about 600 yards off the fort, she fired broadside after broadside with her eight- and nine-inch guns with such devastating effect that the gunners had to take to their bombproofs. For 25 minutes she remained almost stationary. By this time every gun on every ship within range was firing as rapidly as possible. Fort Walker was being smothered by shells. The *Wabash* alone fired 880 rounds during the engagement, and the *Susquehanna* immediately astern fired over 750 shots from her big guns.[13]

In the meantime the gunners within the fort were having trouble. Shortly after the action started, two of their rifled and most effective guns were rendered useless—the shells would not go down the barrels. The heavy ten-inch gun and two 42-pound guns were also incapacitated. Consequently, the fire power of the fort was materially reduced, primarily because of defective ammunition. Early in the engagement a 32-pound gun was hit directly by one of the broadsides and disabled. But even with nearly half of their fire power knocked out, the gunners continued fighting.

Meanwhile, the gunboats had taken up stations from which they could throw an enfilading fire into the fort. Without traverses, the gunners had no protection from this devastating cross fire. The gun that should have been mounted on the northern flank had not been placed in position, for it had arrived without a carriage. In spite of the broadsides from the entire fleet, the garrison stood by their guns like veterans, although for most of them it was the first fight. At one time in the battle as many as 60 heavy shells a minute, ranging in size from eight to 11 inches, were being poured into the fort, filling the air with fragments of gun carriages, timbers, clouds of sand, and bodies. The noise from the concentration of gunfire was so great that it was heard as far away as Fernandina, Florida. A naval officer viewing the scene from the bridge of the *Wabash* said later: "I can bear tribute to the great gallantry of the men who fought the battery at Fort Walker; they stood to their guns like men and fired rapidly and accurately." [14]

Later in the morning the commanding officer of the fort, Col. John A. Wagener, was stunned by a bursting shell and forced to turn over the command to Maj. Arthur M. Huger. Although the situation was hopeless, "the fort was simply fought as a point of honor," and the three remaining guns on the Sound side fired until the ammunition was nearly exhausted. Only then, having been under a deadly fire for over four hours, did the garrison retreat. They had lost nearly all their equipment, which by this time was buried under the debris of gun carriages and sand, and they therefore had to leave their dead. The retreating garrison had to cross a field between the fort and the nearby woods. Carrying their wounded, they ran across, endeavoring to dodge the hail of fire being poured upon them from the broadsides of the fleet, which by now had closed in. A Northern army source says that the retreat was a panic. From the sending end of a cannon it probably looked that way, but it would be hard to imagine a group of men calmly strolling across an open space with 60 heavy shells per minute bursting among them. The supporting infantry, which was in the comparative safety of the woods, also beat a precipitous retreat. Their fear was that Du Pont's gunboats might cut them off at the ferry when they attempted to cross to the mainland. Expecting the gunboats momentarily, the soldiers discarded much of their equipment along the six-mile walk over sandy roads to the ferry. They hurriedly boarded the steamers and flats that were waiting for them and were carried over to safety, but they had left two light field pieces on Hilton Head Island. Seeing the two guns, Lieutenant Johnson, an officer of the "mosquito fleet," went ashore. He respiked the improperly disabled artillery and succeeded in dismounting one and throwing it overboard.[15]

When the fort no longer replied, Comdr. John Rogers of Du Pont's staff was rowed ashore in a boat carrying a white flag. He was followed by acting Lieutenant Barnes, U.S.N., with a detachment of enlisted men. The officers were the first to enter the deserted fort. As Barnes put it, "the scene inside baffles all descriptions. Five guns were dismounted and lying in a heap of fragments about their respective position in battery. Near each, one or two dead, horribly mangled, were lying, crushed out of all semblance to the human form divine, a mere miserable dusty heap of gory clothes and flesh." The heavy shells from the ships had done their work well. The dead were collected and buried in a deep trench, and the navy chaplain read the burial service over them.[16]

At dusk the army landed "amidst the wildest confusion and in a most beautiful disorder," and then Comdr. C. R. P. Rogers, U.S.N., the captain of the *Wabash*, turned Fort Walker over to Brig. Gen. H. G. Wright.[17]

Fort Beauregard had also been badly damaged, although it had received only a fraction of the shells Fort Walker had. The best rifled gun in the fort exploded on the thirty-second discharge; most of the others were smooth bores, and the range was too great for them. Some had faulty ammunition. Thus little, if any, harm was done to the fleet. The last gun was fired from Beauregard at 3:35 P.M. When cheers were heard from the fleet, the garrison knew that Fort Walker had fallen. Fearful of being cut off—Fort Beauregard was also on an island—the garrison retreated. At sunset some of the fleet discovered that the fort was apparently abandoned, but, since no one was certain that the entire garrison had evacuated, no landing was made until sunrise the following day. A little later the fort was officially turned over by the navy to Brig. Gen. Isaac I. Stevens.[18]

The credit for the abandonment of the two forts was due to the naval force, acting according to the plans of Flag Officer Du Pont.

The Battle of Port Royal was the first major Union victory in the war.[19]

It was a common occurrence for brothers to fight on opposite sides during the war. In the Battle of Port Royal, the commanding officer of the Confederate forces was Brig. Gen. Thomas F. Drayton, whose plantation was on Hilton Head Island. His brother, Comdr. Percival Drayton, a Union naval officer, commanded the *Pocahontas*, one of the attacking ships. Because of a breakdown of her machines, the *Pocahontas* arrived after the fight had started. This caused Commander Drayton some concern; he was afraid that Du Pont and his officers might think that he had purposely delayed because he did not want to fight against his brother. Immediately upon arrival, he closed in on Fort Walker and kept up a heavy enfilading fire, getting off 70 shots in a little over an hour; his ship caused a tremendous amount of damage to the interior and also helped to dislodge the gunners.

General Beauregard was criticized by the state convention for his plan of the defense of Port Royal. Because he was in Virginia at the time, he was unable to appear before that body, but John A. Calhoun explained that Beauregard had "declined for a long time to furnish a plan" and had done so only at the urging of "some of the most prominent citizens of Charleston and Beaufort." Why this controversy should have arisen is something of an enigma. On June 20, 1861, Governor Pickens wrote Secretary of War Mallory in Richmond: "Under the scientific examination of General Beauregard I have ordered the State engineer to commence forts at Hilton Head and Bay Point, the entrance of Beaufort Harbor." Apparently, when the criticism was being leveled at Beauregard, the governor kept a discreet silence.[20]

Some were also critical of the apparent lack of defense of the forts, but this criticism was not shared by the Confederate military authorities. Later when the steamer *Planter* was abducted by her crew, a memorandum was found in her cabin which read: "The troops of the fort [Walker] fought with great courage and determination. At Bay Point [Beauregard] the order to retreat was felt to be judicious, but the soldiers were anxious to remain and battle it out to the last." General Ripley used the *Planter* as a dispatch boat to take him to the fortifications around Charleston. The memorandum must have been written either by him or by one of his staff. The garrison of Fort Walker consisted of companies A and B of the German Artillery of Charleston. Upon returning to the city after the fight, they were encamped on Marion Square and at their first parade Colonel Wagener, their commanding officer, commended them for their gallantry. The state legislature, which was then in session, passed a similar resolution.[21]

When the news of Du Pont's victory at Port Royal reached Charleston, the people were thrown into a panic and rumors swept the city: the enemy were marching on it; traitors were going to burn it to the ground and destroy all the railroads so that there could be no escape. One person wrote: "there is great terror prevailing here and no preparation—neither troops nor defense. I regard the city in hourly peril. I believe it could be taken in six hours." Those who could fled or sent their valuables to places of greater safety.[22]

Three days after the battle, Brigadier General Trapier—Ripley was with General Lee at Coosawhatchie—wired the secretary of war for authority to proclaim martial law. Two days later he received a reply that the decision was up to General Lee.[23] Martial law was not put into effect, however, because Gen. Thomas W. Sherman made no attempt to land troops and march against Charleston; he remained on Hilton Head Island establishing his base camp.

With the fall of Port Royal, more of the sea island region, which constituted one of the richest portions of the state of South Carolina, fell into Federal hands, along with large quantities of cotton and thousands of Negroes.

2

On November 5, 1861, under Special Order No. 206, a new military department was created consisting of South Carolina,

Georgia, and East Florida.[24] The man assigned to its command was little known, despite his brilliant performance in the Mexican War. This man was Robert Edward Lee, a general in the Confederate States Army. He arrived in Charleston on November 6, but, hearing that Port Royal Sound was full of ships and an attack expected momentarily, General Lee proceeded by a special Charleston and Savannah Railroad train to Coosawhatchie, the station nearest to Port Royal Sound.[25]

On the evening of the battle, when Lee was on his way to Port Royal Sound, he met General Ripley, who was returning from Fort Walker. Ripley briefed him as to the size of the Union fleet and informed him that both forts had been evacuated and that the fleet had entered the sound. Ripley also reported that the two regiments had lost all their equipment while evacuating the island and were retiring to Garden's Corner. Anticipating that the gunboats and the transports would press on and attempt to sever the Charleston and Savannah Railroad, General Lee did everything he could with his limited resources to defend the rail line as well as implement the defenses of Charleston and Savannah.[26]

Governor Pickens apparently wanted to play soldier again, for on November 9, Judah P. Benjamin, acting secretary of war, wired him that "General Lee is in command of the department" and "has full power to act, and it would be well to send him a copy of this dispatch, that he may not scruple in using all the means of the Government within his reach for your defense." It will probably never be known what motivated this telegram, because Benjamin burned all of his papers just before the evacuation of Richmond. To make sure that General Lee knew of the telegram to Pickens, Benjamin sent one two days later to the general, authorizing him to use all the resources of South Carolina and Georgia under control of the Confederate government.[27]

Anticipating an attack, but not knowing from which direction it would come, General Lee did everything within his power to prepare for it. Capt. Henry J. Harthstene, C.S.N., was requested "to close the inland passes to Charleston and to prepare the water defenses and batteries," and General Ripley in Charleston was

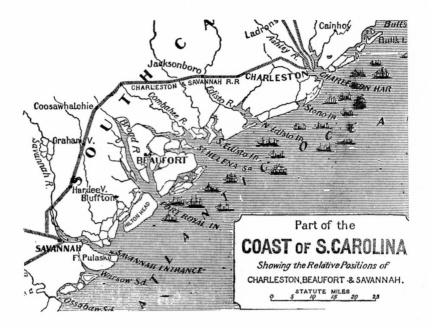

Part of the

COAST of S.CAROLINA

Showing the Relative Positions of

CHARLESTON, BEAUFORT ·& SAVANNAH.

STATUTE MILES
0   5   10   15   20   25

informed that General Lee was "desirous that defenses should be constructed as soon as practicable upon Charleston Neck." [28]

The coast of South Carolina is a complicated series of barrier islands and waterways interspersed with inlets. Many of the inlets are navigable, though dangerous. Consequently, in theory, each one should be defended. Because of this unusual topography, the Charleston and Savannah Railroad was located on the mainland some distance from the inlets. After learning of the effect of the devastating naval gunfire on the earthwork fortifications at Port Royal, Lee wrote to Governor Pickens that the Federal transports, loaded with troops and covered by the guns of the fleet, "can be thrown with great celerity against any point, and far outnumber any force we can bring against it in the field." With a shortage of guns, powder, and troops, it was essential in Lee's plan of defense to keep the Charleston and Savannah Railroad intact. It was the lifeline of his coastal defenses; if it continued to function, troops could be rushed from either Savannah or Charleston to the threatened point. The cutting off of this rail line became the prime target for the Union forces for the rest of the war.[29]

Shortly after his arrival, General Lee, disturbed by the lack of troops, wrote a rather sharp letter to the state adjutant general: "there are no means of defending the State except with her own troops, and if they do not come forward, and that immediately, I fear her suffering will be greatly aggravated. . . . the backwardness in entering for the war is indefensible, for whether it lasts twelve months or twelve years, it cannot be arrested, and all are pledged to its termination." Some men were finding out that war, with its accompanying hardships, was not as glamorous as it first appeared. Furthermore, it was easier to enlist for six months or a year in the state forces than for the "duration" in the Confederate service. Unusual conditions were required to raise the anger of General Lee. But he got results. A few days later Lee wrote Pickens that he was glad to hear that the regiments he was organizing would soon be ready for service in the field, but that he would not arm them unless they "entered the Confederate service for the war." The time for playing soldier had passed.[30]

In the early part of January, 1862, General Lee wrote to the adjutant general in Richmond, giving him a frank estimate of the situation: "Our works are not yet finished; their progress is slow; guns are required for their armament, and I have not received as many troops from South Carolina and Georgia as I had expected." He went on to say that "wherever his [the enemy's] fleet can be brought, no opposition to his landing can be made except within range of our fixed batteries. We have nothing to oppose to its heavy guns, which sweep over the low banks of the country with irresistible force. The farther he can be withdrawn from his floating batteries, the weaker he will become." In other words, Lee felt that it was essential to withdraw his men and guns from the range of naval gunfire.[31]

Upon receipt of General Lee's communication, Adjutant General Cooper must have had a conference with the acting secretary of war, Judah P. Benjamin, and possibly with President Jefferson

Davis, for on February 18, 1862, the following order was sent to General Lee by Benjamin: "Withdraw all forces from the islands in your department to the mainland, taking proper measures to save artillery and munitions of war." The next day, in a letter to General Ripley in Charleston, Lee gave his reason for the withdrawal, though he did not mention that he had received direct orders from Benjamin. "I am in favor of abandoning all exposed points as far as possible within reach of the enemy's fleet of gunboats and taking interior positions where we can meet on more equal terms." [32]

Had General Thomas W. Sherman, with his 13,000 men and the overpowering guns of the fleet, made a sudden attack on the mainland and cut and held the railroad, the results would have been disastrous for General Lee. Instead of making a frontal attack, Sherman first established a base camp at Hilton Head Island and then sent out reconnaissance parties to investigate and to ascertain the number of Confederate troops on the nearby islands. The first expedition, headed by Capt. Q. A. Gillmore, went to Braddocks Point, overlooking Calibogue Sound, on November 10–11, 1861. There they found the earthworks deserted and the tents still standing. But more important, they discovered four cannon and with some ammunition, indicating that the Confederate forces had left hurriedly. [33]

When General Lee issued his order for the withdrawal of all troops and arms from the outer islands and more exposed areas, he did so without much loss. However, this left the rich cotton plantations with their crops completely at the mercy of marauding parties and looters, who took full advantage of the opportunity. For the rest of the war, most of these islands became something of a "no man's land." [34]

3

Military activity was not the direct cause of the conflagration that occurred in Charleston on December 11, 1861, though it may indirectly have occasioned the disaster. But the fire did have a direct effect on the citizenry; it destroyed many residences in a city that was already becoming crowded by refugees from the nearby Sea Islands. The conflagration actually began with a small cooking fire belonging to some slaves who had accompanied their master from one of the outlying plantations and who were refugees in the city.

It was almost a year after the signing of the Ordinance of Secession. Port Royal had fallen the month before. Thousands of Union troops were stationed at Hilton Head, and the inhabitants of the coastal islands had fled because of frequent raids. The war had been brought home. December 11 was a clear and surprisingly mild day with no wind.[35] General Robert E. Lee had just completed his tour of inspection and was dining at the Mills House. Everything seemed calm and peaceful. The sash and blind factory of H. P. Russell, at the foot of Hasell Street just east of East Bay, was busy making articles for the Confederate army. Presumably, Mr. Russell, after checking everything carefully, locked the door of his factory that night and returned to his home thinking that nothing was amiss. However, some slaves from the outlying area had started a small fire on the factory property. The fire got out of hand, igniting the factory. At 8:30 that night the alarm bells rang and a red lantern was suspended from a pole extending in a northeasterly direction from the steeple of St. Michael's Church to show which way the fire was. No one gave it any serious thought, thinking that it was just another unimportant blaze. However, in a few minutes the wind began to rise and with it the flames, burning steadily and inexorably in a southwesterly course. People started to realize that something serious was happening. The fire soon jumped East Bay, and the wind, which by now had reached gale force, carried it down as far as Market Street. One or two houses were saved by the diligent work of some of the fire companies who knew their owners. The Pinckney Mansion at the northwest corner of East Bay and Market Street (actually Ellery Street) was destroyed, but most of its contents were saved by Capt. John Rutledge—a cousin—and the crew from the *Lady Davis*. The elderly Mrs. Pinckney was taken to

the Rutledge home on Tradd Street, which also burned later in
the night. The Mariner's Church and a bakery were saved by the
crew of the school ship *Lodebar* under the command of Captain
M. L. Aimar. However, sparks ignited the roofs of the wooden
houses on the south side of Market Street, and soon they too were
lost.

About this time General Ripley arrived and ordered several
wooden buildings on State Street blown up. Unfortunately, his
orders were not carried out; if they had been, the fire might have
been contained. The wind carried sparks high in the air and
deposited them on every roof lying in its path. Soon the South
Carolina Institute Hall, where the Ordinance of Secession had
been signed, was blazing, together with the Circular Congregational Church next door, both on Meeting Street. Meanwhile, the
fire had been fanning out as it progressed, destroying homes and
places of business on Hayne and Pinckney streets. Soon the Gas
Works on Church Street was engulfed in flames, and the burning
gas added to the fury of the blaze. Most of the paintings in the
Carolina Art Association were burned, along with the building
housing the Apprentices' Library. The Charleston Theater was
the next to go. The nearby Mills House was saved, however; wet
blankets were hung out the windows and water was poured on
them. About 3 A.M. the steeple of the Circular Church fell, with
its huge bell, which made a loud crashing sound as it broke into
fragments on the cobblestones far below.

Then the wind suddenly died down and a light rain began to
fall. But the hope this aroused was short lived. The rain stopped
and the wind began to rise again, fanning the burning buildings
into fresh blazes and scattering sparks on more roofs, which
quickly ignited, creating a hurricane of flame.[36] General Ripley
now gave orders that 14 houses on the north side of Queen Street
be blown up in order to save the Roman Catholic Orphan House
and the Marine and Roper hospitals. This time his order was
carried out, but the Orphan House caught fire three times, and
each time was put out by the soldiers. However, sparks from it
fell on the roof and the steeple of the nearby Cathedral of St. John

and St. Finbar, and it, too, burned furiously. Many people had stored their goods there, thinking that it was fireproof. But soon the roof of the cathedral caved in, and everything that had been placed in it for safekeeping was burned. The insurance on the building had lapsed the previous week. The intense heat from the cathedral soon ignited nearby St. Andrew's Hall.

The fire continued relentlessly, fanned by the gale. Friend Street (now Legare) down to Tradd was burned, as well as both sides of Broad Street. The large residence on the northeast corner of Tradd and Logan streets was saved by the servants, who managed to climb to the roof with buckets of water and extinguish the sparks as soon as they landed. Still moving forward, the fire destroyed some houses on Limehouse, Greenhill, Savage, New, and Council streets. By daylight it had subsided; there was nothing else to burn. As far as one could see the scene was one of utter desolation; the few buildings that miraculously had escaped stood among smoldering ruins.

People had raced before the fire trying to save their possessions, but the blaze spread with such rapidity that most of them lost all of their furniture, even after moving it two or three times. The draymen, realizing that they had the people at their mercy, asked for and received large sums for hauling household articles to places of safety.[37]

It is possible that the fire could have been arrested if the regular firemen had responded. Unfortunately for the city, most of the former firemen were in the uniform of the Confederate States Army. The people of Charleston rose to the occasion: planters sent in produce for the needy, committees were established to house the homeless, and soup kitchens were set up to feed the hungry. Money poured in from all over the South, and Jefferson Davis ordered an advance payment of money due to the state of South Carolina so that some of it could be used for the needy. Everyone did everything possible to help. The following Sunday, because so many of the churches were burned, congregations had to double up. In the Hibernian Hall the Roman Catholic Bishop preached to his parishioners on the second floor while the members of the Circular Congregational Church held their services on the first. Naturally, the Northern press was elated with the disaster; they said that the fire had been sent by the Lord in retribution for the boast of the inhabitants that Charleston was the "Cradle of Secession."

The burned area covered 540 acres.[38] The chimneys left standing remained a stark reminder of the catastrophe during the entire four years of the war and for many years afterwards.

4

On April 19, 1861, President Lincoln issued a proclamation stating that a blockade of the Southern ports was in effect. This was little more than a paper blockade, for the Federal government had few warships at that time, and many of them were scattered around the world. The first blockading vessel to arrive off Charleston was the frigate *Niagara*, which appeared on the morning of May 11. Since there were four ship channels leading into Charleston, though the Main Channel was by far the best, the effect of the *Niagara* was negligible. Blockade-runners brought in war supplies and other necessities and left with cotton and naval stores almost at will. Gradually, additional ships were sent to accompany the *Niagara*, but the blockade was far from effective.[39]

It occurred to Gustavus V. Fox, assistant secretary of the navy, that sinking ships at the mouths of the harbors might increase the effectiveness of the blockading vessels. Professor A. D. Bache, superintendent of the United States Coast Survey, agreed. Bache was the foremost authority on this subject, for in many cases he had made the surveys himself. On September 4, 1861, Bache wrote to Capt. Samuel F. Du Pont, U.S.N., saying: "I think well of Fox's ideas of closing up that [Charleston] entrance and will bring you the evidence for examination tonight." The plan not only appeared feasible but was approved by higher authority. On October 17, 1861, Secretary of the Navy Gideon Welles gave orders to Guy D. Morgan to purchase 25 old vessels as "secretly as possible before any knowledge is obtained that Government is in the market." [40]

Morgan apparently had no difficulty purchasing old whaling ships berthed in New Bedford, Massachusetts, and New London, Connecticut. By this time the whaling industry was on the decline and the owners were probably delighted to unload these old ships on the government. One was so old that it is remarkable that it was able to remain afloat; it had been captured from the British during the Revolution. These ships were stripped of all of their gear, loaded with granite, and fitted with a pipe and valve so that they could be flooded with ease. When the first fleet departed from New London, signal guns were fired as they passed down the bay, led by the revenue cutter *Varing*.

Capt. Rodney French was appointed "Commodore of the fleet." He wanted the skippers to sail down the coast in a unit, but this was a hard-headed group, and each ship sailed independently for Savannah. In some respects, the trip became a race to see who would be the first to reach his destination.[41]

In a letter of November 17, the secretary of the navy wrote to Flag Officer Du Pont: "It is believed that a new channel now exists bearing about due east from the light [Morris Island]. If this can be thoroughly closed, and only a few vessels sunk in the intricate channel of Sullivan's Island, Charleston as a harbor will no longer exist." [42]

The Stone Fleet, so designated because the ships were loaded with granite, reached its destination singly or in small groups, many of the vessels much the worse for wear. On arrival some grounded, and one or two went adrift. And Commodore J. S. Missroon, the senior officer present, had received no notice of their coming. Someone had failed to forward the information. Apparently he was not pleased with the prospect of looking after a group of hard-bitten New England sailing masters and would assume no responsibility for them. Harsh words passed between some of the captains and Commodore Missroon. One of them criticized him "unsparingly," because he "seemed indifferent to the purpose and safety of the fleet." The same captain went on to say that "he had been heard to express Southern sympathies." Relations were decidedly strained.[43]

The original plan was to sink the first Stone Fleet at the mouth of the Savannah River in order to block Savannah. But the Georgians, in an effort to keep out the Federal fleet or at least make it more difficult for them to enter, had already sunk several old vessels at the mouth of the channel. Once this was known, it was decided to divert the ships to Port Royal, South Carolina, and sink them off Charleston.

At Port Royal they were held up for several days by bad weather. The "sinking" operation was under the command of Capt. Charles Henry Davis, U.S.N., chief of staff of the South Atlantic Blockading Squadron, who had a distinct distaste for the job. On December 2 he wrote to his family: "The pet idea of Mr. Fox has been to stop up some of the southern harbors. . . . I had always a special disgust for this business. . . . I always considered this mode of interrupting commerce as liable to great objections and of doubtful success." His predictions proved correct. Fortunately for him a copy of the letter did not reach Mr. Fox, the assistant secretary of the navy. A decade before, Davis had commanded a ship surveying both Charleston and Savannah for harbor improvements; he had valid reason for his "disgust." [44]

The Stone Fleet set out from Port Royal on December 19 and headed for Charleston. The weather was clear, but the wind was so light that many of the heavily loaded old hulks were unable to cross the bar without aid. Many of the blockading squadron were called upon to act as tugs to get them under way. Finally they all cleared the bar and straggled in to Charleston.

Once there, they looked in vain for the lighthouse on Morris Island. It had been destroyed by the Confederate forces so that no accurate bearing could be gotten from it for the sinking of the fleet. But its destruction did not hinder the pilots from locating the main channel; they were able to locate its ruins with ease. Several of the blockading squadron gave them protection, though they were out of gun range of the forts and there was no Confederate navy present to sally out and disperse them.[45]

The sinking of the vessels began late in the afternoon of December 19 and continued through most of the next day. Some went down by the bow, others by the stern, and some even lay across the channel. Before being sunk, they had been dismasted, except for the *Robin Hood*. She was to be the repository of all the old sails and any other unusable material. Finally she was towed into position and set on fire as she began to go down. This was at 6 o'clock in the evening, and she burned briskly until she sank at midnight. The 16 ships had been sunk in checkerboard fashion across the mouth of the main channel leading to Charleston. As the reporter of the New York *Herald* who was present wrote: "One feels that at least one cursed rathole has been closed and one avenue of supplies cut off by the hulks. . . ." An editorial appeared a few days later in the same paper saying: "Charleston, so far as any commerce is concerned except that in small coastwise vessels, may be considered 'up country.' "

Flag Officer Du Pont also felt that the blockade was effective. Three days after the fleet was scuttled, he wrote to the secretary of the navy about the successful obstruction of the main channel leading to Charleston.[46]

Ironically, one of the vessels destined for destruction was the *Margaret Scott*, whose home port was New Bedford, Massachusetts. She had been seized by the government a short time before on the charge that she was being fitted out as a slave ship. She had, it appeared, run some of her cargoes in the ports she was slated to blockade.

General Robert E. Lee was on a tour of inspection when the sinking occurred. When he heard the news, he wired Confederate Secretary of War Benjamin that the vessels had been sunk in the main channel, but that the north channel and Maffitt's Channel were still open. He went on to say: "This achievement, so unworthy of any nation, is the abortive expression of malice and revenge of a people which it wishes to perpetuate by rendering more memorable a day hateful in their calendar. It is also indicative of their despair of ever capturing a city they design to ruin. . . ."[47]

The Charleston *Mercury*, edited by fiery Robert Barnwell

Rhett, came out the next morning with a mildly worded article in an obscure part of the paper. It read: "On the occurrence of the first heavy northeaster, after the sinking of the wrecks, the force of the wind, the heave of the sea and the action of quick-sands, will according to all previous experiences dissipate the Yankee obstruction." The prediction proved true.[48]

The closing of the main channel was considered a success, and it was decided to close some of the other channels leading into Charleston. First, however, it was necessary to purchase another "Stone Fleet." But this time it was more difficult to procure old hulls; Morgan said that he had "cleared the ports." He had to travel as far as Maine to procure the vessels and in some cases had to pay much more than he had for the first ones. Finally he acquired a sufficient number, though there were less than in the first fleet. These, too, were loaded with granite and headed South. They arrived off Charleston on January 20, 1862, but a heavy northeaster set in and caused three of the hulks to lose their anchor chains during the night. Two returned quickly, but the third one was blown out to sea and was missing for several days. Although the weather continued inclement, half the fleet was sunk the first day. Fourteen vessels in all were scuttled in an attempt to close Maffitt's, or Sullivan's Island, Channel. This was a fairly deep channel used by the blockade-runners to slip in and out of Charleston; in addition, it was protected by the batteries located on Sullivan's Island. Flag Officer Du Pont seemed to be satisfied with the disposition of the ships in spite of the difficulties encountered. Capt. G. B. Balch said: "I can confidently state that a very great obstruction has been placed between the land and Rattle Snake Shoal." The "rathole" was finally stopped up.[49]

There was one thing, however, that the North had not counted upon. This was the storm of criticism that arose from the press, ship-owners, and the foreign office when the news reached England. Even France was extremely critical of the action taken. The venerable London *Times*, usually so staid in its editorials, became almost vitriolic in its criticism. A sampling of the remarks indicates the tone: "Among the crimes which have disgraced the history of mankind it would be difficult to find one more atrocious than this." "People who would do an act like this would pluck the sun out of heaven and put their enemies in darkness. . . ." "If it does not call down universal opposition it is only because this enterprise is believed to be as impossible as its design is execrable." The ship-owners of Liverpool were so disturbed that they sent a memorandum to Earl Russell of the Foreign Office. And in a reply to Lord Lyons, the British minister in Washington, the Foreign Office wrote: "Told that such a cruel plan would seem to imply despair at the restoration of the Union . . . and could only be adopted as a measure of revenge and irremediable injury against an enemy." This was strong language from a diplomatic source.[50]

Secretary of State Seward felt it necessary to placate the French and especially the British by saying that it was "all a mistake" and that the plan had not been devised to permanently injure Charleston harbor. The Northern press must have been taken aback by Seward's statement after all the buildup given to the "Stone Fleets" and blocking the "rathole." Seward's statement was simply diplomatic double talk. On February 17, 1862, he had received full reports as to the extent of the obstructions in the approaches to Charleston.[51]

Actually the furor was all for nothing, because in a short time not a vestige of any of the Stone Fleet could be found; it sank slowly into the mud, where it still lies.

Only five days after the sinking of the first fleet, General Ripley reported: "From such observations as have been lately made the sunk fleet is gradually disappearing." It not only disappeared, but the high tides and strong winds carved out new channels, and navigation was quickly resumed.

5

During most of his stay in South Carolina, General Lee maintained his headquarters in Coosawhatchie, almost exactly midway between Charleston and Savannah. From this strategic position

between the two cities and near Port Royal Sound, he could keep
an eye on the movements of the Union forces. Beauregard had
planned most of the defenses in and around Charleston, and since
his departure for Virginia, General Ripley had gone a long way
toward completing them, or at least toward getting them ready
for fighting.[52] The defenses in Savannah were not as far advanced, in spite of the efforts of Gen. Alexander R. Lawton.
Consequently, General Lee gave considerable attention to the
Savannah defenses as well as to the inner lines to which he had
withdrawn his forces after receiving instructions from Secretary
of War Benjamin. It is certainly true that "the credit for the
defense system that balked the combined Federal land-and-sea
forces in front of Savannah belongs to Lee more than anyone
else." Lee was aided in this work by Capt. John McCrady, chief
engineer for Georgia.[53]

Lee moved his heavy guns into position—old hulks had already been sunk in the channel to hinder the advance of the
Federal gunboats—and used contact torpedoes (mines) as well.
On February 13, 1862, a Naval reconnaissance party was sound-
ing the Savannah River near the mouth of Wright's River in an
attempt to find a channel that would lead to the city. The group
saw objects resembling empty tin cans floating nearby, but ignored them as trash. One officer from the U.S.S. *Seneca* found
five cans attached to a line stretched across the channel in such a
way that it could be seen only at low tide. The next day boats
with grapnels were sent out to investigate; one mine was
towed ashore, and destroyed by small-arms fire. That night
the launch from the U.S.S. *Susquehanna*, towing an ammunition barge, detonated one of the mines; there was a loud explosion, but no damage to either the launch or the barge.[54] A month
later, Gen. Thomas F. Drayton, whose headquarters were at
Hardeeville, South Carolina, reported that "Captain Ives informed me that he was ready to supply me with torpedoes, but no
powder. I have made requisition upon General Ripley for 1,200
pounds of blasting powder, the better quality being so scarce."
General Lee apparently intended to plant mines (torpedoes) in

the navigable rivers to keep out the Federal gunboats, but when he first reached South Carolina he had written that "the deficiency in powder is a serious calamity." [55]

With a large Federal force on Hilton Head and Port Royal Sound, and with reconnaissance parties going out farther and farther, work on the inner defenses was continuing at an accelerated pace. Suddenly, on March 2, 1862, General Lee, who was in Savannah at the time, received the following telegram from Jefferson Davis: "If circumstances will, in your judgment, warrant your leaving, I wish to see you here with the least delay." The following day he left for Richmond, never to return to his former command. [56]

Lee's successor was Maj. Gen. John C. Pemberton, who had been assigned as a Brigadier General to General Lee's command and had recently been promoted. The day after the departure of General Lee he assumed command of the district and set up his headquarters at Pocotaligo Station, South Carolina, on the Charleston and Savannah line. Along with Brig. Gen. N. G. (Shanks) Evans, Pemberton had been assigned to General Lee's command directly by Jefferson Davis. [57]

Just before leaving, Lee wrote to Pemberton that before they attacked either Charleston or Savannah, the Union forces "would attempt to seize the line of the railroad both east and west of the waters of the Broad River, so as to isolate your force." General Lee also wrote Governor Brown of Georgia that the only way to get troops to Charleston was by the Augusta and Savannah Railroad to Augusta, Georgia, and from there by the South Carolina Railroad to Charleston. This was a long, circuitous route in time of an emergency. [58]

Shortly after taking command, Pemberton wrote to Isaac W. Hayne in Charleston telling him that he had examined the defenses on James Island and had directed Ripley to do the work, but had been informed that he did not have the necessary labor. He went on to ask Hayne for his cooperation, or, if necessary, that of the executive and council, "to enforce the supply of labor which General Ripley may require." Lack of sufficient labor was the

major problem in completing the defenses. Pemberton also requested that a connection be made in Charleston between the
Charleston and Savannah Railroad and the South Carolina Railroad as a military necessity. The terminus of the former was on
the south side of the Ashley River, and there was no bridge to the
city.[59]

At the end of March, 1862, Pemberton ordered Col. Arthur M.
Manigault, commander of the First Military District, which included Georgetown, South Carolina, to dismantle his batteries
and abandon his position. The work was to be done at night and
"heavy logs" were to be placed in position as each gun was
dismounted. The heaviest guns were to be removed first, and all
were to be shipped to Charleston. When the work was completed,
Colonel Manigault was to report with his troops to Ripley in
Charleston. The planters in the area of Georgetown resented this
action; it left them with even less defense. Actually, there were
1200 infantry and 400 cavalry in the area for "local defense." In a
letter to the assistant adjutant general in Richmond, Pemberton
stated that he had told General Gist, the inspector general of the
state, that he was thinking seriously of withdrawing the batteries
from Georgetown and that Gist had so informed the governor and
council. Having heard nothing from them, Pemberton had issued
the order of removal.[60]

General Drayton was still trying to get powder for his torpedoes when he heard from Pemberton that "the only reason why
the powder for torpedoes was not sent was because I found when
in Charleston that the amount in hand was not sufficient to admit
of it." The powder situation was still critical.[61]

On March 27, 1862, Pemberton issued an order to Ripley
which had far-reaching results: to withdraw the guns from the
batteries on Cole's Island. These guns controlled the entrance of
the Stono River; if the Union gunboats could ascend the river, the
results could be extremely serious for the over-all defenses of
Charleston. When Governor Pickens heard the news of the impending move, he immediately wired General Lee in Richmond
that if Cole's Island was abandoned before the inner lines were

prepared, it opened the approach to the city to the enemy. General Lee replied diplomatically that such a move could only be decided by the officer in command of the department.[62] But Lee did recommend to Pemberton that he comply with Governor Pickens' suggestion to defer the abandonment of the defenses of Georgetown and Cole's Island until the planters could remove their property to safety. General Lee concluded: "It is respectfully submitted to your judgment whether in order to preserve harmony between the State and Confederate authorities, it would not be better to notify the governor whenever you determined to abandon any position of your line of defenses." General Lee, who had had experience with Pickens, was telling Pemberton to be more diplomatic. But the inhabitants of Charleston had already heard the news and were reacting in panic. One Charlestonian wrote in his diary "Our troops have evacuated Coles Island and Battery Island at the mouth of Stono river. This is another example of weakness and vacillation in our military leaders; one erects a fortification at enormous expense and another destroys it. Our waggon has a team hitched to each end and they draw in opposite directions—what will become of the waggon?" [63]

It is possible that Ripley added fuel to the fire; anyone who disagreed with him, especially a superior officer, became the victim of his wrath. Ripley disliked the mild General Lee and wrote many vituperative letters; only at the insistence of Governor Pickens did he desist. Pemberton wrote to Ripley: "You are so confident of being able to hold Cole's Island, that I will not insist on the removal of the guns from there until they can be fought at Elliott's Cut." Ripley was sure he could hold the island, though Pemberton thought otherwise.[64]

Relations between Ripley and Pemberton must have grown worse; on May 26, 1862, Ripley was relieved of his command. The Charlestonian mentioned earlier wrote in his diary: "Ripley had outlived his popularity." However, the people's confidence in Pemberton was badly shaken. To add to his trouble, the steamer *Planter* was abducted by her crew, along with the guns from Cole's Island. The worst, however, was that Pemberton had said that he was "decidedly of opinion that the most effectual defense of the city of Charleston can and should be made from and around the city itself," and that "the forts should not only be dismounted but destroyed." [65] Governor Pickens wanted him removed from command and brought so much political pressure to bear that he eventually got his wish.

On May 12, 1862, the small but fast shallow-draft steamer *Planter* was sent to Cole's Island to take on board four guns that were there, with orders to transport them to Middle Ground Battery (Fort Ripley).[66] Having loaded the guns, the *Planter* proceeded to the city; since it was late, she tied up at her usual berth at Southern Wharf (near the present Shrine Temple on East Bay). In spite of a general order stating that officers were to remain on board during the night, the captain, mate, and engineer left the *Planter* in charge of the Negro crew under the command of Robert Smalls and returned to their homes. Smalls, a man of exceptional ability, planned to abscond with the *Planter* and turn her and the guns over to the blockading fleet outside the harbor. About three o'clock the next morning the crew began to get up steam. They were apprehensive that someone might smell the ship's smoke and, thinking a house was on fire, give the alarm, but either no one noticed it, or those who did ignored it.[67]

When the pressure gauge showed that there was ample steam in the boiler, Smalls backed the *Planter* from her berth, blew his whistle as usual in order to avoid suspicion, and went a little way upstream before turning and heading for the lower harbor. A sentinel about 50 yards away, seeing that everything was being done in a normal way, did not think it necessary to alert the corporal of the guard. Proceeding slowly down the harbor, the *Planter* passed Fort Ripley—her original destination—and in the early morning light steamed by Fort Sumter, over which flew both the Confederate and the state flags. Smalls put on the captain's old straw hat and stood on the bridge; however, he was careful to stand with his back to the fort so that the color of his skin could not be seen, in case someone was watching through a spyglass. As the *Planter* passed the fort, the sentinel called down

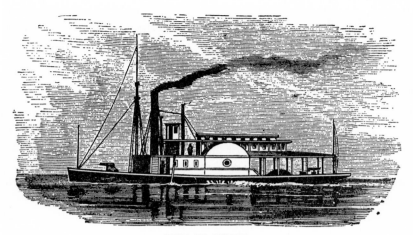

THE *PLANTER*

the fact to the officer of the day, but when her whistle of recognition blew, it was assumed that she was one of the guard ships going to the bar to take up her usual position. In order to reach the bar, a ship normally would have proceeded some distance from Sumter before making a right turn and steaming down the main ship's channel, paralleling Morris Island. But Smalls went straight out to sea through the Swash Channel. By the time anyone on Sumter realized that anything was wrong, the *Planter* was out of range of the guns. Heading for the nearest blockade vessel, the U.S.S. *Onward*, Smalls lowered his two flags and ran up a white sheet. The captain of the *Onward* immediately brought his ship into position so that his port guns could be brought to bear on the oncoming *Planter*. He apparently thought that she was a blockade-runner attempting to get through the cordon of blockading vessels, but the sun was just rising, and it would have been strange for a blockade-runner to make the attempt in broad daylight. When he saw the white flag, the captain held his fire, and as soon as the *Planter* came alongside she was boarded and the American ensign raised. A crew was put aboard, and she went straight to Port Royal.[68]

Smalls was taken to Flag Officer Du Pont; it was at this time that Du Pont first learned that Cole's Island had been evacuated. To ascertain the truth of Smalls's statement, Du Pont ordered the gunboats *Unadilla*, *Pembina*, and *Ottawa* to enter Stono Inlet and proceed up the river. They were not fired on, and they returned to verify Smalls's report.[69]

Smalls was praised by Du Pont for his part in the abduction of the *Planter*, and it was through the insistence of Du Pont that he and his crew received a share of the prize money. Smalls's share amounted to $1500; the other crew members received less.

At first the news of the abduction was not credited, until the *Planter* was seen between two blockaders. But when it was realized what had happened, there was consternation among the authorities. The troops still remaining on Cole's Island "were thrown into a state of excitement" when they heard the news, and "a deep gloom pervaded the community the morning when it was discovered it was clandestinely carried off." General Pemberton was furious; he said it was "the result of the inexcusable and gross neglect of duty on the part of those having charge of the steamer." General Lee wrote Pemberton that he very much regretted the circumstances and hoped that measures would be taken to prevent a repetition; he went on to say that the guilty parties should be punished.[70]

The captain, mate, and engineer were arrested and tried. The first two were found guilty, and the engineer was released because of insufficient evidence. The captain was sentenced to three months in prison and a fine of $500; the mate was to be imprisoned for one month and pay a fine of $100. The decision of the court was brought before General Pemberton for his approval. When the case was reviewed, it was found that the general order stating "that officers are to remain aboard at all times" had never been properly communicated to the officers. In view of this circumstance, Pemberton remitted the sentences, and the men were released.[71]

Smalls was made a pilot by Du Pont. After the war he was elected to the state house of representatives and then to the state senate; later he became a United States Congressman. A high school in Beaufort, South Carolina, bears his name.[72]

The information received from Smalls, confirmed by some deserters from Fort Sumter, caused a modification in the plans for the attack on Secessionville which took place a month later.[73]

While confidence in Pemberton's ability was vanishing, he was having trouble militarily because his troops were being withdrawn in large numbers. Two regiments from Ripley's command were sent to Tennessee, and two more regiments were withdrawn from the Fifth Military District. Shortly afterward, General Lee ordered a good brigade sent to Virginia. When Pemberton requested arms for his new recruits, Lee replied that he had no arms to send except pikes; he suggested that the pikes be given to the artillerymen and that they in turn give their arms to the new recruits. The arms shortage was critical, and whenever the blockade-runners arrived with new ones, they were rushed to Virginia or Tennessee. Pemberton had every reason to be worried about defenses with a total of eight regiments suddenly removed from his department.[74]

With the Federal forces getting closer and closer and the possibility that an attack was imminent, the governor and council passed the following resolution: *"Resolved.* That the governor and Executive Council concur in opinion with the people of South Carolina, assembled in Convention, that Charleston should be defended at any cost of life or property, and that in their deliberate judgment they woud prefer a repulse of the enemy with the entire city in ruins to an evacuation or surrender on any terms whatever." The language may have seemed flowery to some, but it was clear that Charleston, the "Cradle of Secession" was to be surrendered under no circumstances.[75]

In order to strengthen the harbor defenses, Dr. John R. Cheves was charged with the supervision of the chain and boom obstructions as well as the submarine batteries. The latter were large mines which could be detonated from shore.[76]

The powder situation was still bad. In a letter to Lt. Col. C. K.

Huger at Fort Pemberton, located on the Stono River, Pemberton told him to "take the blasting powder out of the torpedoes and mix with other powder for the mortars, and if you have none other, for the 24-pounder also." Obviously the Stono River had been heavily mined with some of Captain Ives's contact mines.[77]

Governor Pickens was sure the attack would be a naval one as "it is too late in the season for the enemy to send any land forces to invest Charleston regularly." [78] The governor meant that at this time of year the troops would be exposed to malaria. But the governor was wrong in his prediction; the attack came by land.

6

If the Battle of Secessionville had been a Union victory, and if the victorious troops had pushed forward across James Island and captured Fort Johnson from the rear, there is no telling what would have happened to Charleston. Had Charleston fallen in 1862, the entire course of the war could have been changed, and in all probability it would have been greatly shortened. With its deep-water harbor and its railroads leading into the interior, Charleston would have given the Union armies an excellent staging area. If a well-equipped Union force had started from Charleston at that time, marching into the interior of the state, the withdrawal of Confederate troops from Virginia and other places would have been necessary to meet the threat, and the results might have been disastrous to the South.

Gen. Robert E. Lee, who well knew Charleston's strategic position, wrote General Pemberton: "The loss of Charleston would cut us off almost entirely from communications with the rest of the world and close the only channel through which we can expect to get supplies from abroad, now almost our only dependence." General Lee then strongly admonished Pemberton to defend the city to the last extremity: it is "to be fought street by street and house by house as long as we have a foot of ground to stand upon." [79]

Fortunately for Charleston and the South, the Union forces

were repulsed at the Battle of Secessionville. Brig. Gen. Johnson Hagood, C.S.A., who participated in the battle, later said that this little known engagement could be regarded as one of the decisive ones of the war. A Northern source said: "The battle of Secessionville has been shamefully slighted by compilers of history." [80]

The battle took place at a small breastworks situated on a narrow peninsula on the seaward side of James Island, nearly opposite Lighthouse Inlet, which separates Folly Island from Morris Island. Secessionville consisted of a small cluster of summer homes belonging to the planters of James Island. The tradition is that it got its name because a group of younger married planters "seceded" from the older people; the name had nothing to do with the Secession talk engaged in by Southerners for so many years before the outbreak of hostilities.[81] General Beauregard had stated that James Island was the key to Charleston, and the Union forces also realized this. In fact, Brig. Gen. Horatio G. Wright, U.S.A., who commanded the first division of the Federal forces during the Battle of Secessionville, stated: "Taking posession of the Stono [River] solves the question of the taking of Charleston." He was badly mistaken.[82]

In fact the Northern press was so sure that the expedition to capture Charleston would be successful that the following appeared in the New York *Tribune* for June 9, 1862:

"Doom" hangs over wicked Charleston. That viper's nest and breeding place of rebellion is, ere this time, invested by Union Arms—perhaps already in our hands. If there is any city deserving of holocaustic infamy, it is Charleston. Should its inhabitants choose to make its site a desert, blasted by fire, we do not think, many tears would be shed. Travellers of to-day are quite undecided as to the location of ancient Carthage; travellers of 2862 may be in the same doubt about Charleston.

With the capture of Port Royal the previous November, the Union forces had an excellent staging area. But except for an occasional foray against the Charleston and Savannah Railroad, very little activity had taken place since then. With the fall of

Port Royal, however, the Confederate forces realized that Edisto and John's islands, lying to the south of Charleston, were untenable. They therefore withdrew their troops from these positions and evacuated the planters and their families. When General Pemberton ordered the abandonment of Cole's Island, the Union forces took advantage of this by overrunning Edisto and John's islands. With the Confederate guns gone from Cole's Island, Union gunboats could steam up and down the Stono River, thus exposing the southwestern shore of James Island to their fire. This gave them a considerable advantage, for at Port Royal it had been demonstrated that shore batteries could not withstand naval gunfire.

Hilton Head, South Carolina, was full of well-trained and well-equipped Federal troops who had been there all winter and had seen only an occasional skirmish against the enemy. Maj. Gen. David Hunter, commanding officer of the district, wrote in June, 1862, to Secretary of War Stanton in Washington: "I left here for Stono River with an expedition against Charleston . . . and I have not the least doubt if we had the steamers belonging here and those for which I applied that we should to-day be in possession of Charleston." [83]

It seems strange that General Hunter wanted more steamers, for he had taken almost every available man with him and left only 600 effective troops at Hilton Head to look after the military materiel stored there. The officer left in command was extremely worried that he might not have enough troops to repulse a determined Confederate attack; fortunately for him, there was not one. [84]

On June 2, 1862, General Pemberton wired Jefferson Davis that there were 20 vessels in Stono Inlet. On the same day Jefferson Davis wired Pemberton asking that more troops be sent to Virginia. This was a usual request; the Charleston district was regularly ordered to send troops to other areas. [85] In addition to those on the transports lying in Stono Inlet, other Union troops stationed on Edisto Island were ferried across to Seabrook's Island and marched across John's Island to Legareville, from which point they were transported across to James Island for the assault on Charleston. A vivid description of the march across John's Island is given by a member of the Third New Hampshire Regiment who participated in it. He writes that the temperature was 100° and that hundreds of men fell out from heat exhaustion, and he goes on to say that "whiskey was given to the men to enable them to perform the journey; and many fell to the rear, apparently exhausted for the sake of whiskey. Consequently, a few were very much overcome by the relief and could not march." It is strange that whiskey was given for heat exhaustion, but apparently at that time whiskey was the anodyne for all ills. Then, to add to their misery, heavy rains "descended and the floods came, and it really seemed as if it had never rained before." But finally the regiment arrived in Legareville.[86]

Col. Johnson Hagood harshly criticized Brig. Gen. N. G. Evans, C.S.A., who had several regiments of troops on the upper end of John's Island, for not attacking the exhausted and drenched Union troops as they trudged across John's Island. Undoubtedly the Union troops were in a precarious position, drawn out in a long line with hundreds of stragglers. But, for reasons which are not clear, though they were vulnerable to attack, no move was made against them. While the various regiments were straggling across John's Island, "a constant and careful watch was kept" by the Union forces to ascertain where the Confederate forces were; they expected an attack any minute.[87]

Realizing that an assault through James Island was imminent, General Pemberton was preparing for it. But Pemberton also had other concerns. In addition to Jefferson Davis's call for more troops to be sent to Virginia, Governor Pickens was doing all he could to have Pemberton removed from command, on the charge that he was incompetent. To further add to his problems, he was short of ammunition and men; to remedy this situation, he wired Savannah to send him 100,000 rounds of ammunition and as many Enfield rifles as possible. Many of the latter had come through the blockade. He even warned Brig. Gen. States Rights Gist at Secessionville not to waste ammunition. He also wired

Brigadier General Mercer in Savannah to have "all of your command ready to move at the shortest notice." This, of course, outraged the mayor of Savannah, who argued that the city would be left undefended. On June 8, General Pemberton informed W. J. Magrath, president of the Charleston and Savannah Railroad, that "the enemy in large force is preparing to attack Charleston —Probably through James and John's Islands," and requested that Magrath have several trains ready to move at a moment's notice "for or with troops." [88]

As late as June 15, General Pemberton wrote Governor Pickens that he had on James Island only 6,500 effective men.[89] The Union generals estimated that the Confederate forces on the island numbered at least 12,000 effective troops.[90] Their information apparently came either from prisoners or deserters. Throughout the campaign against Charleston, the Union intelligence consistently overestimated the number of available Confederate troops. The situation was critical—Stono Inlet was filled with transports and gunboats—but even now, although he had told Jefferson Davis that he could spare no troops, Pemberton received a similar request from George W. Randolph, secretary of war. Pemberton did prove to be a poor general, but it must be admitted that he had other things to occupy his mind besides fighting an enemy.[91]

On June 2, Union troops landed on the southwesternmost tip of James Island at the plantation of Thomas Grimball. Why a more determined effort was not made by Confederate forces to stop the enemy on the shore line is not clear, though the Union reports state: "We landed in the face of a severe fire from the enemy." Perhaps the answer lies in the indirect fire of the gunboats. A clear report of their firing is given by Lieutenant Howard, acting signal officer, who was aboard the gunboat *Unadilla*. He was in constant communication with Lieutenant Keenan, who went ashore with the troops. Because of this, they were able to maintain a devastating fire at targets out of sight of the gunboats. This method proved highly successful; a statement by Howard testifies to this success: "These vessels after the occupation of James Island fired hardly a shot except under my direction." The Union forces were met by heavy fire, and a skirmish took place, but the landing was made. Colonel Hagood, who came under the indirect fire from the gunboats, comments that he was "subjected to a rapid fire of gunboat shells, which threatened as much damage from the falling limbs cut from trees as from themselves." He and his men were in a densely wooded area with 11-inch shells bursting all around.[92]

The advance guard of the Union forces pushed ahead for about a mile. Some, in order to get out of the rain, took shelter in sheds and corn cribs. As one of them wrote later, it was an education, "For it taught us not to suppose we were the sole occupants, though apparently we were. The other tenants were there on a permanent basis." Many of them probably preferred the rain to the dry, but flea-infested shelter.[93]

In the next few days troops from both the transports as well as those who had come across John's Island were landed on James Island. One officer sarcastically wrote: "We are credibly informed that we and the rebels were the joint occupants of the same island, that the latter was strongly fortified, that James Island was the direct and substantially the only path to Charleston, that Charleston was only about 8 miles away, that the rebels would without doubt interpose objection to one walking right over them or even around them." And they did. Realizing that the main attack might be directed against the breastwork at Secessionville, General Pemberton instructed Brig. Gen. W. D. Smith to hold at "any cost" the woods west of Secessionville. General Pemberton knew that the Union forces were going to make an all-out attempt to capture Charleston, and he was making every effort to meet the attack.[94]

On June 10, Pemberton ordered the Confederate lines to advance in order to establish a battery of heavy guns on the edge of Grimball's plantation with a view to driving the gunboats from the immediate area and making landing hazardous. Colonel Hagood started advancing with the First South Carolina and a battalion of the Fourth Louisiana on the right flank, and Colonel

Williams with the Forty-seventh Georgia on the left flank. Williams ran into the Union forces in the thick woods. The Georgians made "a gallant advance and fought with great vigor, but their lines being disorganized, advanced in squad strength where they were repulsed and badly cut up." Again the indirect fire of the gunboats played an important part in the repulse of the Confederates. Brigadier General Wright reported of the skirmish: "The Naval vessels in the river kept up a continued fire over the heads of our men, and as their practice was excellent it must have occasioned much loss to the enemy's reserve." [95]

During the next few days, the Union forces were busy unloading supplies and troops; the Confederate forces were working to strengthen their lines and secure additional ammunition. On June 14, General Evans assumed command on James Island and spent the next two days inspecting the lines. He knew an attack was coming, but he did not know at precisely what point to expect it. He decided, however, to fortify one of the larger breastworks, which lay across a small peninsula on either side of which was a marsh. The peninsula at this particular point was approximately 125 yards wide. Just beyond it was the cluster of summer homes known as Secessionville.[96]

In spite of feverish activity, this breastwork was incomplete at the time of the attack. Col. Thomas G. Lamar, who was in command, had pushed his men to the point of exhaustion. Finally, at 3 A.M. on the morning of June 16, he allowed his worn-out men to sleep. This was the only time they had been permitted to do so without arms in their hands, and it was almost disastrous. They were barely asleep when they were awakened by an assault by a brigade of Union troops. Colonel Lamar in his official report stated that he was alerted when the Union forces were three quarters of a mile away. However, Colonel Hagood said that Lamar told him that he had fallen asleep on the parapet after superintending the working parties most of the night and that he was awakened by the sentry when the Union forces were only about 50 yards away. The Union forces were actually 100 yards away when they received the first fire. Since there was little time to give the alarm, Lamar rushed to one of the big guns, already loaded with grape, and pulled the lanyard. The roar of the gun aroused the troops, and the grape tore into the oncoming ranks. The Battle of Secessionville had begun. Actually a 24-pound gun had been fired by Sgt. James M. Baggett a moment before the Columbiad was fired by Colonel Lamar.[97]

By 2 A.M. on June 16 the Federal troops had been "falling in" into two columns. The first or assaulting group consisted of the Second Division, composed of six regiments with some engineers, cavalry, and artillery, under the command of Brigadier General Stevens; this group comprised about 3500 men. Another column, comprised of the First Division, consisting of about 3100 troops, was formed on the left of the Second under the command of Brigadier General Wright. The assaulting group was to advance in silence and make the attack at "first light" with the bayonet; the First Division was to protect the Second from a flank attack by the Confederate troops. The large number of Federal troops should have been more than sufficient to surprise and crush a garrison of 500 men.[98]

About 4 A.M. the movement got under way; the attacking column was led by Lieutenant Lyons and a Negro guide. The morning was dark and cloudy, and it was difficult for the officers to align their troops. About three quarters of a mile from the battery, the attacking forces ran into the Confederate pickets, who fired at them and wounded five men of the Eighth Michigan. All four pickets were captured. Their firing should have alarmed the garrison, but apparently little attention was paid to it. In fact, in his report General Pemberton excoriates them for not having made more noise and given the alarm.[99]

The leading troops consisted of two companies of the Eighth Michigan with some New York engineers, closely followed by the rest of the Eighth, the Seventh Connecticut, and the Twenty-eighth Massachusetts. The Eighth Michigan advanced in regimental front, with the other two regiments close on its heels. The Second Brigade, consisting of the Seventy-ninth New York (Highlanders), the 100th Pennsylvania (Roundhead), and the

Forty-sixth New York, was held in close reserve. All were excellent regiments; the Eighth Michigan and the Seventy-ninth Highlanders were the crack regiments of the entire force.[100]

The troops advanced across the cotton field in good order until they were met by the blast from the Columbiad fired by Colonel Lamar. This blew a gap in the advancing line, but they continued on. Soon they were receiving a devastating fire from the thoroughly aroused garrison. In spite of the fire of grape, cannister, chain, nails, and broken glass, some of the Eighth Michigan managed to climb onto the parapet, where they fought hand to hand with the Confederate defenders. The narrowing of the peninsula at the point at which the battery stood made it difficult for the supporting regiments to maneuver. The fire had cut the regiments in half. The Twenty-eighth Massachusetts took cover in the bushes next to the marsh and fired steadily on the defenders; some of the Seventh Connecticut took cover to the right and in the cotton rows. The remnants of the Eighth Michigan who had gained the parapet were left unsupported.[101]

Confederate troops rushed to the aid of Colonel Lamar's defenders as they were aroused. The first to reach him was the Pee Dee Battalion under the command of Lt. Col. A. D. Smith. Next, from its encampment nearby, came the Charleston Battalion, commanded by Lt. Col. P. C. Gaillard. Finally those of the assaulting troops who had reached the parapet were either killed or repulsed. The Eighth Michigan fell back and re-formed; with the aid of the Second Brigade they charged under fire for 1000 yards, assaulted the works, and again gained a foothold. After more fierce hand-to-hand fighting, they were again pushed back.[102]

In the meantime the Third New Hampshire and some of the troops of the Third Rhode Island of the First Division had marched down the other peninsula, which is separated only by a small creek from the peninsula on which the battery was located. Taking cover in some heavy undergrowth on the edge of the creek, they fired from the rear at the gunners of the battery, forcing them to leave their guns and "take up their rifles." Some of the Charleston Battalion were sent to meet their threat. Meanwhile, the situation on the parapet was precarious, as reinforcements were slow in coming to the beleaguered garrison.[103]

Two things helped turn the battle in the battery's favor. Lt. Col. J. McEnery, commanding a battalion of Louisiana troops, had been aroused by Colonel Hagood and sent to Secessionville. McEnery and his men, who were encamped some distance away, started toward the battery, but, as they were unfamiliar with the country, they became confused when they came to a crossroads. This delayed them for a few moments. Once on the right road, they advanced to Secessionville over the bridge, nearly a mile long, that extended from the opposite part of the island to the rear of the battery. They arrived on the run yelling "Remember Butler" (General "Beast" Butler had just occupied New Orleans) and gave considerable assistance in repulsing the Third New Hampshire, which was pouring a deadly fire into the rear of the battery. Another factor was two small field guns at two different locations, one manned by Lieutenant Jeter, the other by Lt. Col. Ellison Capers. Both men fired their guns with excellent effect into the Third New Hampshire and helped to hasten their withdrawal. Meanwhile, the hand-to-hand fighting continued until the assaulting troops were again repulsed.[104]

A two-gun battery of 24-pounders was placed in front of E. M. Clark's house, later known as Battery Reed, for the purpose of enfilading an enemy attack on the breastwork at Secessionville a mile away. At the time of the attack, Lt. Colonel Ellison Capers, later an Episcopal Bishop, was with Colonel Hagood. When Hagood did not hear the battery open fire, he ordered Col. Capers to find out the trouble. When Capers arrived there, he found Lt. J. B. Kitching with about 15 men belonging to Colonel Lamar's regiment. Colonel Capers wanted to know why the battery had not fired. Kitching informed him that he and his men had just returned from the country, had no orders, and knew nothing about loading and firing a cannon. However, he said, they would gladly cooperate if Capers would instruct them. Capers loaded and fired one of the guns; the shell hit in the area right behind G.

W. Hill's house, which was occupied at the moment by a Federal regiment. Kitching and his men were soon loading and firing like veteran artillerymen. One gun recoiled off its carriage, but the other was fired throughout the engagement; one shot killed a captain and a sergeant of the Third New Hampshire. A few days later, Capers received a note from Brigadier General Smith commending him for his "efficient and distinguished service," and Lieutenant Kitching, the substitute artilleryman, was cited by Lamar for gallant conduct.[105]

Having had such excellent support from naval gunfire at the landing at James Island, General Benham decided to use it again in his assault against Secessionville. The gunboats *Ellen* and *E. B. Hale*, both light-draft boats, were assigned this duty. They had to use the upper reaches of Lighthouse Inlet, which was very shallow and interspersed with mud flats. Lieutenant Howard was assigned to the *Ellen*. General Benham stated in his official report: "The gunboats . . . did great execution among the ranks of the enemy." Like many official reports, Benham's gave the impression of success. But some of the men of the Third New Hampshire who participated in the attack had a different idea; their report stated: "The gunboat now began to shell at long range, and mostly by guess, as a mile or more of woodland intervened. These shells struck as often around Federals as Rebels." [106]

By this time Colonel Lamar, who had received a Minié ball through the neck and was suffering from loss of blood, turned the command over to Lieutenant Colonel Gaillard, who, in turn, when he was wounded in the knee, gave the command to Lt. Col. T. M. Wagner. Once more the Federal forces regrouped and attempted a third assault, but by now the Confederate reinforcements had made themselves felt and the assault failed.[107]

After almost two and a half hours of hand-to-hand fighting Brigadier General Benham ordered a general retreat; both divisions returned to their base camps. For a short battle the losses were heavy. The Union dead and dying were piled up in the small area in front of the battery. The Eighth Michigan had borne the

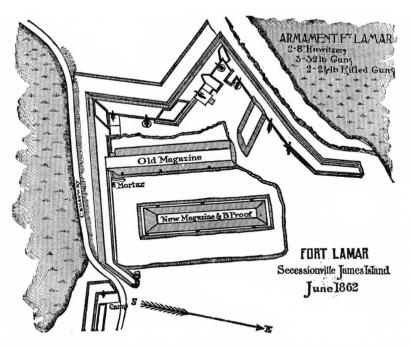

brunt of the fighting; it returned to camp with 33 percent casualties among the enlisted men. The Seventy-ninth Highlanders also suffered heavy losses. Their commanding officer, Lt. Col. David Morrison, although wounded in the head, actively participated in the hand-to-hand fighting on the parapet.[108] Total Union casualties, including killed, wounded, and missing, were almost 700; those of the Confederates came to slightly over 200. Most of the casualties occurred in an area about 125 yards wide immediately in front of the battery and on the battery itself.[109]

Before the attack, the battery was known to the Union as the Tower Battery, because of the proximity of a look-out tower erected by Confederate forces on the peninsula opposite. Apparently, at the time of the attack, the Confederate authorities had given it no specific name. After the battle, however, it was named Battery Lamar. Lamar died the next year of fever contracted on the island.[110]

In spite of the fact that there were four Confederate generals in the district, none participated in the battle. Brig. Gen. N. G. Evans was in command of the troops on James Island, but for some reason did not arrive at the battery until after the fighting was over.

General Benham's strategy was basically sound. With excellently disciplined and well-equipped troops, he planned to overwhelm the garrison by sheer numbers. Had it not been for the magnificent fighting abilities of the defenders, he probably would have succeeded. A member of the Third New Hampshire may have hit on the cause of the failure when he stated: "The fight seems on the whole to have been a poorly-managed one, as the forces were apparently put in small lots at intervals. . . ."[111] To the Confederates there appeared to be three distinct assaults; to the Union forces it was one sustained assault which, because the forces were not committed simultaneously, evolved into three waves of troops.

After the valiant defense of the battery, the Confederate Congress passed the following resolution: "That the thanks of Congress are due and are hereby tendered to Colonel Thomas G. Lamar and the officers and men engaged in the gallant and successful defense of Secessionville against the greatly superior numbers of the enemy on the 16th day of June, 1862."[112]

When the news of the repulse of the Federal forces reached Charleston, the citizens were elated, but when the casualty list arrived including the names of many Charlestonians, one commentator wrote: "a Gloom has been cast over our City by the death of many fine young men."[113]

After the battle, a young Confederate officer who had been wounded in the leg was asked by a Charleston girl, "When you were so outnumbered, did you not think of retreating?" The officer answered, "Where could we have gone other than the bottom of the Ashley River, for had we crossed over to the city, you would have beaten us out of it with your broomsticks." The indomitable spirit of the women added greatly to the fighting abilities of the troops.[114]

The Confederates immediately buried their own and the Union dead. The wounded prisoners were taken to hospitals in the city, where they were well cared for.

A Federal burying party came across a Confederate soldier—though it is not clear how he got so close to their lines—and were about to put him in the ground when, to their amazement, he opened his eyes. He was offered a drink of whiskey, but he refused until one of the burying party had first taken a drink. When he was asked why he would not drink until one of them had first done so, he told them that he thought the whiskey was poisoned.[115]

For having lost the battle, General Benham was ordered to Hilton Head and placed under arrest.[116] Brig. Gen. Horatio G. Wright was given command of the forces stationed on James Island, more than 9,000 well-equipped and now battle-seasoned troops. Three days after the Battle of Secessionville, General Hunter, placing General Wright in command, gave the following specific instructions: "You will not attempt to advance towards Charleston or Fort Johnson till largely re-enforced and until you receive express orders from these headquarters." [117] Apparently General Hunter did not want a repetition of Secessionville. He went on to say: "Should you deem your present position untenable you will immediately make all the necessary disposition for abandoning James Island. . . . Your front being completely covered by the gunboats of the Navy, you can make the retrograde movement, should you deem it necessary, without losing a man or a pound of supplies." Again naval gunfire was of the greatest importance.

Expecting an attack momentarily, General Wright strengthened his camp at Grimball's plantation. No attack came because, in all probability, he had more troops than the Confederates had on James Island; furthermore, the gunboats were lying in the Stono River at his rear to give him fire support. Had an attack been made by the Confederates, it would have been costly and would probably have accomplished nothing. After a few days, puzzled as to why he and the troops were left on the island, General Wright wrote to General Hunter: "I am bound to say in all frankness that I do not understand the object of the occupation at all, unless the command be sufficiently re-enforced to enable us to prosecute the attack upon Charleston." He stated that to ensure the success of the expedition he would need 40,000 men with a suitable complement of heavy and light artillery.[118]

On June 27, General Wright received orders from General Hunter to abandon James Island and go "to some more healthy location." In order to cover up his movements from the Confederates, Wright had his bands play almost the entire time to drown out the noise of his packing up and embarking. The Confederate pickets were puzzled; they were unable to tell whether the troops were embarking or reinforcements were arriving. Finally, by July 9, the evacuation was completed without the loss of a man or any supplies.[119]

Thus ended the abortive "expedition against Charleston." General Samuel Jones, C.S.A., who late in the war succeeded General Beauregard at Charleston, said of the Battle of Secessionville: "The assault which had resulted so disastrously, narrowly missed a brilliant success." A Northern source said: "The battle became a massacre."[120]

The Battle of Secessionville was a sorry day for generals. Pemberton received no acclaim in spite of the Confederate victory —actually it was all over before he got the full details at his headquarters. All the honor went to the actual combatants. This is unusual in any war. Political pressure was still being exerted for Pemberton's removal, and soon after Secessionville he was transferred to the Department of Mississippi, Tennessee, and East Louisiana and promoted to lieutenant general. He was the commanding officer when Vicksburg fell to General Grant and was captured and exchanged.[121]

When a battle is lost, it is customary for the commanding general, unless he has powerful political friends, to receive the blame. Brig. Gen. Henry W. Benham received all the blame and the stigma attached to the loss.

Maj. Gen. David Hunter was the Union Commander for the

Department of the South, with headquarters at Hilton Head. On June 2 he sailed from there "with an expedition against Charleston." He notified Secretary of War Stanton to that effect and told him that if he had the steamers he had applied for "we should today be in possession of Charleston." In the same letter he wrote: "I deem it a duty I owe to myself frankly to state our situation, as I have before frequently done, that reverses may not be attributable to me." Why General Hunter should have wanted more transportation is not clear; he had with him almost every available man stationed at Hilton Head, leaving scarcely enough to protect the supplies located there. The secretary of war wrote back to General Hunter: "It could not have been expected that a general of your experience would undertake at his own discretion, without orders and without notice to the Department, a hazardous expedition, with 'fear of failure' for want of adequate transporation, and it is therefore hoped that the statement in your letter in the last respect may be unfounded." General Hunter had approved of the "expedition against Charleston." But, realizing that the expedition might not be successful, he turned over the command to Brigadier General Benham and returned to Hilton Head. He wrote to Benham: "You will make no attempt to advance on Charleston or to attack Fort Johnson until largely re-enforced or until you receive specific instructions from these headquarters to that effect." [122]

After the battle Benham was ordered to Hilton Head, where he was placed under arrest by General Hunter for disobedience of orders and sent North by steamer. He waited for months, but no charges were brought against him, though he pleaded with Secretary of War Stanton to bring charges and let him stand trial. The *New York Times* became involved, as well as Major General Halleck, the chief of staff. On August 7, 1862, General Halleck, with the approval of Secretary Stanton, recommended "that Brigadier General Benham be mustered out of the service as a brigadier general of volunteers." Benham was reduced to his original rank, major of engineers. Benham was from New Hampshire, and the governors of all the New England states signed a letter to

President Lincoln stating that they felt Benham should stand trial and that it was unjust for him to be "deprived of his rank and command without trial." In response to this political pressure, Lincoln on January 3, 1863, recommended to the judge advocate general that Benham be restored to rank. For the balance of the war he had an excellent military record; he finally retired with the rank of colonel in 1882.[123]

7

General Pemberton had won the battle of Secessionville and inflicted heavy casualties on the Union forces, which finally brought about their withdrawal from James Island, but Governor Pickens was still determined to have him removed. Upon receiving another letter from Pickens, Jefferson Davis ordered Adjutant General Cooper from Richmond to look into the situation. The governor expressed a wish that Huger, Magruder, or Longstreet be sent as a replacement for Pemberton. General Lee said that Huger, a native South Carolinian, could be spared from his command, but Pickens changed his mind and Huger remained in Virginia.[124] On his arrival in Charleston, Cooper made an inspection of the defenses; writing his findings to Davis, he said: "General Pemberton was doing all that a zealous, active, and intelligent officer could do with the means placed at his command to defend the city against the approaches of the enemy, both by land and water." There was no ambiguity or censure in his statement. Cooper also stated that he had had a conference with Pickens and that his strong feeling against the general impaired Pemberton's usefulness. Therefore, Cooper thought it best not "to retain him in his present position against such a weight of opposition." Cooper closed his report by saying that he had great confidence in the zeal and untiring efforts of General Pemberton.[125]

A week after Cooper's letter to the president, Pemberton wrote to the governor: "It is useless to undertake this work [on fortifications around Charleston] unless an ample supply of labor is sent here. So far from being able to furnish it from what is now at my disposal, the force laboring here on the many indispensable works is entirely inadequate." It was up to the governor to furnish the necessary labor; Pemberton was placing the blame where it should be. Pickens, however, was implacable. On July 5, 1862, Pemberton received a communication from Cooper that if the Union forces had been withdrawn from James Island, it would be well to occupy Cole's and Battery islands, Bull's Bay, and Georgetown. Cole's Island was fast becoming a *cause célèbre*. Pemberton replied that it was impossible to put guns on Cole's Island or Battery Island; the enemy's gunboats could always prevent it. On July 12, Pemberton sent a dispatch to Cooper saying, "Shall I go on to Richmond at once?" He received the following reply: "Do not proceed to this place until you receive further orders. General Gustavus W. Smith reports himself unfit for duty." Another general decided that the climate of the Carolina low country did not agree with his health.[126]

At the first opportunity, Capt. William H. Echols, the engineering officer of the district, made an inspection of Cole's Island and reported that its reoccupation was "impracticable!" Jefferson Davis wrote Pickens on August 5: "With respect to the reoccupation of Coles and Battery Islands, the opinion of military men are so different that I should be unwilling, while at a distance from the locality, to decide the question. The matter may be left open for further consideration or for the decision of a new commander." Cole's Island had become an obsession with Pickens. Regarding the removal of the commanding officer, the president went on to say: "I am desirous of obliging you and would be glad also to secure the services of General Pemberton elsewhere. I have tried to get a competent officer, whose assignment to the position would be satisfactory, and will not relax my efforts to that end. My own confidence, however, in General Pemberton is such that I would be satisfied to have him in any position requiring the presence of an able general." A few days later Pemberton went to Richmond for a conference with the president. After this meeting Davis wrote Pickens: "I have recently had a long interview with General Pemberton, and received a full exposition of his views relative to the defenses of the coast of South Carolina. I find that his determination to hold the city of Charleston is as fixed as you could desire it to be. I do not find it practicable to send in his place another general who would equally well answer for the command." [127]

Finally, on August 29, 1862, under Special Order 202, Gen. P. G. T. Beauregard was assigned to command the Department of South Carolina and Georgia. Beauregard was at Bladen Springs, Alabama, where he had gone to recover his health. Pemberton probably welcomed the change in command, but he wrote to the adjutant general requesting that he be ordered into the field for active service, as it would be humiliating in the extreme if he were reduced to a subordinate position under Beauregard. As to his unpleasantness with the governor, he said: "my arrangements for the defense of Charleston and Savannah have been made, whether judiciously or not, at least uncontrolled by the interference of others." Pemberton was relieved of command on September 17, 1862. When he left, there were 241 guns in the harbor or the immediate vicinity, a formidable defense which was to be further strengthened by Beauregard. Prior to assuming command, Beauregard went with Pemberton on a detailed inspection of the defenses of Charleston and Savannah and the intervening points. Finally, on September 24, 1862, Beauregard assumed command. [128]

Beauregard had just settled into his new duties when he received a letter from Pickens. The governor wrote: "It strikes me that the defense of Charleston is now of the last importance to the Confederacy, and in our very full interview yesterday, I took the liberty of urging that Fort Sumter was the key to the harbor." He declared that he was glad to have Beauregard. Pickens was running true to form in harassing the commanding officer. [129]

Beauregard lost no time strengthening the defenses; changes were made in both Sumter and Moultrie, and because of the "inefficiency of the boom" more heavy guns were requested to control the harbor. Pickens wrote directly to Davis asking that Ripley be reassigned to Charleston. Then Beauregard, in an effort to keep the governor quiet, did something he probably regretted. He wired the adjutant general in Richmond: "I would be pleased to have General Ripley assigned to my command for defense of Charleston." [130]

Beauregard took seriously the resolution that the city would not be surrendered. On this matter he wrote Pickens: "As I understand it is the wish of all, people and Government, that the city shall be defended to the last extremity; hence, I desire to be in all respects ready to make its defense equal to that of Saragossa." He went on to say that the governor should see that proper places be found to house the noncombatants. Captain Echols, the chief engineer, was ordered to submit a plan for defending the streets and squares of the city proper from an attack from the gunboats in case any should reach the inner fortifications, as well as a plan for the construction of bombproofs for the garrison. [131]

In mid-October the secretary of war notified Beauregard that he had received information that Admiral Du Pont would attack Charleston within the next two weeks. Beauregard replied: "We will endeavor to give Commodore Du Pont as warm a reception as circumstances will permit." [132] Actually, it was not until six months later that Du Pont got his "warm reception." The district was enlarged, thereby giving Beauregard's command a part of Florida. During the next few months the Union forces on Hilton Head Island sent out parties probing for a weak spot in the defenses along the Charleston and Savannah Railroad. Everyone was on the alert; no one could tell whether a major engagement would develop.

Governor Pickens was not quiet long. On November 5, 1862, he wrote a long letter to Beauregard telling him about the guns and booms at the mouth of the harbor and how useful the two gunboats would be in case of an attack; he also gave his opinion that a land attack could not be made on the city "unless Lee's army is first disposed of." There is no record of a reply. [133]

In early July the critical powder shortage was somewhat alleviated when the blockade-runners *Hero*, *Memphis*, and *Leopard*

eluded the blockading squadron and brought in 237,000 pounds
of powder as part of their cargo. A little later the *Scotia* got
through with 1000 barrels. Now that there was sufficient powder,
the guns on Sumter and Moultrie and all the batteries on Morris
Island were ordered to be kept supplied with 200 rounds of
ammunition.[134]

Beauregard's command was constantly being stripped of
troops. Casualties were heavy in the other theaters of war, and in
order to fill the ranks Davis suggested to Pickens that he immediately call out all men up to the age of 45. Even at this early date
the manpower shortage in the Confederacy was making itself
felt.[135]

Work continued uninterrupted on the defenses in and around
Charleston, but the pace was slow because of the shortage of
labor. The Neck Battery on Morris Island was incomplete. This
small sand fortification, later known as Battery Wagner, was to
play an important part in the defenses in the next few months.[136]

Beauregard wanted to hold off Du Pont's fleet, but he did not
have much faith in the heavy boom made for that purpose. On
December 7, 1862, he ordered John R. Cheves to continue in
charge of the torpedoes being constructed for the entrance of the
harbor. He also ordered his chief engineer, Maj. D. B. Harris, to
see that contact mines were laid in some of the rivers south of the
city. Because of rope obstructions and the fact strong winds and
high tides had broken up the boom, Cheves reported that it would
be useless to put down torpedoes; the drifting timber would
detonate the contact mines.[137]

In order to accommodate the recently commissioned gunboats,
orders were given to deepen Wappoo Cut to 13 feet, "For the
passage of gunboats—rams from the Ashley to the Stono, in
order that they may operate in either river according to circumstances; we will thus be enabled to retake possession of and hold
Cole's Island, thereby doing away with the necessity of keeping
so large a force on James Island as is now required for the
protection of the city. . . ." However, the underpowered rams
were of little use in the defenses of the city.[138]

On November 29, 1862, Beauregard advised Ripley that Du Pont's fleet had left Hilton Head and that he should be prepared to "meet him at all fronts." Troops were to be issued three days' rations, and railroad cars were to be ready to move them in any direction at the shortest notice. Beauregard thought the attack would be made at Georgetown.[139] Actually, the fleet was headed for the coast of North Carolina to act in conjunction with the Union's expedition against Goldsboro. General Whiting at Wilmington, who had been asked to send aid to stop the advance on Goldsboro and was fearful of a land attack on Wilmington, called on Beauregard for aid. Troops were rushed to Wilmington by rail from both Savannah and Charleston. Since Du Pont's fleet was no longer in Port Royal Sound, no imminent attack on the Charleston and Savannah Railroad was feared. When the Union expedition against Goldsboro was repulsed, the troops were returned to their various military districts.

In December, 1862, Milledge L. Bonham was inaugurated as governor of South Carolina.

3

The Navy in Action

1

EVER SINCE THE FEDERAL GUNBOAT *Isaac Smith* HAD BEEN launched, things seemed to go wrong. She was originally built as a river steamer, driven by propeller instead of by the customary paddlewheel, but she was requisitioned by the Federal Government as soon as she was completed, converted to a gunboat, and armed with a main battery of eight eight-inch guns in addition to a 30-pounder on her bow. Because she drew only nine feet and had a speed of 12 knots, she was admirably suited for patrolling the rivers along the South Carolina coast.[1]

The *Smith* was one of the fleet of 15 warships that had accompanied Flag Officer Samuel F. Du Pont on his successful Port Royal expedition. On the way there the ships were caught in a bad storm off Cape Hatteras. Seeing that the transport *Governor*, with 600 marines aboard, was sinking, the *Smith* immediately went to her aid. The *Smith* was rolling so much that her skipper,

Lt. J. W. A. Nicholson, U.S.N., afraid of capsizing, was forced to jettison his main battery. With superb seamanship, he got a line aboard the *Governor*. This soon parted. With great difficulty, another was made fast. The *Sabine*, also a member of the armada, gave assistance, and all but seven men were saved. All of the equipment was lost. The *Smith* made it to Port Royal, though part of her deck was cut away, her engine frame was loose, the engine was out of line, and only her bow guns remained. When Lieutenant Nicholson reported to Du Pont on the condition of his ship and the reasons for it, Du Pont praised him and even wrote a letter of commendation to the secretary of the navy. Du Pont knew that Nicholson wanted to get into the battle, but he could be of little use with only his bow gun. Du Pont ordered the *Smith* to tow the (sailing) sloop *Vandalia*, armed with 21 guns, and assigned them to bring up the rear of the column of ships that were to engage Fort Walker at close range. During the battle the crew of the *Smith* vigorously worked its single gun, getting off 31 shots.[2]

After the fight the ship was repaired, given a new battery of eight-inch guns, and assigned to patrol duty off Charleston. With other gunboats, she ranged up and down the Stono River, shelling the shore batteries on James Island with her new guns; no Confederate troops could show themselves without receiving a salvo from her alert gunners. The Confederate forces, exasperated with her forays along the Stono, decided to set a trap for her. General Beauregard called in Brigadier General Ripley for consultation, and the two of them assigned the task to Lt. Col. Joseph Yates, a top artillery officer. The idea for the trap may even have originated with Yates.[3]

At times the *Smith* would anchor in various parts of the Stono River, almost as if there were not a Confederate gun within miles. Sometimes she went as far up as Fort Pemberton, just below Wappoo Cut, and anchored just beyond the range of its guns. Yates knew her habits, and his first plan was to load barges with troops, approach the *Smith* at night with muffled oars, and attempt to take her by surprise. This plan, however, was aban-

GUNBOAT *ISAAC SMITH* CAPTURED IN THE STONO RIVER, S.C. *Drawn by Emmett Robinson*

doned; it was too risky and had little chance of success. A second plan was devised which called for the establishment of masked batteries of field guns on both sides of the river. The *Smith* would be permitted to go up the river as far as she liked; but when she anchored or started down, the nearest battery would open up and she would be forced to run past the other batteries, each of which would open up as she neared.

With utmost secrecy, Colonel Yates assigned several companies of artillery and a company of sharpshooters to the task. One of the batteries, which was within sight of patrolling gunboats, had to place their guns at night. The sharpshooters were assigned to shoot the helmsman and any members of the crew who showed themselves above deck. The trap was set, and the *Smith* floated into it unsuspectingly. Proceeding up the river, she anchored in her usual manner and was immediately fired upon by the battery located near Grimball's plantation on James Island. Quickly getting under way and returning a heavy fire, she passed the batteries on John's Island, which in turn opened up on her. Finally getting as far down as Legare's Point Place, she was disabled by three shots that struck her "steam chimney." With her engine room full of steam and with no power, she dropped anchor and surrendered unconditionally. Her entire crew of 119 officers and men was captured. Colonel Yates stated in his official reports that 25 members of her crew were killed or wounded and that he had lost only one man. Acting Lt. F. S. Conover, the captain of the *Smith*, was among those captured. He stated that the only reason he did not blow her up to keep her from falling into Confederate hands was because of the many wounded men lying on her deck who would have been drowned.[4]

Colonel Yates had a valuable prize, but he also had a problem: getting her to a place of safety. He had used almost all of his ammunition, and he had no way to tow the *Smith*. Yates made plans to blow her up. As anticipated, the Federal gunboat *Commodore MacDonough* started up the river to her aid, but was turned back by the batteries who still had ammunition left. The steamer *Sumter* rushed from Charleston, took the *Smith* in tow, and anchored her under the protection of the guns of Fort Pemberton farther up the Stono River.[5]

As the draft of the *Smith* was nine feet, she had difficulty getting through Wappoo Cut, which had not been deepened. Only by unloading her main battery was she sufficiently lightened, and it took four days to warp her through. She was then towed to the Commercial Wharf in the city, repaired, rechristened the *Stono*, and, under the command of Capt. Henry J. Hartstene, C.S.N., used as a guard boat in the harbor. Capturing a heavily armed man-of-war by land batteries of field guns is uncommon, if not unique, in the annals of naval warfare.[6]

Because of her excellent speed, however, it was decided to convert the rechristened *Smith* into a blockade-runner. On her first attempt to run out of the harbor, however, she was discovered, chased by the blockading fleet, and stranded on the breakwater near Fort Moultrie. Apparently she was refloated and used as a gunboat, because she was reported burning when the United States navy steamed into the harbor on the morning of the evacuation of Charleston.[7]

2

At the outbreak of hostilities, the Confederate government had no navy and only a few ships that could be converted into privateers. Moreover, since the South was an agrarian area, there were almost no facilities for constructing warships. Those that were built were usually of makeshift material, and the greatest problem was that of getting suitable engines. With the fall of Port Royal in November, 1861, it was realized that, if the rivers and adjacent area were to be protected, some heavily armored gunboats would be needed. On February 12, 1862 (Lincoln's birthday, ironically) the South Carolina Executive Council appropriated $300,000 for the construction of a gunboat; at the same time it asked for estimates "for ten first-class Gun Boats of the strongest model for our water." [8]

Two weeks later the following short item appeared in the *Courier:* "Cannot the women of Charleston give an order for a gunboat?" It has not been ascertained who was responsible for the question, but it had far-reaching results. The women of Charleston immediately accepted the challenge; in fact, women all over the state responded. The idea caught fire, and money poured in. Vases, silver, gold bracelets, paintings, watches, and diamonds were sold or raffled. Even the Negro slaves contributed to the fund. A Columbia firm sent in two 100-dollar Confederate bonds; they felt that it was "better by far that we spend our last dollar as a means of resistance than to suffer subjugation." [9]

The editor of the *Courier* received five dollars "from a little girl eleven years old" and seven dollars from ladies refugeeing from Beaufort. In one issue he asked his readers to be patient; he had received over 100 letters containing contributions, but lack of space prevented his publishing them. In early May a fair was held at Hibernian Hall for the benefit of the gunboat; everyone who could walk attended. One lady asked to have the privilege of making the flag for the new gunboat. The efforts of the women of the state not only raised a large sum of money, but proved conclusively that they were wholeheartedly behind their men, the war effort, and the cause for which they fought. [10]

The keel of the first of the gunboats was laid in March, 1862; the contract for its construction had been awarded to Messrs. Marsh and Son. A month after the Executive Council had appropriated the money for its construction, it was informed that the Confederate government expected to pay for it. A motion was then made "that the money, lately put at the disposal . . . for building a Gunboat . . . be recalled from them as they said Captain Ingraham had lately received orders from Richmond to have a Gunboat built for the same purpose at the expense of the Confederate Government." With the release of the funds, it was quickly decided that another gunboat should be built; the contract for its construction was awarded to J. M. Eason. The keel was laid on the ways located on the Cooper River at the east end of Broad Street. During the time of its construction, it was usually spoken of as the "State Gunboat." At first neither gunboat had officially been given a name.[11]

Work progressed steadily on the two boats; the two construction crews were vying to see which would finish first. When Eason had trouble getting timber, the Executive Council authorized him to cut timber "wherever most accessible." When the armor plating failed to arrive, the governor was requested to write to the secretary of the navy in Richmond to ask him to expedite its shipment. Eason had the better crew; his gunboat was launched on August 23, 1862, and the governor and other notables attended the ceremony. Until just before the launching the gunboat had no name. On August 12, the Executive Council instructed the "Chief of Military together with the Committee, to select a name for the State Gun Boat." The name chosen was *Chicora*, and she was commissioned the following month. An effort was made to secure a pledge from the secretary of the navy that he would not remove the *Chicora* from South Carolina waters, but he would make no such promise.[12]

Meanwhile, the other gunboat, still unnamed, was being rushed to completion. At the time the *Chicora* was named, Richard Yeadon wrote to the secretary of the navy asking that the other gunboat be christened the *Palmetto State*. In reply the secretary stated: "Captain Ingraham, before the receipt of your letter, had been instructed to name the vessel the 'Charleston,' but in deference to the wishes of the noble women in Carolina, this order is revoked, and he has this day been directed to call her the 'Palmetto

State.' " The ladies turned over to the Confederate government the funds they had raised from raffles, fairs, and contributions. The commissioning ceremony took place on October 11, 1862. Yeadon gave the address and was welcomed on board by Capt. D. N. Ingraham. General Beauregard, with some of his staff, put in an appearance and was "welcomed with hearty and long continued cheers." As the ceremony was being concluded, the *Chicora* came steaming up the river, flags flying fore and aft, and gave a salute to the newly commissioned ship. Standing on her deck with the officers was her builder, Mr. Eason. As she neared the *Palmetto State*, "the assembled multitude broke forth in loud and prolonged cheers for the *Chicora* and her energetic builder." [13]

At the end of December, 1862, both gunboats were manned and ready for action. By this time the Federal blockading fleet was becoming more and more effective; ships had been added to it and fewer blockade-runners were able to get through the cordon of ships guarding the channels leading into Charleston. Throughout the month of January, 1863, both gunboats remained at their wharfs. People began to wonder why they did not go out and engage the blockading vessels. Finally, on January 28, the following article appeared in the *Courier:*

Mess'rs Editors: —Why is it that with—gunboats at this port well armed, manned, and officered, and "spoiling for a fight", we do not clear the blockade?

Why is it that so much material, gallant officers and men, and scientific accomplishments and preparation, should be wasted in doing nothing, and should not protect the very large and singular important trade to this port in its egress and ingress?

[signed] A. MARINER

This feeling among the people had its effect. Flag Officer Ingraham the senior naval officer present, after consultation with General Beauregard, decided to start an aggressive action against the blockading vessels. Orders were given to the two gunboats to engage the entire Federal fleet, which consisted of nine vessels.

At 11 o'clock on the night of January 30, 1863, the *Palmetto State* and the *Chicora* slipped quietly down to the lower harbor. They were painted a pale blue or bluish gray, probably one of the earliest attempts at ship camouflage, and their armor was coated with grease to deflect cannon balls. Because of their excessive draft, caused by the weight of armor and armament, they had to wait until flood tide to cross the bar.[14]

The gunboats had been built for harbor defense and were far from seaworthy. Fortunately, the ocean was calm. Before sunrise, the area was covered with a heavy haze, which enabled the attacking gunboats to approach the blockading vessels closely before being detected. About 5 A.M. the *Palmetto State*, commanded by Lt. Cmdr. John Rutledge, with Flag Officer Ingraham aboard, headed for its nearest opponent, the *Mercedita*. The Union ship was taken by surprise; the watch hailed the approaching gunboat: "What steamer is that? Drop your anchor or you will be into us." [15] The Confederate ship replied: "This is the Confederate States steamer, *Palmetto State*."

The gunboat was so close that it was impossible to depress the guns; she rammed the *Mercedita* and fired from her bow gun. The shot went through the *Mercedita*'s boiler, causing a tremendous explosion and tearing a hole in the Union ship. Two of her crew were killed and many others badly scalded by escaping steam. Rutledge called out: "Surrender or I will sink you. Do you surrender?" The attack came so suddenly that several members of the crew of the *Mercedita* came on deck nearly undressed. Her commander, Capt. H. L. Stillwagen, appeared on the quarter deck in his peacoat to announce the surrender of his ship. Lieutenant Commander Abbot, executive officer of the *Mercedita*, rowed over to the *Palmetto State* to arrange the terms. In the excitement, the men lowering the small boat had forgotten to put the plug in and only strenuous bailing kept her afloat. Abbot said that when he left, the water was over the floor boards of the engine room and that the ship was doomed. He asked if the *Palmetto State* would take the entire crew of the *Mercedita* aboard. Flag Officer Ingraham replied that it was impossible, as there was not enough room and, furthermore, he had no small boats to help in rescuing them. Moreover, Lieutenant Commander Abbot, speaking for all the officers and crew of the *Mercedita*, gave his word that "they would not take up arms against the Confederacy unless regularly exchanged as prisoners of war." [16] However, the *Mercedita*'s wound had not been fatal, and she was able to return to Port Royal under her own power.

The firing of the shot into the *Mercedita* had alarmed the other vessels of the blockading squadron, and they were fully prepared for the *Chicora*, which was going farther out to sea. She sighted a ship and quickly fired into her, and it is believed that the ship caught on fire. Almost immediately she engaged another vessel of the squadron and fired three shots into her; this ship, which turned away into the haze, may have been the *Quaker City*, which took a shell in her engine room. [17]

The *Chicora* then engaged the *Keystone State*, which caught on fire and was temporarily disabled. One shot of the many that hit her pierced the port steam chimney; the boiler emptied, filling the forward part of the ship with steam and giving the ship a heavy list to starboard. Twenty of her crew were killed and about the same number wounded or scalded. There was a foot and a half of water in her hold, and her condition was so grave that her captain struck her colors and threw overboard his signal book and some small arms. [18]

The *Chicora*, about 200 yards astern, had the *Keystone State* completely at her mercy. Some of the Union crew held out their arms and begged the *Chicora* not to fire any more. Cmdr. John Randolph Tucker, captain of the *Chicora*, ordered Lieutenant Bier to lower a boat and take charge of the prize. While this was being done, it was discovered that the *Keystone State* was trying to escape by working her starboard paddlewheel; the port one had been disabled by gunfire. The *Chicora* started in pursuit, but even with only one paddlewheel the *Keystone State* was able to outdistance the Confederate gunboat and escape.[19]

The *Chicora* next engaged four vessels, but did not have sufficient speed to bring any of them to close quarters. At 7:30 A.M., at the orders of Flag Officer Ingraham, the action was broken off. Neither of his gunboats could catch any of the blockading fleet. On his return, Commander Tucker stated in his official report that "leaving the partially crippled and fleeing enemy fleet about seven miles clear of the bar," he returned to Charleston.

The two gunboats had to wait in the Beach (Maffitt's) Channel for several hours for high water before they could return to the city. On their way in, they received salutes from the various batteries and forts they passed. And when the news reached the city, the people went wild. As one of them wrote, "the excitement in the city was almost equal to the day of the Battle of Fort Sumter." [20] The following Tuesday the people of Charleston publicly celebrated the victory with a ceremony at St. Philip's Church at which the *Te Deum* was sung.

Commodore Ingraham reported to General Beauregard that the blockading fleet had been dispersed and that several vessels had been sunk. The facts later revealed that Ingraham had assumed too much. At the time of the attack, there were nine vessels in the blockading fleet. The *Mercedita* limped off to Port Royal under her own power. The *Keystone State*, which had been badly damaged, was taken in tow by the *Memphis*. The *Augusta* was dispatched to Port Royal to carry the news to Admiral Du Pont. Just before leaving, Captain Parrot of the *Augusta* reported to Captain Taylor (the senior officer present) that the *Mercedita*, the *Flag*, the *Stellin*, and the *Ottawa* were nowhere to be seen. Captain Taylor on the *Housatonic* reported that he was steaming southward to overtake the *Keystone State* when the *Quaker City* signaled that she had received a shell in her engine room.[21] Thus every vessel can be accounted for.

If the blockade had been broken, it would have been necessary legally to establish a new blockade and officially notify foreign powers of its establishment. Because of the slow method of communication, the port of Charleston would have been open for weeks, and blockade-runners would have been able to run in and out at will with supplies.

On the day of the engagement General Beauregard and Flag Officer Ingraham issued a proclamation stating that the naval forces of the Confederacy had that morning attacked the United States blockading fleet off Charleston "and sunk, dispersed, or drove off and out of sight for the time the entire hostile fleet." [22]

At the time of the action, the British man-of-war *Petrel* was in port at Charleston. When the news arrived, she took the British consul, Mr. Bunch, on board and went out to see if the blockade was really broken. She went five miles beyond the usual anchorage of the fleet and reported that she could see nothing of them even with glasses. Later General Ripley took the French and Spanish consuls so that they, too, could see that the blockade was no longer in existence. That evening the three consuls met with Captain Watson of the *Petrel* and apparently decided that the blockade "was legally raised as claimed by the proclamation," though no formal statement was issued to that effect. In the meantime, Judah P. Benjamin, secretary of state for the Confederacy, was apprized of the proclamation. Quick to see the opportunity given him, he immediately informed the foreign consuls in Richmond. He also sent a dispatch by ship to James M. Mason and John Slidell, who were representing the Confederate government in London, with instructions to submit it to Earl Russell, British minister of foreign affairs. Russell refused to accept the view that the blockade had been broken. The blockade was re-established late the afternoon of the day of the attack, when four of the vessels returned to their stations, and Russel may have known this.[23]

The incident occasioned many denials and recriminations. Admiral Du Pont, who was in Port Royal at the time of the attack, immediately denied that the blockade was ever broken. The *Mercedita*, as well as the *Keystone State*, both reported by Flag Officer Ingraham as being sunk, made port. The *Keystone State* was so badly damaged that she had to be sent to Philadelphia for repairs. The other damaged vessels were able to make temporary repairs and return to their stations.[24]

The captains of the blockading vessels off Charleston all denied that they had left their posts. Actually, every ship in the blockading squadron had slipped her anchor in order to maneuver against the gunboats. Consequently, when the foreign consuls made their inspection, all of the Union fleet was either "hull down" or steaming for Port Royal.[25]

In *The Story of the Eleventh Maine Regiment* the following statement appears: "The rams dispersed the fleet, after disabling two or three vessels, two of which struck their colors, but were left behind when the rams steamed back to Charleston." Obviously the Union forces, at least for a while, were under the impression that the blockade had been broken.

Commander Tucker of the *Chicora* in his official report made some scathing remarks about the behavior of the captain of the *Keystone State:* "While the boat (to take a prize crew aboard) was being manned, I discovered that she was endeavoring to make her escape. She then hoisted her flag and commenced firing her rifled guns; her commander, by this faithless act, placed himself beyond the pale of civilized and honorable warfare." At that time the word of an "officer and a gentleman" was regarded as his bond. This was quite in contrast to the behavior of the captain of the *Mercedita;* when the *Augusta* hailed him as he was steaming away to Port Royal, he said he could give no orders because he was under parole.[26]

In any event, the attack startled Washington, and the Northern newspapers heaped invectives on the government, but the blockade continued.

3

With the withdrawal of most of the Union forces from eastern North Carolina and with Du Pont's fleet returning to Port Royal Sound, it was only a question of time before an attack would take place. While it is generally known that Charleston was heavily fortified against a naval attack, it is not so well known that there was also an excellent defense system against land attacks, regardless of the direction from which they were launched. It is doubtful if any city in the Confederacy had more or stronger defenses than those around Charleston. But there was one problem—lack of troops.

The outer harbor approaches were guarded by Sumter and Moultrie and several powerful batteries on Sullivan's and Morris islands. The mouth of the harbor was protected by booms and torpedoes. Should Union ironclads break through the outer defenses, they would meet resistance from batteries on James Island, overlooking the harbor, and two smaller fortifications, Fort Ripley and Castle Pinckney. Pilings had been driven in the shallower parts of the harbor, and the river channels were mined with frame torpedoes; the city itself was surrounded by batteries located on the waterfront. White Point Gardens (the Battery) housed several heavy guns protected by large earthworks. If Du Pont's fleet managed to break through all these obstructions, and if enough ships were still afloat and a landing was effected, the city was to be fought "street by street."

The defenses against land attack were also well planned. A heavily manned line extended across the lower central part of James Island. The extreme lower part of the island was indefensible because of the evacuation of Cole's and Battery islands. On the upper part of the peninsula above the city, known as "the Neck," entrenchments had been dug from river to river. In the Revolution, the British, after an unsuccessful attack by water in 1776, returned and laid siege to Charleston from the rear, finally forcing the surrender of the city in 1780. The Confederate forces did not want a repetition of this; therefore they had located their lines far enough above the city proper to keep it from being bombarded as the British had done and, with a sufficient number of troops, could have repelled an attack.

In Christ Church Parish, about five miles above Mt. Pleasant, where the headwaters of the Wando River near the small ocean inlets, another line was built across the entire peninsula. The trees felled in order to provide lanes of fire were thrown with their branches outward, making it almost impossible for troops to advance if they left the main approaches that were covered by the guns.[27]

Bee's Ferry, which crosses the upper reaches of the Ashley River, where the British crossed in 1780, was heavily fortified, as was the road leading to it. Wherever the road crossed a swamp, breastworks were erected on the opposite side. The Charleston and Savannah Railroad, as well as the main roads leading to the city, were protected in the same way. The inland waterways were not only mined, but obstructions such as pilings or sunken barges were placed in their channels, and wherever the waterway neared the mainland a small fortification was erected. If some of the outer defenses were assaulted and lost, there was the inner line to be captured before reaching the city. In Charleston and the immediate vicinity there were approximately sixty batteries within a ten-mile radius.

In anticipation of the possibility that Du Pont's ironclads might break through his outer defenses, Beauregard instructed Ripley to organize at least "six boarding boat parties." They were to attack the ironclads at night. The crews were to be "provided with blankets with which to close all apertures; also iron wedges and sledges to stop the tower from revolving, with bottles of burning fluid to throw into the tower, with leather bags of powder to throw into the smoke-stack." Beauregard had said that he would give Du Pont a "warm reception." [28]

At the end of January, 1863, Beauregard wired General Mercer in Savannah that 40 transports, four frigates, and four gunboats were at Hilton Head. Nine Rains torpedoes were placed in the channel of the Ogeechee River in Georgia, close to Fort McAllister; when the fort was attacked by the ironclads one of them (the *Montauk*) was almost entirely blown up when she detonated one. General Whiting in Wilmington returned a brigade that he had borrowed and held another in readiness to send at a moment's notice. Encouraged by the repulse of the ironclads at Fort McAllister, Beauregard ordered that volleys should be fired against the turrets of the ironclads and stated that he was putting "Rains torpedoes in every direction." He closed a letter to Congressman W. Porcher Miles in Richmond: "At all events my friends may rest assured that the defense of Charleston with or without additional troops shall be worthy of a few pages in the history of this revolution. The enemy may destroy this city, but they shall not take it so long as I have any troops to defend it with." The city authorities were asked to remove all noncombatants, and officers and soldiers on furlough were recalled. Then Beauregard issued a rather effusive proclamation: "Carolinians and Georgians! The hour is at hand to prove your devotion to your country's cause! Let all able-bodied men, from the seaboard to the mountains, rush to arms. Be not exacting in the choice of weapons; pikes and scythes will do for exterminating your enemies, spades and shovels for protecting your friends. To arms, fellow citizens! Come to share with us our dangers, our brilliant success, or our glorious death." Actually, the mention of weapons, or rather the lack of them, was not mere rhetoric; some of the North Carolina troops sent as reinforcements arrived without arms.[29] Congressman Miles wrote to the secretary of war about the lack of troops: "I do not know any other city in the Confederacy that has been obliged to call out (not for a day or two, as in Richmond, but for months) its exempt population and keep them under arms to defend it against the regular army of the enemy." Somewhat later President Davis wired the mayor that "it is very desirable that all the citizens of Charleston able to bear arms and not subject to enrollment for military service should be promptly organized for local defense." With few troops available, it was up to the Charlestonians to defend themselves.[30]

Every brigade between Charleston and Savannah had detailed plans of what to do in case of attack; if they were forced back by superior forces, routes of retreat were outlined. It is doubtful if any anticipated battle in the entire Confederacy was planned for more carefully. Beauregard's strategy was above reproach. All indications were that Charleston would be attacked. And Beauregard was prepared, except for one thing—he did not have fully armed troops!

4

"This Department has determined to capture Charleston as soon as Richmond falls." These optimistic words were written on May 13, 1862, by Gideon Welles, secretary of the navy, to Flag Officer S. F. Du Pont, who was commanding the South Atlantic blockading squadron with headquarters at Port Royal. Welles had a long wait before his desires were fulfilled. But he was a determined man. On January 3, 1863, he again wrote to Rear Admiral Du Pont (since promoted) that he was sending him the *New Ironsides* and four monitors so that he could enter the harbor of Charleston and "demand the surrender of all its defenses, or suffer the consequences of a refusal." He went on to say that General Hunter would be sent to Port Royal with over 10,000 troops to help, but the "capture of this most important port, however, rests solely upon the success of the naval forces, and it is committed to your hands to execute." [31]

The *New Ironsides* was one of the most powerful warships existing. Her fourteen 11-inch guns, along with the 15-inch guns of the monitors, constituted a formidable armada. Welles was set on the capture of Charleston and had sent the cream of his navy to accomplish this purpose.

General Beauregard was thoroughly prepared for the attack when it came. The whole channel was carefully buoyed so that the gunners on Fort Sumter, Morris Island, and Sullivan's Island could always know the exact range of the attacking ship. Booms had been strung across the channel between Fort Sumter and Fort Moultrie and mines placed where the ships had to pass over them.[32] The secondary line of defense consisted of the inner fortifications of Fort Ripley, Castle Pinckney, and the James Island batteries. If the fleet succeeded in pushing past these, then it would have to fight it out with the guns mounted in the city. If a landing was effected, the city was to be fought "street by street and house by house."

Two days before the attack, Admiral Du Pont's fleet lay lazily at anchor off the bar. People within the city were going about their business as usual with serenity; they had unbounded confidence in the defenders. General Beauregard had issued an order for the women and children to leave the city, but it had been generally disregarded.

On the morning of April 7, 1863, activity by the fleet was observed, and everyone realized that the test of strength was about to begin. Ambulances were standing by on East Bay to carry the wounded to the hospitals; people were collected in groups, talking in low voices; women were preparing lint for bandages; the impoverished shops were still open. It hardly seemed possible that one of the most powerful fleets in the world was just outside the harbor entrance threatening destruction of the city before nightfall. A reporter for the *Illustrated London News* was present; just before the attack, he wrote: "But I have every faith in the results of the coming encounter, for never at any time have the Confederates been more determined to do or die than they express themselves now."

After some delay, caused by the fact that the raft (to sweep up the mines) attached to the monitor *Weehawken* became entangled, the fleet steamed slowly toward the harbor in line of battle. Word was quickly flashed to headquarters in the city by Colonel Rhett on Fort Sumter. All of the defenses and the city were surprised to hear the 13 shots from Fort Sumter and the strains of "Dixie" floating over the water with the sound of the salute. The state and regimental flags were quickly raised, and the gunners ran to their guns.[33]

Steaming slowly and majestically up the main ship channel, the fleet approached. The lead ship was the monitor *Weehawken*, which was followed by three other monitors, the *New Ironsides*, and four more monitors. The total armament of the ironclads consisted of twenty-two 11-inch guns; seven 15-inch guns; and three 8-inch rifle Parrott cannon. It is doubtful if any fleet had ever carried heavier metal. The reserve squadron of five ships never entered the action. Admiral Du Pont's flag was flying from the *New Ironsides;* he thought he could signal the others better from the center of his fleet.[34]

Finally, at three o'clock in the afternoon, Fort Moultrie fired one of her heavy guns at the lead ship. However, realizing that the range was too great, she suspended fire. When the *Weehaw-ken* reached a buoy in the channel, the gunners on Sumter, knowing her exact range, began firing by battery. As the fleet advanced steadily, the guns from Fort Moultrie, batteries Bee and Beauregard on Sullivan's Island, and batteries Gregg and Wagner joined with those of Sumter, pouring a devastating stream of shells from their 76 guns. None, however, had the weight of the guns of the fleet.[35]

The monitors continued onward; they took a severe pounding and got off comparatively few shots at Fort Sumter. Because of their heavy armor, they suffered little damage in the initial phase of the action, but as they came nearer and nearer, the shells from the concentrated fire of the guns began to have a telling effect. The day was mild and clear and the water perfectly calm, which should have enabled the gunners in the fleet to fire with great accuracy. As each monitor came within range, she fired her guns and turned away to reload, each time nearing or receding a little from the forts in order not to present a fixed target. The gunners in Sumter cheered between every salvo.[36]

A mine exploded near the *Weehawken;* it lifted the vessel a little, simply throwing up a huge column of water.[37] As she was the lead ship, she received most of the gunners' attention. In his report, her captain stated: "The accuracy of the shooting on the part of the rebels was very great." The *Passaic,* under the command of Capt. Percival Drayton, then steamed in, and she in turn received most of the fire. After getting off four shots from her 11-inch gun, she received two shots in quick succession; they hit the lower part of her turret, smashing in the plates and forcing together the rails on which the gun carriage worked, totally disabling it. Her pilot house was also crushed, and she had to drop out of action and anchor below Fort Moultrie. The *Passaic* was struck 35 times in 35 minutes.

By this time all of the monitors were engaged. Along with the others, the *Nahant* took a frightful pounding. Shells hitting the pilot house caused the bolt heads to fly in all directions; the pilot was knocked senseless, the quartermaster was wounded, and only the commander was left in the pilot house, with the steering gear disabled. After circling for some time, she was brought under control; then she too retired from the action.

Meanwhile, the *New Ironsides* was having trouble on her way in. Because she drew nearly 16 feet, she became unmanageable in the shoal water, collided with the *Catskill* and *Nantucket*, and finally anchored to keep from running aground. Though Du Pont was unaware of the danger, the *New Ironsides* was directly over a large mine that was to have been fired from shore. At the end of the cable leading to the mine, Assistant Engineer Langdon Cheves was trying to detonate it, but because of the excessive length of the cable nothing happened. In his report, Cheves said "that for ten minutes he could not have placed the *Ironsides* more directly over it [the mine] if he had been allowed to, but the confounded thing, as is usual, would not go off when it was wanted." Although the *New Ironsides* did not participate in much of the action, she received the attention of the gunners, especially from Fort Moultrie. She received 50 hits, but because of her heavy armor, none penetrated.[38]

Because the *New Ironsides* had to anchor, the four monitors comprising the second division were delayed about 20 minutes. For this reason vessels of the first division received most of the fire, which disabled many of them. The last in line of the second division was the double-turreted ironclad *Keokuk* which, in spite of the heavy fire, steamed ahead of the others until she was only 900 yards from Fort Sumter. Her audacious captain brought down upon his ship the concentrated fire of almost every available gun from the forts and batteries. In short order 19 shots pierced through her at and just below the water line. Her turrets were riddled, her guns were incapacitated, and she got out of control. She was hit 90 times in all but was able to limp away. Her skipper, Commander Rhind, succeeded in keeping her afloat only for a short while; she sank the next morning off Morris Island.[39]

In the meantime, Fort Sumter was receiving the attention of the fleet. Though the fort was hit repeatedly, comparatively little damage was done. Some straw bedding was ignited, but the fire was quickly brought under control. The gunners serving the barbette guns were having difficulty seeing their targets because of the smoke from the guns in the lower tier—there was only a light breeze at the time. For this reason orders were given to fire

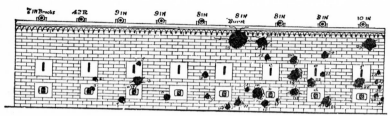

EASTERN OR SEA-FACE OF FORT SUMTER AFTER DUPONT'S ATTACK

the guns singly whenever a target presented itself instead of by batteries. This probably made for greater accuracy. Another feature of the guns was an invention of Lt. Col. Joseph A. Yates, First Regiment of South Carolina Artillery. He had devised a means by which the guns could be easily traversed so that they could quickly follow the movements of the fleet and remain "on target." [40]

Fort Moultrie was hit a few times by shells from the fleet. There was only one casualty there; a man was killed when he was hit by the flag staff, which was cut down by a lucky shot. When the flag fell, Capt. W. H. Wigg promptly picked it up and held the flag himself until the shattered staff could be repaired. The guns of Moultrie were fired by battery at the nearest ship.[41]

Since all of the heavy guns of Fort Johnson were trained on the inner harbor, they could not be brought to bear on any of the fleet.

The gunners fired a couple of times with their ten-inch mortar, but found the range too great.[42]

The people of Charleston hurried to the waterfront. The High Battery and every wharf were jammed with spectators, as were every rooftop and window that commanded a view of the harbor. Because of the clear weather, the watchers could see the near hits as they struck the water.

The monitors continued firing, but their fire was becoming slower and slower. Finally Admiral Du Pont signaled the order of withdrawal. The remaining six monitors maintained their fire until 5:25 P.M., when they withdrew out of range and anchored. The *Passaic* was immediately towed to Port Royal; the *Keokuk* sank the next morning, and two other monitors were so severely damaged that they had to be repaired.

The Confederate gunners were remarkably accurate. They had fired a total of 2209 shots and registered 520 hits.[43]

With the withdrawal of the fleet, Capt. Charles Inglesby, officer of the day at Fort Sumter, made his tour of inspection. One of the gunners gravely asked him, "Mr. Officer of the Day, have you seen an eight-inch Columbiad running around anywhere that you have been?" Inglesby asked tartly, "What do you mean?" The gunner pointed to his gun carriage, which was empty, and said, "We fired our gun just now, but when we started to sponge her for a new load we saw that she had gone!" The gun had burst. Part of it had leaped forward over the front of the fort; the rest of it had fallen into the parade ground 60 feet below.[44]

Two days later Brigadier General Ripley received an admonition from the chief of staff saying that he had wasted ammunition, especially from batteries Bee and Beauregard, which had fired at extreme range with little effect.

When the fleet finally weighed anchor and departed for Port Royal, the garrison at Fort Sumter turned out for a dress parade, which was followed by another salute of 13 guns, with all flags raised in honor of the event.[45]

Brig. Gen. Quincy A. Gillmore, U.S.A., writing of the attack, said that Fort Sumter had "defied the assault of the most powerful and gallant fleet the world ever saw." His statement was probably correct, which is certainly high praise for the Confederate defenses.[46]

That night Admiral Du Pont called his captains together for a conference. After hearing their reports of the conditions of their ships, he decided not to renew the attack. This was a sensible but costly decision. Had he renewed the attack, he probably would have lost more of his ships, but his failure to renew it angered the secretary of the navy and eventually caused his removal from command.[47]

The day after the attack, Du Pont wrote to Maj. Gen. David Hunter, who was in command of more than 12,000 troops which

THE MONITOR *PASSAIC*

had been dispatched to aid in the capture of Charleston, that "I attempted to take the bull by the horns, but he was too much for us. These monitors are miserable failures where forts are concerned; the longest one hour and the others forty-five minutes under fire, and five of the eight were wholly or partially disabled." This was a remarkably frank admission of his casualties.[48]

General Hunter wrote to Admiral Du Pont on April 8 (their communications must have crossed): "I cannot but congratulate you on the magnificent manner in which the vessels under your command fought. A mere spectator, I could do nothing but pray for you . . . and for all the gallant men under your command who sailed so calmly and fearlessly into and under and through a concentric fire which has never heretofore had a parallel in the history of warfare." He ended his letter with, "God bless you and keep you safe, Admiral, and believe me, with the highest esteem, ever your true friend and servant." Admiral Du Pont was deeply touched by the letter and said that he would have it read on every ironclad in the fleet. The next day the admiral wrote to General Hunter "that a merciful Providence permitted me to have a failure instead of a disaster." Later he said: "I am now satisfied that that place cannot be taken by a purely naval attack." He also stated that he was withdrawing his vessels. When the remaining monitors started for Port Royal to be repaired, three of them were so badly damaged they had to be towed.[49]

The secretary of the navy was stunned when he received the news of the failure; he had been determined that the navy should capture Charleston. He even got President Lincoln to instruct Admiral Du Pont: "Hold your position inside the bar near Charleston, or if you shall have left it, return to it, and hold it till further orders. . . . I do not herein order you to renew the general attack. That is to depend on your own discretion or a further order." The following day the president wrote a joint letter to Admiral Du Pont and General Hunter saying that "no censure upon you or either of you is intended." The letter arrived too late; the admiral had already withdrawn his ironclads.[50]

A large number of war correspondents had been assigned to the fleet to cover the story of the glorious victory of the navy and the capture of Charleston. The entire North had been in a state of suspense over the approaching attack, and word of the repulse was received by the Northern press with dismay. The New York *Herald* described it, "though almost bloodless, as one of our most discouraging disasters." The Baltimore *American* denounced it as "a shameful abandonment of the siege" and continued: "Oh! that we had a Farragut here to take command at once, and do what has been so weakly attempted by Admiral Du Pont." The article also commented on his fear of torpedoes. But Du Pont had every reason to be fearful of mines. The following entry is found in the log of the British man-of-war *Petrel*, which had been in Charleston for two months: "February 17, 1863: Confederates laying down nets and torpedoes." Shortly afterwards the *Petrel* sailed for Fortress Monroe, Virginia, and upon arrival reported that the entrance of the harbor of Charleston was "filled with torpedoes."

The attack by the press became so vituperative that six of Admiral Du Pont's captains signed a statement to the effect that the articles were incorrect. The admiral himself wrote that the Baltimore *American* article was "injurious to myself, unjust to the officers whom I had the honor to lead, derogatory to the reputation of the naval service and utterly false in its most important particulars." But someone had to take the blame, and Admiral Du Pont was the man.[51]

The losses of the fleet were so severe that the secretary of the navy wrote to Du Pont on May 15, 1863, that he had not published his reports "because in my judgment, duty to my country forbade it. They may justify the failure at Charleston and excuse your abandoning, after a single brief effort, a purpose that the nation had at heart, and for which the department had, with your concurrence and supposed approval, made the most expensive and formidable preparation ever undertaken in this country." The secretary was angry, and it was not until eight months later that he let the true losses be known.[52]

Admiral Du Pont tried to justify his withdrawal and his decision not to renew the attack the following day, but his fate was already decided. On June 3, 1863, he received a letter from the secretary which read: "From the tone of your letter it appears that your judgement is in opposition to a renewed attack on Charleston, and in view of this fact, with your prolonged continuance on the blockade, the Department has concluded to relieve you of the command of the South Atlantic Squadron."[53]

Major General Hunter was an old hand at army politics. He had saved his own skin at the Battle of Secessionville by laying all the blame on Brigadier General Benham, and now he tried to do the same kind of thing. After writing the admiral a letter praising his action and professing great friendship, he wrote directly to President Lincoln: "on the day of that attack, the troops under my command held Folly Island up to Lighthouse

Inlet. On the morning after the attack we were in complete readiness to cross Lighthouse Inlet to Morris Island, where once established, the fall of Sumter would have been as certain as the demonstrations of a problem in mathematics." Actually, General Hunter had over 12,000 available troops trained in "surf-boat exercise" ready for the amphibious assault. At the height of the attack, Brigadier General Seymour (who had been with Anderson at Fort Sumter) begged Hunter to let him cross Lighthouse Inlet and attack the southern end of Morris Island. Hunter refused; he "thought the attempt too hazardous." Seymour was disgusted by his refusal. Hunter was exaggerating in his letter to Lincoln; it was to take General Gillmore, who relieved him, two months of intense fighting to capture Morris Island, and even then he was unable to take Fort Sumter. General Hunter went on to say: "The sacrifice would be of no avail without the aid of the Navy, and I have been painfully but finally convinced that from the Navy no such aid is to be expected." But this letter did not save Hunter; he, too, was relieved of command in June, 1863.[54]

Six months after the attack, Secretary of State William H. Seward tried to explain the failure of the ironclads. He said that the attack "failed because the rope obstructions in the channel fouled the screws of the iron-clads, and compelled them to return after passing through the fire of the batteries. . . ." This statement drew immediate response from Brigadier General Ripley and Col. Alfred Rhett; almost everyone who had participated in the fight had something to say about it. General Ripley bluntly said, "The statement is simply false." Colonel Rhett, who had been standing on the parapet of Fort Sumter during the entire engagement, wrote, "It is incorrect throughout." Furthermore, the injured *Keokuk* drifted in with the tide to within 30 yards of the obstruction before getting under way and going out of the conflict; she was the only ship that came anywhere near the boom.[55]

After the war, General Beauregard said that, if the fleet had attacked at night, they could have destroyed Fort Sumter and the other fortifications. "Such a result at that time," he said, "would have been necessarily followed by the evacuation of Morris and Sullivan's Island and soon after by Charleston itself." [56]

Colonel Davis of the 104th Pennsylvania, an interested spectator, said: "In point of strength this was the mightiest Armada the sea had ever borne upon its surface, and these few mailed ships could have vanquished in conflict the proudest wooden navy the world had ever seen. . . . The firing, while it lasted, was the most terrific kind, probably never equalled in the annals of naval warfare." [57]

The first great attempt to capture Charleston had ended in a miserable failure. Later the Confederate Congress passed a resolution thanking General Beauregard and his troops "for their brilliant and signal defeat of the ironclad fleet." [58]

5

Good seamanship and the fact that the sea was perfectly calm enabled Captain Rhind, the skipper of the *Keokuk*, to get his ship under control and out of the battle of April 7. The crew worked all night trying to plug the numerous holes in the hull. Early the next morning, with the wind freshening and the sea becoming rougher, more and more water poured in. At 7:30 A.M. Captain Rhind flew a signal of distress. Fortunately, the tug *Dandelion* came to his aid and took aboard the entire crew without the loss of a single life. The *Keokuk* sank in about 18 feet of water (high tide); only the stack was visible above the surface. [59]

In writing his report of the battle the day that it occurred, General Ripley said the *Keokuk* was "probably for sale." Admiral Du Pont sent down divers to examine the wreck, and they reported that she was unsalvagable. Furthermore, since the sunken ship was only 1300 yards off Morris Island, which at that time was in Confederate hands, it would have been hazardous to maintain a crew to work on her. In order to keep her from falling into Confederate hands, efforts were made to blow her up, but these apparently were not too successful.

A week later, Lt. W. T. Glassell, an officer on the Confederate gunboat *Chicora*, visited the sunken *Keokuk* to observe the effects of the shells against her heavy turrets; he came away with two United States flags and some signal pennants. Other Confederate officers visited the *Keokuk* as well; two naval officers pronounced her two 11-inch guns unrecoverable. However, Maj. D. B. Harris, chief engineer, and Lt. S. Cordes Boyleston thought otherwise and convinced General Beauregard that such a feat was possible. The general sent some qualified mechanics along with the necessary guard boats to make the attempt. All the work had to be done at night, as the Federal fleet was constantly on patrol off the bar.[60]

Adolphus W. La Coste, a civilian employed by the ordnance department, was an able rigger, skilled in moving heavy guns and other large objects. General Beauregard placed him in charge of the hazardous operation. As part of his crew La Coste selected his brother James, along with several other civilians, a few soldiers from the garrison of Fort Sumter, and one Negro, Edwin Watson.[61]

The *Keokuk* had gone down in relatively shallow water, but her two turrets, each containing a huge gun, were exposed only at low water; the salvage party, therefore, had only about two and a half hours a night in which to work. Furthermore, the sea had to be calm for them to maintain a footing on the slippery turrets, and they had to be ready at any moment to jump into the guard boats and row for the Morris Island beach and the protection of the Confederate guns. As the work progressed and the possibility of success increased, the working party was enlarged. In order to give them additional protection, one or both of the Confederate gunboats would take a covering position and, if necessary, engage the Federal fleet long enough for the working party to get to the Morris Island beach.

On April 20, 1863, the Federal fleet fired on the boats containing the men who were working on the wreck. The guard ship, which at that time was the Confederate gunboat *Chicora*, exchanged shots with the fleet at long range, but for some reason the ships in the fleet did not press the attack. No definitive explanation has ever been given as to why the blockading squadron was not aware that something important was taking place at the wreck; the crews aboard the Union vessels must have heard the sound of hammering as the turrets were being cut open to get at the guns. Sound travels long distances over water, especially on calm nights.[62]

In spite of the fact that the work was being done in late April and early May, the water was still cool. The men must have suffered greatly from the cold. Nevertheless, the crew started cutting through the heavily armored turrets with sledge hammers and chisels, wrenches and crowbars. Finally, a hole was cut in the top of the turrets large enough to allow the removal of the 11-inch guns, which were over 13 feet long and weighed 16,000 pounds. The first gun was rigged and ready to be taken out of the turret and placed on an old hulk. To counterbalance the weight of the gun, 1500 sandbags were placed in the bow. The crew warped the hulk alongside the wreck and secured the tackle in order to lift the gun off its bed and swing it aboard. Up to their waists in water, the men took up the strain, and gradually the gun was lifted. The breech came out first, the muzzle still swinging in the turret. Gradually the gun was raised higher and higher until the lifting blocks touched, and it could be lifted no more. The muzzle did not clear the turret, and with the blocks touching there was no way of elevating the gun further. La Coste ordered the sandbags shifted from the bow to the stern of the hulk. As the bags were being carried aft, the bow began to rise slowly, but even with the flood tide the muzzle would not swing clear. Daylight was approaching, and it was only a short time before the working party would be discovered by the blockading vessels. Fortunately for La Coste and his crew, a large wave lifted the hulk, the derrick, and the gun just enough for the muzzle to swing free and clear the turret. At long last the effort was successful. The men got under way as quickly as possible. As they headed toward the city with their salvaged gun, they were cheered by the garrisons of Sumter and the batteries.[63]

The second turret was hacked open, and the salvaging of the

second gun was comparatively easy. By this time Adolphus La Coste had become ill from exposure, but his brother James took over, and it was under his supervision that the second gun was recovered. By their daring, perseverance, and skill the Confederate forces acquired two valuable and badly needed heavy guns. One of these guns can be seen to this day (1970) on White Point Gardens (the Battery); it was formerly used on Sullivan's Island.

Few episodes of the war exceeded in daring the raising of the *Keokuk's* guns. The men worked feverishly for nearly three weeks, soaking wet and cold, under the eyes of the Federal fleet. On May 5, 1863, General Beauregard wrote to Secretary of War Seddons in Richmond that the two 11-inch guns from the *Keokuk* had been recovered.[64]

No mention of the operation had appeared in the local press while the work was in progress, but when the second gun was brought into the city, the press proudly proclaimed the accomplishment. When the news reached Secretary of the Navy Welles in Washington, he wrote a letter of severe censure to Admiral Du Pont, stating in part: "The duty of destroying the *Keokuk* and preventing her guns from falling into the hands of the rebels devolved upon the commander in chief rather than on Chief Engineer Robie. . . . The wreck and its important armament ought not to have been abandoned. . . ."[65]

The withdrawal of the fleet left over 12,000 Union troops with their surf boats on Folly Island. Unaware of the tremendous damage sustained by the ironclads and thinking that they were still capable of supporting an amphibious assault, Beauregard thought that a landing would be made at Bull's Bay, about 20 miles above Charleston, and an attempt made to take Sullivan's Island from the rear.[66]

Gradually some of the Federal troops withdrew from Cole's and Seabrook's islands, and it was reported that the monitors had returned to Port Royal. Beauregard, therefore, felt justified in returning part of a brigade that had been rushed from Wilmington, North Carolina, and some infantry who had been sent from Georgia. He also received information that troops were being withdrawn from Folly Island, but, had he known the number that remained, it is doubtful that he would have returned the troops sent to aid in his defense. Actually, on April 30, 1863, there were over 4,000 Union troops on Folly and over 3,000 on Seabrook's Island. With this number of men accompanied by gunboats a serious demonstration could have been made in any area.[67]

After Du Pont's attack Beauregard wrote to Col. John Forsyth in Mobile, Alabama, who had a similar problem of defense, that he placed great reliance in three things: heavy guns, Rains torpedoes, and deep-water rope obstructions.[68]

Things were getting worse in the West for the Confederate army, and the Union forces were abandoning their attack on the eastern seaboard; therefore, Secretary of War Seddons ordered Beauregard to send with the "utmost dispatch" 8,000 or 10,000 men to General Pemberton's relief. A week later he ordered him to send another 5,000, if Evans' Brigade had been returned to him from North Carolina. Beauregard remonstrated with the secretary of war, telling him that two brigades had been returned to North Carolina, that he was sending over 5,000 men to Pemberton and had only 10,000 men left for the defense of all of South Carolina and Georgia, and that if any more were sent he would have to abandon the Charleston and Savannah Railroad.[69]

Meanwhile, the Union forces were digging in on Folly Island and were doing so "without attracting too much attention." General Seymour wanted the north end of Folly Island held securely, "yet quietly." Even at this early date a build-up was being made preparatory to the amphibious assault on the southern end of Morris Island.[70]

During April and May, in spite of the constriction of the blockading fleet lying off the Charleston bar, 15 blockade-runners entered the port and 21 departed, carrying over 10,000 bales of cotton. By this time cotton had become scarce, and the English mills were clamoring for it.[71]

In the meantime, the Union forces were sending raiding parties up the rivers. Apart from these raids, things were relatively quiet. In the middle of June, Capt. John C. Mitchel reported that he observed "symptoms of work on Little Folly Island," and that he had begun shelling it slowly. Since he received no answer from the island, he assumed that very little activity was taking place there. He was badly mistaken, however; three weeks later 47 guns opened up there at first light.[72]

4

Morris Island

1

"WAGNER WAS ONE OF THE MOST TERRIFIC BATTLES OF THE war; the numbers engaged were but a fraction of the numbers at Gettysburg and Spottsylvania and Cold Harbor, but the fierce fighting and heroism at Wagner was not excelled upon any battlefield in the War." [1] Why, then, is so little known about this battle and even less said about it? The main reason is that it was not an overwhelming Northern victory. Had it been, and had it caused the fall of Charleston, it would probably be better known today. In addition, it occurred at a time when both the Northern and Southern press were full of stories of Vicksburg, Gettysburg, and the New York draft riots. A Northern source said that "Morris Island has not received much attention from historians." [2]

Morris Island is a small, low island on the south side of the mouth of Charleston harbor; it runs in a northeasterly to southwesterly direction. It is approximately 6500 yards long and the upper end is almost treeless. Water is obtained by sinking shallow wells, and it has an unpleasant taste. The upper part of the island had been used as a quarantine station and a burial ground. It was altogether an uninviting and desolate place.

Strategically, Morris Island was of less importance than James Island or Sullivan's Island. When Cole's Island at the mouth of the Stono Inlet was ordered abandoned by General Pemberton on March 27, 1862, the way was opened for Federal forces to occupy both Cole's and Folly islands without having to fight for them.[3]

The previous year General Beauregard had written that, as soon as Fort Sumter was repaired (after it was evacuated by Major Anderson), he would withdraw all of his troops and guns from Morris Island; at that time he believed that Charleston could be held against all attacks without the island being in Confederate hands. This ultimately proved to be the case. But at the time Beauregard had no idea that Federal forces would be able to occupy Folly Island unopposed. Two years later, with the buildup of the Federal forces on Folly Island, General Beauregard said: "I think it is more probable they will move from Stono Inlet along Folly Island, thence Morris Island, to endeavor to take Fort Sumter *à la* Pulaski; but they may find that to be a piece of folly." Again his prediction was correct; that is exactly what the Federal forces did.[4]

General Pemberton had ordered the construction of a battery across the narrowest part of Morris Island, about 1300 yards from Cummings Point; this battery was known as the "Neck Battery." Because of lack of labor, work on it had been slow, and it was far from completed. Consequently, when the Federal forces occupied Folly Island, since it was not known whether they would strike at James Island or Morris Island, every effort was made to get the battery in fighting order.[5]

The dimensions of the battery within the interior slope were 630 feet from east to west and 275 feet from north to south; it covered an area of about 3 acres. The smallness of the battery should be kept in mind. It was named after Lt. Col. Thomas M. Wagner of the First Regiment of South Carolina (regular) Artillery, who lost his life on Fort Moultrie by the bursting of a gun. At the time of the first attack, its armament consisted of 13 guns, the heaviest being a ten-inch Columbiad.[6]

Shortly after his return to Charleston, General Beauregard gave orders to have the southern end of the island fortified, but misunderstandings and delays caused work to progress slowly. However, by the middle of June, 1863, it was almost completed, and Capt. John Mitchel, who was stationed there, shelled Little Folly Island from there. He received fire from some gunboats which had gone up Folly River, but none from Little Folly.[7]

Brig. Gen. Quincy A. Gillmore assumed command of the Department of the South on June 12, 1863; he had just been promoted for his part in the quick reduction of Fort Pulaski at Savannah. His plan of attack was: (a) to take possession of the lower end of Morris Island; (b) to reduce Wagner; (c) to batter Fort Sumter with his heavy guns—as he had Fort Pulaski—until it was a ruin; and (d) to make it possible for the fleet to run by the other batteries and obstructions and reach the city, which in turn would compel the evacuation of Sullivan's Island, after which James Island would be of little value to the Confederate forces. Gillmore accomplished his first two goals, but the battering of Fort Sumter did not have the desired effect; the troops in the fort refused to be beaten and had no thought of surrendering.[8]

At the end of June, 1863, General Gillmore wrote to General Halleck in Washington that in less than a week he hoped to be in possession of a part or the whole of Morris Island. It was to take him a long time and there were to be many casualties before he accomplished his objective. In explaining why he did not attack by way of James Island instead of Morris Island, Gillmore said: "The answer is simple. The enemy had more troops available for the defense of Charleston than we had for the attack." He was badly mistaken. At the time of the amphibious assault on July 10, he actually had a numerical superiority of two to one. Union intelligence always greatly overestimated the number of Confederate troops in the Charleston District and underestimated their fighting abilities.[9]

In order to take the island, General Gillmore had 11,500 crack troops with 98 pieces of artillery, some of the heaviest used in warfare. In addition, he had the close cooperation of a large armored fleet under the command of Admiral Dahlgren; the fleet carried 11- and 15-inch guns. The Union troops were of the finest quality, all volunteers with two years of service. As one Northern source said, "General Gillmore was supplied with material for carrying on a siege probably superior to those which any General had ever possessed in all history of war." [10]

On the other hand, General Beauregard was continually losing troops as they were ordered to reinforce General Lee in Virginia and General Pemberton in Tennessee. On July 10, 1863, the troops in the First (Charleston) Military District were distributed as follows:

James Island	2906
Morris Island	927
Sullivan's Island	1158
City of Charleston	850
Total	5841 [11]

General Gillmore planned two feints to throw Beauregard off: to land a force on James Island and to attempt to burn the Charleston and Savannah Railroad bridge across the Edisto River. On July 9, General Terry landed on James Island with nearly 4000 troops, and Col. Thomas W. Higginson attempted to destroy the railroad bridge across the Edisto River. The James Island landing was a serious threat to Charleston, and the cutting of the railroad would have disrupted the sending of reinforcements between Charleston and Savannah and transportation in general. General Beauregard was fully aware of the seriousness of these two maneuvers. [12]

On the night of July 8–9, a party under the command of Capt. Charles T. Haskell, Jr., while scouting Little Folly Island, discovered several Federal barges collected in the creeks approaching Lighthouse Inlet. [13] The scouting party also heard the sound of chopping coming from Little Folly. The next night, Colonel

Graham of the 21st South Carolina volunteers, anticipating an attack, alerted his troops. At first light the small trees and bushes on Little Folly were cleared away and 47 guns of all caliber opened fire on the Morris Island troops with their 11 guns. Each of the Federal guns had 200 rounds of ammunition to expend against Confederate forces during the next three hours. Though smothered by artillery fire, the Confederate troops stood gallantly by their guns. Admiral Dahlgren aboard the *Catskill*, followed by the monitors *Nahant*, *Montauk*, and *Weehawken*, steamed in close to shore and at 6:05 A.M. with their 11-inch guns opened a devastating enfilading fire on what was left of the Confederate forces. According to the admiral, he had to use his 11-inch shells to dislodge the gunners from their pieces.[14]

In the meantime troops of the Third New Hampshire, Sixth and Seventh Connecticut, Ninth Maine, 76th Pennsylvania, and four companies of the 48th New York had been sitting quietly in the barges in the marsh on the edge of Little Folly Island waiting for the signal to advance. After nearly three hours of gunfire from the 47 guns and mortars there was a sudden silence; the time to make the assault had arrived.[15] As soon as the barges rounded the end of Little Folly they were seen by the remaining Confederate troops, but because most of the troops' guns had been dismantled or the gun crews annihilated, the firing was inaccurate, and only one barge was sunk.

When the Union troops landed, the Confederate forces slowly gave ground, those who could retreating to the safety of Battery Wagner. The Federal forces, consisting of 2000 men, were able to cross the inlet in a short time and moved along the beach with the monitors shelling the ground ahead of them. Approximately 700 Confederate troops opposed the landing, sustaining casualties of 42 percent and losing their 11 guns.[16]

Brigadier General Strong was in one of the first boats to approach Morris Island. Thinking that the water got shallow near shore, he jumped from the boat but the beach shelved off abruptly. Strong went down, and nothing could be seen but his hat drifting down the inlet. When he surfaced, he was hauled out and carried ashore. As his boots were full of water, he had them taken off and led the troops in his stocking feet. After a while he commandeered a small donkey and continued leading the advance bootless and hatless.[17]

The monitors, meanwhile, had moved ahead, throwing their heavy shells in front of the advancing troops, until they had gotten close to Battery Wagner, which opened up on them with good effect. The first three shots from Wagner hit the *Catskill*, which, flying Admiral Dahlgren's flag, received most of the attention from the gunners. Before the monitors withdrew, the *Catskill* had received 60 hits. The *Nahant* had been hit only six times and the *Montauk* twice. It is the opinion of some that if the Union forces had pursued the retreating Confederate troops and stormed Battery Wagner, they probably would have taken the battery and the island.[18]

After a desperate stand under overwhelming fire, the Confederate forces gave way and the Federal forces were firmly established on Morris Island. It was, however, to take them two months to reach the upper end of the island, a distance of only 1300 yards, and it was to cost them nearly two casualties for every yard gained.

Sailors from the fleet manned some of the barges used in the amphibious assault. One of them got ashore, captured a stray mule, and brought it on board. Riding the mule on the barge, he loudly proclaimed that it was the first craft he had ever commanded and that, he therefore, had the right to ride on the quarter deck.[19]

The 21st South Carolina Volunteers under Col. R. F. Graham were among the troops stationed at the lower end of the island at the time of the amphibious attack of July 10. When they retreated, they were unable to take their baggage with them and they apparently lost most of their clothing. The following appeal appeared in the *Courier* a few days later:

The brave soldiers of the 21st Regiment, SCV (Graham) were among those that fought desperately to save us and our homes and their loved soil on Friday. Owing to the excessive heat of the weather, the men had stripped themselves as far as possible, and in the fight they lost their clothing and nearly all their baggage.

We shall deem it a privilege to receive and apply any donations in money or clothing, which may be left at the *Courier*'s offices for the men of the 21st Regiment.[20]

General Beauregard was severely criticized by some for not sending for reinforcements to prevent the Federal forces from getting a foothold on Morris Island. However, as he always maintained, James Island was the key to Charleston. At the same time the Federal forces under General Terry, consisting of approximately 3800 men, had landed on James Island. General Beauregard had only 2900 men under the immediate command of Brig. Gen. Johnson Hagood to oppose General Terry. Beauregard did not know whether the Morris Island attack was merely a feint and James Island would be the main attack; he could ill afford to reduce his small garrison on James Island to reinforce the troops on Morris Island.

Many have said that the attack on the southern end of Morris Island was a surprise. In one sense it was, as the Confederate scouts had no idea how many guns General Gillmore had concentrated on Little Folly. However, the day before the attack General Beauregard had sent a communication to Charles Macbeth, mayor of Charleston, stating: "The papers herewith will show you that an attack is impending on the Morris Island outworks." On the same day Beauregard had alerted the troops at Adams Run and Pocotaligo to be ready to come to Charleston at a moment's notice.[21]

Brigadier General Strong, after his successful amphibious assault, ordered an attack on Battery Wagner to take place the following morning (July 11). However, in the meantime the garrison had been reinforced by troops hurriedly brought over from Georgia (the railroad bridge crossing the Edisto River had not been burned). Consequently, they were ready for the assault.

At daylight the attack was made by four companies of the Seventh Connecticut supported by the 76th Pennsylvania and the Ninth Maine. They advanced quietly with fixed bayonets, their pieces loaded and primed, until they were a short distance from the works. There they received their first fire. With a loud cheer they immediately advanced and rushed the works. By this time fire was pouring on them not only from the cannons but from the riflemen on the parapet as well. The Federal forces charged over the outer works and across the moat to the crest of the parapet. Here they waited for the two supporting regiments, so close to the Confederate troops on the other side of the parapet that if anyone lifted his head he was shot at directly. Actually, because of the proximity of these opposing forces, it was difficult for either one to dislodge the other even with hand grenades. The two supporting regiments broke under the terrific fire they received when they reached the ditch in front of the battery, leaving the Connecticut troops completely isolated. When this happened, the entire garrison turned its attention to dislodging them. At length the order for retreat was given, and those left alive started for the rear through a rain of shot. When a roll call was taken at camp, only 88 of the original 196 answered.[22]

In his report of the action, made two days later, Sylvester H. Grey, the surviving captain of the Connecticut battalion, speaks bitterly of the two supporting regiments; he says that they "broke and fled." Apparently the two regiments ran into the concentrated fire coming from Battery Wagner and, being severely cut up, were forced to fall back. The 76th Pennsylvania sustained 180 casualties, while the Ninth Maine had 56. These, along with the casualties of the Seventh Connecticut, made a total of 339 for the short but fierce fight.[23]

Brigadier General Strong's report of the action states that within 200 yards of Battery Wagner "the Seventy-sixth Pennsylvania halted and lay down upon the ground. . . . The causes of their failure, and hence the failure of the assault, were, first, the sudden, tremendous, and simultaneous fire which all encountered, and second, the absence of their colonel, who was taken ill before the column was put in motion." [24]

On the other side, the Confederate troops in Battery Wagner had been reinforced by the time of the attack. They were even

BATTERY WAGNER—SEA-FACE BASTION, POINT OF FIRST AND
SECOND ASSAULTS

looking forward to it. Because they were fighting from a protected position, their total losses amounted to only 12 killed and wounded. The first assault on Battery Wagner had failed.

A member of the Third New Hampshire who did not participate, but was being held in reserve, wrote feelingly about the attack: "The troops all fell back to their former positions of the day before, with the same accompaniment of hot sun, hot sand, hot shot, and hot shell." [25]

The Charleston *Daily Courier*, describing the attack of July 11, magnanimously stated: "The front line advanced bravely up the battery, our men, according to previous orders reserved their fire until the enemy had gotten within musket range, when a terrific fire of grape, canister, and musketry opened upon the advance." The "enemy" here, of course, is the Seventh Connecticut, which led the charge.[26]

The diversionary attack against the railroad bridge on the Edisto River was not successful. Ascending the river in a dense fog, the steamers got close to Willtown Bluff before they were seen. After a brief artillery duel, the Federal troops landed. However, they had to wait until enough of the pilings that had been driven across the river could be removed in order to proceed. This was a costly delay; it enabled the Confederate forces to hurriedly bring in some artillery farther up the river. The two steamers and the tug were close to the railroad bridge when they were turned back by another battery. On the way back down the river, one of the steamers ran into some of the piles and, as the tide was ebbing, had to be abandoned and burned. Casualties on both sides were negligible.

The other diversionary attack occurred on James Island. Under cover of the gunboats furiously shelling both banks of the river, 13 transports loaded with 3800 troops under Brigadier General Terry landed on the afternoon of July 9. General Beauregard frankly stated that he did not have troops enough to prevent a landing. Brig. Gen. Johnson Hagood was in command of the 2900 Confederate troops stationed on the island at the time of the landing. Two days later he received reinforcements of troops from Savannah and Wilmington. Even with these, it is doubtful that he had numerical superiority over the Federal forces. No real battle took place, though there were several skirmishes. Finally, on July 16 there was a skirmish which eventually caused the Federal forces to fall back under the protection of their gunboats anchored in the Stono River. As had been the case the previous year, the land-directed fire of the gunboats was accurate and devastating. Embarking on July 17, Terry's troops returned just in time to march the length of Folly Island, ferry across Lighthouse Inlet, and walk two-thirds of the length of Morris Island to participate in the second assault of Battery Wagner.[27]

While this was going on, General Beauregard called a council of his generals to discuss the idea of trying to push the Union forces off Morris Island. It was estimated that this would require 4000 troops, but it would be impossible to maneuver that number on the narrow island. Furthermore, there was not enough transportation available to move them to the island during the night in order to make the assault at daybreak. If the crossing was made in daylight, most of the troops would have been annihilated by the concentrated fire of the Federal fleet anchored just off shore. Consequently the idea was abandoned, and it was decided to hold the island as long as possible and make the assault a costly operation for the attacking forces.[28]

On the night of July 14–15 Brig. Gen. William B. Taliaferro, who had just assumed command of Morris Island, ordered Maj.

James H. Rion with 150 men to make a raid on the Union pickets in the rifle pits they had constructed about 200 yards from Battery Wagner. A lively action took place for a short time, then Major Rion retired with two prisoners. Casualties were light on both sides.

Because conditions in Battery Wagner were crowded, and in order to disperse the troops to keep casualties to a minimum, Brigadier General Ripley ordered several hundred rice casks sent to Morris Island. These were sunk in the loose sand and were called "rat holes," forerunners of the "fox holes" of World War II.[29]

On July 16, General Beauregard wired General Cooper in Richmond that he was expecting another attack on Battery Wagner and that he was preparing for it. On that same day the *Courier* stated: "A forest of masts present themselves to our view just outside the bar, mortar boats, gunboats, and monitors, lie within range of our guns on Morris Island." Something was about to happen, and the Confederate forces crouched in Battery Wagner and in the "rat holes" did not have long to wait.[30]

After the unsuccessful attack of July 11, General Gillmore started bringing his heavy artillery over from Little Folly Island and established one of his batteries only 1330 yards from Battery Wagner. As soon as the battery was set up, the men began hurling shells; the fleet opened fire, too. This went on for a week, until noon of July 18.

Two days before the assault, General Gillmore had a conference with Admiral Dahlgren aboard his flagship. After the meeting, the admiral wrote in his diary: "I thought the General much too sanguine."

By July 17, General Gillmore's engineers had established four batteries containing 40 guns of various types and caliber on Morris Island in preparation for the assault.[31]

2

There were about 1300 men at Battery Wagner at the time of the second assault. Their positions are important: On the extreme right was the Charleston Battalion under the command of Lt. Col. Palmer C. Gaillard; the 51st North Carolina under Col. H. McKethan was in the center; and the 31st North Carolina, under Lt. Col. Charles W. Knight, was assigned to the ocean or left side of the battery. In addition, there were several companies of South Carolina artillery, all under the command of Brig. Gen. William B. Taliaferro.[32]

General Gillmore had planned the attack for the previous day, but heavy rains had dampened the powder and inundated some of his batteries, and the attack had to be postponed.

At 10 A.M. on July 18 the Union batteries opened fire with 15 large mortars and 25 guns of various caliber. At the beginning of the bombardment the rate of fire was fairly slow, but it was greatly increased as the day went on. Admiral Dahlgren moved in with his fleet, consisting of five monitors, five gunboats, and the *New Ironsides*, and his 11- and 15-inch guns added to the heavy fire of the land batteries.

General Beauregard said that there was an average of 14 shells a minute throughout the day and that the shelling was "unparalleled until this epoch of the siege in the weight of projectiles thrown." General Taliaferro, who was on the receiving end, estimated that 9000 shells were fired at Wagner during the day, and Maj. Alfred Rhett from his vantage point on Fort Sumter noted that at the height of the bombardment as many as 27 shells per minute were seen over the battery.[33]

The North Carolina troops sought protection from the hail of destruction by going into the bombproofs. Because there was not enough room there, the Charleston Battalion had to seek the protection of the parapets. Some of the other troops were very wisely ordered to the nearby sandhills and "rat holes"; consequently their casualties were light. Before the attack, the Confederates had buried some of their lighter guns in the sand to protect them from the devastating fire; these guns, being undamaged, were unearthed and used with deadly effect against the assaulting troops.[34]

During the day the tempo of the firing increased, until 5 P.M., when all guns were ordered to fire as rapidly as possible. Thousands of shells were fired at the battery. Admiral Dahlgren, who was watching from his flagship just off Wagner, stated that "the fort was soon overpowered by the weight of metal and did not respond with spirit." At five o'clock, when the tide began to rise, the monitor *Montauk* closed in until she was only 300 yards away, pounding the earthworks with her big guns. The *New Ironsides*, with her fourteen 11-inch guns, also closed in, shooting over the *Montauk* with great accuracy. The admiral went on to say, "We had it all our own way." By this time many of the guns in Battery Wagner had been disabled, and the artillerymen were making no effort to respond.[35]

In the early part of the bombardment a shot from the *New Ironsides* cut the halyards of the garrison flag flying over Wagner. Thinking that the flag had been hauled down in token of surrender, the Union troops cheered loudly, but to their great disappointment they saw a member of the garrison standing boldly on the parapet holding the flag out to the breeze. The records state that the flag was replaced by Maj. David Ramsay, Sgt. William Shelton, and Pvt. John Flynn, all of the Charleston Battalion, and Lt. W. E. Readick of the 63d Georgia; but the records do not give the name of the brave man who held the flag until a new pole could be erected.[36]

For ten hours shells descended on Battery Wagner. At dusk General Gillmore, thinking that Wagner had been thoroughly devastated and every gun disabled, ordered the attack. One of the troops who participated in the attack wrote: "No one would suppose that a human being, or a bird even, could live for a moment upon that fort." [37]

Gillmore had prepared for this assault 6000 troops, who were divided into three brigades. The commander of all the troops was Brig. Gen. Thomas Seymour (who had been on Fort Sumter with Major Anderson). The first brigade, consisting of six regiments, was under the command of General Strong, the one who had led the attack of July 10 in his stocking feet. The second brigade was commanded by Col. H. S. Putnam, who had four regiments, while the third brigade, consisting of "four excellent regiments," was led by Brig. Gen. T. G. Stevenson. An imposing force gathered together to make the assault on 1300 shell-shocked troops.[38]

Some of the men stationed at Wagner had had almost no sleep for six nights. Furthermore, many of those who were in the bombproof were fainting from the extreme heat and lack of air. However, this was not apparent to the assaulting troops at the time of their attack.[39]

General Gillmore, having reduced Fort Pulaski so easily, seems to have assumed that he would simply overwhelm the garrison in Wagner by sheer force of numbers. He gave no special instructions to the troops, and no specific plan of action had been adopted, except to commit brigade after brigade. No provisions had been made for cutting away obstruction, for filling the ditch in front of Wagner, or for securing scaling ladders.[40]

The Confederate signal corps had intercepted a message from General Gillmore to Admiral Dahlgren stating that the assault was to be made at dusk. There is some question as to whether this communication ever reached General Taliaferro. Actually, it would have made no difference; it was obvious to everyone that something big was about to happen.

At dusk the fire of the Union batteries, as well as that of the fleet, ceased. Nevertheless, the guns from Fort Sumter, Battery Gregg, and the batteries on James Island opened up on the beach in front of Battery Wagner.

Men were massed in a solid column a mile long down the beach. In the dim light the first assault wave could be seen advancing. It consisted of the 54th Massachusetts regiment of over 600 men deployed in two lines, followed by the Ninth Maine and 76th Pennsylvania, with the Sixth Connecticut on the right and the Third New Hampshire and the 48th New York on the left. By this time the tide was fairly high, and the beach was narrow; some of the men had to walk in water up to their knees. As they advanced, they were met by fire which tore huge holes in their ranks and cut them down like grass. The column reeled but continued onward. Wagner became a mound of fire from which poured a steady stream of shot and shell, making it almost as light as day.[41] In the advance many men fell into the large craters that had been created by the 11- and 15-inch shells from the fleet, and the dead and dying were piled in heaps.

A few of the 54th Massachusetts followed their colonel to the top of the parapet, where almost all of them were killed. The rest broke and fled, going through the lines of the Ninth Maine and 76th Pennsylvania and throwing them into confusion. General Strong was left with less than half of his brigade, but he proceeded on under the intense fire. The Confederate light artillery which had been dug up, played havoc with the advancing troops. In addition, the garrison had been reinforced by the men who had spent the day in the "rat holes" and sand dunes.

The second brigade was ordered to the attack, but Colonel Putnam, the brigade commander, refused to order his brigade forward for about 15 minutes. This left General Strong with only the Sixth Connecticut and the 48th New York, and the latter was being badly beaten. The 31st North Carolina regiment refused to come out of the bombproof and fight, leaving the left or ocean salient of Battery Wagner undefended.[42] Consequently, some of the Sixth Connecticut and the 48th New York were able to enter the battery. However, by this time General Seymour had been carried from the field, General Strong had received a mortal wound, Colonel Shaw of the 54th Massachusetts had been killed, and Colonel Emory of the Ninth Maine and Colonel Barton of the 48th New York had been wounded. With the exception of Captain Little, who commanded the 76th Pennsylvania, all of the commanding officers in the First Brigade had been either killed or wounded.

The regiments had been ordered to remove the caps from their rifles and rely solely on the bayonets. All of them carried out the order except the 100th New York of the second brigade. Colonel Dandy, their commanding officer, said that it was not necessary for his men because they "never fired without orders." However, when they arrived at the edge of the ditch in front of Wagner, in their excitement they fired a heavy volley into their friends in front, who happened to be the Third New Hampshire and the 48th New York, and they wounded Colonel Barton. This not only caused heavy casualties but added greatly to their demoralization. One of the survivors said: "Men fell by scores on the parapet and rolled back into the ditch; many were drowned in the water, and others smothered by their own dead and wounded companions falling upon them." [43]

The delay in the arrival of the second brigade created a hazardous situation for the remnants of the Sixth Connecticut and the 48th New York. As they were partially protected by a salient in the battery, it was difficult for the garrison to dislodge them. Fierce hand-to-hand fighting took place with every weapon available. Captain Ryan of the Charleston Battalion was killed leading his company in an effort to dislodge the invaders.

In about 15 or 20 minutes the second brigade arrived, and along with the remaining troops of the first brigade, who were lying down in front of Wagner, they stormed the works. Because the left salient was still undefended, many were able to get into the battery, where the fighting continued. Orders were sent out to Brigadier General Stevenson of the Third Brigade to advance with his "four excellent regiments." But for some reason, not clearly explained, he never arrived and consequently took no part in the assault.

By this time Brig. Gen. Johnson Hagood had arrived with reinforcements—the 32d Georgia, which aided considerably in eliminating the Union troops inside the battery.

Orders for a general retreat were given, but this in no way affected the troops who had penetrated the battery and continued fighting fiercely. Though they soon realized that their situation was hopeless because no reinforcements could reach them, they fought on until they were all killed, wounded, or captured. It took the Confederate forces three hours to liquidate the rest of the assaulting troops. Out of the several hundred who had gotten into the fort, only 140 left unharmed. [44]

Except for the 31st North Carolina, Confederate troops behaved laudably. In light of the situation their losses were remark-

ably few—188 were killed and wounded—though they too lost
some excellent officers. On the other hand, the losses of the Union
forces were appalling. Few of the regimental commanders came
out of the fight without a wound. The Union casualties totaled
over 1500, including 111 officers. While this does not compare
numerically to the huge losses sustained in some of the other
areas of the war, it was an extremely high percentage.[45]

Even the *Courier* paid tribute to the bravery of the attacking

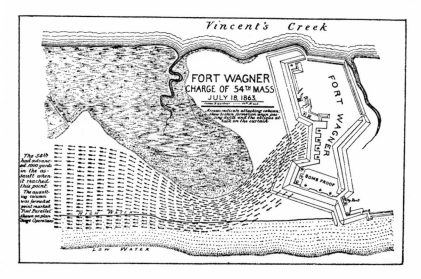

troops: "These repeated the experiment that had just been termi-
nated so disastrously to their companions, and with a bravery that
was worthy of a better cause dashed upon the work." [46]

When the tide rose, many of the wounded were drowned. An
officer of the Third New Hampshire who was wounded in the foot
gives a graphic description of the frightful scene.

As he was making his way to the rear, shots ploughed the sand
near him several times. Near the shore, he "saw a sickening sight.
It was of several unfortunate men lying upon the beach, some
dead and others dying, the rising tide slowly but surely drowning
those that lived." [47] He went on to say that when he had advanced

halfway between Wagner and his lines, he heard the "yell of victory and defiance from Wagner's garrison." Apparently by this time the last of the Union troops had surrendered. As he advanced near his lines, he said:

It became apparent that another scene of bloodshed was going on at this point. It appears that a company of light artillery had been stationed between the batteries [Union] and the ocean to arrest those who retreated without orders. They had been furnished with whiskey and were . . . too drunk to know or do their duty. As the troops arrived in the gap, these drunken artillerymen used their sabers quite lively, cutting right and left. No arguments were of avail. A colored man was sure to be cut down and a white man unless wounded was not suffered to pass unmolested. Soon the pressure became so great that the artillerymen were overborne by the crowd.[48]

The retreat became general, and the assaulting troops returned to the lower end of the island. As it was night, there was much confusion, and most of the regiments, except those of the third brigade, were hopelessly mixed up. The wounded were making their way back as well as they could. By this time the tide was ebbing, which possibly saved the life of some of those who were lying in the surf.

With daylight the following morning, the scene before Wagner was fully visible. Hundreds of corpses mixed with the severely wounded were piled up three deep in some places. Because of the close fighting, many were blown completely to pieces. Blood, mud, and partly dismembered bodies were mingled indiscriminately in the ditch in front of Wagner. The moans of the wounded calling for water had been heard all through the night.

In viewing the ghastly scene the next morning, the correspondent of the *Courier* wrote: "Probably no battlefield in the country has ever presented such an array of mangled bodies in a small compass as was seen on Sunday morning." [49]

The day after the battle, a truce was declared so that both sides could bury the dead and take the wounded to the hospital in Charleston. General Beauregard issued a directive "that special care be taken of the wounded captured at Wagner, as men who were brave enough to go in there deserved the respect of their enemy." [50]

In spite of the intense feeling against the enemy, the Charleston ladies went to the hospital to minister to the sick and dying. This brought down the wrath of one of the daily newspapers, which, in an article entitled "The Yankee Sympathizers," commented: "We understand that the petticoat sympathizers with the Yankee prisoners were again busy in their shameful vocation yesterday." This blast from the newspaper in no way affected the ladies; they continued to nurse the wounded. Every available doctor in the city was called in to help. Because of the great number who had been wounded at close range by the cannon fire, there were many amputations; it is said that amputated limbs were piled high outside the hospital door. [51]

Shortly after the attack, General Gillmore wrote to Admiral Dahlgren that unless the Navy could furnish sailors and marines for one of the attacking columns, he could do nothing more until he received reinforcements because 33 percent of his force was killed, wounded, captured, or sick. He went on to say that he could furnish reinforcements with either muskets or lances. It would have been interesting to see a column of sailors armed with lances making an assault on Wagner. [52]

Three days after the assault, General Gillmore wrote General Halleck "that his losses are not yet accurately reported, but have been very heavy." It was quite some time before he finally released his casualty list and the reports of his regimental commanders.

The 48th New York went into action with nearly 500 men and 16 officers. The next morning at roll call only 86 men answered to their names; 15 of the 16 officers had been either killed or wounded. Some of the other regiments sustained casualties of over 40 percent. [53]

The attack on Fort Wagner failed for several reasons. Probably the most important one was the delay of the second brigade in reinforcing the first, and of the third in reinforcing the second.

Had all three brigades been committed closely together, the outcome might have been considerably different. If the left salient of Wagner, unguarded because of the defection of the 31st North Carolina, had been penetrated by several hundred Union troops, the results might have been disastrous to the defenders. Gen. Thomas Seymour reported that "the failure must be ascribed solely to the unfortunate delay that hindered Colonel Putnam from moving promptly in obedience to my orders, and his not being supported after he had essentially succeeded in the assault." [54]

Colonel Putnam was unable to give an explanation, much less defend himself, because the back of his head had been blown off after he had fought his way into Wagner. When General Seymour ordered him to commit his brigade, Colonel Putnam had refused to move; he said that he could not do so until he had received specific orders from General Gillmore, with whom he had just had a conference. Finally, after 15 or 20 minutes, he ordered his brigade to advance to the assault. While the actions of Colonel Putnam can never be fully explained, a light can be thrown on them by a statement made by one of his officers (Putnam was colonel of the Seventh New Hampshire, but was placed in temporary command of the brigade): "About sundown General Gillmore called up his brigade commanders; and on Colonel Putnam's return, we learned that an assault had been determined on—contrary to his advice as he said. 'I told the General,' said he, 'I did not think we could take the fort so; but Seymour overruled me. Seymour is a devil of a fellow for dash.' " To Major Henderson, Putnam remarked: "We are going into Wagner, like a flock of sheep." [55]

Another factor which contributed to the failure of the attack on Wagner was the breaking of the 54th Massachusetts, who led the assault. That demoralized the Ninth Maine and the 76th Pennsylvania. The 54th regiment consisted of free Negroes led by white officers. Though it was spoken of as a Massachusetts regiment, it was composed of troops from Pennsylvania, New York, Rhode

Island, and other places as well. Its commanding officer was Robert Gould Shaw, son of a prominent abolitionist family of Boston. It has been said that the 54th was given the honor of leading the attack because they were Negroes. They were not actually part of the First Brigade, but only attached to it temporarily for the assault.[56]

Some, if not all, of General Stevenson's third brigade had been on James Island with General Terry on the morning of the assault; consequently, they had to march the entire length of Folly Island, be ferried across to Morris Island, and walk another couple of miles, all under a broiling sun. Actually, the third brigade was moving into the attack when the orders were countermanded.[57]

3

On the day following the repulse, General Gillmore's engineers erected a palisade across the lower end of Morris Island to stop any sortie by the troops from Wagner.

When General Halleck in Washington heard the news of the bloody repulse of the Union troops, he wrote to General Gillmore that his letter had "caused much embarassment"; he continued: "Had it been supposed that you would require more troops, the operation would not have been attempted with my consent or that of the Secretary of War." General Gillmore had asked for 8,000 additional troops for Morris Island. At least he fared better than his predecessor General Benham, who had been arrested and subsequently reduced in rank for his unsuccessful attack at Secessionville.[58]

Now that General Gillmore knew that Wagner could not be captured by a frontal assault, he settled down to siege operations. He had 41 pieces of heavy artillery, including several 200- and 300-pound Parrott guns, as well as the 11- and 15-inch guns of the fleet. He decided, therefore, that he would pound the fort to pieces. Again he had underestimated the stubbornness and fortitude of its defenders; it took him nearly two months and thousands of rounds of ammunition to achieve his objective, and even then the fort was evacuated by the defenders and not taken by assault.[59]

The morning after the assault of July 18, General Beauregard instructed General Ripley to hold "Morris Island at all costs for the present." General Gillmore immediately erected new batteries, which added their fire to those already concentrated on Wagner. It was now a question of how long the garrison could hold out against such overwhelming odds. Day and night the shells fell on Wagner. Every morning the fleet would close in and pound it with their heavy guns.[60]

During the day a force of 500 troops was kept in Wagner; the rest of the men were withdrawn to the protection of the sand hills and "rat holes." In this way casualties were greatly reduced. The 500 men were considered a sufficient number to hold an assault in check until the others could arrive.[61]

In early August, Capt. Samuel LeRoy Hammond of the 25th South Carolina Volunteers suggested a plan to kidnap General Gillmore out of his bed some dark, rainy, disagreeable night so that he could enjoy the hospitality of the "city by the sea," which he seemed so determined to reach. General Taliaferro, however, quickly disapproved of the scheme; it was, he said, "altogether impracticable."

The siege continued, and General Beauregard ordered General Ripley's force reduced to 1000 men; this, he felt, was "quite sufficient," though Ripley should be ready to throw in a larger force in the event of an assault. In spite of the small size of the force opposed to him, General Gillmore feared a sortie. On the night of August 11 the gunners at Wagner opened up with grape and canister. Fearing an attack, Gillmore signaled Admiral Dahlgren to have the fleet open up with their guns. Not only had palisades been erected across the entire width of the island, but a boom had been constructed across Vincent Creek in order to prevent a Confederate amphibious assault. The garrison, expecting an attack and fearing that the fighting would be at short

OCCUPATION OF CASTLE PINCKNEY BY THE CHARLESTON MILITIA,
DECEMBER 26, 1860.

FORT JOHNSON (oil by C. W. Chapman, courtesy The Museum of the Confederacy).

ARTILLERY PRACTICE UPON THE MARSH FRONT AT FORT MOULTRIE, CHARLESTON, SOUTH CAROLINA, BATTERY

BOMBARDMENT OF PORT ROYAL, NOVEMBER 7, 1861—FORT WALKER, *left*; FORT BEAUREGARD, *right* (courtesy New-York Historical Society).

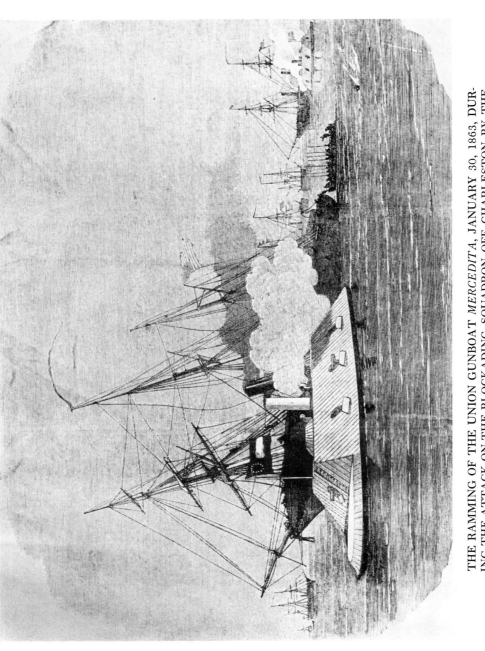

THE RAMMING OF THE UNION GUNBOAT *MERCEDITA*, JANUARY 30, 1863, DURING THE ATTACK ON THE BLOCKADING SQUADRON OFF CHARLESTON BY THE CONFEDERATE GUNBOATS *PALMETTO STATE* AND *CHICORA*.

CAPTAIN WIGG ACTING AS A HUMAN FLAGPOLE AT FORT MOUL-
TRIE DURING THE ATTACK OF DU PONT'S FLEET, APRIL 7, 1863.

THE IRONCLAD *KEOKUK* SINKING ON THE MORNING AFTER THE
BATTLE AT CHARLESTON, APRIL 8, 1863.

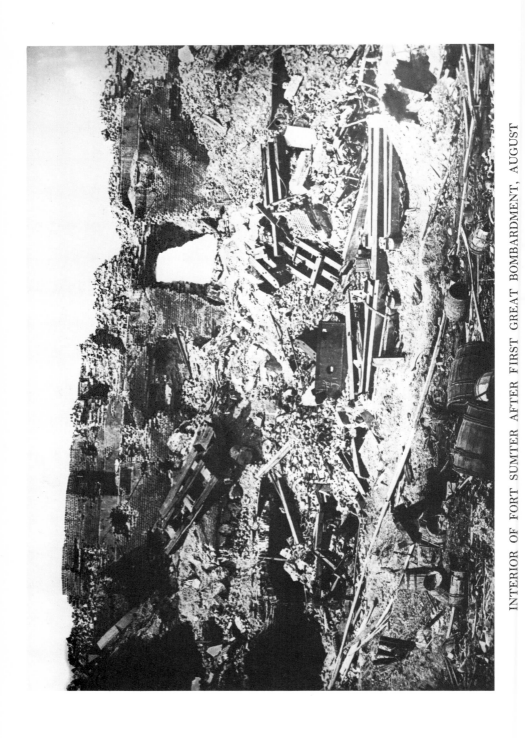

INTERIOR OF FORT SUMTER AFTER FIRST GREAT BOMBARDMENT, AUGUST

THE MAGAZINE OF FORT MOULTRIE EXPLODED BY A SHELL FROM
THE GROUNDED MONITOR *WEEHAWKEN*, SEPTEMBER 8, 1863.

GUNBOATS IN CHARLESTON HARBOR—1863 (painting by C. W. Chapman,
courtesy The Museum of the Confederacy).

THE BOAT ATTACK ON FORT SUMTER.

range, ordered a shipment of double-barrel shotguns—lethal weapons, but legitimate at that time.[62]

The fleet gunners became expert with their fire, which they suspended only during lunch time. Because they were virtually unopposed, they could place one of their shells almost anywhere they wanted, except in the center of Wagner. However, they devised a way of ricocheting their shells off the surface of the water into the center of the battery. This could only be done on calm days, but when it did occur, it caused serious trouble for the men inside. One day a shell ricocheted into a school of mullet, bouncing one of them into Wagner and almost into the lap of Capt. Robert Pringle, who politely thanked the gunners for sending him such an appetizing breakfast. Shortly afterward, a shell ricocheted into the battery and killed him instantly.[63]

Morris Island is extremely low, and large areas of it are flooded at exceptionally high tides. A "full moon tide," which causes the water to rise higher than usual, occurred in the latter part of August, completely flooding the lower part of the island so that the Union troops had to stand in water until it receded. This must have caused them discomfort, as well as damage to their equipment. The troops in Wagner were not greatly affected, as they were in a built-up battery.[64]

Several mounted couriers were assigned to carry messages between Wagner and Battery Gregg, on the extreme upper end of Morris Island. This was necessary because by this time the Union signalmen were probably reading the signals sent by the Confederates. The Confederates had long since acquired the code and were reading with ease the signals sent between General Gillmore and Admiral Dahlgren. The distance between Gregg and Wagner was not great, but getting messages through became something of an obstacle race. The guns of the fleet would open up on the mounted carriers as soon as they departed. The gunners undoubtedly were laying wagers on which one would hit him, while the men in Wagner, protected by one of the salients, would cheer madly for the courier. If he should be injured, or if his horse tumbled into a newly created shell crater, one of the troops, with no thought of his own life, would rush out to save him. This at least broke the monotony of the continuous shell fire.[65]

General Gillmore steadily pushed his lines forward. His first batteries were located 1,300 to 1,600 yards from Wagner. By a series of zigzagged trenches or saps he extended his lines closer and closer, erecting new batteries as he advanced, always bringing more guns to bear on beleaguered Wagner. But this was not done without loss and great difficulty. The guns not only from Wagner but from the batteries located on James Island and Fort Sumter caused great discomfort to the digging troops. Furthermore, because the island was so low, it was difficult to dig any distance without striking water. Many of the batteries located in soft mud had to have stable foundations under them to support the heavy guns. Moving his 300-pounder Parrott guns, weighing a total of 26,600 pounds, into position must have posed a tremendous problem to Gillmore's engineers, but it was accomplished in a remarkably short period of time. At times as many as 100 men would drag the guns through the heavy sand, horses and mules being impractical because of the nearness of the lines.[66]

The Confederate sharpshooters armed with Whitworth rifles equipped with telescopic sights constantly harassed the digging troops. Their range was deadly up to 1,000 yards. It was suicide for a man to show himself for over a brief moment; he was bound to be shot at and almost invariably hit. A Confederate sharpshooter could always be distinguished by a bruise on his right cheek caused by the recoil of his rifle from shooting the extra load necessary for the extra distance.[67] These sharpshooters became such a nuisance and caused so any casualties that General Gillmore decided to have some sharpshooters of his own. Most of them were enlisted from the ranks of the New England troops because many of them were country boys who were familiar with rifles.

A beach can be cool in summer, when the ocean breeze can be felt, but it can also be quite hot. The fact that the men in Wagner stayed there, crouched behind the parapets and at times jammed into the bombproofs, is a high tribute to their fortitude. The fleet moved in almost every morning to deliver broadsides of heavy shells, and the coehorn mortars threw shells that descended vertically and almost noiselessly into the center of the fort. The men were subjected to almost incessant day and night bombardment. The blazing sun reflected from the white sand intensified the heat. In addition, an intolerable stench hung over Wagner, caused by the decomposing bodies of men and horses, as well as by barrels of putrid meat thrown out on the beach. This stench attracted a large, brilliantly colored kind of fly, whose bite caused great discomfort to the suffering men. It was said that water was scarcer than whiskey. When shallow wells were drilled, the water was so contaminated from dead bodies that it was unfit to drink, though the men who were driven by overwhelming thirst to drink it survived. Food was in good condition when it started off for the garrison. Sometimes, however, it took 48 hours in intense heat to reach its destination, and by the time it had been transported across the harbor to Cummings Point and carried under shell fire to Wagner it was usually decomposed.

Dead bodies and amputated limbs were buried in the nearby sand hills, and they were frequently disinterred by the shells from the heavy guns. The situation was so intolerable that the human body could stand it for only a short period of time; consequently, the infantry was relieved every three days. But those who returned always came back ready to fight. And the siege continued day and night, with General Gillmore moving his lines closer and closer to Wagner.[68]

Two Confederate officers suffering from the heat decided to take off their uniforms and plunge into the ocean. While enjoying the refreshing surf, they were spied by the lookouts from the fleet. These, in turn, alerted the gunners, who opened up on the two bobbing heads with their heavy guns. Naturally the two officers rushed to the safety of the sand hills, arriving unharmed but badly shaken. History does not reveal how or whether they recovered their uniforms, which they had left lying on the beach.

One of the guns at Wagner fired a shell which traveled the

length of the island with a horrible screeching noise. A member of the Third New Hampshire wrote that it made "it lively for poor Yankee 'we-uns.' " [69]

In order to delay Gillmore's engineers in their approach to Wagner, the Confederates planted torpedoes in front of Wagner. These land mines did cause some casualties, but did not seriously hinder the advance. When one of the approaching men tripped one of the torpedoes, the force of the explosion hurled him several feet into the air, tore off all his clothes, and deposited him naked some distance away with his elbow resting on the trigger of another torpedo. When the trench got close to Wagner, a large American flag was kept flying at its head so that the guns of the fleet would not fire on it. This, of course, gave the Confederate gunners a target, but they were only at times able to slow down, never to completely stop, the work. As the digging men approached Wagner, they ran into the decomposing bodies of the men who had been hastily buried after the assault of July 18. At first they tried to reinter the bodies, but, finding this impossible, they merely used bodies, arms, legs, and sand as part of the sides of the trenches, a ghastly but necessary procedure.

On the seaward side of Wagner the Confederates had only one ten-inch Columbiad to answer the gunfire of the entire fleet. One day, after it had drawn fire from almost the entire fleet and been slightly disabled, the officer in command of the gun reported to his superior that the heavy shells had caused "some inconvenience to his gunners." This was certainly an understatement. The fire from this gun was remarkably accurate; had it been one of General Gillmore's 300-pounder Parrott guns, the vessels in the fleet would have suffered serious damage. As it was, Admiral Dahlgren, in reporting the actions of the fleet at Morris Island, stated that they fired 8026 rounds and received 882 hits. But because of their heavy armor, the ships of the fleet were not in any way incapacitated.[70]

All during the time that he was pushing his lines and batteries forward toward Wagner, General Gillmore's engineers were skillfully erecting other batteries, which, as soon as completed, opened up on forts Sumter and Moultrie. One which was eventually completed was called the "Marsh Battery"; its 200-pounder Parrott gun fired into Charleston on the night of August 22, a distance of nearly four miles.[71]

Being continually short of lead and other material needed for ammunition, the Confederate government offered to pay the troops on Morris Island for collecting Minié balls and shell fragments that had been fired at them by the Union forces. The troops being held in reserve fanned out over the sand dunes picking up material that would eventually be shot back at their enemies.[72]

General Gillmore was not only having trouble subduing Wagner; he was also having difficulty with the newspaper correspondents who were covering the siege. Apparently they were very critical of the operation and their articles angered Secretary of War Stanton. Stanton ordered General Halleck to instruct Gillmore to "arrest all newspaper correspondents in your command and keep them in confinement at Hilton Head until your operations against Charleston are concluded." General Gillmore ordered them confined, but if they languished in the brig until his "operation against Charleston" was concluded, they had a pleasant wait of over a year and a half.[73]

The siege continued, the Union lines being pushed closer and closer and the condition in Wagner growing worse and worse. With the incessant pounding from the big guns, Wagner was beginning to show signs of disintegrating. It was increasingly difficult to get food and ammunition into the fort. Realizing this, General Gillmore increased his efforts. He knew that it was now only a matter of time before the fort would be so weakened and its defenders so exhausted that he could make another assault and this time carry it by storm.

A private stationed at Wagner, in a letter written to his family, gives a graphic account of conditions just before the end. He says that his regiment was stationed there for six days and nights, instead of the customary three, and that they got only about six hours sleep the entire time. Of the heavy bombardment he said that the bombardment of "Vicksburg sinks into insignificance along side of it." The casualties became so heavy that for 36 hours three surgeons did nothing but amputate limbs, dress wounds, or pronounce soldiers dead, many of whom were their close friends. There were some Georgia troops present who had been in all the big battles in Virginia; they all said "that nothing they ever experienced could approximate conditions" at Wagner. While water was practically nonexistent for the garrison, the Union troops could get a glass of beer almost anywhere in camp, as well as iced lemonade.[74]

In order to aid his gunners and sharpshooters, General Gillmore had several large calcium lights placed near Wagner. These not only blinded the defenders but illuminated the whole fort as clearly as daylight. Any man who exposed himself trying to make repairs was bound to be shot down. Except for one man, an entire detachment manning the parapet was annihilated. Before it was silenced, the mortar in Wagner was firing at such close range that fragments from the bursting shell came back into the battery.[75]

The sap was by now so close to Wagner that the men's voices could be heard. Furthermore, an increase in the tempo of the bombardment informed the garrison that an assault was in the making. On September 2, the effective strength of the Confederate troops at both Wagner and Gregg was 1,656, apparently the largest number ever on the island. In order to reduce his casualties, General Beauregard ordered a gradual withdrawal. At daylight three days later all of Gillmore's batteries, aided by the 11-inch and 15-inch guns of the fleet, opened up on Wagner and kept up a constant stream of shells for 42 hours. General Gillmore said, "The spectacle presented was of surpassing sublimity and grandeur." The men on the receiving end would have expressed it differently. Col. L. M. Keitt, who was then in command of Wagner, got a message through on September 6 to the effect that if the bombardment continued Wagner would be almost a ruin, that he had only 900 troops with him, and that he had already suffered 100 casualties and they were increasing steadily. During the day he sent another message through saying that he now had only 400 effective troops. If they could not be evacuated that night, rather than see them annihilated, he preferred to make a sortie with them against the 11,000 Union troops on the island; he said he would do it at 4 A.M. on September 7. By this time Wagner was unable to answer with a single gun.[76]

General Beauregard ordered the evacuation to take place that night. As soon as it was dark, the sick and wounded were sent to Cummings Point, gradually followed by various units from the garrison. In the meantime, General Gillmore had given orders for an assault to be made on Wagner at 9 A.M. the next morning with 3,000 troops. To prevent the guns and ammunition from falling into their hands, Beauregard ordered the magazines blown up and the guns spiked. It was difficult to spike the guns in such a way that the noise would not alert the Union troops, who were only a few feet away. Fuses were carefully laid and lighted, but they were defective and went out before igniting the magazines. All but 46 men were safely evacuated from Morris Island.[77]

General Beauregard, speaking of the evacuation, said, "The operation is one of the most delicate ever attempted in war." At 1:15 A.M. on September 7, General Gillmore flashed a signal to Admiral Dahlgren: "A deserter just in reports Wagner evacuated." Four hours later he sent another signal: "The whole island is ours, but the enemy have escaped us." The first to enter the beleaguered battery was Captain Randlett with two companies of the Third New Hampshire, though there are others who claim the distinction. They proceeded cautiously until they realized that all of the troops had been evacuated. One of their number said: "Dead bodies long unburied, heads, arms, feet (with the shoes still upon them) lay strewn all around—the stench was almost unbearable." [78]

After 58 days and nights under incredible conditions, subjected to possibly the heaviest artillery fire ever experienced in such a small area, Wagner stood defiant until the end. A small garrison, usually consisting of less than 1,000 men, held off a well-equipped force of 11,000 fighting men armed with some of the heaviest artillery then known and aided by a fleet of heavily gunned and armored vessels. The garrison had the will to fight, and fight they did.[79]

General-in-Chief Halleck wrote to Secretary of War Stanton in high praise of General Gillmore's operation: "He had overcome difficulties almost unknown in modern sieges. Indeed, his operation on Morris Island constituted a new era in the science of engineering and gunnery." Colonel Davis of the 104th Pennsylvania, who was to have participated in the third great assault, said: "Thus ended the most memorable siege ever undertaken on this continent." However, one Union survivor wrote that it was the "most fatal and fruitless campaign of the entire war." Another best expressed it by saying, "The truest courage and determination was manifested on both sides on that crimson day at that great slaughter-house Wagner." [80]

One of the last to evacuate Wagner was a soldier from Georgia, who, arriving safely in Charleston, said he wasn't "afeared of hell no more, it can't touch Wagner." [81]

4

On the night of August 30–31 the steamer *Sumter*, substituting for the disabled steamer *Chesterfield*, made a trip to Cummings Point with a load of troops to relieve those who had been stationed on Morris Island. The returning troops, consisting of the 20th South Carolina Volunteers and the 23d Georgia Volunteers, were slow in arriving to embark.

Because of this delay, when the *Sumter* was ready to leave, the tide had ebbed to such a degree that it was impossible to return to Sullivan's Island by her usual route, which ran behind Fort Sumter. Consequently, it was decided to return by the main channel or on the outside of the fort. In their hurry to get under way, and with the tide fast leaving them, no one thought of notifying the forts. This could have been done easily by sending word to the telegraph operator stationed at Cummings Point.[82]

The batteries on Sullivan's Island had been alerted for another attack of the monitors expected that night, but postponed because of rough weather. The men were sleeping by their guns, and when the sentinels reported a blacked-out ship approaching through the main channel, they had every reason to assume that it was one of the monitors. The batteries opened fire. The civilian skipper of the *Sumter*, Capt. James R. Riley, lit a candle, apparently the only available light on board, hoping to signify that he was friendly. But the light was so dim that some of the gunners thought it was coming through a crack that had not been completely darkened and intensified their fire.[83]

When this occurred, Lt. Col. O. M. Dantzler, who was in command of the troops on board, ordered the light extinguished, feeling that it was giving the gunners aid in sighting their guns. This was a grave error. Some of the battery commanders were beginning to wonder whether they were firing on a monitor, but when the light went out they were convinced that it was an enemy vessel and continued firing.

Almost immediately after being fired upon, the *Sumter* ran aground on the sea end of the shoal off Fort Sumter and a small boat was sent to Sullivan's Island to tell them to stop shooting. The ship's whistle was blown but, because of the wind coming from Sullivan's Island and the roar of the guns, was not heard by the gunners. However, Col. William Butler and some of his officers on the island suspected that something was wrong, and the firing was slowed down. When Captain Riley finally managed to communicate to them that they were shooting at the wrong vessel, the guns were ordered silenced.[84]

Only two men were killed and one wounded on the *Sumter*. Small boats under the command of Capt. C. C. Pinckney were sent to their aid.[85] The tide was low, and some of the men had abandoned ship and were standing on the shoal in two feet of water. Most had lost all of their equipment, and all were thoroughly bedraggled. The *Sumter*, which had been "hulled" several times in addition to having run aground, capsized a few hours after she was abandoned.

An investigation was immediately ordered, and after reports were received from everyone involved, it was found that the responsibility rested on the post quartermaster, who was aboard and in charge of the *Sumter*, for not having informed the forts of her change of course.

With Morris Island evacuated and Fort Sumter reeling from its first great bombardment, many of the inhabitants thought that it was just a question of time before Charleston would be forced into surrendering. Fearful of what would happen to the city when occupied by Federal troops, a group of leading citizens, headed by the Honorable Robert N. Gourdin, had the body of John C. Calhoun removed in the dead of night from its grave in the west cemetery of St. Philip's churchyard and reinterred in an unmarked grave in the east cemetery. It was many years later before the body, in its metal casket, was returned to its original resting place.[86]

5

Sumter Bombarded

1

EVERY STUDENT OF AMERICAN HISTORY IS FAMILIAR WITH THE bombardment of Fort Sumter which took place on April 12–13, 1861, and the gallant defense made by Major Anderson before he was forced to capitulate. However, few are aware that later in the war Fort Sumter was subjected to three major bombardments that dwarfed into insignificance the initial bombardment suffered by Major Anderson. It has been said that until the time of the Gallipoli campaign in 1915 (Turkey in World War I), the defense of Fort Sumter ranked as one of the greatest in the world against a combined army and navy attack.[1]

Subjected to gunfire from a heavily armored fleet, bombarded by heavy artillery that consisted of some of the most accurate rifled guns then known, assailed by amphibious forces, battered into a shapeless mass of brick and rubble, with pestilence raging among its garrison, with every gun dismantled or removed, at one

183

time holding off the Federal forces with four Whitworth shoulder rifles mounted with telescopic sights, the garrison never surrendered. Fort Sumter was the symbol of the Confederacy. The first question asked by daily papers North and South was: "Is Fort Sumter still holding out?" The flag flying from it was also a symbol, and, though it was shot down repeatedly, it was always replaced by some member of the garrison. If Fort Sumter fell, so would the Confederacy.

General Gillmore, while constructing batteries on Morris Island in order to subdue Battery Wagner, was keenly aware that occupation of the island alone would not give his army and Admiral Dahlgren's fleet, probably the most powerful in the world at that time, access to Charleston. Consequently, he ordered the building of several batteries to house his heaviest guns to batter down the walls of Fort Sumter and secure its quick surrender, as he had done with Fort Pulaski the previous year.

Anticipating a bombardment, General Beauregard and his district engineer, Lt. Col. D. B. Harris, decided to fill in the casements and other areas of Fort Sumter with wet sand and bales of cotton soaked in salt water. Two feet of sand was first laid on the floor; then bales of wet cotton were placed two feet apart and the sand filled in between them until the entire area had been filled. The original sallyport faced Morris Island, but, since this area would receive the brunt of the shelling, a new one and a wharf were constructed on the west (city) side of the fort. In addition to strengthening various parts of the walls, 20,000 bags of sand had to be brought from the city during the night and placed in position before daylight. All the work being done was under the supervision of Lt. John Johnson, the engineer in charge of the fort, with a gang of men varying in number from 300 to 450.[2]

Another engineering task was the removal of some of the heavy guns. This, as well as the strengthening of the fort, was started at the time that the Federal forces made their successful amphibious assault on Morris Island. More than 20 guns and mortars were withdrawn and placed in various batteries on James Island and in the inner harbor. Log "Quaker" guns were put in their place. At the time of the first great bombardment, the armament of Sumter consisted of 38 guns of various kinds and caliber and two ten-inch mortars.

In the latter part of July and early August, there was some preliminary firing on Fort Sumter by General Gillmore's batteries so that they could sight the guns and see the effect of the shells. However, at daylight on August 17, 1863, Battery Brown tried her two eight-inch Parrott rifles against the gorge wall of Sumter. One fired solid shot, the other percussion shells. This firing was immediately followed by the other batteries on Morris Island, including a "naval battery" consisting of two eight-inch Parrott rifles and two 80-pounder Whitworth rifles. This battery was manned by sailors from the fleet under the command of Cmdr. Foxhall A. Parker. At the beginning, 11 heavy guns were aimed, as anticipated, at the gorge wall of the fort, shooting a distance of from 3,400 to 4,200 yards. As the heavy rifled guns were placed in position, they joined in the bombardment, until finally a total of 18 participated. Had all the advance preparations not been made, it is doubtful whether the Confederate forces could have held Sumter.[3]

By mid-morning of the first day, the monitors *Passaic* and *Patapsco* had joined in the bombardment with their 15-inch guns. Their fire was returned by the 11-inch gun that had been raised from the ironclad *Keokuk* and mounted in Sumter. Heavy firing continued until dusk, when it slackened considerably, but it was maintained all night. During the first 24 hours of the bombardment nearly 1,000 shells of various sizes were fired at the fort. Seven guns had been disabled, and the masonry had suffered heavy damage. That night Colonel Harris, district engineer, and Col. Alfred Rhett, the fort's commanding officer, made a tour of inspection. It was obvious to them that it was only a matter of time before the entire brickwork in the fort would be destroyed; the only course for its defenders was to hold out as long as they could and save as many of their guns as possible.[4]

The second day was almost a repeat of the first, only the fleet did not participate in the bombardment; however, three heavy rifled guns were added to the others. Inside the fort, the destruction was becoming more apparent. The western barracks were a ruin, the casemates on the harbor side were extensively damaged, and a crack developed in the main wall. More guns were disabled and the garrison flag was twice cut away, but each time it was gallantly replaced.

The number of shots fired on the second day was only 876, somewhat less than on the first. An exceptionally high tide pushed by a northeast gale flooded most of Morris Island and inundated the batteries for several hours before it receded. This caused a slowdown in the rate of fire.[5]

Day after day the thunder of the bombardment continued, and the destruction of the fort became more and more obvious. On August 21, since its guns were not replying, General Gillmore thought the fort was completely demolished and demanded its immediate evacuation, as well as that of Morris Island. He declared that, if the demand was not complied with, he would bombard the city of Charleston. One thing General Gillmore had not bargained for was the courage of the garrison and the indomitable spirit of the people of Charleston. General Beauregard replied that "neither the works on Morris Island nor Fort Sumter will be evacuated on the demand you have been pleased to make." The bombardment of the city began soon after midnight on August 22, from an eight-inch Parrott rifle, which had been given the nickname "Swamp Angel," [6] in the Marsh Battery.

Before daylight on the morning of the sixth day of the bombardment, five monitors anchored about 800 yards off Sumter and opened up with their 11- and 15-inch guns. The abortive attack of April 7, 1863, had given the men on the monitors a healthy respect for the guns of Sumter. Consequently, they had placed sandbags around turrets and other vulnerable parts of the ships, which gave them a strange appearance.[7]

The fire from the monitors was returned by the guns of Sullivan's Island and Battery Gregg. Fort Sumter got off six shots from the only two guns that were able to reply, one of which, ironically, was the 11-inch *Keokuk* gun. Those were the last guns fired from the fort. The last day of the first great bombardment was similar to the previous one; Sumter looked more and more like a huge mass of rubble. One shell went through the floor of the upper tier and caused masonry to fall into of the lower rooms, where some officers were eating dinner. Colonel Rhett's hand was cut when his dinner knife broke, and his dinner companions suffered slight wounds.

During this time the flagpole had been shot away twice and the garrison's flag had been cut away seven different times. Each time it was replaced by a member of the garrison.[8]

General Gillmore wrote General Halleck in Washington on August 24, 1863: "Fort Sumter is today a shapeless and harmless mass of ruins." He then quoted Col. J. N. Turner, his chief of artillery: "By a longer fire it could be made more completely a ruin and a mass of broken masonry, but could scarcely be made more powerless for the defense of the harbor." In General Gillmore's opinion, it "was reduced to the condition of a mere infantry outpost, alike incapable of annoying our approaches to Fort Wagner or of inflicting injury upon the iron-clads."[9]

While it was true that the fort did resemble a "mass of ruins" and was incapable of returning any fire, General Gillmore had overlooked one thing in his calculation—the defenders of the fort.

On August 28, 1863, General Foster wrote from Fortress Monroe, Virginia, to General Halleck that a steamer had just arrived from the fleet off Charleston with the news that Sumter and Wagner "had been reduced, and that our own troops now occupied those forts." The news was jubilantly received by the Northern press.[10]

In his official reports, General Gillmore showed that 5,009 projectiles, weighing over half a million pounds, had been fired at Sumter during the seven-day period. No wonder the fort looked like a mound of bricks. The initial phase of the first great bombardment was over.[11]

The second phase was primarily a navy show; the army felt that Sumter was nothing but a mass of ruins without a gun with which to reply and devoted most of their energies to subduing

Wagner. For the next six days Fort Sumter received only a desultory fire, which was merely for annoyance and to keep the garrison from remounting their guns.[12]

General Beauregard, anticipating an all-out attack, issued orders that the fort "shall be held and defended to the last extremity." On August 30, firing by the land batteries was resumed for two days in anticipation of a naval attack by the ironclad fleet under Dahlgren. The admiral thought that Sumter still had a few serviceable guns, while General Gillmore was equally certain that they had all been dismounted by the shells from his guns. This firing on Sumter was even more destructive than the earlier firing because by this time General Gillmore had mounted a 300-pounder Parrott gun. Its 250-pound shell pulverized Sumter and made life even more miserable for its garrison.[13]

Admiral Dahlgren had planned a night bombardment on August 30–31, but the weather was so rough that it had to be postponed. Finally, on the night of September 1–2, the weather was moderate enough to suit the admiral, who signaled that his six monitors would assemble punctually at 9:30 P.M. in preparation for the attack on Fort Sumter and that they would move up the channel to a position near the fort, following in close order behind the *Weehawken* and anchoring across the channel. The admiral also instructed his men to fire at any "floating obstruction that may appear in the channel." In spite of General Gillmore's statement that Sumter did not have a gun that was able to fire, the admiral was apprehensive that the fort would open up on him. At 11:30 P.M., the five monitors were within 500 yards of Sumter when the guns on Sullivan's Island opened up, with the *Weehawken* as their main target. They continued a sustained and rapid fire, which probably would have been devastating had it not been for the "obscurity of the night," which interfered with the accuracy of their aim. Finding that Sumter was unable to reply, the monitors came nearer and nearer, pounding it unmercifully with their 11- and 15-inch guns, aided by the broadsides of the *New Ironsides*, which by this time had joined them. When the tide began to change, Admiral Dahlgren ordered the "cease fire" and the ships returned to their anchorage. On their way there, the *Lehigh* and the *Passaic* collided.

The five monitors and the *New Ironsides* pounded Sumter with impunity, engaging the batteries for approximately five hours, during which time they fired 245 shells from their heavy guns and received 71 hits. Considering that the fleet could only be dimly seen, the Confederate gunners shot remarkably well. A round shot struck the base of the turret of the *Weehawken*, driving in a fragment of iron which broke the leg of Fleet Captain Badger.[14]

The bombardment of Sumter on the night of September 1–2 was longer than any previous naval attack and far exceeded in severity the one of April 7, 1863. The constant roar of the heavy guns aroused the sleeping citizens in the city and sent them scurrying to White Point Gardens (the Battery) to see what was going on. When the *New Ironsides* opened up with her broadsides, "the whole horizon at times seemed to be on fire." [15]

The east wall of the fort was badly damaged; some shells even went completely through and damaged the west wall. Crossing the parade ground, Colonel Rhett narrowly missed serious injury from one of the exploding shells. He himself was unharmed, but his orderly was slightly wounded. The second phase of the first great bombardment, which lasted a total of sixteen days, was over.[16]

2

Knowing that Battery Wagner had been evacuated, Admiral Dahlgren thought it time to try to take Fort Sumter. The navy had played an important part in the subjugation of Morris Island, but the burden of the fighting had been carried by the army, and the next move was up to the navy.

Since every gun on Fort Sumter was dismounted or incapacitated, Beauregard decided to make the fort an infantry outpost. He put Col. Alfred Rhett in charge of the inner fortifications and selected Maj. Stephen Elliott as his successor at Sumter. In offering him the command, General Beauregard said: "You are to be sent to a fort deprived of all offensive capacity, and having but one gun—a 32-pounder—with which to salute the flag, morning and evening. But that fort is Fort Sumter, the key to the entrance of this harbor. It must be held to the bitter end: not with artillery, as heretofore, but with infantry alone; and there can be no hope of reinforcements. Are you willing to take the command upon such terms?" After inspecting Sumter, Major Elliott replied: "Issue the order General; I will obey it." [17]

On the night of September 6–7, Morris Island was successfully evacuated by the Confederates; only a few troops were captured. When this occurred, Admiral Dahlgren became more determined

THE MONITOR *WEEHAWKEN*

than ever to take Sumter. "I immediately designed to put in operation a plan to capture Sumter." [18] As a preliminary, on the morning of September 7 he ordered the monitor *Weehawken* to pass through a narrow winding channel around Cummings Point in order to cut off communications between the Confederate forces. It is not clear precisely what he had in mind at that particular time, for there were no Confederate troops on Morris Island; they had all left the previous night. The waters between Cummings Point and Fort Sumter are treacherous; therefore, the *Weehawken* was instructed to mark the channel with buoys. The tide was low, and the *Weehawken* anchored in order not to run aground; swinging with the tide, she touched bottom, but as soon as the water rose was able to get under way. However, because of the shoal water, she had difficulty steering and ran hard aground. In the afternoon at high water she failed to get off. The Confederate gunners on Sullivan's Island could see her, but did not fire because of the extreme range and because of her heavy armor; they did not realize that she was in serious trouble.[19]

However, seeing her predicament, Admiral Dahlgren ordered a diversionary attack against the Sullivan's Island batteries. About 6 P.M. on September 7, the *New Ironsides* and five monitors engaged the batteries in a spirited fight that lasted until it was too dark for either side to see their targets, when the fleet returned to its anchorage. Meanwhile everything possible was being done to extricate the grounded *Weehawken*. Tugs were sent to help haul her off; coal and ammunition were removed to lighten her. Nothing worked. Maj. Stephen Elliott, sitting helplessly by on Fort Sumter, reported that he distinctly heard hammering during the night, though he apparently did not realize that the *Weehawken* was stuck hard and fast on a shoal.[20]

The following morning (September 8) she was still aground. After working most of the night in an endeavor to free her, Comdr. Edmund R. Colhoun, her captain, ordered the crew to get some sleep. The outer harbor was covered by a light fog, and Major Elliott did not discover the *Weehawken's* plight until 7 A.M., at which time he signaled the information to the batteries.

Elliott did not have a single gun to shoot, and here was a grounded monitor on the shoal within excellent shooting distance. As soon as the fog lifted, about 8:30 A.M., the Sullivan's Island batteries, as well as those of Fort Johnson and Battery Simkins, opened up on the *Weehawken*. But ammunition was scarce and the ship was heavily armored, so the gunners fired with deliberation, aiming at her bottom, which was exposed because of her heavy list.[21] Admiral Dahlgren ordered another diversionary attack, hoping to draw the fire away from her to his fleet. Again the *New Ironsides* and five monitors steamed within range of the several batteries on Sullivan's Island and opened on them.

In the meantime, Captain Colhoun saw that his crew had breakfast before ordering them into action. The second shot from his 15-inch gun bounced off the muzzle of an eight-inch Columbiad in Fort Moultrie into a box of ammunition; this caused an explosion which killed 16 men and wounded 12. For quite some time Fort Moultrie was unable to reply.[22] The *New Ironsides* and the monitors were pouring a devastating fire on the batteries. The broadsides of the former were particularly destructive; they tore through the buildings in Fort Moultrie.[23]

The Confederate gunners, on the other hand, were firing slowly and with great accuracy. Major Elliott on Fort Sumter was able to report the hits, of which there were many. Fortunately for the *Weehawken*, one of the most effective guns that could have been used against her, an eight-inch gun on Shell Point, had burst the previous night.[24]

The *New Ironsides* was not only heavily sandbagged, but had green hides spread over her deck to help deflect the shells. The firing continued without letup for five hours, and the ship was hit again and again.

At the same time Capt. John C. Mitchel, in command of the artillery at Fort Johnson and Battery Simkins, was concentrating all of his available guns on the grounded monitor. He opened up on her with his eight-inch naval shell gun; however, since it was mounted in a shattered carriage, it was impossible to shoot accurately with it. His three ten-inch mortars and ten-inch Columbiad had been sighted in on Morris Island. When Mitchel realized that the mortar fire was ineffective on the armor of the *Weehawken*, he discontinued the firing. He worked feverishly to mount his most effective gun, a Brook rifle, during the day, but succeeded in getting off only four shots from it before the monitor made her escape.[25]

Throughout the engagement, Major Elliott was deploring the fact that the batteries were firing at individual ships in the fleet rather than concentrating on the *Weehawken*. This, of course, was just what Admiral Dahlgren had hoped would occur.[26]

During the entire five hours of fighting, the *Weehawken* was firing away with both her 11-inch and 15-inch guns despite her severe list.

At 1:05 P.M. Major Elliott reported that the *New Ironsides* was withdrawing, followed by the monitors. The reason she withdrew was because she had completely expended her ammunition. By 2 P.M. the firing by the batteries on Sullivan's Island ceased, as the entire fleet had withdrawn out of range.

Shortly afterward, the *Weehawken* floated and, though badly battered, managed to make her escape. The *Courier*, writing of the engagement, stated: "The Monitor that had been aground all the morning was got off between three and four o'clock, firing a parting gun, as if in triumph, at Fort Moultrie." The newspaper continued: "The dense volume of smoke at times enveloped the whole island, and obscuring the Monitors from the sight of the gunners." [27] As the *Weehawken* passed through the fleet on her way to her anchorage she was cheered by the crew of each vessel. Ten days later Commander Colhoun received a letter of commendation from the secretary of the navy in Washington. [28]

The *New Ironsides* and the monitors took a bad but not a fatal pounding during the engagement of the previous evening and in the morning action. Statistically, during both engagements the *New Ironsides* fired 635 shots from her 11-inch guns and was hit 94 times; the *Passaic* fired 49 shots from her 15-inch and rifled guns and was hit 51 times. [29] The other monitors were not so badly battered. The damage to the batteries, which were constructed mostly of sand, was not extensive; two guns were disabled in Fort Moultrie, one being the eight-inch Columbiad that was hit by the lucky shell from the *Weehawken*.

At the height of the morning's fight, seeing that the *Weehawken* was in serious trouble, Admiral Dahlgren signaled Captain Colhoun: "Well done, *Weehawken;* don't give up the ship. We may lose the service of this vessel—I hope not—but the honor of the flag will be maintained." [30] The *Weehawken* was hit 24 times, but her crew suffered only 3 casualties. During the fighting she fired 83 shots from her two big guns. After her lucky shot at Moultrie and when the fleet closed with the batteries on Sullivan's Island, Captain Colhoun directed his fire at Sumter, making it look even more like a rubble heap. During the entire time that the *Weehawken* was aground every Union soldier on Morris Island was watching from the sand hills. [31]

Some authorities have said that the shells of the evening and morning bombardment constituted the greatest weight of metal ever fired up to that time by an American fleet.[32]

3

Fort Sumter was nothing but a heap of rubble, and Admiral Dahlgren thought that its garrison had been battered into complete submission; he therefore demanded its surrender. Major Elliott quickly replied to the demand with, "Inform Admiral Dahlgren that he may have Fort Sumter when he can take it and hold it." Thinking that it was nothing but an advanced infantry fort—which, in fact, it was—Dahlgren decided to take it by an amphibious assault.[33]

The admiral was under the impression that the taking of Sumter would be an easy task. He assigned Comdr. T. H. Stevens to command the expedition. When Stevens told him that he knew nothing about conducting an amphibious assault, the admiral replied: "There is nothing but a corporal guard at the fort and all we have to do is to go in and take possession." Apparently this idea prevailed throughout the entire fleet. A mail sack that had drifted ashore on Sullivan's Island contained a letter dated August 29, 1863, written from aboard the *Ottawa*, which read: "Fort Sumter has still a small garrison of a few men stowed away somewhere at night as an excuse to keep a flag flying, although the sides nearest us present nothing but a mass of shapeless ruins and the work [of destruction] goes on steadily and surely." [34]

By this time relations between Admiral Dahlgren and General Gillmore were becoming strained. The latter, now that he had at long last occupied Morris Island at a terrific cost, was needling the navy to push in past Fort Sumter and take the city. This prompted Dahlgren to make the amphibious assault; General Gillmore planned a similar attack on the same night.[35] The two were competing to see who would conquer Sumter, for the one who captured the historic fort would gain national acclaim. At the last moment, finding that the navy was going to make the assault, General Gillmore demanded that the entire expedition be placed under army command. This the admiral promptly declined to do, and the army then refused to participate.[36]

General Gillmore had been so certain of success that, in a special order designating the troops who were to participate in the attack, he said: "After the capture of the fort, the force will return at once, leaving 100 men as a garrison." [37]

Major Elliott, in anticipation of an attack, had procured from the city a supply of hand grenades and fireballs and had one-third of the garrison manning the parapet, with the remainder posted so that they could reinforce the others wherever necessary. In addition, wire entanglements and other obstacles had been placed on what remained of the parapet so that it would be difficult to scale.

On the afternoon of the attack, a signalman on the gunboat *Chicora* intercepted the signals being sent by Admiral Dahlgren to the effect that an amphibious assault was planned that night against Fort Sumter.[38]

Admiral Dahlgren assembled 500 sailors and marines of the fleet. On the night of September 8–9, 1863, they were put in small boats, towed within 400 yards of the fort, and cast loose. They rowed toward Sumter, unaware that they were under constant surveillance. Instead of only a "corporal's guard" opposing them, they were soon to find Major Elliott and the Charleston Battalion, 320 strong and anxious for a fight.[39]

The point of landing was to be on the southeastern and southern face. There was some confusion among a few of the boats, but the rest came in as planned. Major Elliott ordered that fire be withheld until the boats were only a few yards away, when they were met by a withering blast. Continuing gallantly on, the sailors effected a landing and sought entrance into the fort. When they stepped ashore, they were met by a deluge of hand grenades, fireballs, brickbats and other objects, in addition to an increasingly heavy fire. The gunboat *Chicora*, anchored nearby, opened up on them, as did the guns from Moultrie and Johnson, which had been sighted in for just such an occurrence. Finding it impossible to scale the walls, the sailors took shelter in its recesses, but even the select men of Admiral Dahlgren's fleet could not hold out under such a devastating fire. With no hope of reinforcements getting through to them, those who could surrendered. Realizing that they had fallen into a trap, the supporting boats withdrew without attempting a landing. The gallant but abortive amphibious attack on Fort Sumter was over. The garrison sustained no casualties, but the assaulting forces suffered a loss of 127 in killed, wounded, and prisoners,[40] according to Elliott's report.

The prisoners were treated considerately. Their baggage and medical supplies for the wounded were brought to them under a flag of truce. The navy must have been extremely sure of success. Among the articles brought in were two boxes: one was addressed to Lt. E. P. Williams, commanding Fort Sumter; the other to Ens. Benjamin H. Porter, Fort Sumter. The boxes contained many delicacies, "and were probably intended to grace a festival in honor of the capture of the fort." [41]

In addition, the amphibious force lost five boats and five stands of colors. One of the flags captured was said to be the garrison flag carried from the fort when it was evacuated by Major Anderson. If this is correct, it has never been admitted by the United States authorities. The day after the attack General Beauregard wired General Cooper in Richmond: "Can I be authorized to present to State of South Carolina garrison flag captured yesterday, intended by enemy to float over ruins of Sumter? Am informed it is the same which floated there when that fort surrendered to me in 1861." His request was approved by the secretary of war, but it is not known what eventually happened to this huge garrison flag.[42]

As it turned out, the assault was a matter of no great importance, though it humiliated Admiral Dahlgren. Had it been successful, it would have had far-reaching effects. General Gillmore laconically stated that it "was repulsed with considerable loss." [43] If his forces had participated along with those of the navy, and if a concerted attack had been made on all sides of the fort simultaneously, there is a possibility that a foothold might have been gained. But even then, there would have been no assurance of success, for the Charleston Battalion was not easily subdued.

4

The mighty force of the combined Union army and navy had been blunted against the defenses of Charleston. True, Morris Island had been captured after two months of terrific fighting, but there stood Sumter, still defiant, though frightfully mauled. Since another attack was inevitable, orders were given that the garrison on Sumter be supplied with at least one month's provisions. With a lull in the bombardment, efforts were made to strengthen its defenses. Guns were remounted and special attention was given to the chevaux-de-frise—called by soldiers "Sugary Freeze"—to resist an amphibious assault. Realizing the seriousness of the situation, the authorities in Richmond belatedly sent Anderson's brigade of Georgia troops, which had been with the Army of Northern Virginia to bolster the defenses, and Wise's brigade, composed of Virginia troops.[44] Both arrived after the bloody fighting on Morris Island. Realizing that a Union raiding party might break through the thinly defended line along the Charleston and Savannah Railroad and make a sweep around the outer defenses, Gen. G. J. Rains, head of the Torpedo Bureau, proposed that land mines be laid on the roads leading into the city. The men were to put down the mines whenever a raid was expected, but, for the safety of the citizens, the mines were not to be activated until it was known that the raiding party was coming. Land mines had been used successfully in Virginia the previous year.[45]

The Moultrie House on Sullivan's Island, a favorite place for Charlestonians to spend the summer, was still standing, though much battered. Apparently General Ripley wanted it razed, but orders were given to let it stand, as "it serves as a good object to draw the enemy's fire." Situated near Fort Moultrie, it made a good point of aim for the Federal gunners on Morris Island. But it was far enough away from the fortifications that most of the shell landed in the sand, doing no damage.[46]

Because of the tremendous amount of ammunition being used on the battlefields of Virginia and Tennessee, orders were given to economize on ammunition in every possible way. When Colonel Gorgas, chief of ordnance in Richmond, read in a Charleston newspaper that a 21-gun salute had been fired to commemorate General Bragg's premature victory at Chickamauga, he was furious. Needless to say, salutes were discontinued.[47]

In the meantime, with a comparative lull in the bombardment of Sumter, the work of strengthening the defenses was continued, especially on the batteries in the city proper. A huge Blakely gun had just arrived and had burst while being tested. Apparently General Ripley was responsible. Colonel Gorgas wrote to General Cooper in Richmond that "the destruction of this formidable gun was due to a want of forethought, unpardonable in an officer as experienced as General Ripley." Another Blakely gun arrived and was mounted in White Point Gardens (the Battery).[48]

General Gillmore was busy strengthening the defenses on Morris Island and fortifying the north end of Kiawah Island to prevent any damage to his shipping in Stono Inlet. It is not clear what he had in mind, because the three Confederate gunboats were too underpowered and cumbersome to negotiate the channel of the Stono River. And if the torpedo ram *David* had gotten into the inlet, she would have been an extremely difficult target with her low silhouette. At the end of September, Gillmore had more than 22,000 men stationed on Morris and Folly islands, but except for an occasional reconnaissance party they remained inactive.[49]

During this period Gillmore seems to have spent considerable time casting aspersions on Admiral Dahlgren. Gillmore, who had suffered heavy casualties on Morris Island and knew that Sumter did not have a single gun, expected the fleet to push by the defenses. Feelings between the two became so bitter that President Lincoln wrote his secretary of war that the secretary of the navy wished "that General Gillmore will courteously confer with and explain to Admiral Dahlgren." The secretary of war passed the message on to General-in-Chief Halleck, knowing that he in turn would tell Gillmore to act with more restraint.[50]

Gillmore's espionage was excellent, and he quickly received accurate information as to what was going on in Charleston. As soon as Anderson's brigade arrived, he knew that it had been part of Longstreet's corps and he was quickly informed about the damage to the large Blakely gun. In some cases espionage was not necessary; all he had to do was to read the Charleston *Mercury:* "GREAT BALL OF THE GERMAN VOLUNTEERS LATELY RE-TURNED FROM VIRGINIA will be held in the Hibernian Hall, on Thursday, the 8th of October, 1863. All friends are invited to attend. Commences at 8 P.M. Muller's Musical Band is engaged for the evening. THE COMMITTEE." He must have known fairly accurately the number of troops Beauregard had in the area.[51]

Beauregard had already given his opinion as to the worthlessness of the three gunboats lying in the harbor. He must have gotten Maj. Gen. J. F. Gilmer, who had been assigned to his command, to write to the secretary of the navy for authority to transfer five guns from the gunboats to some land batteries on the shore overlooking the river harbor and further west and to ask that "the batteries armed by the naval guns . . . be commanded by naval officers and seamen." [52] As nothing came of the request, the secretary of the navy must have refused to grant it.

The situation in Charleston had eased, and after less than a month, Anderson's brigade was sent to Lieutenant General Longstreet of the Army of Tennessee. In releasing Anderson and his men, Beauregard was careful to stipulate that the brigade was being lent and had to be returned "when called for here." Beauregard was always loath to release any troops that might weaken his defenses.[53]

In early October, the Confederate torpedo ram *David* crept out of the harbor on a dark night and rammed her spar torpedo into the side of the Federal man-of-war *New Ironsides*. The force of the explosion nearly swamped the *David*, which limped back into port minus half her crew, while the *Ironsides*, though damaged, did not have to leave her station outside the bar.[54]

The Confederate defenses were being strengthened daily, and additional contact mines were laid in the Stono River and Wappoo Cut, which made it almost impossible for a Federal gunboat to navigate the upper reaches of the river.[55] But the comparative quiet was rudely shattered early one morning by the thunder of guns coming from Morris Island.

5

On October 26, 1863, battle was resumed and the harbor and the vicinity reverberated with the deafening thunder of cannon. This lasted unremittingly for 41 days and nights. The second great bombardment of Fort Sumter had begun. Major General Gillmore—promoted from Brigadier for having conquered Morris Island—wrote to General Halleck in Washington that his reason for the bombardment was the fact that the Confederates were erecting guns on the northeast face of the fort. The heavy guns mounted on Wagner (renamed Fort Strong), Gregg (renamed Fort Putnam), and the center battery on Morris Island blasted away on the already ruined fort. In addition, the monitors *Patapsco* and *Lehigh* concentrated their fire on the sea face of the fort, which still bore some semblance of its original shape.[56]

The day before the bombardment, General Gillmore asked Admiral Dahlgren to assist him in subduing the fort. The admiral, as usual, said that he would be glad to help in every possible way, but he wrote in his diary: "Rather singular, when the General was so much exercised because I asked him to do that very thing in order to enable me to go in. What does this change mean?" By this time relations between the two had become very strained.[57]

General Beauregard wrote to Brig. Gen. Wilmot G. DeSaussure, in speaking of Sumter, that ". . . the eye of the whole country is now fixed . . . upon it." A little later he said: "The ruins of the fort will be defended to the last extremity." [58] Sumter was in for it, but there would be no capitulation. The firing continued inexorably, and this time the guns kept on throughout the night. Between the crossfire of the monitors and the big guns on Morris Island, the top row of arches on the sea face of Sumter was cut down, as was the gorge wall. Much of the rubble fell outward, making it possible for assault troops to secure a foothold and enter the fort. Major Elliott, fearing a repetition of the naval amphibious assault of September 8–9, asked that guard boats be stationed between Sumter and Cummings Point to signal the approach of assaulting barges. [59]

During the night of October 31, 13 members of the Washington Light Infantry, composed of Charleston men, who were posted in one of the barracks that was still standing by the sea face of the fort in readiness to climb to the top to repel a boat attack, were crushed to death when a heavy shell broke a girder and caused the roof to fall in. In spite of the efforts of their companions to dig them out, all of them died. This loss of so many Charleston natives cast a pall over the entire city. [60]

General Gillmore, again writing to General Halleck, spoke of Sumter as a ruin able to reply only with musketry fire and said that he would probably make an assault. [61] The incessant firing of the heavy guns continued, aided by that of the monitors, and the remnants of the wall continued to crumble with the explosion of the shells, hurling brick, mortar, sand, timber, and splinters high into the air. An officer standing on Wagner (Fort Strong) wrote that the sight was sublime. His thoughts were undoubtedly not shared by those crouching in the bombproofs of Sumter. All during the bombardment, guns from the Confederate batteries on Sullivan's and James islands kept up a fire on the Morris Island batteries as well as on the monitors. However, the latter remained at extreme range and, when they were hit, the "shots glanced from them as pebbles from an alligator's back," doing no appreciable damage. The flagstaff on the fort was shot away so frequently that at one time the battle flag of a Georgia Battalion stationed in the fort was used in place of the garrison flag until the regular staff could be repaired. On some days of the bombardment as many as 1,000 shells were hurled at the beleaguered fort, and on one day the huge 300-pounder on Morris Island fired 15,000 pounds of metal into Sumter.[62]

In the midst of all this, on November 2, Jefferson Davis visited Charleston. He was met at the depot by General Beauregard and a group of citizens. With honors befitting his position, he was escorted to City Hall, where he delivered an eloquent and patriotic address. He spoke on almost every topic of the war, but he made no mention of the siege of Charleston nor of the officers and men who had distinguished themselves in its defense, except Maj. Stephen Elliott.[63] When he had finished speaking, former governor Aiken, with whom he was staying, invited the ranking officers present and the leading citizens to dine with the president. General Beauregard refused. Later the president made a tour of inspection of James and Sullivan's islands accompanied by General Beauregard, but by this time they were hardly on speaking terms. The Union troops were puzzled by the cessation of fire from the Confederate batteries on James Island until they learned that the president was on his tour of inspection. During his entire stay in Charleston Davis was never out of earshot of the incessant roar of the guns.[64]

In a conference with Admiral Dahlgren, General Gillmore told him that his guns were wearing out; they were bursting with annoying regularity.[65] Nonetheless, the furious firing continued. The admiral wrote in his diary that "the only original feature left [of Sumter] is the northeast face; the rest is a pile of rubbish." In contrast to the first great bombardment, which was carried out at a longer range, the second consisted predominantly of mortar fire. It was not only deadly accurate, but devastating; the fuses were cut short so that the shells would explode a second or two after impact.[66]

At this time the only offensive weapons on Sumter were four Whitworth rifles equipped with telescopic sights; these were used effectively by the sharpshooters on the gunners at Cummings Point, a distance of over 1,300 yards. The Union troops congregated on the sand hills and the beach of Morris Island to witness the effect of their shells on Sumter, but the audience was promptly scattered by the Confederate sharpshooters.[67]

Expecting an amphibious assault on Sumter any moment, the chief of staff requested Captain Tucker, C.S.N., to have one of his ironclads anchored so that it could sweep the area between Sumter and Cummings Point in case of such an assault. For this eventuality 200 men in rowboats were ordered held in readiness at Fort Johnson and an equal number on Sullivan's Island to go to the aid of the garrison. A special order was issued that at no time would the garrison consist of over 300 men.[68]

General Gillmore wrote to his mentor General Halleck: "Of the practicability of carrying the place by assault, I entertained but little doubt, but I have never seen any necessity for doing so, while its sole power of doing harm consists in the protection which its infantry garrison affords the channel obstructions." This seems a strange statement in view of the fact that Fort Sumter had been Gillmore's objective ever since he assumed command of the South, and, if it were captured, the people of the North would have been elated. General Halleck did not bother to reply.[69]

On the night of November 11, heavy musket fire was heard coming from Cummings Point. Apparently one detachment mistook another for a Confederate amphibious assaulting force and each fired into the other.[70] Northern sources are singularly quiet about the incident. The next night a calcium light was erected on Cummings Point. The Confederates thought the light was put up for the sole purpose of "illuminating our works and preventing the location of obstructions upon the slopes." Actually it served a dual purpose; it would equally well have illuminated a Confederate assaulting force.[71]

At daylight on the morning of November 16, the Confederates saw the monitor *Lehigh* aground about a mile away and immediately opened fire on her. Admiral Dahlgren ordered three monitors to her aid. Transferring in his barge to the monitor *Nahant*, he pushed in close to the stranded *Lehigh*, and had a hawser passed to her. This was immediately shot away. Another was passed, and that one, too, was severed. Finally, a third was gotten to her. She backed her engines and the *Nahant* pulled. At high tide the *Lehigh* was floated after being under heavy fire for four hours. The supporting monitors succeeded in getting off 50 shots, concentrating their fire at Fort Moultrie; they dismounted one of the guns and killed one and wounded three of the garrison. One of the 15-inch shells entered a large traverse on the east salient of the fort and created a nine-by-four-foot crater. As usual, the Morris Island batteries fired on Sumter during the day, getting off 406 rounds.[72]

Taking General Beauregard's orders literally, that "the fort be defended to the last extremity," Major Elliott constructed a new system of interior defense. If the Union forces effected a landing, the fort was to be fought foot by foot; holes for infantry fire had been placed in every area that had a view of the interior, and every night a 12-pound howitzer loaded with grape and canister was put in one of the arches, from which it could sweep the parade ground. For the final effort, the batteries on Sullivan's and James islands were aimed at the parade ground.

On the night of November 30, the moon was down and the weather was favorable. Major Elliott broke out the whole garrison under arms. At 3 A.M. a detachment of Union barges approached the fort; because of the darkness Elliott was unable to determine their number. Approaching within 300 yards of the fort, they opened fire with musketry, and in spite of Major Elliott's instructions, the recently awakened troops returned a random fire. Meanwhile the batteries on Sullivan's Island opened up with their guns, as did those at Fort Johnson and the gunboat off Fort Johnson. Realizing that they were no match for the fire power of the defenders, the barges withdrew. In his report, Major Elliott said that the fire from Sullivan's Island "was very handsome. The fire from Fort Johnson was very bad, the balls passing directly over the fort." General Gillmore said of the attack: "I ordered a reconnaissance of the place last night, of the nature of a simulated attack, with a view to compel the garrison to show its

UNION BATTERIES ON BLACK ISLAND, FOUR AND A HALF MILES FROM
CHARLESTON.

BOMBARDMENT OF THE CITY OF CHARLESTON.

FORT SUMTER AFTER SECOND GREAT BOMBARDMENT, DECEMBER, 1863 (from a drawing by Lieutenant John R. Key).

GUNS ON WHITE POINT GARDENS (courtesy the National Archives).

SUBMARINE *HUNLEY* (oil by C. W. Chapman, courtesy The Museum of the Confederacy).

THE TORPEDO-RAM *DAVID* (oil by C. W. Chapman, courtesy The Museum of the Confederacy).

FLAG OVER FORT SUMTER (oil by C. W. Chapman, courtesy The Museum of the Confederacy).

INTERIOR OF FORT SUMTER AFTER THIRD GREAT BOMBARDMENT
(oil by C. W. Chapman, courtesy The Museum of the Confederacy).

PART OF THE CITY BURNED IN THE FIRE OF DECEMBER, 1861
(courtesy the National Archives).

NORTHEASTERN RAILROAD STATION AFTER THE EXPLOSION (courtesy
the National Archives).

strength." But General Gillmore had sent 250 troops to make the "simulated attack," an unusually large number.[73]

All during the second great bombardment the flagstaff had been shot away with monotonous regularity and the flag always replaced. One gunner on Morris Island, a member of the Third

FORT SUMTER: REPLACING THE FLAG ON THE GORGE-WALL

Rhode Island Heavy Artillery, became so adept that he could shoot down the flagstaff almost at will.[74] A striking incident occurred on the morning of November 27. Seeing that the flag had been shot down, Pvt. James Tupper, Jr., of the 27th South Carolina Volunteers coolly walked out on what was left of the parapet and tried to raise it. Finding the staff too short, he proceeded to splice it, aided by some men of the same command. While they were doing this, a shot cut the flag out of their hands. It took them about 15 minutes to erect a new staff and raise the flag, all of the time under intense fire. At times the smoke from bursting shells completely hid them from view. When the job was completed, two of the group politely tipped their caps to the gunners on Morris Island.[75]

At the end of November, General Gillmore reported to General Halleck: "I fire but slowly at Sumter, and that simply to prevent work being done inside while the Navy are getting ready." On the same day, General Halleck replied to General Gillmore's request to come to Washington: "your absence from there would furnish an excuse to the Navy for doing nothing." [76] On December 2, Admiral Dahlgren wrote in his diary: "It is admitted now that the Rebels are snug in the ruins. Shot and shell will not drive them out." Actually, in spite of the fury of the bombardment, the Confederate forces had managed to mount a three-gun battery on the northeast face of the fort, overlooking and dominating the approaches to the inner harbor. These guns, along with those on Sullivan's Island, would have made it even more difficult for Admiral Dahlgren's fleet to have passed through the Confederate guns without sustaining heavy losses.

Brig. Gen. J. W. Turner, chief of artillery on Morris Island, said: "The precision of fire of the Parrott rifles was remarkable, probably excelling any artillery ever before brought on to the field in siege operations." The firing by the Confederate gunners was equally as accurate; in a 24-hour period, out of 235 shells fired at Wagner (Fort Strong), 185 burst inside the fort, wounding 16 men. The distance was about two miles and the shells were dropped in an area of approximately one acre.[77]

There was a marked decrease in the number of shots fired at the fort in the early part of December. Finally, on December 6, the fury of the bombardment ceased and sudden quiet prevailed after 41 days and nights. During this time eight of General Gillmore's heavy guns had burst.

Confederate casualties amounted to exactly 100, which seems remarkably light in view of the intensity of the firing—18,677 shells. The second great bombardment of Fort Sumter had ended, leaving the fort looking more like a "volcanic pile" than a fortification.[78] A week later Sumter was racked by an internal explosion so severe that it nearly caused its evacuation.

6

Whiskey has been the downfall of many a man. Whiskey has lost battles. But it is doubtful if whiskey has ever been responsible for the loss of a fort. Fort Sumter was holding out against the incredible odds of the combined might of the Union army and navy. The garrison deep down in the rubble dug tunnels within the ruin. These tunnels were not only for the purpose of fast communication between different parts of the fort, but also served as living quarters and storage space.

On the morning of December 11, 1863, an explosion took place deep within the fort, killing 11 men and burning or wounding 41 others.[79] For a time no one knew exactly what had happened. Men emerged from the tunnels and fought to get away from the flames and smoke. The official records state that the fort "caught fire from accidental explosion of small-arms ammunition depot." The unofficial report is that fumes ignited from a candle held too close to an open barrel of whiskey and caused it to explode.[80] This in turn ignited the small-arms depot next to it. Because it occurred in a confined area, the intensity of the explosion was extreme. If the candle story is not correct, it is possible that the explosion was caused by a spark from the pipe of one of the men waiting in line to draw his rations; or possibly a spark fell on some loose powder leading to the storage depot. The actual cause of the accident will never be known; those who could have told were all killed. Capt. Edward D. Frost, assistant quartermaster, was one of the dead.

The fire became a raging inferno, and since it was underground, there was no way to combat it. A boat from one of the nearby gunboats was sent over with water buckets, and a fire engine was ordered to be sent from the city, but all these efforts were futile. The fire burned steadily, and walls and arches crumbled under the intense heat. The men living in the lower casemates had to evacuate the area, and those in the upper ones were completely cut off. The only way they were saved was by dropping ladders on the outside of the walls and climbing out. Strenuous efforts were made to barricade the passageways to contain the fire, but the barricades soon crumbled under the heat. Nothing could be done to arrest the fire, and it was left to burn itself out.

For a time neither the Union forces stationed on Morris Island nor the forts and batteries on Sullivan's realized that anything was wrong. Because the fire was underground, only a comparatively small amount of smoke was seen. But when the Union forces did realize that something of a serious nature had occurred, they opened up on the burning fort with every available gun and mortar. During the next few hours, over 200 shells were fired at Sumter. In order to try to slow down the Union fire, the mortars on Sullivan's Island opened up on Battery Gregg (Putnam). Colonel Elliott was wounded slightly by one of the Federal shells.[81]

As soon as some semblance of order had been restored, to show that the fighting spirit of the garrison was still intact, although many at that time were unarmed, Colonel Elliott brought his band out on the parapet and had them play "Dixie." When the strains of the music carried to Morris Island, the Union soldiers ceased firing and cheered the garrison.[82] It is possible that this act on Colonel Elliott's part convinced the troops on Morris Island that nothing too serious had occurred within the fort.

The heat of the fire was so great that it was ten days before the brick and rubble had cooled sufficiently for the men to enter the area and search for the charred bodies.[83]

The troops had lost most of their equipment and were defenseless; that night 200 muskets were sent down from the city with thirty days' rations.[84] Capt. John Johnson, the engineer in charge, made a tour of inspection and reported that the condition of the fort had reached a crisis. Had the Union guns on Morris Island and the big 15-inch ones of the monitors kept up a sustained fire for several days, the garrison might have been forced to evacuate the fort.[85]

By December, General Gillmore had increased the number of troops on Morris and Folly islands to more than 27,000 men. They were well armed, volunteers, and excellent fighters. In the middle of the month he wrote General-in-Chief Halleck that he had a "new program" to operate against Charleston either by way of Bull's Bay or by way of James Island. In spite of having such a heavy concentration of troops on the nearby islands, he requested that an additional 10,000 or 12,000 good infantry be sent to him.[86] He wanted to be sure of success and not have a repetition of Secessionville and suffer the fate of General Benham. But he did not get his troops; they were needed in other theaters of war.

With Fort Sumter under bombardment, the city under the fire of long-range guns, and 27,000 troops standing by, Beauregard had plenty with which to occupy himself. But, in addition, he was having trouble with Ripley, who was highly critical of his operation on Morris Island, especially the failure to repulse the amphibious assault on the lower end. Instead of going through regular channels, Ripley apparently had written directly to the secretary of war. Beauregard wrote Ripley concerning this: "I am informed, to my utter surprise, that the honorable Secretary of War is of the following opinion relative to the attack of the enemy on Morris Island on the 10th Ultimo." [87] Several letters were exchanged between the two; Beauregard asked specific questions of Ripley, who gave evasive replies. From then on a feeling of animosity developed between the two, and Ripley's usefulness gradually declined. Actually, two months before the amphibious assault, Beauregard had warned Ripley to "give special attention to the east [lower] end of Morris Island to prevent the crossing of the enemy. . . . otherwise Fort Sumter might run great danger from batteries of long-ranged, heavily rifled guns, placed on the northern extremity of Morris Island." Ripley was in command of the district that included Morris Island.[88]

To add to Beauregard's trouble, the brigade of Brig. Gen.

N. G. (Shanks) Evans had deteriorated, due to poor leadership, to such an extent that it was no longer useful as a combat unit. Evans was arrested, subsequently court-martialed, but acquitted. After his acquittal, he went to Cokesbury, South Carolina, where he remained under arrest for nearly three months. When he did not hear from Beauregard, he wrote directly to Adjutant General Cooper in Richmond, asking to be restored to the command of his brigade. Evans' letter to Cooper reached the desk of President Davis, who suggested that Evans appear before an examining board and that "he be immediately released from arrest." An inquiry into the condition of his brigade was instituted by Beauregard through his assistant inspector general; the resulting recommendation was that "Evans be at once relieved from his command and assigned to other duties." [89]

The year 1863 ended in comparative calm. Beauregard not only lost the usefulness of two of his generals, but the Federal army and navy were ready to resume operations at a moment's notice.

6

The Blockade:
Torpedoes and the Submarine

1

IT IS NOT CLEAR WHO WAS THE ACTUAL INVENTOR OF THE TOR-
pedo ram, with its spar torpedo attached to its bow; there were
several who claimed to be. The preponderance of the evidence
would make it appear that Capt. Francis D. Lee, Corps of Engineers, C.S.A., if not the actual inventor, was certainly one of the
early advocates of its use by the Confederate government. Actually, the spar torpedo was invented in 1801 by Robert Fulton, but
it was not used successfully until the Civil War. The torpedo
ram, as originally designed, was a low, fast, heavily armored
steamer, with no guns, but with a spar torpedo attached to its
bow. The torpedo contained a heavy charge of powder which
exploded when rammed into the side of, and below the water line
of, an enemy craft.[1]

As early as October 8, 1862, General Beauregard wrote Governor Pickens of South Carolina about the possibilities of a torpedo ram designed by Captain Lee; in his opinion, he said, it would be worth several gunboats. At this time, the gunboats *Palmetto State* and *Chicora* were being built in Charleston. General Beauregard was so favorably impressed with the torpedo ram that he immediately dispatched Captain Lee to Richmond to confer with William Porcher Miles, congressman from South Carolina, who introduced Captain Lee to Secretary of the Navy Mallory. Upon his return, Captain Lee wrote Brigadier General Jordan, Chief of Staff, that Mr. Mallory had "expressed deep interest in the undertaking and his entire willingness to furnish everything in his power to make its accomplishment as early as possible." Shortly afterward, General Beauregard wrote to Mr. Mallory: "I thank you for your prompt and favorable support you have given me in the desire to construct one of Capt. F. D. Lee's marine torpedo rams, which I think is destined ere long to change the system of naval warfare." [2]

The South Carolina Executive Council, acting with great promptness, authorized the sum of $50,000 for the "construction of a 'ram and submarine torpedo' recommended by F. D. Lee, Captain of Engineers, and approved by General Beauregard." Work on the torpedo ram began the following month in Charleston under the supervision of Captain Lee. The hull was built by F. M. Jones, ship carpenter, and the machinery was installed by Cameron & Company. The boiler and the engine were taken out of the steamer *Barton*, which was lying in Savannah. As it later developed, they were almost worn out at the time they were installed in the torpedo ram. General Beauregard was still enthusiastic on November 8, 1862, when he wrote Governor Pickens: "Moreover one of these rams can be furnished in at least half the time required for an ordinary sized gunboat ram." [3]

On February 17, 1863, while the torpedo ram was being built, Captain Lee sent a request to Brigadier General Jordan that he be allowed to experiment "with spar torpedoes with this view of using them on small boats against the Iron-clads." By this time the Federal blockading fleet, which formerly had consisted of wooden vessels, was being supplemented with ironclad monitors, and the blockade was becoming more and more effective. Captain Lee was authorized to proceed with his experiments. He found that a light-built canoe (probably a dugout) about 20 feet long, with a spar torpedo submerged six feet below the surface on a pole 22 feet long, had devastating effects when exploded against the side of an old hull. More important still, the explosion did not swamp the canoe or injure its occupants. General Beauregard was so impressed that he recommended to Commodore Duncan Ingraham, C.S.N., that "at least one dozen should be fitted up at once with Captain Lee's spar-torpedo." [4]

On the night of March 18, 1863, Lt. William T. Glassell, C.S.N., with a rowboat and a crew of seven, went out to attack the blockading fleet. With only one spar torpedo, they had to try to ram it into the first vessel they encountered. Lieutenant Glassell acted as coxswain, with one man forward to lower the spar torpedo when they approached a ship and six men rowing. The attack was a failure. In his official report, Lieutenant Glassell stated that the rowboat ran aground on Drunken Dick Shoals, was nearly swamped, and had to return. It was not until many years later that he told the true story of what took place: He and his crew started out about 1 A.M. with the low tide, looking for a vessel to attack. The crew had been carefully instructed that, regardless of the circumstances, they were to continue rowing until they rammed their torpedo home. That night everything favored their success; the moon had set and the sea was calm. Their intended victim turned out to be the steamer *Powhatan*, one of the blockading vessels. Approaching steadily, they were discovered 200 or 300 yards away and hailed by the watch to halt and be recognized. Lieutenant Glassell kept giving evasive answers and told the watch that he was coming on board; at the same time, he was urging his men to row as hard as possible. They were within 40 feet of the *Powhatan*, aiming at a spot directly under the gangway, when one of the rowers started backing water and stopped the boat's headway. This caused the others to cease rowing. As they drifted by the stern of the *Powha-*

tan, they were interrogated by the officer of the deck, who wanted to know who they were and what they were doing. No mention of the incident is noted in the ship's log. In the meantime, the rowboat drifted off into the night. The oarsman who had backed water had thrown his revolver overboard and was trying to get hold of that of the man next to him and do the same thing with it. Lieutenant Glassell goes on to say that the man went into a state of panic and afterward was ashamed of himself. Shortly afterward he deserted by swimming to one of the Union vessels lying at the mouth of the Edisto River.[5]

Captain Lee, greatly disturbed by the fact that the mission had been unsuccessful, wrote to the chief of staff: "As the inventor of the mode of attack, and consequently responsible in a greater degree than any other party for its successful operation, I would most respectfully protest against so unfair a test as the sending of a single boat unsupported against the fleet." It would appear foolhardy to send eight men against a fleet, but, if the attack had been successful, it might have had far-reaching results.[6]

Captain Lee was not only having difficulties in getting iron plating for the armor of his torpedo ram, he could not get adequate machinery to go into it. The Confederate government, hard pressed for guns and other war material, would not divert the necessary iron for the armor. General Beauregard became so exasperated by the delay that he suggested that some of the torpedo rams be built in Europe. The local authorities, at General Beauregard's insistence, had spar torpedoes installed not only on the gunboats but on "every available steamer and small boat in the harbor." [7]

Realizing that the construction of the torpedo rams would be greatly delayed because of the lack of armor plating and wishing to do everything in his power to raise the blockade, General Beauregard proposed a plan to Captain Tucker, C.S.N. He suggested towing out several rowboat torpedo rams and letting them attack the blockading vessels, which now included several of the new monitors recently added to the fleet. Captain Tucker instructed Lieutenant Dozier to prepare the crews of the rowboat torpedo rams and gave the following instructions for boarding: "The parties to be divided into tens or twenties each under a leader. One of these parties to be prepared with iron wedges to wedge between the turret and the deck [thus preventing the turret from turning]; a second party to cover the pilot-house with wet blankets; a third to throw powder down the smokestack or to cover it; another provided with turpentine or camphene in glass vessels, to smash over the turret, with an inextinguishable liquid to follow it; and still another to watch every opening in the turret or deck, provided with sulphuretted cartridges, etc., to smoke the enemy out." Light ladders were to be carried to reach the tops of the turrets.[8]

The attack was to have been made on the night of April 12, 1863. About 15 of the rowboats were assembled behind Cummings Point at the mouth of Charleston harbor. The plan was to row quietly off the front beach of Morris Island until almost opposite the blockading fleet and then to dash out and make the surprise attack. Two boats were to concentrate on each vessel, and each commander was instructed not to return until his torpedo had been exploded.[9] However, this plan was frustrated by the sudden withdrawal of most of the monitors either for overhaul or to take on supplies. It was less than a week after the repulse of the ironclads by Sumter and Moultrie, and most of them had taken a heavy beating. When this news was obtained, at the last minute, the attack was called off. A rowboat attack was never again attempted against the blockading fleet. One was planned against some vessels lying at the mouth of the Edisto River, but it was discovered that a deserter had given the vessels warning of the attack, so that, too, was called off. The warning was given by the same man who had accompanied Lieutenant Glassell on his unsuccessful attack on the *Powhatan*.[10]

In the meantime, Captain Lee was still having trouble securing armor for his torpedo ram. The shortage had become so critical that Brigadier General Jordan wrote on May 6, 1863, to Major L. Heylinger in Nassau, B.W.I., who was procuring supplies for the Confederacy, asking that 300 tons of "iron mailing plate" now in Nassau be brought in by the blockade-runners and that he make a formal demand on each captain of the blockade-runners to bring in an amount predicated on the size of the vessel, not exceeding 25 tons. If a captain refused, he would be told that everything possible would be done to keep him from getting a return cargo of cotton and naval stores. The Confederacy was willing to pay a freight charge not exceeding 30 pounds per ton and to pay 60 pounds per ton for the armor.[11]

Captain Lee's torpedo ram was so thoroughly believed in by the people of Charleston that on June 6, 1863, John Fraser and Company, the largest exporting firm, wrote to Lee: "The undersigned, in connection with other merchants in the city, propose the construction of a marine torpedo steamer abroad, and desire your service for carrying the work into effect. Arrangements have been made for placing the necessary funds at your disposal in Europe." [12] Going through proper channels, General Beauregard wrote Colonel Gilmer, Corps of Engineers, asking that Captain Lee be sent to Europe. The request was approved, but apparently he did not go, for nothing more is heard of the project. International complications may have caused its abandonment.

On July 11, 1863, the same day the first assault was made on Battery Wagner, Captain Lee wrote General Beauregard: "I am making preparations to launch the torpedo-boat at 3 o'clock." The boat was launched, but with no armor, for no "iron mailing plate" had been brought in from Nassau. Two weeks later a survey was made "to ascertain if she was fitted to the service for which she was proposed." Apparently she was, for the command was given to James Carlin, captain of the blockade-runner *Ella and Annie*. Lee's torpedo ram at this time was under the jurisdiction of the army rather than the navy, probably because it was General Beauregard's pet project.[13]

In the hope of stimulating interest, although General Beauregard and Captain Lee were already working hard at this, Theodore D. Wagner of John Fraser and Company, along with his copartner, offered a reward of $100,000 for the sinking of the *New Ironsides* or the *Wabash* and $50,000 for a monitor. The gunfire from the *New Ironsides* had been devastating at Battery Wagner.[14]

Admiral Dahlgren of the blockading fleet must have had a good source of intelligence; on August 5 he told his fleet that "it is rumored that the enemy have a ram near Fort Johnson." His report was accurate; on the night of August 20–21, Captain Carlin with Lee's unarmored ram, which had acquired the name *Torch*,[15] slipped quietly out of the harbor with the *New Ironsides* as his intended victim. Passing Fort Sumter, he obtained a guard of 11 soldiers under the command of Lt. E. S. Fickling. Continuing down the main ship channel, he passed all of the booms and at about midnight sighted the *New Ironsides* lying at anchor in the channel off Morris Island, with five monitors moored about 300 yards away. Within a quarter mile of her, Captain Carlin lowered his torpedo and proceeded directly for the ship; he was fully confident of ramming his spar torpedo into her side with devastating effect.[16] When about 50 yards away, he received a hail demanding his identification. He replied, "The steamer, *Live Yankee*." At this particular moment the *New Ironsides* was lying across the channel. When he was within 40 yards, Captain Carlin ordered the engines stopped and the helm put hard to starboard. The quartermaster misunderstood his order and, though he repeated it three times, Carlin realized that he would be unable to strike the *New Ironsides* with his spar torpedo, for she was swinging with the ebb tide. Afraid that he would foul her anchor chain, Carlin ordered the engine stopped. He was drifting by the bow of the *New Ironsides* when he gave orders to go ahead. About this time he was hailed again, and this time he said he was from Port Royal. In the confusion, Captain Carlin received a report that he was being boarded. What happened was that he had come so close to the *New Ironsides* that his guard could see the sailors looking out of the portholes. Wondering why his order had not been carried out, Captain Carlin went to the engine room and found that the engine had stopped on "dead center." For several minutes they drifted helplessly. Finally the engines were started, and they lumbered away into the darkness.

Immediately the *New Ironsides* started shooting in the opposite direction, afterward sweeping the horizon with shots, two of which missed the *Torch* by about 20 feet. Captain Carlin's intention was to attack one of the nearby monitors, but, having had such disastrous results with his engine, in addition to the fact that his ship was leaking badly, he decided to return to port.[17]

Considering the circumstances, the report of Captain Rowan of the *New Ironsides* is rather amusing. He states: "A very low and apparently swift steamer came up under the stern of the ship, gave her name as the *Live Yankee* and made her escape." Inasmuch as the *Torch* was drifting helplessly with her engine in dead center, it is ironical that she is spoken of as a "swift steamer." Upon his return from the abortive attack, Captain Carlin strongly condemned the use of the *Torch:* "I feel it my duty most unhesitantly to express my condemnation of the vessel and engine for the purpose it was intended, and as soon as she can be docked and the leak stopped would advise making a transport of her." [18]

General Beauregard and Captain Lee must have been disappointed at the failure of their pet scheme. Captain Carlin was prevailed upon to retain command of the *Torch*. Apparently her name was little used; she is generally spoken of as the "torpedo-ram." Shortly afterward, General Beauregard wrote Flag Officer J. R. Tucker, C.S.N.: "It is my wish to turn over to you the torpedo ram steamer . . . until it may be found convenient and judicious to mail armor and arrange her as originally designed." From this point on she figures very little in the history of the defense of Charleston.[19]

On July 25, 1863, Captain Lee wrote to Captain A. N. T. Beauregard, aide to the general: "I would further state that the small torpedo steamer [Winan's model] now building in Cooper River, is nearly complete, and we have good reason to expect will aid materially in the defense of this city." Ross Winan of Baltimore—a Southern sympathizer—was an inventor of many things, notably steam locomotives. During the war his talents turned to ships and apparently he came up with the idea of a fast, cigar-shaped steamer. A model of it is now in the possession of the Maryland Historical Society.[20]

The small "torpedo steamer" referred to by Captain Lee was being sponsored by a group of Charleston businessmen who were quietly having it built at Stony Landing near the headwaters of the western branch of the Cooper River about 30 miles from Charleston. Theodore D. Stoney put up $25,000 towards the cost of construction, and the rest was paid by Theodore Wagner and some of his colleagues.[21] Dr. St. Julien Ravenel was its designer, and he actually used Winan's model as his prototype.[22]

The small steamer was 54 feet long and $5\frac{6}{10}$ feet wide.[23] Security and censorship being almost nonexistent, it was decided to build this torpedo ram, later known as the *David*, at some distance from Charleston. It is not recorded when the work was first started. D. C. Ebaugh was head mechanic, Samuel Easterby the master carpenter, and John Chaulk was in charge of installing the machinery; the labor was done by Negro plantation hands. The work was supervised by Dr. Ravenel, who had received permission from General Beauregard to be away from his official duties at the hospital in Columbia, South Carolina.[24]

All machinery in the South was woefully deficient, if not totally lacking. An old engine belonging to the Northeastern Railroad was commandeered by Dr. Ravenel, with General Beauregard's blessing, and put in the *David*.[25]

Upon her completion, with the aid of all available plantation hands, she was warped on to flatcars and taken to Charleston, where she was launched at Atlantic Wharf at the east end of Broad Street. Much to the relief of those interested, she floated as designed—deeply submerged, with only her funnel and a few inches amidship showing. At the suggestion of his wife, Dr. Ravenel named her *David*. She is now generally spoken of as the "Little David." [26]

The *David* was placed under the command of Lt. W. T. Glassell, and James H. Tomb volunteered as assistant engineer. Captain Lee gave his "zealous aid" in fitting on a spar torpedo, as he had already had much experience in this type of work. The rest of the crew consisted of J. Walker Cannon, who served as pilot, and James Stuart, who volunteered as fireman. Stuart is always spoken of as "alias Sullivan." He may have been a Northerner with Southern sympathies.[27]

On her trial trips it was found that the *David* responded satisfactorily; she was able to attain a speed between six and seven knots. Heavily ballasted to keep her low in the water and camouflaged a bluish color, she crept out of the harbor on the night of October 5, 1863, headed for the *New Ironsides*. Passing Fort Sumter undetected, she slipped down the main channel at the last of the ebb tide. Fortunately the sea was smooth. Steaming along the inside of the bar and waiting for the turn of the tide, Lieutenant Glassell had ample opportunity to reconnoiter the whole fleet at anchor between him and the camp fires of the Union troops on Morris Island. Having been informed from some recently captured prisoners that the fleet was expecting an attack from a torpedo boat, Lieutenant Glassell expected a hot reception if he was perceived. He was not disappointed.

Glassell thought that if he could disable the officer of the deck, it would cause some confusion and delay, which would give him a greater chance of escape. Each member of his crew carried a revolver and a shotgun loaded with buckshot.[28] Steering with his feet in order to have his hands free, he directed his engineer and fireman to go below and give him flank speed. As anticipated, about 300 yards away from the *New Ironsides* Glassell received the hail: "Boat ahoy! Boat ahoy!" The officer of the deck made his appearance and loudly demanded, "What boat is that?" Receiving no reply, the sailors opened up on her with small-arms fire. By this time the *David* was about 40 yards away and had plenty of headway; Lieutenant Glassell let go with both barrels of his shotgun, mortally wounding the officer. He then ordered the engine stopped and immediately rammed his torpedo into the side of the *New Ironsides*. The force of the explosion rocked the *David*, and some of the ballast jammed the machinery, rendering her completely helpless. In addition, the tremendous volume of water, estimated by Engineer Tomb to have reached a height of 100 feet, went down the stack, putting out the fires in the boiler.[29] Glassell immediately gave orders to back off, though he was unaware that the fires were out, the machinery was jammed, and the little ship was helpless. A general alarm had been sounded aboard the *New Ironsides*, and Glassell responded by giving orders to abandon ship; he ordered Tomb to scuttle the *David*.[30]

Lieutenant Glassell, believing that everyone had abandoned ship, took a cork float and leaped overboard. Tomb and Sullivan also took to the water, but the pilot, J. Walker Cannon, who could not swim, remained on board. Seeing that the *David* was drifting clear, Tomb swam back to her and was helped aboard by Cannon. These two men managed to unjam the machinery, raise steam, and bring the *David* safely into Charleston. Glassell thought that flood tide would bring him near Fort Sumter, but the wind held him out; numbed by the cold, he called out and was picked up by a boat from a coal schooner. Sullivan saved himself by hanging on to the rudder chain of the *New Ironsides*.[31]

When the explosion was heard, the Union troops on Morris Island were alerted; they stood in line until midnight before they were allowed to return to camp.[32]

Admiral Dahlgren was not happy that one of his officers had been killed by a load of buckshot. He ordered Lieutenant Glassell placed in irons on board the *Ottawa;* if he offered any resistance, he was to be double ironed. Glassell, a former officer in the United States Navy, found an old friend in the captain of the *Ottawa*, Capt. W. D. Whiting, who released him when he promised that he would not attempt to escape from the ship.[33]

Sullivan was also put in irons, kept in a dark cell, and, along with Lieutenant Glassell, taken to New York, where, as reported by some Northern papers, they were to be tried for using an engine of war not recognized by civilized nations. However, inasmuch as the Federal government now had a torpedo corps, Glassell and Sullivan were never brought to trial; instead they were confined in prison at Fort Lafayette and Fort Warren. After being kept there for several months, they were exchanged for the captain and a sailor from the steamer *Isaac Smith*, which had been captured in the Stono River in January, 1863.[34]

Lieutenant Glassell was promoted to commander, and Tomb became a lieutenant. After the attack, everyone in Charleston was elated because they thought the *New Ironsides* had been badly damaged. While she was greatly shaken by the explosion, she was not incapacitated. However, six weeks later, Captain Rowan of the *New Ironsides* told Admiral Dahlgren that when the coal was removed from the bunker, it was discovered that the injury from the torpedo was very serious.[35] While the *David* is generally known for her attack on the *New Ironsides*, she also made attacks on some of the other vessels in the blockading squadron, but bad luck always seemed to prevent her carrying out her designs.

By January 15, 1864, James H. Tomb was in command of the *David*. The next month General Beauregard asked Flag Officer Tucker if the *David* could be used in the Stono River; he wanted to destroy the Federal gunboats *Pawnee* and *Marblehead*, which were ranging up and down the river making things uncomfortable for the shore batteries. Because there was no suitable pilot familiar with the mudbanks in the river as well as the torpedoes that had been planted in it by the Confederates, it was decided not to risk the *David* in these treacherous waters.[36]

The *David*, meanwhile, was being covered with quarter-inch steel above the water line in order to deflect small-arms fire, and a new spar attachment was placed on her to permit the spar to be lowered to any depth and to be controlled from the pilot house. In addition, a shield was put over her stack to keep out the water in order to avoid a repetition of what had happened when she attacked the *New Ironsides*.

On the night of March 4, 1864, the *David* steamed slowly down the North Edisto River with the steamer *Memphis* as her intended victim. J. Walker Cannon was again her pilot. When she was near enough to see the Union ship's lights, the *David*'s pumps failed and she had to return to Church Flats. The next night, about the same time and the same place, the pumps again failed; but this time they were repaired, and the *David* proceeded on. The watch on the *Memphis* saw her when she was within "hailing distance," but, when she did not respond to his hail, the *Memphis* opened up on her with small arms, which struck her new armor, doing no damage. The *David* rammed her torpedo into the *Memphis* on her port quarter about eight feet below her water line; it was a perfect hit, but nothing happened. By this time the *Memphis* had slipped her cable and gotten under way. The *David* then made a sharp turn to port and again rammed her in her starboard quarter. Again nothing happened. While she was passing under the counter of the *Memphis*, a portion of the *David*'s stack was cut away. By this time the *Memphis* was gathering speed and made good her escape, firing with all her guns; she was not, however, able to depress them sufficiently to hit the *David*.[37]

When it returned to Church Flats, the torpedo was carefully examined. It was found that the glass tube containing the acid was broken, but it was defective and had failed to explode the 95 pounds of powder contained in the warhead. Had it done so, it would have blown a huge hole in the *Memphis*, probably causing her to sink at once.

When the *David* returned to Charleston, it was fitted with a new torpedo. A few weeks later she steamed out of the mouth of the harbor again. This time she was discovered by the watch of the frigate *Wabash* when she was about 150 yards away. Three times the *David* headed for her, but each time the heavy swells rolled over her, forcing her to return to port. In the meantime, Captain DeCamp of the *Wabash* maneuvered his ship so that the bow was always headed toward the *David*; this made her a very difficult target. Had Tomb and his crew been successful in sinking the *Wabash*, they would have been richer by $100,000, the reward offered by John Fraser and Company.[38]

On October 15, 1863, Captain Lee wrote to Captain Beauregard, the general's aide, that he was enclosing a hasty sketch of a "cigar steamer for carrying spar torpedoes."[39] On the same day General Beauregard endorsed the letter, saying that he would "like much to have one dozen, at least, of these boats." The following month, the general wrote Theodore D. Stoney, secretary and treasurer of the Southern Torpedo Company, who had asked him to give the company his "official sanction." General Beauregard said that he was delighted to give it his official blessing and ended his letter: "In conclusion, I will be most happy to afford the company all the facilities in my power to carry into effect their proposed plans and operations [to build *Davids*], and may fortune smile on their patriotic efforts." [40]

On December 20, 1863, Captain Lee wrote to Col. D. B. Harris that W. S. Henerey had patterns for double engines which were exactly suited for torpedo boats and that he had ordered 20 of them. He also said that the engines could be "readily transported by railroad to the points where the boats may be constructed." Apparently Lee had forgotten to go through official channels by first consulting Major Chambliss, commanding officer of the arsenal. When Major Chambliss heard what had happened, he objected vehemently to the idea of Henerey devoting all of his time to building engines, when, in his opinion, guns and shells were of greater importance. Major Chambliss used such strong language that General Beauregard instructed his chief of staff to offer him an opportunity to withdraw his statements. Major Chambliss replied that the engineering department (Lee) had entered a field exclusively under the control of the ordnance department (Chambliss), but that "no one can be more desirous of conforming to military subordination and courtesy than myself." By negotiating directly with Henerey, Captain Lee had offended Chambliss. On January 5, 1864, General Beauregard wrote that Captain Lee must have his engines made in some place other than Charleston.[41]

By January 26, 1864, Theodore D. Stoney wrote the chief of staff that the Southern Torpedo Company expected to have "two more steamers afloat tomorrow or next day." The following day Lt. Col. A. L. Rives wrote to Captain Lee: "Inclosed I send you orders placing you in charge of the construction of torpedo-boats." He also said that as soon as plans were received from him,

Lieutenant Colonel Sheliha would "commence the construction of torpedo-boats at Mobile." A private company and the Confederate government were both building torpedo boats.[42]

Admiral Dahlgren had such respect for the Confederate rams that on January 13, 1864, he wrote to the secretary of the navy in Washington, urging him to employ torpedo boats in Charleston. He even suggested "a large reward of prize money for the capture or destruction of a 'David.' I should say not less than $20,000 or $30,000 for each. They are worth more than that to us."

On May 1, 1864, General Beauregard instructed Brigadier General Wise to be on the lookout for "three army torpedo boats under the control of Mr. Theodore Stoney, leaving this city to-morrow by inland navigation for operation against the enemy fleet in the waters of Port Royal." Two of these boats had been built by the Southern Torpedo Company; the other was the *David*. The boats built by the Southern Torpedo Company were commanded by Capt. Augustus Duqucron and Capt. E. R. Mackay. Somewhere along the inland waterway they were forced to return because of engine trouble. The *David* proceeded alone, but finally she, too, apparently turned back.[43]

The two company-built boats were placed under the command of General Beauregard. The *David* was under navy command. Beauregard wrote General Whiting in Wilmington, North Carolina: "The navy has the real *David* in its possession, but it seems to have exhausted itself in its attack on the *Ironsides*. It now keeps company with the gun-boats." He seems to have been disgusted at the *David*'s apparent lack of aggressiveness.[44]

Meanwhile, the Confederate government was trying to build torpedo boats, but lack of suitable machinery greatly delayed their construction. On March 18, 1864, Flag Officer Tucker wrote from Charleston to Captain Hunter, C.S.N.: "The station is building two of these boats to be turned over to me when completed, but I fear that will be some time yet." Another was being built at the Confederate shipyard on the Pee Dee River in South Carolina. Some boats of this class were being built in Savannah, and the engines were probably being built in Augusta,[45] though there is apparently no record that any were completed. On April 16, 1864, Secretary of the Navy Mallory wrote to Commander Bullock, the Confederate representative in England, asking him to "have twelve small marine engines and boilers built for torpedo boats." If they were completed, as far as is known, none ever arrived in a blockade-runner.

Just how many boats were built and put into operation before the end of the war is not certain. Apparently there were quite a number, for on February 16, 1865, the day before Charleston was evacuated, President Jefferson Davis wired General Beauregard: "What's to be done with the torpedo-boats?" [46]

When Admiral Dahlgren arrived in Charleston after its evacuation, he wrote to Commodore George S. Black about "a torpedo boat, being one of nine found here, and of two that were raised by the squadron divers from the bed of the Cooper River, where they had been sunk just before we entered. It was such a boat as this that exploded a torpedo under the *New Ironsides*." [47]

Why the spar torpedo boat was not more effective is not clear. Certainly it was not for want of a crew. After the attack on the *New Ironsides*, General Gillmore gave Admiral Dahlgren some calcium lights, which he had placed on the *New Ironsides*. In addition, nets extending on booms surrounded her and two tugs circled her at night. These measures made it almost impossible for a torpedo boat to approach the fleet unseen and may have accounted for their mysterious inadequacy.

Some thirty years later, W. P. Poulnot, executive officer of the *Torch* at the time of her attack on the *New Ironsides*, gave a different version of the incident, which appeared in the local press. He said that as they were approaching the *New Ironsides*, Captain Carlin ordered him to lower his two torpedoes, each weighing 75 pounds. The spars to which they were attached were lowered into the water to a depth of 12 feet, and the guys were pulled tight. Poulnot said that they struck the *New Ironsides* squarely amidship on the port side; however, nothing happened except that the officer of the deck was alarmed. The officer inquired who they were and what they were doing, to which Captain Carlin replied, "The *Live Yankee* from Beaufort." After more interrogation, Carlin said that they were on their way to Wilmington, but had run out of coal. This gave Carlin and Poulnot the chance to hold the *Torch* off in order not to get entangled in the lines of the *New Ironsides* as they were drifting past. As soon as they got by her, she opened up with her guns. Poulnot goes on to say that they put rosin in the boiler, which caused a dense smoke and helped them escape. As they passed Fort Sumter on their way in, the *Torch* stopped to let off her "volunteer marine corps," who were sent back to their barracks "agreeing that they had a splendid trip and enjoyed the fun."

When they returned to Charleston and tied up at North Atlantic Wharf, the torpedoes were examined. Instead of 75 pounds of gunpowder, they were found to contain sand and sawdust. Further investigation revealed that the "maker of the torpedo," a Bostonian by the name of Ruck, had loaded them with sand and sawdust because he could not be guilty of such a crime as manufacturing a death-dealing instrument to kill his own people.

Poulnot speaks of the torpedo ram as the *Live Yankee*, but he adds that "some time afterwards she was called the *Torch*." He also says that Captain Carlin was an Englishman and that after the war he acquired a sugar plantation in Louisiana, probably from the profits he made successfully running the blockade.[48]

2

The story of the *Hunley* boat is one of enigma, tragedy, and courage: enigma, because it is not known how many times she sank during her trial trips, nor are the accurate dimensions of the small submarine known; tragedy, because so many men lost their lives as members of her crew; and courage, because crew after crew voluntarily stepped forward to take the place of the dead men as they were taken out of the submarine and finally to sink the Federal sloop-of-war the *Housatonic* on the night of February 17, 1864.

During the Revolutionary War, David Bushnell devised a

form of submarine which was tried unsuccessfully against the British Fleet lying at anchor in New York harbor. Robert Fulton, an advocate of the steamboat, built a successful submarine, which he tried, unsuccessfully, to sell to the French government. The concept of the submarine was not new, but operating one successfully against an enemy was.[49]

The prototype of the *Hunley* boat was built in New Orleans, but it was never put into operation because the city was captured by Federal forces in 1862. To prevent her falling into Union hands, she was scuttled. Years later she was raised, and today she can be seen in the Louisiana State Museum in New Orleans. Her designers and builders, along with the machinery used in her construction, were moved to Mobile, Alabama. There another submarine was constructed, but she sank on one of her trial trips in Mobile Bay. Apparently she was not recovered, and a third boat was built. This one was sent to Charleston on completion.

The small submarine could dive, stay under until the oxygen was exhausted, and maneuver while submerged. To make the boat run, a crank attached to the propeller was turned by eight men. The three-bladed propeller was covered with a metal band to keep ropes from fouling it. In calm water her best speed was about four miles an hour; when bucking a strong tide, she was almost helpless. Conrad Wise Chapman of Virginia, who was stationed in Charleston for part of the war, made a painting of the *Hunley* when she was on the wharf at Mt. Pleasant at the mouth of Charleston harbor. From this painting and a description of her given by W. A. Alexander, a former member of her crew, it has been estimated that she was between 35 and 40 feet in length. Her main hull was made out of a boiler. In order to increase her height, the boiler was cut lengthwise and a longitudinal strip 12 inches wide was added to it. A pointed bow and stern were attached to the boiler. Alexander, many years afterward, made a drawing from memory which shows the bow and stern to be fairly blunt. The painting, however, made from the original, shows them to be not so blunt, giving the boat a more streamlined appearance. She had two fins, which could be controlled from the inside. These enabled her to rise or dive. In order to submerge, ballast tanks were flooded; these were pumped out in order to surface. The tanks were the weak points in the construction of the boat. In addition, there were two pipes which could be raised when she was just under the surface to get air. The crew entered by two hatches about 14 feet apart. Alexander gives these dimensions as 12 inches by 16 inches, though in the painting by Chapman they appear circular, which would have made it possible for a slender man to get in and out with difficulty. Each hatch had a combing of 8 inches and a small glass window, from which one could see when running partially submerged. The eight men who turned the crank and a pilot made up the crew. It was so crowded inside that the men had to use both hatches to get in and out.

As originally designed, she was intended to tow a torpedo about 200 feet behind and dive under her victim; when the torpedo came in contact with the hull, it would explode. In theory this was fine, but because of her slow speed, if the tide was strong, it was almost impossible for her to outrun the torpedo she was towing. Consequently, a spar torpedo on a long pole was attached to her bow, and she was to ram it into a vessel. This, too, was a good idea, but apparently it did not work when she made her final attack on the sloop-of-war *Housatonic*.

General Beauregard, anxious to destroy some of the blockading vessels, asked that the submarine be sent to Charleston. In his usual impatient manner, he sent a wire on August 7, 1863, to all railroad agents between Charleston and Mobile to expedite the movement of the "Whitney Submarine boat," which was loaded on two flat cars.[50] B. A. Whitney, one of her co-owners, came with the boat from Mobile.[51] She must have arrived in Charleston by August 15, for on that date Brigadier General Jordan, chief of staff wrote to Whitney, "In Charge of Submarine Torpedo-boat, Charleston, S.C.," about the $100,000 reward offered by John Fraser & Co. for the sinking of the *New Ironsides* or the *Wabash*. Jordan went on to say: "Steps are being taken to secure a large

sum to be settled for the support of the families of parties, who
. . . shall fail in the enterprise, and fall or be captured in the
attempt." This was a lucrative and unusual offer.[52]

In spite of the secrecy, news must have leaked out; Admiral
Dahlgren of the blockading squadron wrote on August 11 to the
secretary of the navy requesting that a submarine be built. This
could not have been pure coincidence. Dahlgren had an excellent
source of information about what was going on in and around
Charleston the entire time he was stationed there.[53]

Apparently the military authorities were not satisfied with the
boat. On August 23, Brigadier General Clingman, whose headquarters were on Sullivan's Island, wrote to Captain Nance, assistant adjutant general: "The torpedo-boat has not gone out. I do
not think it will render any service under its present management." On the same day he wrote Captain Nance again: "The
Torpedo-boat started out at sunset, but returned, as they state,
because of an accident. Whitney says that though McClintock is
timid, yet it shall go tonight unless the weather is bad." [54]
McClintock was one of her designers and probably came from
Mobile shortly after the arrival of the submarine and Whitney.
Things must have gotten worse, for Theodore A. Honour wrote
from Legare Point, James Island, on August 30, 1863: "You
doubtless remember and perhaps you saw while in the City the
iron torpedo boat which certain parties brought from Mobile to
blow up the Ironsides. They have been out three times without
accomplishing anything, and the government suspecting something wrong, proposed to them to allow a Naval Officer to go with
them on their next trial, which they refused. The boat was therefore seized and yesterday nine men from one of the gunboats were
placed in her to learn how to work her and go out and see what
they could do." [55] On August 30, 1863, Lt. John Payne, C.S.N.,
and a crew were aboard the submarine when she was swamped
while tied up to the wharf at Fort Johnson. A small notice of the
accident occurred in the daily report of Col. Charles H. Olmstead,
commanding officer at Fort Johnson: "August 30 . . . an unfortunate accident occurred at the wharf yesterday, by which 5

seamen of the Chicora were drowned. The submarine torpedo-boat became entangled in some way with ropes, was drawn on its side, filled, and went down. The bodies have not been recovered." [56] The Charleston *Daily Courier* carried the following account on August 31: "UNFORTUNATE ACCIDENT, on Saturday last, while Lieutenant PAYNE and HASKER, of the Confederate Navy, were experimenting with a boat in the harbor, she parted from her moorings and became suddenly submerged, carrying down with her five seamen, who were drowned. The boat and bodies had not been recovered up to a late hour on Sunday. Four of the men belonged to the gunboat *Chicora*, and were named FRANK DOYLE, JOHN KELLY, MICHAEL CANE, and NICHOLAS DAVIS. The fifth man, whose name we did not learn, was attached to the *Palmetto State*." For security reasons, no mention of the kind of boat appeared in the newspaper article.

What actually happened was that the steamer *Etiwan* was tied up at the dock at Fort Johnson. When she moved off without notice, her ropes became entangled with the submarine, which was also tied up at the dock, with her hatches open. This capsized her, trapping the five men before they could get out of the small openings.[57] In the same letter in which he refers to the government taking possession of the boat, Honour describes the accident. He ends the description with the statement, "They had not up to last night recovered the boat or the bodies—poor fellows they are five in one coffin."

Lt. C. L. Stanton, C.S.N., a shipmate of Lieutenant Payne aboard the *Chicora*, barely missed being aboard the *Hunley* when she sank. Stanton had guard duty aboard the gunboat *Chicora* and was unable to accept Lieutenant Payne's invitation to go with him when he took the *Hunley* on a trial run before tying up at Fort Johnson. Lt. Charles H. Hasker volunteered to go in his place. As the *Hunley* started going down, Lieutenant Payne got out of the forward hatch and two other men got out of the other hatch. With the water pouring through the hatches, Lieutenant Hasker climbed over the bars which controlled the diving fins and pushed his way through the column of water that was flooding the boat. Just as he reached the hatch, it came down on his back. He forced it open and got almost through, but the hatch closed on his left leg. Held in this manner, he was carried to the bottom with the boat in 24 feet of water. As soon as the *Hunley* reached bottom, the water pressure became equalized. Lieutenant Hasker released his broken leg, managed to reach the surface, and was rescued. Later Lieutenant Hasker said, "I was the only man that went to the bottom with the 'Fishboat' and came up to tell the tale." [58]

Shortly after the accident, Admiral Dahlgren received a communication dated September 1 from the secretary of the navy, telling him that he had received information from Nassau about a "submarine machine." Obviously, one of the sailors from a blockade-runner had talked too much. [59]

In the meantime, Lieutenant Payne was having difficulty raising the boat because General Beauregard had his chief of staff write to Brigadier General Ripley on September 9, suggesting, "if the submarine torpedo boat is not already raised, that Lieutenant Payne shall be relieved, and that the work of raising the vessel shall be placed under the direction of Ferguson, Mathews, or other competent persons, as you may determine." [60]

The boat was finally raised, and on September 24 General Beauregard directed Brigadier General Ripley to appoint a board "to estimate the value of the submarine torpedo-boat at the time she was taken possession of by the military authorities." It is not revealed at what price she was appraised, but this confirms Honour's statement that she was taken over by the Confederate authorities. [61]

Nothing more is heard about her for the next few weeks. Horace Lawson Hunley, who put up most of the money to build her, came from Mobile and was in Charleston by September 19, for on that date he wrote to General Beauregard, proposing that if the submarine were placed in his hands, he would bring a crew from Mobile who were "well acquainted with the management and make the attempt to destroy a vessel of the enemy as early as practicable." Beauregard accepted his offer. In training his crew, he made many trial trips with the submarine in Charleston Harbor. However, on a morning in October, something went wrong; the submarine dove under the *Indian Chief* and failed to surface. The report of its loss appears in the *Journal of Operations in Charleston Harbor:* "October 15, 1863—an unfortunate accident occurred this morning with the submarine boat, by which, Capt. H. L. Hunley and 7 men lost their lives, in an attempt to run under the Navy receiving ship. The boat left the wharf at 9:25 A.M. and disappeared at 9:35. As soon as she sunk, air bubbles were seen to rise to the surface of the water, and from this fact it is supposed the hole in the top of the boat by which the men entered was not properly closed. It was impossible at the time to make any effort to rescue the unfortunate men, as the water was some 9 fathoms deep." Three days later, "Mr. Smith, provided with submarine armor, found the sunken submarine boat today in 9 fathoms of water." [62]

The morning after the accident, the following article appeared in the Charleston *Daily Courier:* "MELANCHOLY OCCURRENCE— On Thursday morning an accident occurred to a small boat in Cooper River containing eight persons, all of whom were drowned. Their names were: Captain HUNLEY, BROCKBANK, PARK, MARSHALL, BEARD, PATTERSON, MC HUGH, and SPRAGUE. Their bodies, we believe, have all been recovered." Again the press maintained censorship by speaking of the submarine as a "small boat." Actually, three weeks passed before the boat was raised and the bodies recovered.

W. A. Alexander, who helped build the submarine and later became a member of her crew, gives a rather graphic account of his experiences in Charleston. He arrived shortly after this last accident, and probably before the boat was raised. He said that the boat was on the bottom at an angle of 35 degrees with her bow deep in the mud. When she was raised, it was found that the "holding-down" bolts for each hatch had been removed. Captain Hunley's body was found with his head in the forward hatch and his arm over his head; he apparently had been trying to raise the hatch. His left hand held a candle that had never been lighted.

The ballast tank was wide open, and the wrench lay on the bottom of the boat. Park's body was found with his head in the other hatch, also with his right hand over his head, as if he, too, was attempting to raise the hatch in order to escape, but the pressure of 54 feet of water was too great. Alexander thinks that Hunley and Parks were asphyxiated and the others drowned.[63]

The boat was at last raised, taken to Mt. Pleasant, and hoisted on a wharf so that the bodies could be removed and the boat overhauled. This is where she was when Chapman did his painting. On the back of the painting he wrote, "Submarine Torpedo Boat H. L. Hunley Dec. 6, 1863." [64]

After these experiences, General Beauregard was deliberating as to whether or not the submarine was too dangerous and whether it ever would be an efficient fighting machine. Lt. George E. Dixon helped him come to a decision. Dixon, a lieutenant in the 21st Alabama Volunteers, had been seriously wounded at the battle of Shiloh. Returning to Mobile, he became familiar with the submarine. According to Alexander, when news of the fatal dive under the *Indian Chief* was received, he and Lieutenant Dixon volunteered to go to Charleston and operate the boat. Their offer was accepted, and they were ordered to report to the chief of staff.

On December 14, 1863, under Special Order 271, Lieutenant Dixon was ordered to "take command and direction of the submarine torpedo-boat H. L. Hunley, and proceed tonight to the mouth of the harbor or as far as capacity of the vessel will allow, and will sink and destroy any vessel of the enemy with which he can come in conflict." The order also stated that "all army officers are commanded and all navy officers requested to give all possible assistance to Lieutenant Dixon." [65]

Headquarters were established at Mt. Pleasant, and another crew was gotten together. Before this was done, General Beauregard, after many refusals, allowed Lieutenant Dixon to go aboard the *Indian Chief* for volunteers, with the firm admonition that he fully inform them about the previous history of the boat. Fearing that she would meet with another catastrophe by diving, he gave instructions that she be used with a spar torpedo in the same manner as the *David*. Apparently a full crew could not be obtained from the *Indian Chief*, for one of the crew members was Cpl. C. F. Carlson, of Company A, German Artillery.[66]

During the month of December the weather was windy, and it was often impossible to use the boat. One night the *David* towed her to the harbor entrance. Somehow her torpedo got adrift and nearly blew up both boats. This practice was immediately discontinued.[67]

By this time the captains of the blockading vessels, who knew what was going on, were anchoring farther and farther off shore, which made it increasingly difficult for the submarine, because of her slow speed, to reach them. She was therefore moved to Breach Inlet, between Sullivan's Island and the Isle of Palms, and left under guard of the troops stationed at Battery Marshall, on the upper end of Sullivan's Island. For some time the crew had to march from their headquarters at Mt. Pleasant to Breach Inlet, a distance of several miles along the beach, operate the boat, and march back again.

In the meantime, Admiral Dahlgren was receiving accurate first-hand reports of the ship's activities from deserters. Expecting an attack momentarily, he issued the following orders on January 7, 1864: "There is also one of another kind, which is nearly submerged and can be entirely so. It is intended to go under the bottoms of vessels and there operate." A week later the admiral wrote to the secretary of the navy that the "Diver" was at Mt. Pleasant and described her method of attack.[68]

Dahlgren ordered all ironclads to have their own boats in motion, their fenders rigged with netting dropped overboard from the ends, the howitzers loaded at all times, and a calcium light ready. He ended his instructions with this statement: "It is also advisable not to anchor in the deepest part of the channel, for not leaving much space between the bottom of the vessel and the bottom of the channel it will be impossible for the diving torpedo to operate except on the sides, and there will be less difficulty in raising a vessel if sunk." In his reports he spoke of the submarine as the "American Diver." [69]

Some time in January, 1864, Lieutenant Dixon moved his headquarters from Mt. Pleasant to the upper end of Sullivan's Island, where he found it bitterly cold and miserable.[70] The probable reason for the move was to eliminate the long walk back and forth from Mt. Pleasant. Finally the break in the weather for which he had been waiting came.

SLOOP-OF-WAR *HOUSATONIC. Drawn by Emmett Robinson*

On the night of February 17, 1864, he slipped away from his dock with the ebb tide and steered his craft through the tortuous channel of Breach Inlet, heading for the open sea and the nearest blockading vessel, the sloop-of-war *Housatonic*. Partially submerged, with only his two conning towers showing, he crept up to the ship, ready to ram the torpedo into her hull. Unfortunately for Lieutenant Dixon, "the night was bright and moonlit" and the sea was calm. When he was about 100 yards away, he was discovered by the watch and the alarm was given immediately. However, he approached so rapidly that they could not bring a gun to bear on him. In the meantime, the Union crew were frantically slipping the cable, and the engines were backed. As the submarine was approaching the *Housatonic*, she was met by small arms fire, which probably did no damage. Just as the *Housatonic* began to move backward, the torpedo was rammed home into her starboard quarter, blowing away the after part of the ship and causing her to sink immediately. Captain Pickering, having followed Admiral Dahlgren's instructions, was anchored in only 27 feet of water. Consequently, when the *Housatonic* hit bottom, her masts and spars were above water. Most of the crew climbed the rigging and were rescued by boats from the *Canadaigna*, which was anchored nearby. Only five men were lost.[71]

Two days after the attack Lt. Col. O. M. Dantzler, whose headquarters were at Battery Marshall, Sullivan's Island, wrote to the acting assistant adjutant general to tell him that the torpedo boat "stationed at this port" had not returned. The following day General Beauregard endorsed the message: "As soon as its fate shall have been ascertained, pay a proper tribute to the gallantry and patriotism of its crew and officers."

Finally, on February 21, 1864, General Beauregard wrote: "a gunboat sunken off Battery Marshall. Supposed to have been done by Mobile torpedo-boat . . . which went out for that purpose, and which, I regret to say, has not been heard of since." A week later, he wrote to General Cooper in Richmond that prisoners reported that it was the *Housatonic* which had been sunk by the submarine torpedo-boat. He went on to say: "There is little hope of safety of that brave man and his associates, however, as they were not captured."[72] Admiral Dahlgren was under the impression that the *Hunley* was "another 'David' torpedo boat." This assumption on his part has led to much confusion between the two types of boats since.

The following November, Admiral Dahlgren ordered W. L. Churchill to examine the wreck of the *Housatonic* with the idea of raising her. Churchill made the examination with his divers and reported back on November 27, 1864, that she was so badly damaged that it was useless to bother attempting to raise her. However, in his report was a statement that was of even greater significance: "I have also caused the bottom to be dragged for an area of 500 yards around the wreck, finding nothing of the torpedo-boat." [73]

In 1872 divers went down to examine the wreck of the *Housatonic*, which was a menace to navigation, and reported that they had found the *Hunley*, turned her propeller, and seen the skeletons of the crew. Many others have accepted this as an absolute fact.[74] It seems strange that after such a length of time the divers could turn her propeller, which by this time must have been deeply buried in the sandy mud. It also seems unusual for them to have seen the skeletons of the crew.[75] If the submarine was still intact and the skeletons were still inside, the divers with their heavy diving equipment would not have been able to squeeze through the 12-inch by 16-inch hatches without becoming wedged in them. In 1872 powerful underwater lights were unknown; consequently, if they had peered down the hatches, they could have seen almost nothing. On the other hand, if the submarine had had a large hole in her, the bodies would probably have floated out with the action of the waves and tide and been carried away. In only 27 feet of water, the wave action in a heavy blow, and especially in a hurricane, would have been very strong. In addition, it cannot be overlooked that 20 vessels of the "Stone Fleet" had been sunk close by and had disappeared without a trace into the sand and mud bottom.

On September 20, 1872, the bid of Benjamin Maillefert was accepted by the United States Engineers for the removal of "the wrecks Weehawken, the Housatonic, and the torpedo-boat to a depth of 20 feet." In Major Gillmore's report, dated August 28, 1873, the following appears: "The wooden gun-boat Housatonic sunk outside the bar in 4½ fathoms of water, was removed to a low water depth of 20½ feet. The torpedo-boat, sunk at the same time and place, could not be found." [76]

At that time only the upper part of the *Housatonic* had been removed to a depth of 20½ feet. In 1879, however, the main channel was changed with the building of jetties, and ships entering the harbor hit their keels on her wreck. For years a buoy was placed over her, and she was shown on the charts as the "Housatonic wreck." Finally, in July, 1908, divers examined the wreck and made a chart showing the exact location of the *Housatonic;* it does not show the wreck of the *Hunley* boat.[77] An article appeared in the *Sunday News* of July 12, 1908, describing the divers' examination of the *Housatonic*, but it made no mention of the *Hunley*.

The contract for removing the wreck was awarded to William H. Virden, who began work on February 19, 1909. He "blasted the boilers, which was practically all that remained of the wreck." At first he was unable to remove enough of it to get the channel to its required depth, but after more blasting he finally succeeded. It is possible that the *Hunley*, which had been made out of a boiler, was mistaken by Virden for one of the boilers from the *Housatonic* and blasted along with the others.[78]

No two *Hunley* authorities can agree on the number of times the submarine was lost on her trial trips in Charleston harbor. It is now generally accepted that the submarine that was lost on her trial trip in Mobile Bay was not the same boat that was sent to Charleston. That boat, therefore, can be discounted.

The *Official Records of the War* reveal that the *Hunley* sank twice on her trial trips prior to the night she went down with the *Housatonic*, February 17, 1864. The records state that she was lost on August 30, 1863, at Fort Johnson, and again on October 15, 1863, when diving under the *Indian Chief* in Charleston harbor.

General Beauregard said the "fish torpedo-boat" went down twice on her trial trips, once at Fort Johnson, the other time when diving under the *Indian Chief*.[79] As he was vitally interested in her, it seems unlikely that he was mistaken. Commodore D. M. Ingraham says she sank twice.[80] Even though the submarine was manned by naval officers only part of the time she was in operation, he must have been aware of what was going on from the moment she arrived until the time she was lost on her final trip.

The Charleston newspapers contain only two accounts of her

sinking. Both are fairly detailed, though the submarine is not spoken of by name.

On March 3, 1864, J. D. Breaman wrote from Mobile to his wife. The letter was captured and thus saved. It reads in part:

. . . among the number, however was a submarine boat, built in this place, of which Whitney and myself bought one-fifth for $3,000.

We took her to Charleston, for the purpose of operating there, and a few days after her arrival there, she sunk through carelessness and her crew of 5 men drowned.

Another crew of 8 men went on from here, raised her, and while experimenting with her in the harbor, sunk her and all 8 were drowned.

Lieutenant Dixon then went on from here and got another crew in Charleston. A few nights ago he went out, attacked and sunk the steam sloop of war *Housatonic*, but unfortunately (like his predecessor in this desperate and untried adventure), fear that he and his crew were all lost . . .[81]

Here is a statement from a man who was a co-owner and who accompanied the submarine, along with Whitney, to Charleston. His statement that she sank through carelessness a few days after her arrival and again when experimenting in the harbor agrees perfectly with the *Official Records*.

Lieutenant Stanton, C.S.N., said she was sunk at Fort Johnson, again while diving under the *Indian Chief*, and finally with the *Housatonic*. As he was closely associated with Lieutenant Payne and stationed on the *Chicora*, he must have been fully aware of the activities of the *Hunley*, or, as he spoke of her, the "Fishboat." [82]

Col. Charles H. Olmstead of the First Georgia Volunteers, who was commanding officer at Fort Johnson when the *Hunley* sank at the dock, stated that she was twice sunk on her trial trips before sinking with the *Housatonic*.[83]

In 1899 a drinking fountain with a tablet was erected at White Point Gardens (the Battery) in Charleston to commemorate the deeds of these brave men, along with others. Among the names on it is that of Horace L. Hunley, and under it, "inventor of the Hunley submarine."

In Mobile, Alabama, there is a tablet which reads:

The Hunley

The first submarine successfully used in warfare was completed at this site in 1863. Designed by James McClintock and Baxter Watson, and financed by Horace L. Hunley, it was built by W. A. Alexander at the Mobile machine shop of Park and Lyons. After trials in Mobile River and Bay it was sent by rail to Charleston, where, on February 17, 1864, it sank the U. S. S. Housatonic.

Park lost his life along with Hunley on October 15, 1863, and with him is buried in Magnolia Cemetery. James McClintock operated the submarine when she first arrived in Charleston. W. A. Alexander, along with Lieutenant Dixon, was a member of the crew for some time, but he was ordered back to Mobile. It seems to be the general consensus that Horace L. Hunley, who lived most of his life in New Orleans—he was only 35 years of age at the time of his death—was the main person to finance the building of the boat. Some credit James McClintock, a young steamboat captain, as the sole designer. Apparently the people in Mobile give equal status in this regard to Baxter Watson. In the *Official Records of the Navy*, the designers are given as Hunley, McClintock and Watson.

3

A week after the first shot was fired at Fort Sumter, President Lincoln proclaimed a blockade of the South Carolina ports. At first it was only a paper blockade because the Federal government had no ships to enforce it; most of its men-of-war were on distant stations or being overhauled. Consequently, merchant ships continued to enter the so-called blockaded ports on regular schedule.

When news of the blockade was received, a wave of anger swept the South, but soon it became obvious that it could not be enforced.

When news of the blockade reached the heads of state in Europe, they were puzzled; they did not see how it was possible for a nation to blockade its own ports. Previously the use of the blockade had been recognized only between independent nations. Did this mean that the North recognized the South as an independent nation? If not, the Federal government should merely have stated that it was closing its ports because the nation was in a state of insurrection. Furthermore, it was one thing to issue a proclamation of a blockade, but to be effective it had to be enforced. Secretary of State William H. Seward received some scathing criticism from his fellow cabinet members for his bungling. They charged that he had placed the United States in an embarrassing position in the eyes of the world, but nevertheless, the blockade remained in force and the South was never recognized as an independent nation.

Lincoln realized that the South was an agrarian area and had almost no factories. If the Confederacy was to put up any kind of resistance, it would be entirely dependent on outside sources for munitions. The sooner these sources could be cut off, the quicker the end of any organized resistance would come.

For the first three weeks after the proclamation of the blockade, ships came in and went out of the port of Charleston as usual. One, the schooner *Mary Haley*, 14 days out of Boston, arrived on April 20. On the morning of May 11, 1861, the U.S.S. *Niagara* appeared off the bar.[84] The blockade was being put into effect. The *Niagara* was ill suited for this type of work; she had a draft of 24 feet 5 inches, and it was impossible for her to maneuver except in the deep water at the mouth of the main channel.[85] There were three other channels leading into Charleston that could be used by vessels of lighter draft.

On the morning of May 12, the *Niagara* stood offshore, apparently to warn some vessels away. Seeing her off station, the *A and A*, 42 days out of Belfast, took the opportunity to slip into the harbor. The *Niagara* gave chase, but the *A and A* was empty and consequently drawing little water; she hugged the shore, and the *Niagara* dared not follow for fear of running aground. The race between the two vessels was watched by people on the wharf as well as by a party in the pilot boat *Rover*. The following morning the *A and A* was successfully towed into port by the steamer *Gordon* and thereby became the first ship to enter Charleston since the blockade was physically established.[86]

While the *A and A* was making port, the *Niagara* was warning off other ships attempting to enter. One, the *General Parkhill*, from Liverpool, was warned to keep off the coast. Nevertheless, she kept edging into shallow water and communicating by means of signal flags with someone on shore. The *Niagara* sent out a boat, and the *Parkhill* was taken as a prize and sent to Philadelphia.[87] As soon as she had left Liverpool, the American ensign had been lowered and the Palmetto flag hoisted in its place.

The British ship *Susan G. Owens* left Charleston on May 13 bound for Liverpool, and apparently was allowed to proceed by the *Niagara*. It appears that the first vessel to actually run the blockade was the steamer *Ella Warley*, loaded with cotton bound for Nassau. In Nassau she took on a valuable cargo, and managed to slip by the harassed *Niagara* and return safely to Charleston.[88]

The area at the mouth of Charleston Harbor is large. A 12-mile arc extends from Lighthouse Inlet to Breach Inlet. As the efficacy of the blockade increased, the blockade-runners began to use the shallow and dangerous channel that ran close to Sullivan's Island. Since most of the blockading vessels were heavy-draft ships, highly unsuited for the work, it is understandable that so many vessels, even sailboats, were able to slip by. As the number of ships off the bar increased, the use of sailing vessels as blockade-runners was gradually discontinued. It was thought, quite logically, that the faster the vessel, the greater its chances of success. But several steam-propelled vessels of slow speed made many successful runs before being captured.

While speed was the primary requisite and the efficiency of the crew was extremely important, much depended on the captain of the runner. Cold nerve was probably the greatest asset, in addition to excellent seamanship and a thorough knowledge of the channels and landfalls along the coast. Many captains who ran into Charleston fulfilled these qualifications. Among the most notable were Thomas J. Lockwood, Robert W. Lockwood, Louis M. Coxetter, James Carlin, H. S. Lebby, and F. W. Bonneau. One night when Captain Coxetter was trying to slip through the cordon, he was not satisfied with the amount of speed his engineer was giving him. He sat at the head of the ladder leading to the engine room with a Colt revolver in his hand and demanded more speed, his ship successfully eluded the blockading vessels.[89]

Both sides thought the war would be short and therefore made but little effort to establish credits with foreign nations. Early in the war Beauregard suggested that the Confederacy purchase some British-built vessels to use for shipping cotton to England.[90] His idea, however, was vetoed, either by Jefferson Davis or his cabinet. Consequently, blockade-running was left in private hands until almost the end of the war. John Fraser and Co. of Charleston, with its subsidiary Fraser, Trenholm and Co. of Liverpool, was probably the leading blockade-running company in the Confederacy, and Fraser-owned ships always returned with the greater part of their cargo consisting of munitions. So much money was being made by speculators that the South Carolina legislature was forced to place restrictions on the exportation of cotton as early as April, 1862.[91] As the war continued, and all goods became scarcer, prices skyrocketed. Consequently, the temptation was great to bring in merchandise rather than war supplies. It was generally conceded that, if a blockade-runner could make two round trips, the profits could pay for the ship.[92] One man purchased a share in a runner for $3200. Two months later he received a dividend for $500 and shortly afterward sold the share for $6000.[93] British Colonel Freemantle, who visited Charleston in June, 1863, commented on the blockade-runners: "They are seldom captured and charge an enormous price for passengers and freight. It is doubtful whether the traffic of the private blockade runner doesn't do more harm than good to the country by depreciating its currency, and they are generally looked upon as regular gamblers, speculators. I have met many persons who are of the opinion that the trade ought to be stopped, except for government stores and articles necessary for the public welfare." [94]

One of the most successful runners was the *Herald*, formerly a liner on the Glasgow-Dublin run. She made 24 trips before being captured. Her first skipper was Coxetter, who was considered by the officers and crews of the blockading vessels as one of the most skillful masters engaged in blockade running. [95]

In spite of the increase in the number of blockading vessels, the runners managed to get through the cordon with regularity. As one Charlestonian wrote, "The steamers are now running between Charleston and Nassau as regular as packet boats." The runners would usually wait until dark before attempting to make the run. In early 1862, one person wrote, "The *Isabel* and three schooners got out two nights ago, and five more are to go out tonight." [96] One evening a woman was in a rowboat in the harbor when a runner passed close by bound for Nassau. She gave the following description of the ship:

She looked like a veritable phantom-ship of tradition as she glided past. No ghost could have moved more silently, or looked more mysterious; and we all felt a sort of mystical enchantment as we watched her rapid, stealthy progress. She was painted a smoky gray color, and could scarcely be distinguished in the light mist which enveloped her. Not a lamp gleamed aboard; no sound could be heard, except very faint echoes from her revolving wheels, and no smoke seemed to be thrown out by her engines. Everything to ensure a successful trip had been carefully studied and prearranged. She passed like a spirit through the midst of the blockading squadron, and twenty-four hours later dropped anchor in the sparkling tropical waters of her Nassau haven. Three requisites were needful in this dangerous traffic to ensure success; these were, a bold captain, a swift steamer, and a noiseless crew. [97]

Blockade-running by now was a fine art.

The *Kate*, owned by John Fraser and Co., was under the command, most of the time, of Thomas J. Lockwood. She was named after the wife of George S. Trenholm. She was rather slow, but it is said that she made 40 trips through the blockade, reaping a fortune for her owners.[98]

As the war continued and prices rose, running the blockade became a lucrative business. Many of the runners were ships built by Clyde Bank (Scotland), they were usually British owned, and they were frequently commanded by British naval officers, who obtained leaves of absence solely for the purpose of running the blockade. Most of them probably did it for the excitement, but they could not have been unmindful of the tremendous profits involved if they were successful. One officer said that it had the excitement of fox-hunting, only they were the foxes. In spite of the remonstrances of United States Minister Charles Francis Adams in London that the British government was violating its neutrality by allowing ships to be built and used for this purpose, their construction continued. The crew of a blockade-runner was usually a motley collection. A crew list has survived which gives the different nationalities of its men: Italian, French, Irish, English, Canadian, South African, Cuban, Prussian, and one from New Providence (Bahamian). Obviously these men were in it solely for profit. Wages were quite high, amounting to $100 a month, payable in gold, and a $50 bounty at the end of each successful trip. Captains and pilots received as much as $5,000. Frequently a round trip could be made in seven days. The Confederate representative in Nassau wrote to Secretary of War Randolph: "Four of the Charleston branch pilots arrived on the *Kate* this morning. They have fixed their demands at $1,500 to be paid here [Nassau] and $3,500 at home. We have offered the exorbitant rate of $1,000 here and $3,000 on arrival, which they have thus far refused." While it is not recorded what rate was settled upon, it is safe to assume that the pilots got their $5,000 for their trip.[99] The masters made a great deal of profit on their investments of sorely needed merchandise, which they sold for as much as seven times the original cost. One captain of a runner gives a vivid description of conditions in Nassau. "Money was almost as plentiful as dirt," he says, and at times even the bank vaults could not hold all the gold, which was dumped down by the bushel and guarded by soldiers. Nassau was a wide-open town, with gamblers, speculators, and women from all the dives of Europe to relieve the sailors of their gold. In the latter part of the war, when quinine was almost nonexistent in the Confederacy, it was said that ten dollars invested in it at Nassau would bring four hundred to six hundred dollars in Charleston.[100]

The *Margaret and Jessie* was another successful blockade-runner; it is said that she paid her owner ten times over. Her captain was Robert W. Lockwood, noted for his nerve and seamanship. One night, loaded with munitions, the *Margaret and Jessie* arrived off the bar. The night was clear, and before Lockwood knew it, he was seen by the five blockading vessels, who opened up on him with every available gun. With no chance of reversing course, he headed straight for the harbor at full speed. Later he estimated that between 100 and 150 shots had been fired at his fleeing ship from a distance of 200 feet. However, he arrived in Charleston without a man wounded and his ship hit in only five or six places without any serious results. It was probably his nearness to the blockading vessels that saved his ship; it was impossible for them to depress their guns, and most of the shots must have gone over his ship. The *Margaret and Jessie* made 18 trips before she was finally captured off Wilmington, North Carolina.[101] After being condemned as a prize, she was purchased by the United States Navy, renamed the *Gettysburg*, and sent to Charleston as a blockading vessel. As she had a shallow draft and a speed of 15 knots, she was successful in capturing several runners before the war ended.[102]

In February, 1864, the British-built blockade-runner *Presto* was run aground on Sullivan's Island as she attempted to enter the harbor. She saw the wreck of the runner *Minho* on the way in, but was slow to respond to her helm; the *Presto* struck the wreck with such force that a hole was knocked in her bottom, and her captain had to beach her. At daylight the Federal batteries on Morris Island immediately opened up on the grounded vessel, and the monitors moved in for the kill. The gunners noticed that

BLOCKADE-RUNNER *PRESTO. Drawn by Emmett Robinson*

soldiers were frantically trying to remove her cargo in spite of their heavy fire, which somewhat puzzled them. The *Presto* had several barrels of liquor as part of her cargo, and the soldiers were doing their best to salvage it—for themselves, of course. Col. W. W. H. Davis of the 104th Pennsylvania troops, who were stationed on Morris Island, wrote regretfully: "The troops on Sullivan's Island got hold of the liquor on board of her and had a 'grand drunk,' and it is alleged that 300 men at that time could have taken the island, but unfortunately it was not known until the opportunity had passed." [103]

Vessels were constantly being added to the blockading fleet, but in spite of this the runners continued to elude the vigilance of the officers and men. Admiral Dahlgren wrote that "previous to the 10th of July 1863, the blockade of the port [Charleston] was so imperfect that vessels entered and departed with so little risk that the export of cotton and import of supplies did not suffer any material interruption." Sixteen months later he said: "So many steamers [blockaders] were repairing as to make even the blockade inefficient." While the captains of the runners were having trouble trying to get past the increasing number of ships, Admiral Dahlgren was also having trouble trying to catch them. Toward the end of the war the blockade increased in stringency. [104]

After the fall of Fort Fisher, which took place on January 15, 1865, closing the port of Wilmington, the only remaining port open to the runners was Charleston. Since the mouth of the Cape

Fear River no longer required guarding, many of the ships which had been used in this duty were ordered to Charleston.[105] However, as late as January 20, 1865, a month before the evacuation of Charleston, vessels were still entering and leaving the port. In the first week of February, four runners successfully got through the blockaders and two got safely out of the harbor.[106]

The last runner to enter Charleston, discharge her cargo, and take on an outward-bound one was the *Hattie*, under the command of H. S. Lebby. A Scottish-built ship with powerful engines, she had made many successful trips. One night in February, 1865, she started to go through the double cordon of vessels lying off and inside the bar. Captain Lebby, with his runner recently painted a blue-white in order to look as much like the mist as possible, slowed his speed so that the noise of his engines could not be heard and let the tide and the wind drive him forward. He got through the first line of blockaders without being seen, drifting by two of them at a distance of not over 300 feet. However, when he tried to pass through the second line, one of the vessels opened fire at a distance of 200 feet and sent up rockets to illuminate the area. As soon as he was discovered, Captain Lebby rang for full speed, but for the next ten minutes every gun that could be brought to bear opened up on him. Miraculously, the *Hattie* was not hit. Just below Sumter, two barge-loads of men were stationed on picket duty, and as the *Hattie* sped by they opened up with musketry fire, wounding some of the crew. Captain Lebby hurriedly took on another cargo and slipped back past all 26 of the blockading vessels without being detected.[107]

Charleston was evacuated on February 17, 1865. On the night of February 17–18, the runner *Chicora* steamed into the harbor before realizing that the city was no longer in Confederate hands. The sailors on the guard ships were probably too busy celebrating to pay any attention to a runner's attempting to slip by. When he realized what had happened, the captain of the *Chicora* turned her around and again slipped through the surrounding ships, arriving safely at Nassau. The *Fox* also ran into Charleston not knowing that the city was in Union hands. Unlike the *Chicora*, she was seized before she could turn around and make a dash for freedom. When the Federal troops entered the city, two blockade-runners were lying at the docks.[108]

Great efforts were made by the Union navy to capture the runners, with ships of every size and description, but they were not very successful. From 1861 through 1865, 87 percent of the steamers and 81 percent of the sailing vessels which attempted to run in and out of the ports of Charleston and Wilmington escaped capture.[109] These figures explain why blockade-running was such an indispensable factor to the Confederacy. With practically no factories capable of turning out large quantities of war material, the armies of the Confederacy would have been conquered quickly if it had not been for the cargoes brought in by the blockade-runners. Specifically the runner *Minho* in one trip brought in over 7,000 rifles, 2,100 swords, and nearly 100 cases of ammunition.[110] Those amounts multiplied many times give an idea of the amount of war supplies that slipped through the blockading squadrons.

7

The City Besieged

1

WHEN GENERAL GILLMORE WAS ERECTING BATTERIES ON Morris Island to house his large siege guns to force Battery Wagner and Fort Sumter into submission, he ordered his engineers to erect another some distance away to house a 200-pounder Parrott rifle gun to throw shells indiscriminately into the city of Charleston at a distance of four miles.[1] On August 21, 1863, he sent a communication to General Beauregard demanding "the immediate evacuation of Morris Island and Fort Sumter." In the demand Gillmore said: "should you refuse compliance with this demand, or should I receive no reply thereto within four hours after it is delivered into the hands of your subordinate at Fort Wagner for transmission, I shall open fire on the city of Charleston from batteries already established within easy and effective range of the heart of the city." [2] General Gillmore must have known when he sent the demand that it would be almost impossible to receive a reply within the stipulated four hours. This involved sending the note from Wagner to Cummings Point, finding a boat to take it across the harbor, getting it to General Beauregard's headquarters—with the possibility that he might not be there—and then reversing the entire route. The note finally arrived at 10:45 P.M. without General Gillmore's signature, and was immediately returned. Three hours later, General Gillmore opened fire on the city with his 200-pounder Parrott rifle gun.

It so happened that General Beauregard was away inspecting some of the fortifications when the demand arrived. Upon his return, he wrote General Gillmore: "Among nations not barbarous the usage of war prescribes that when a city is about to be attacked, timely notice shall be given by the attacking commander, in order that non-combatants may have an opportunity for withdrawing beyond its limits." General Beauregard said that at least one to three days notice was usual, but that General Gillmore had given only four hours' notice. He continued: "It would appear, sir, that despairing of reducing these works, you now resort to the novel measure of turning your guns against the old men, the women and children, and the hospitals of a sleeping city, an act of inexcusable barbarity . . ."[3] Gillmore granted a 24-hour respite, but his reply was couched in vituperative terms.[4]

The first shell fell at 1:30 A.M. on August 29; it landed on Pinckney Street and started a lively blaze. The first fire company to reach the scene was one composed of free Negroes, who all through the war did valiant service in fighting fires started by shells. All the time they were fighting the fire, they kept muttering "cussed bobolitionists" (abolitionists).[5]

A war correspondent staying at the Charleston Hotel gives an amusing account of what took place when the first shot exploded on Pinckney Street. The night of August 21–22 was extremely hot. Unable to sleep, the correspondent was reading and could hear the monotonous sound of the cannonade, when he was startled by a noise that "resembled the whirr of a phantom brigade of cavalry galloping in mid-air," followed by a crash and a deafening explosion near his window. Looking out, he saw smoke and fire coming from the house that had been hit and a policeman running down the street. He struck his club against the curb, a signal of alarm practiced by the local police. At first the correspondent thought a meteor had fallen, but soon another shell exploded nearby, and he knew what was going on.

The hotel was filled with speculators who had been attracted to the city by the sale of some blockade cargoes. As they were aroused by the sound of the explosion, the hotel corridors became filled "with these terrified gentlemen rushing around in the scantiest of costumes and wildest alarm." One fat individual wearing almost nothing trotted back and forth with one boot on and the other in his hand. In the excitement of the moment, he had forgotten the number of his room, and his distress was ludicrous. Another, almost naked man dragged an enormous trunk from his room in an effort to get it to the staircase. Pandemonium reigned, and everyone cursed General Gillmore. When the third shell "swished" over the roof, everyone fell to the floor, among cigar butts and tobacco juice. The correspondent, who had no admiration for the speculators, remarked: "If a shell could have fallen in their midst and exterminated the whole race of hucksters, it would have been of great benefit to the South." [6]

By this time the lower part of the city was awake, and people were streaming into the streets. Women with children in their arms made their way to the upper part of the city, where they could find refuge from the shells; others wandered around aimlessly. The sick were carried out of houses on mattresses and taken to places of safety.

The next morning, under a flag of truce, the British consul went over to Morris Island to protest to General Gillmore. Gillmore refused to see him. In the meantime, many of the noncombatants who had means left the city, but hundreds unable to do so had to remain and endure the bombardment for the next year and a half. While the bombardment at first created excitement and panic among some of the people, after the initial shock it caused only bitter scorn and indignation. [7]

Four days after the bombardment began, Fire Chief M. H. Nathans recommended "that a supply of water be kept on hand to extinguish the fire of the enemy's incendiary shells exploding in the city." The local press, incensed at the bombardment, stated that "Gillmore was a second Butler, and the Yankees expect him to excel Butler in brutality to South Carolinians." The Butler referred to was General "Beast" Butler of New Orleans fame.[8] A correspondent of the *Illustrated London News* who was in Charleston covering the war was so shocked that he wrote: "The Federal General was guilty of that barbarity which disgraced him as a soldier." [9]

General Gillmore said: "No military results of great value were ever expected from this firing . . . the results were not only highly interesting and novel, but very instructive." While it was novel to the citizens of Charleston, it was definitely not appreciated by them. The local press said that inasmuch as the city was merely a military post, the bombardment was an "experimental school of practice in developing new results in artillery," which was close to the truth.[10]

After the brief respite granted by General Gillmore, the 200-pounder Parrott rifle gun again began lobbing shells into the city. The Charleston *Mercury* stated: "From thirteen or fourteen eight-inch incendiary shells fell into the City. . . . No damage was done. It is unnecessary to make any comment upon this act." Apparently even for the *Mercury*'s vociferous editor, Robert Barnwell Rhett, words failed.[11]

The men who fired the gun were a volunteer detachment from Company D of the 11th Maine, under command of Lt. Charles Sellmer, brought to Morris Island from Fernandina, Florida. Upon arrival, Lieutenant Sellmer was placed in charge of the "Marsh Battery," which consisted of only one gun. On the evening of August 21–22, 1863, he was ordered to open fire on the city, with St. Michael's Church steeple as his point of aim. Since neither the city nor the church steeple could be seen from the battery, Lieutenant Sellmer got into a position from which he could see the steeple to take a compass bearing on it. In this way he was able to aim his gun with accuracy, an early instance of indirect fire. At 1:30 A.M. he gave the order to fire. The aim was badly off, for the shell struck a storehouse on Pinckney Street, some distance north of St. Michael's Church. After the second shot, as the night was quiet, Lieutenant Sellmer and his gun crew could hear the ringing of the fire bells in the city.

The battery, which had been built in the marsh upon logs laid crossways (grillage), was literally floating on the mud, and at every shot the entire structure swayed. This may have caused the pintle holding the gun to loosen with each shot; with the sixteenth one, it became so dangerous that Lieutenant Sellmer gave the order to cease fire. When daylight came, the gun was inspected by Chief Engineer Col. Edward W. Serrell, who determined that it would take two days to repair it. This was why General Gillmore was so magnanimous in giving General Beauregard time to evacuate noncombatants.

The Confederate batteries on James Island opened up a heavy fire on the battery. While the aim of the mortars was good, the timing of the fuses was poor, and all of the shells landed in the mud and then exploded rather than bursting in the air over the battery. Consequently, the only effect on the gun crew was that mud was spattered on them and on their gun.

When the carriage was repaired, the firing resumed, this time with shells of Greek fire, which in theory were to make Charleston a raging inferno. But the shells were defective, and many exploded before leaving the gun. After 19 shots, the gunner informed Lieutenant Sellmer that he could not get his priming wire down, which indicated that the gun had moved in its jacket. This probably happened because 20 pounds of powder were being used instead of the customary load of 16 pounds. Realizing that the gun was about to burst, Lieutenant Sellmer ordered his men outside of the battery for protection just before it was fired. But Sellmer wanted to see what time it was, and he could do this only by the flash of the gun. When the order to fire was given, the whole battery became a sheet of flames. The "Swamp Angel" had burst on the thirty-sixth discharge, hurling itself forward and

SWAMP ANGEL

completely off its carriage. Lieutenant Sellmer's hair and eyebrows were badly singed as a result, and his left ear was injured. But "the shot itself went smoothly to the city, as if nothing had happened to the gun." [12]

Most people think that with the bursting of the "Swamp Angel" the bombardment of Charleston ceased. Actually, the shells from the Angel were only a forerunner of what was to continue for the next year and a half. General Gillmore immediately ordered a four-gun battery erected on Black Island, close to the site of the "Swamp Angel," to throw shells into the city.

The official name of the location of the gun was the "Marsh Battery"; the nickname "Swamp Angel" was given the gun by Sergeant Fitter of the New York Engineers. It is still known by that name, and the burst cannon can now be seen at Trenton, New Jersey.[13]

Writing to General Halleck in Washington, General Gillmore said of the bombardment: "The projectiles from my batteries entered the city, and General Beauregard, himself designates them as 'the most destructive missiles ever used in war.' " [14]

No shells were fired at Charleston during the month of September, and only three in October. It is possible that the heavy rifled guns on Morris Island were wearing out from their sustained firing at Wagner and Sumter. Sand blowing into the barrel seems to have been one of the factors in their excessive wear and subsequent bursting. However, by the middle of November the bombardment started in earnest, and the guns began to throw shells into the city with regularity.[15]

During the early part of the bombardment, the Union gunners continued to use the steeple of St. Michael's as their target. The church itself was hit many times, and the interior, the chancel, and the organ were completely wrecked. The South Carolina Society Hall on Meeting Street received several shells that penetrated its roof. By this time the citizens who had remained were reconciled to the incessant shelling and showed little emotion. Almost all of the people had either retreated into the interior of the state or moved farther uptown out of range of the shells.[16]

Shortly after midnight on Christmas night, several guns opened up on the city, again aiming at St. Michael's steeple. Shells rained on Charleston from five guns on Morris Island in the most severe bombardment the city had yet experienced.[17] Fire broke out in a building on Broad Street and spread rapidly to some of the nearby buildings. Soon afterward a fire was discovered on the corner of Church Street and St. Michael's Alley and before it was brought under control, it had spread to five other buildings and the Cotton Press. In addition, the Germans' Turners Hall between Church and Meeting streets and the kitchen and outbuildings of the old Bath House began to burn furiously. Capt. T. S. Hale, who used St. Michael's steeple as an observation point not only to count the number of shells fired into the city but also to see where they landed, reported that he saw a man with a torch set fire to Turners Hall.[18] Between the fire started by the shells and the one set by an incendiary, the firemen were busy. Members of the First Regiment of Artillery under the command of Col. Alfred Rhett were called out to help fight the blaze.

The gunners always increased their rate of fire when they saw a blaze, but in spite of the shells bursting near their engine, the firemen worked uninterruptedly. Four firemen and four soldiers were injured in fighting the fire, and a little farther up the street an 83-year-old man had his leg shot off at the knee. It was a memorable Christmas night; 134 shells fell into the city.[19]

A Confederate soldier stationed on James Island at the time of the Christmas bombardment described it in detail in a letter to his mother: "The Yankees as soon as they saw the light of the fire poured their shells like rain around the neighborhood of the fire . . . and yet for all this, the people in the city is [sic] as unconcerned as if there was not a Yankee within a hundred miles. . . . With such people left to protect our City, I have no fear of any such thing as surrendering it." [20]

The bombardment began in earnest in January, 1864. Within a period of nine days, 1,500 shells were fired at the city. The intensity of fire was not as great during the rest of the month, but the few people who had remained in the lower part of the town were forced to evacuate their houses. Places of business also had to be moved out of range of the shells, and the hotels closed. The lower part of the city looked deserted. The next month was almost a repetition of the former; nearly a thousand shells were hurled into the battered but defiant city.[21]

Although the "Swamp Angel" burst early in its career, one of General Gillmore's guns, mounted on Cummings Point, had a remarkable record of endurance. Sixty-nine days elapsed between the first and last discharge of the gun, during which time it had fired 4,253 shells that landed in the city. Gillmore was so pleased with its performance that he wrote it up in detail, stating that the gun was usually fired at an elevation of 40°. Most of the other guns burst after firing about 300 shells.[22]

Believing that the extreme lower part of the city was in ruins, and finding that many of their shells were falling in the "Burnt district" (caused by the conflagration of December, 1861), the gunners shifted their sights to the spire of St. Philip's Church. The story is told that one Sunday morning the rector, Mr. Howe, was midway in his sermon when a shell passed over the roof and exploded in the western churchyard; the congregation remained calmly seated until the service reached its proper close.[23] Because of the danger, the Episcopal congregations went to St. Paul's, which was out of range of the guns, and united there for worship. The rectors of the abandoned churches took turns officiating. The same thing was done by other denominations. The interior of St. Philip's was badly wrecked, having received ten or more shells in the heavy bombardment. The military headquarters also were moved out of danger of the falling shells to former governor Aiken's mansion on Elizabeth Street.[24]

The bombardment continued relentlessly, and fires broke out almost daily. The fire department always responded promptly and effectively. During one of the fires caused by the shells, at the corner of Elliott Street and Gadsden Alley, "the engine of the Phoenix Company was struck by a shell and blown to atoms," injuring several firemen.[25]

The Northern press gave a rather vivid account of the situation in Charleston: "block by block of that city is being reduced to ashes, and by a process as steadily inexorable as that which *Gill-more* humbled Pulaski and Sumter." It is amazing that more people were not killed. The local press related how a "shell passed through a bed containing three children and exploded in the next floor," and that "no one was injured is regarded as miraculous." Another shell struck a house on Calhoun Street, went through the bed between a man and his wife, and then passed through into the cellar. Again no one was injured.[26]

Day after day, month after month, the bombardment continued, sometimes with great severity; on other days hardly a shell was fired into the city, and on some days none at all. Brig. Gen. John P. Hatch, in a report on activities along the coast, said: "a few shells are daily thrown into the city of Charleston, not with the expectation of doing serious injury, but with the hope of annoying them and delaying movements of the railroad trains." [27]

Sure by now that the entire lower part of the city was thoroughly destroyed, the Federal gunners changed their point of aim to the Second Presbyterian Church, just above Calhoun Street.

This apparently was the maximum distance for their guns; though some shells fell as far north as John Street.[28]

In early 1865 the bombardment was still in progress. General Foster, who had succeeded General Gillmore as commanding officer of the Department of the South, received a communication from O. S. Halsted, Jr., relative to the use of Greek fire. Halsted assured General Foster that it was of superior quality to the kind first used in the early part of the bombardment and promised him that, if he used it, he could burn Charleston whenever he pleased. Halsted continued: "Nothing would suit the people so entirely just now as to hear that General Foster had burned that hot bed of rebeldom—Charleston." General Foster answered that he had no such shells on hand but that if Halsted would send some he would "fire them on Charleston with pleasure." [29]

A Charleston lady who drove from the upper section to the lower part of the city described it as going from life to death. The streets were overgrown with grass, and formerly well-kept gardens were obliterated. She went on to say that the houses were indescribable—all of their windows were broken, many chimneys had fallen and gables were shot out, piazzas were half gone, and the street looked like it was scattered with diamonds from the broken glass. On the way from Calhoun Street to White Point Gardens (the Battery), she saw two people come out, wondering who could possibly be driving by.[30]

2

Concentration of purpose and dedication to a cause elevates people. Men are better soldiers when their homeland is being invaded and the lives of their loved ones are at stake. The troops from Charleston were outstanding on the battlefield, not only because they believed in the cause for which they fought but because they had the unqualified backing of their women.

The spirit of the Charleston women was magnificent during the entire conflict; they made many sacrifices and suffered great hardships. One woman wrote to her husband: "No Charlestonian has any right to be absent. Every son of Carolina should be at his post in the day of trial. May God be your shield and a strong tower of defense in the hour of danger." [31] With that admonition no man dared turn his back to the enemy. A soldier writing to his wife in Charleston from camp on James Island two years after the beginning of the war said: "Remember that we are now fighting for all a man holds dear in the world. Life, Liberty—the honor of our wives, daughters and Sisters, together with all that we are possessed of—and it becomes the duty of our women to encourage by every means in their power our Soldiers to do their whole duty irrespective of any private consideration." [32] The soldiers looked to their women for encouragement. This mutual dependence produced courage and a determination never to surrender, regardless of the cost.[33] This was the major factor in the prolonged and heroic siege of Charleston. As one citizen put it, "We intend to die hard."

For the first two years of the war the blockade was ineffective, and blockade-runners made trips regularly, but nevertheless, ordinary articles gradually disappeared from the stores, and by the end of 1861 shoes had become scarce.[34] Soon everyday merchandise was nonexistent. When a runner arrived from Nassau or Bermuda with part of her cargo consisting not only of luxuries but of articles of wearing apparel, there was a rush on the part of the women to attend the auctions at which they were being sold. A description of one of the sales gives the flavor of these events: "I wish you could have seen the building, crammed with animated faces from end to end, men holding up half-grown girls on their shoulders so the younger members of their household should not be crushed, women wedged against each other and trying to peep over the sea of heads by standing on chairs or any available article that raised their height." The merchandise was not displayed in tempting showcases, "but piled, one over the other, on rough tables, anything and everything, from a household or kitchen utensil to a lady's robe, all tumbled together pell-mell, and all contended for with the same eagerness, all treasured as triumphantly as though fit for an empress. In half an hour the

tables were cleared." One gentleman succeeded in getting boots
of French make for his five daughters. The dress materials were
nothing but simple Scotch ginghams, but the new owners ex-
claimed over them as if they had been the finest silks or velvets;
they "willingly sacrificed luxuries for the simple comforts in these
dark days when the South needed all her children could
contribute." [35]

When called upon by the military authorities, the women always responded. One time Captain Wagner at Fort Moultrie
wanted several thousand cartridge bags in 24 hours. To get them

BLOCKADE-RUNNER *ARIES* WITH COLLAPSIBLE MASTS. DRIVEN
AGROUND AND CAPTURED IN BULL'S BAY, S.C. *Drawn by*
Emmett Robinson

done, many of the women sat up all night; others got up at
daylight to work on them. Within the alloted time the bags were
completed.[36] When sandbags were needed for the fortifications
and none were available, the women supplied bags made out of
their petticoats and pillow cases.[37] The ladies of Baltimore sent
some needles to the Soldiers Relief Association of Charleston,
which was making uniforms. Common pins became so scarce that
they were hoarded like precious jewels. Most of the women spent
most of their time working in the aid societies. As one woman
phrased it, "The war and all that is connected with it seems to
absorb every thought and feeling," but "it is a great satisfaction
to be able to help a little, to do something, if ever so little, for
those who have done and suffered so much for us." [38]

After Charleston and the surrounding countryside were occupied by Federal troops in early 1865, the men located the silver and jewels that, in many cases, had been buried for safekeeping. Their loot would certainly have been greater if the women had not already donated many of their jewels for various patriotic causes.

Up to the very last, Charleston made a show of being carefree, and there was a semblance of social life. Things brightened up perceptibly when Beauregard returned to Charleston to assume command. Balls and parties were given, which were enlivened by the strangers who were in the city. There was a French-speaking battery stationed on James Island and there were many Creoles on Beauregard's staff, and French was heard almost as much as English.[39] Because of the seriousness of the times, the St. Cecilia Society and the Jockey Club gave no formal balls. However, because the horses arrived, the Jockey Club decided to hold its three-day meet.[40] When Fort Sumter was not under bombardment, parties were given at the fort. Steamboats filled with ladies, usually accompanied either by General Beauregard or by Ripley, would leave the city in the afternoon, and when they arrived, a review of the garrison would be held. Afterward the regimental band would play, and there would be dancing and dinner. Occasionally the boat would miss the tide, and the ladies would have to wrap their shawls around them and make themselves as comfortable as possible until the boat floated with the incoming tide. The excursions added greatly to the morale of the men.[41]

But provisions and fuel became harder to get, and a special committee was appointed to look after the women and children who could not leave the city. By early 1862 there was a shortage of shoes. A factory had been built in Raleigh, North Carolina, to manufacture wooden shoes, but whether they were used in Charleston is not recorded.[42] Prices rose with the depreciation of Confederate money. In the spring of 1863, corn was selling for $225 a bushel and bacon was $1.00 a pound. By the next spring bacon had gone up to $5.00 a pound; butter was $6.00 a pound; sugar, $8.00 a pound; fresh shad, $10.00 each; tea, when obtainable, $15 to $25 a pound, according to quality. Along with the increased cost of food and merchandise, men's wages had risen, although they probably did not keep abreast of the inflation. Wages in early 1864 were $10 per day for common labor and $15 for skilled labor, but by this time a pair of boots was bringing $90; later they reached the fantastic price of $250. In spite of the inflation, people managed somehow to find money to make purchases whenever there was anything to buy.[43] During the early winter of 1864, one family was fortunate to procure a keg of salt pork which contained almost every part of the hog. One member of the family wrote: "One day we would have spare ribs and sausage for breakfast and backbone and spare ribs for dinner, and the next day by way of a change we would have sausage and spare ribs for breakfast and spare ribs and backbone for dinner, and so it went on, until we all got dyspepsia, except Anna, who seems to have the stomach of an ostrich." [44] Meat and butter were probably the scarcest commodities. As long as communication with the nearby plantations was open, rice was always available. From the beginning there was little salt. Salt works were established along the coast, and there was one at the foot of the west end of Tradd Street, but their output came nowhere near supplying the demand. The demand for salt became so acute that many of the nearby farmers resorted to digging up the ground of their smokehouses to get the drippings from the meat that had been hung up to cure. To get out the sediment, it was boiled, leaving a brownish-looking salt that was generally used for the stock and frequently for the table. Rice and hominy were boiled in a mixture of fresh water and sea water to make them palatable.[45]

Lead was equally as scarce, only it was used for a different purpose. Every valley of every roof was stripped, as well as every window sash in every window, and the lead was melted down to make bullets. One old lady refugeeing in Sumter somehow managed to get hold of some scrap lead and cast 526 musket balls, which she sent to the military authorities.[46] Brass, copper, and, in fact, every kind of metal were needed for cannon. Many of the churches gave their bells to be melted down, and women from all over the state sent in their preserving kettles to be used for munitions.

With the hospitals in Charleston full of wounded soldiers, and with sheets nonexistent, except those which came through the blockade, churches, public halls, and private dwellings were stripped of their carpets, which were used to cover the troops, and church cushions were used as beds.[47] One man, upon returning to Charleston, was amazed to see how well dressed the women were in spite of the shortage of materials. Every wardrobe had obviously been thoroughly ransacked, and every old dress had been reworked. One lady made hats by ripping up old hats and bonnets, dyeing them, and then remaking them. She had only two styles, the droop and the boulevard. The latter was small and round, turned over the head like a soup plate, and was usually trimmed in rosettes made from the palmetto tree.[48]

With General Robert E. Lee's admonition always in mind that the city must be fought "from street to street and house to house," General DeSaussure, writing to Governor Bonham, suggested that heavy traverses be placed at intervals in the streets and that the upper stories of the City Hall, the Court House, and the Fireproof Building be filled with rubble from the "Burnt district" so that they could be used by the troops as bombproofs in defending the city. The city was to suffer utter destruction before surrendering.[49]

In October, 1864, an epidemic of yellow fever was raging in Charleston, probably brought in by a crew member of a blockade-runner. By this time most of the remaining population was living in the upper part of the city out of range of the big guns, which were almost daily dropping their shells into the city. When the advent of cold weather killed the mosquito, the fever abated.[50]

With the capture of Savannah on December 21, 1864, most of the people in Charleston realized that the situation was becoming desperate. One Charlestonian said: "This has been a very blue Christmas for us as we have had besides the fall of Savannah, very bad news from Hood's Army, which seems to have been utterly routed in Tennessee and today we get news from Confederate sources of the death of General Price. Verily, Calamities thicken about us!" [51] By this time the city was becoming demoralized by the "laxity of morals and intemperance in drink." Yet a doctor on duty on Sullivan's Island wrote: "This ends the year. Our Confederacy is still existing and resolved upon securing her independence. She has met with many reverses lately, but these will only tend to nerve the army to more glorious deeds. God grant that the close of the coming year may meet us enjoying the blessings of peace." The spirit was there, but the Confederacy was fast collapsing and the end was near. [52]

3

"The true nature of the obstructions of Charleston Harbor is the profound mystery of the War." This statement appeared in the *New York Times* some time after the repulse of Du Pont's fleet, which occurred on April 7, 1863. [53] From the Northern point of view, it remained a profound mystery until the evacuation of the city two years later. Mine warfare was not unknown to the people of Charleston. As early as March, 1839, experiments were carried out in the harbor by Messrs. Taylor and Goodyear in their "Submarine Armour." The two divers affixed a keg containing 75 pounds of powder to the bottom of a small schooner with a long attached fuse. Two minutes and 40 seconds after the fuse was lighted the schooner "was torn into fragments, nay, almost atoms, by the explosive force." An interested spectator was Lieutenant R. S. Pinckney of the United States Navy; later to become an officer in the Confederate Navy.

On April 23, 1861, ten days after Major Anderson had surrendered Fort Sumter, Jefferson Davis called to Richmond the internationally known oceanographer Matthew Fontaine Maury, who had just resigned from the U.S. Navy. Davis placed him on an advisory council which was to make recommendations for the protection of the waterways. The Confederacy had no ships, but 3,000 miles of waterways, with numerous bays and rivers; this posed a very difficult defensive problem. Maury reasoned that torpedoes could take the place of heavily armed and armored gunboats—yet to be built—at a fraction of their cost. But he had difficulty selling his plan to the authorities; many felt that it was "unlawful warfare." However, as early as the middle of June, 1861, he gave a successful demonstration of an electrically controlled mine in the James River in Virginia. Maury was promoted to captain, with the title of "Chief of the Seacoast, Harbor and River Defenses of the South." In mid-July, 1861, Maury had already constructed some mines with the idea of destroying the Union men-of-war *Minnesota* and *Roanoke* lying in Hampton Roads, Virginia. Floating contact torpedoes were tied to each end of a rope and allowed to drift with the tide on the anchored ships. The idea was that the rope would foul the anchor chain and that one of the mines would be brought against the side of the ship and detonate, blowing a large hole in it at the water line. The venture was not successful, but two weeks later one of the mines was seen drifting in Hampton Roads, taken ashore, and examined. It was then, for the first time, that the Federal authorities ascertained that the mine was a potent factor and one to be dreaded.

In March, 1862, Jefferson Davis told the House of Representatives in Richmond that the "channels of approach to our principal cities have been and are being obstructed" and "that submarine batteries [mines] have been and are being prepared." His speech put every Union naval officer on the alert to look for mine fields at the entrance of every major harbor.[54]

A month after Davis's speech, an act was passed by the Confederate Congress providing that the inventor of any device that would destroy an enemy vessel be awarded 50 percent of her value.[55] About this time G. W. Randolph, secretary of war, stated: "It is admissible to plant torpedoes in a river or harbor, because they can drive off blockading or attacking fleets."[56] In October, 1862, the Torpedo Bureau was established in Richmond, with Brig. Gen. G. J. Rains at its head; a torpedo station was located at Charleston. The men attached to the bureau were sworn to secrecy and because of the dangerous nature of their duty were granted extra privileges. The Northern press cried out that this type of warfare was inhuman and outright murder, but the following year the Federal government had established its counterpart; the hue and cry of the press came to nothing.[57]

The harbor obstructions in Charleston, other than guns, fortifications, and men, consisted of (a) contact mines that carried a sufficient amount of powder so that, when struck by a vessel, they would blow a large hole in her bottom; (b) electrically controlled mines that could be detonated from shore when the ship was directly over them; (c) booms extending across the channel, so heavily constructed that a ship could not break through by ramming them (some booms had long ropes dangling from them to foul the propeller of any vessel); (d) and piling placed in the shallower parts of the harbor, making it necessary for any ship to remain in the main channel, where it could be destroyed by the concentrated fire of the guns from the various fortifications. In theory these obstructions were impregnable, but actually, because of the lack of suitable material, in addition to the strong winds and tides, they were far from effective. But they did keep a heavily armored and heavily gunned fleet at bay for nearly three years.

By June, 1862, a State Marine Battery Commission had been established, with J. K. Sass as its chairman. On June 26, Sass reported to the Executive Council that a Mr. Johnson had invented a torpedo and recommended its use. The council turned down the proposal on the ground that it would take a longer time for its construction than "our circumstances would allow," but, if it could be done more quickly, they would consider the application.[58] On October 8, 1862 (Beauregard had returned to assume command three weeks earlier), the council authorized Sass to appropriate $50,000 for the construction of a torpedo ram and "submarine torpedo," recommended by F. D. Lee, captain of engineers, and "desired" by General Beauregard. This was part of the money that was received by the state when it sold the gunboat *Chicora* to the Confederate government.[59]

The mine that could be detonated from shore played no part in the defense of Charleston other than psychological, but the contact mine played a tremendously important part. General Rains stated that it was the use of these mines that prevented the capture of the city. This minimizes the fighting done by the Confederate troops, but the famous Union admiral, David Dixon Porter, concurred in General Rains's statement.[60]

On his return to Charleston in September, 1862, General Beauregard, accompanied by General Pemberton, whom he was relieving, made a tour of inspection of the district. Beauregard was greatly disturbed by the incomplete conditions and the defective arraignments of the fortifications and obstructions. On September 29, after Pemberton had left, he held a council of war with his officers. Among the many recommendations was one that the boom be modified and made into smaller sections, and that rope obstructions be prepared; more significantly, Beauregard "determined to make use of floating torpedoes." [61] The construction of them was placed in charge of Capt. Francis D. Lee. As soon as he had a sufficient number completed, Beauregard ordered that "two lines of torpedoes be planted a few hundred yards" in front of the boom. Shortly after they were laid, a blockade-runner attempting to leave the harbor got her propeller entangled in the rope obstruction and, in fear of hitting a mine, dropped anchor until she could be towed to safety to have the ropes removed.[62]

Expecting an attack by the Union fleet, Brigadier General Ripley, who was in command of the Charleston district, issued a circular at the end of December, 1862, giving careful instructions to his fort and battery commanders about what to do and where to aim. At first the fire was to be concentrated on the lead ship. Ripley also said: "The position of torpedoes will be communicated to commanding officers." Apparently the mines had been laid in such secrecy that not even the fort and battery commanders knew exactly where they were.[63]

Dr. John R. Cheves, under whose direction the boom was being constructed, was directed to cease all work on it. The

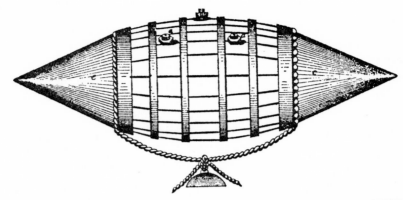

BARREL TORPEDO [MINE], A TYPE USED IN CHARLESTON HARBOR

general requested him to continue in charge of the mines that he was constructing for the harbor. Under his and Lee's direction, mines were being completed as quickly as possible.[64]

In addition to those laid in the main ship channel, General Beauregard ordered his chief of engineers, Major Harris, to have contact mines placed in the Wadmalaw, South Edisto, Dawhoo, and Pon Pon rivers. The object was to sink gunboats and other vessels which had been going up the rivers carrying marauding parties of soldiers. At that time the islands and adjacent areas were regarded as no man's land, and skirmishes frequently took place there.[65]

On the morning of April 7, 1863, General Beauregard wrote to Capt. John R. Tucker, C.S.N., who was in command of the Confederate naval forces in Charleston. Beauregard predicted that "the enemy, for the purpose of exploding our torpedoes, will precede their monitors with one or two armed 'alligators.' " This statement indicates that a large mine field was already present.[66]

It was fear of the contact mine that made Du Pont and his fleet so cautious in their approach to Charleston on the afternoon of April 7, 1863. Du Pont has been severely criticized for his timorous action, but he had every reason for his caution. Undoubtedly he had an excellent source of information and knew that mines

had been planted at the mouth of the harbor. He also knew that
the U.S. ironclad *Cairo* had been blown up by a mine the previous
fall in the Yazoo River and had sunk in twelve minutes, and he
remembered that one of his monitors, the *Montauk*, nearly had
her bottom blown by a contact mine just five weeks earlier. He
did not want the same thing to happen to any of the vessels under
his command this time.[67]

Captain Ericsson, the designer of the *Monitor*, was asked to
come up with some counter measure. He designed a large, cumbersome raft-like attachment that could be fastened to the bow of
a ship to explode mines far enough away so that they would do no
damage. This was called an "alligator." As predicted by General
Beauregard, one was attached to the bow of the *Weehawken* as
she came up the harbor. As the ship proceeded slowly, the "alligator" exploded a contact mine. The force of the explosion lifted the
Weehawken, but no damage was done to her hull. The other
vessels were careful to follow in the wake of the *Weehawken*.[68]

Major D. B. Harris submitted a detailed report of the action of
April 7, 1863, in which he said: "The enemy's evident and just
dread of torpedoes, as evinced in his preparation for their explosion by the 'devil' (alligator) or torpedo-searcher, should induce
us to multiply our defenses of that character in whatsoever manner they can be made available." [69] Quickly taking Harris's advice, Beauregard ordered that mines be placed in the Stono River,
with the hope of restricting the gunboats which were harassing
the Confederate shore batteries.[70] The following month, as soon
as more mines became available, he ordered all of the channels of
the inner harbor to be heavily mined: Two rows were laid in the
Folly Island channel between Castle Pinckney and Fort Ripley;
the Cooper River from near the foot of Broad Street to Shute's
Folly (behind Castle Pinckney) was made impassable; the Hog
Island channel at the west end of Sullivan's Island was also
rendered useless for any vessel attempting to bypass the main
channel; finally, Beauregard ordered "a large number of torpedoes [placed] in front of the obstructions between Forts Sumter
and Moultrie . . . to half way across." [71] The necessity of main-

taining a channel for the blockade-runners to go in and out was
the reason for not placing them all the way across. Later, some of
these mines exploded during the night, which greatly puzzled the
garrison of Fort Sumter. The following morning, however, it was
found that the detonations had been caused by heavy wave action.
At this time Capt. M. M. Gray was in charge of "Submarine
Batteries and Torpedoes" in the Charleston area.[72] Most of these
mines were placed when the ferocious fighting was taking place
on Morris Island. Should Morris Island be lost, and possibly
Sumter, Beauregard was determined that when the ironclads
tried to enter the harbor, few would succeed.

In an attempt to destroy some of the fleet, floating contact
mines were set adrift at high tide at Lighthouse Inlet. Some were
camouflaged to look like driftwood; others were tied at each end
of a rope. On a dark night in August, four lines, each with a mine
attached to either end, were set adrift by Captain Gray. In a few
minutes, three loud reports were heard, but in the darkness he
and his men were unable to see what had caused the explosions or
what damage had been done. The U.S.S. *Pawnee* was anchored
off the inlet directly in line with the drifting ropes. Had it not
been for the keen eye of the lookout on a nearby mortar schooner,
she probably would have been heavily damaged or sunk. One
mine exploded under her counter, blowing to pieces the captain's
launch hanging from her davits, but doing no damage to the hull.
The other mines were towed out of the way to a place of safety.
To prevent a repetition, the Union forces strung nets, buoyed
with fifteen kegs, across the entire inlet. Mines were set adrift in
the main ship channel, too, but with no results. As a counter-
measure, the larger vessels were equipped with net booms, and
tugs slowly circled them on the lookout for the mines.[73]

Even as late as January, 1865, 16 contact mines were laid
between Sumter and Moultrie. It was one of these that blew the
bottom out of the monitor *Patapsco* on the night of January 15,
causing her and 62 members of her crew to sink almost immediately. Many of the contact mines were also constructed by Capt.
Francis Lee.[74]

The electrically controlled mines would have been lethal if proper material had been available in the Confederacy. The weakness was the cable leading to them. One huge mine, made out of an old boiler containing 3,000 pounds of powder, was placed on the bottom in the main ship's channel just before Du Pont attacked with his fleet. During the attack, the flagship *New Ironsides* was directly over the mine for ten minutes while the engineers on Morris Island were trying to detonate it. After the action charges and countercharges were hurled back and forth as to why the mine had not exploded. Sabotage was mentioned; others said an artillery cart on Morris Island had accidentally cut the cable leading to the mine. What really happened, however, was that, when laying the cable, the steamer *Chesterfield* had run out of steam and drifted onto Sumter shoal. Able to move again, she continued laying the cable, but by this misfortune an extra mile of cable was put down. Therefore, instead of one mile of cable leading to the mine, there were nearly two miles. The electric impulse had to travel twice the distance anticipated, and it was too weak to jump the arc necessary to detonate the mine.[75] Another huge mine of this type was placed in "Poor Man's Hole," located off the battery at the confluence of the Ashley and Cooper rivers, on the morning of April 7, 1863, in case Admiral Du Pont succeeded in pushing by the forts and other obstructions. As an attempt was being made to retrieve it, it broke loose and drifted away, and it was lost in the darkness.[76]

Plans were made to lay 50 smaller floating mines that could be fired by electric contact from shore between Sumter and Moultrie, but after three unsuccessful tries the plans were abandoned because of swift current, the depth of the water, and lack of suitable cable.[77] At first the mines were made out of "tin-iron," but they collapsed when placed at a depth of eight feet of water. These were then discarded, and Lager-beer barrels were used in their place, for it was found that they could be submerged to a depth of 24 feet without leaking. In order to streamline them to better resist the current, nose cones were fitted on them, and they were coated with coal-tar and resin to make them waterproof.

They had a 13-gallon capacity and could hold enough powder to cause concern to any ship's captain. This is probably why Beauregard gave orders to Colonel Harris to "place a large number of torpedoes in front of the obstructions [booms with ropes attached to them] between Forts Sumter and Moultrie." These, of course, were contact mines.[78]

In anticipation of the continually expected naval attack, a heavy boom was placed between the two forts. Spars of timber strengthened by railroad iron and held together by large iron links were used in its construction so that it would be strong enough to resist the force of a vessel hitting it while under way. When put to the test, this proved to be inadequate, because the tide and wave action continually broke it up. The hard sand bottom between Sumter and Moultrie made it difficult for anchors to hold it in place in the swift current. Even granite blocks, which were to be used in the construction of the Customs House, were tried, but they, too, proved inadequate. In March, 1863, Beauregard wrote to Congressman Miles in Richmond that the "boom was a failure" and that he needed more guns to defend Charleston.[79]

At the time of the evacuation of Morris Island by the Confederate forces, Admiral Dahlgren wrote to General Gillmore requesting the use of a steamer to ram the obstructions in Charleston harbor. Gillmore curtly replied that he had no steamer to spare.[80]

Pilings were placed across the shallower parts of the harbor, making it almost impossible for any vessel to batter them down; this restricted ships to the channels, where in theory they could be destroyed by gunfire. Wind and tide action, in addition to the marine borer, made it difficult to keep the pilings intact.

Another type of mine was the "frame torpedo," which could be used only in shallow water. This consisted of timbers put together something like a raft, with one end pointing upwards. On the upper end containers were attached, each holding from 25 to 50 pounds of powder, which would explode on contact. This quantity of powder would have completely destroyed any small craft and probably would have done considerable damage to a larger one.

After the evacuation of Charleston, the task of clearing the mines from the harbor and adjacent waters fell to the navy. Two days after the city was evacuated, this hazardous undertaking was begun by M. M. Gray, formerly a captain in the Confederate Torpedo Service, who was employed by the Union navy to carry out this work. Having been imprisoned for six months by the Confederate authorities, ostensibly for irregularities in purchasing rope for the booms, but probably because he was under suspicion, he was released by the Union authorities. In a statement to Admiral Dahlgren, he said that since the previous August he had tried, several times, to desert to the Union navy.[81] Gray removed two contact mines from the ship channel near Fort Sumter. These were probably two of the 16 that had been placed there the previous month. In addition, he found three large electrically controlled mines between Middle Ground and Battery Bee. Gray said that the wires had been cut since the previous August, when he went to jail, but that no one but him knew it. Some floating contact mines were found in the Wando River near Cat Island and at the mouth of the river, where it joins the Cooper.[82] Frame torpedoes were located in the Ashley River; it was one of these that detonated as it was being towed out of the channel by the tug *Jonquil*. The force of the explosion was so great that three of the crew were injured and four fell overboard. The latter were rescued unharmed. In spite of this accident, the *Jonquil* was back on the job the following morning. The *Bibb* exploded a mine on March 17, which caused some damage, and two days later the *Massachusetts* "grazed one." [83]

In all, 61 contact mines, just about ready for use, were found in various locations. All were made out of small casks fitted with nose cones and covered with pitch. Most contained about 70 pounds of powder; a few contained more.[84]

Admiral Dahlgren probably came up with a logical explanation as to why so few anchored contact mines were found in the harbor when the city was evacuated. Of the 16 mines (one of which sank the *Patapsco*) laid the previous month by the Confederates, only two were recovered. Strong currents and wave action probably caused them to drag their anchors. A certain amount of leakage not only dampened the powder but caused them to sink; for this reason they were always having to be replaced. The 61 found on land were intended as replacements rather than for new mine fields.

Two carpenters who did nothing but make casks said that they were called upon to lay mines twice and that as many as four could be placed in position in an hour. Consequently, if the fleet showed any undue activity, mines could be quickly anchored in the main channel.[85]

The placing of the mines seems to have been a well-kept secret. According to Admiral Dahlgren, "the rebels were singularly fortunate in the precaution to keep their own counsel as to the nature of the submerged defenses." This is confirmed by General Ripley's "circular" of December 26, 1862, in which he said: "The position of torpedoes will be communicated to commanding officers." [86]

After the war, Capt. James H. Tomb, who had accompanied Lieutenant Glassell on the *David* when she rammed her torpedo into the *Ironsides* and later became her commander, wrote: "There were three lines of torpedoes between Fort Sumter and Fort Moultrie on Sullivan's Island, and also three [lines of] ropes attached to floats which had torpedoes attached to them. . . . The first line of torpedoes was directly between Fort Sumter and Fort Moultrie, leaving an open space between the torpedoes and the fort in the channel for ships to pass through." [87] General Beauregard, speaking of Charleston, said that he "had planted about one hundred and twenty-five torpedoes." Gen. G. J. Rains, chief of the Confederate Torpedo Bureau, who spent some time in Charleston during the war, was more specific: "There were 123 torpedoes planted in Charleston harbor and Stono River." No one could speak with better authority on the subject than he.[88]

There was much ridicule of the Union fleet, not only by the

Confederate forces but also by Union General Gillmore, who accused Admiral Dahlgren of timidity. It was generally stated that the Union fleet was afraid of empty beer kegs. Actually, the beer keg made an excellent mine, especially when it was loaded with a heavy charge of powder and armed with several detonators that would go off at the slightest touch.

4

On New Year's Day, 1864, not a gun was fired from either side. After five months of almost continuous bombardment, there was silence. But the respite was of short duration; the next day a few shots were fired from one of the Confederate batteries on the Union battery on Black Island. The relative peace was completely shattered when Union guns opened up at long range on the city. The firing was slow at first, but the tempo increased, and in a 9-day period in the middle of January over 1,500 shells were fired at the city. By the end of the month the long-range bombardment

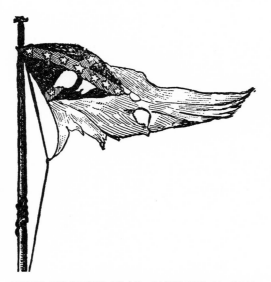

FORT SUMTER'S FLAG, JANUARY 29, 1864

diminished, probably because ammunition ran low and the guns wore out.[89]

For a while there was little activity on the part of the Union forces. Large numbers of troops were being withdrawn and sent to Florida to participate in the so-called "Florida expedition," the objective of which was to dislodge the Confederate forces in the eastern part of the state and maintain Jacksonville as an open port. To keep Beauregard from knowing about the number of troops that were being withdrawn, on February 9 the Union forces under General Schimmelfennig, with 3,000 to 4,000 troops and six pieces of artillery, made a strong demonstration on John's Island, where they were met and repulsed by General Wise's brigade, composed mostly of Virginia troops. Casualties were light on both sides.[90]

To meet the threat in Florida, Confederate troops were being withdrawn not only from the Charleston and Savannah area but from other parts of the Confederacy. Col. W. W. H. Davis, then commanding officer on Morris Island, reported that a regiment camped on Mt. Pleasant had struck its tents and departed and that at least one, if not two, regiments on James Island had done likewise.[91]

In order to keep the Union forces from knowing how many of his troops were being withdrawn, Beauregard ordered every available gun on James and Sullivan's islands to open up on Black Island, a small, marshy island between Morris Island and Fort Johnson, at 2 A.M. on February 12. Shortly afterward, Gen. W. S. Walker, stationed at Pocotaligo, South Carolina, was ordered to throw up rockets and beat drums at night "to prevent him [Union] from sending troops to Florida." This had no effect, however; the Union troops continued to pour into Florida. With both sides rushing men to the scene of action, comparatively few were left in the Charleston area. About the end of February, even Beauregard left Charleston, to assume command of the Florida operations.[92]

On February 17, 1864, the Confederate submarine *Hunley* sank the sloop-of-war *Housatonic*.

In the meantime, Brigadier General Evans, who had been released from arrest while at Cokesbury, South Carolina, had returned to Charleston and was waiting to resume command of his brigade. Beauregard was unable to convene a board of examiners because all the generals senior to Evans were in Florida. He wrote to General Cooper in Richmond about Evans, saying, in part, that "he had become a disturbing element in his brigade, that some of the superior officers in it occupied relations towards him of such fierce personal hostility as to create inextinguishable discord, that the confidence in him of a large number of the officers and men of the brigade had become materially impaired." Shortly afterward Beauregard wrote directly to Evans that he was not opposed to his resumption of his command but that, "for the good of the service," it would be best if the brigade to which he was assigned was in some other department. Beauregard did not want him under his command. Richmond probably had no other officer to send as a replacement and restored Evans to active service, on March 21, 1864, as commander of the First Military District (the Charleston area).[93]

While in Florida, apparently in an attempt to forestall Evans's return to active service, Beauregard wrote to Maj. Gen. Daniel Harvey Hill, who had been a corps commander under Gen. Braxton Bragg of the Army of Tennessee. Relations between Bragg and his officers had reached such a state that President Davis went out to investigate the trouble. Hill, who was probably more outspoken than the others about Bragg's blundering, was relieved of his command and sent to his home in North Carolina. The famous cavalry leader Gen. Bedford Forrest violently refused to serve any longer under Bragg. For his heresy he too was relieved of command and sent to Mississippi.[94] Bragg, who was a favorite of Davis, was allowed to retain his command. General Hill declined the offer to come to Charleston, stating as his reason that he could not do so until his record had been cleared.[95]

Beauregard angered General Bragg in a disagreement over the question of commissary supplies. By this time Bragg was in Richmond and had been promoted by Davis to general-in-chief.

While still in Florida, Beauregard wrote Bragg that, if his requests were denied, "the interests of the country, my own self-respect, nay, a proper regard for my reputation, would require that I should ask to be relieved from the command of this military department." Apparently the incident blew over, for Beauregard retained his command.[96]

By this time the shortage of ammunition within the Confederacy had become critical. Maj. J. T. Trezevant, head of the Charleston arsenal, received orders from General Gorgas, chief of ordnance, to reduce his monthly consumption of lead to 10,000 pounds, regardless of circumstances. The issue to armies "must be limited to 3 rounds per man per month." The firing of the heavy guns was greatly reduced, both for this reason and because they were wearing out. One gun burst after having been fired over 1,700 times.[97]

On April 2, 1864, Maj. Gen. J. F. Gilmer, who was stationed at Savannah and was second in command of the department, was ordered to Richmond to resume his former duties as chief of the Bureau of Engineers. His successor was Maj. Gen. Samuel Jones. Beauregard wrote Gilmer regarding Jones: "I hope he will do, but from what I hear I fear not." He went on to say that none of his officers, even though recommended, ever got promoted, and he spoke of his department as the "Department of Refuge." [98]

Three weeks after Brigadier General Evans had assumed command of the First Military District, Brigadier General Ripley, who was senior to Evans, wrote Beauregard's chief of staff that he intended to resume command of the First Military District. It is not clear what had happened to Ripley in the interim, but it was not unusual for him to disappear for long periods of time. As a way of getting around this embarrassing situation, the First Military District was subdivided. Evans was assigned to the third subdivision, which was composed only of the upper end of Sullivan's Island, "with headquarters within the limit of his command." Beauregard had every reason to call his command the "Department of Refuge"; he should have called it the "Department of the Damned." Evans's stay on the upper end of Sullivan's

Island was short; he and his brigade were soon ordered to Wilmington, North Carolina.[99]

On April 15, 1864, Beauregard received the following telegram from General Cooper in Richmond: "Repair with the least delay practicable to Weldon, N.C., where instructions will be sent to you." Beauregard replied that he was leaving the department "with great concern" and asked that General Hill relieve him and be his second in command. At the time, Hill was in Charleston looking over the situation. Hill, however, declined to accept the wording of his orders and returned to his home in North Carolina. On April 19, General Jones arrived; the following day Beauregard left for North Carolina.[100]

Gilmer was leaving Savannah, and his post was offered to Maj. Gen. Lafayette McLaws. Before accepting the command, McLaws wrote to General Bragg asking if he would give an endorsement and, if possible, that of President Davis to show whether or not his being ordered to Savannah could be regarded as a reflection upon his fitness for a command in the field. Apparently he got the endorsement, for he reported to Jones for duty in Savannah. McLaws had been relieved of active duty with his division, was charged with "neglect of duty to the prejudice of good order and military discipline," tried, and found "guilty of part of specification, and guilty of charge. Sentence: to be suspended from rank and command for sixty days. Proceeding, findings, and sentence disapproved." [101]

General Gillmore, having received a severe setback in his Florida expedition with the overwhelming Confederate victory at Olustee, was ordered to send 7,000 to 11,000 troops to Fortress Monroe, Virginia. This corps, with some additions, was to be commanded by him. Grant was gathering troops for the Battle of the Wilderness, which was to cost him so many lives. Replacements were sent to Hilton Head, but most of them were recruits.[102]

Many of the troops around Charleston were being sent to bolster Gen. Joseph E. Johnston's command at Dalton, Georgia. The withdrawal of most of his troops drew a blast from Ripley.

In this case he had every reason to be worried about the defense-less condition of his district. At this time General-in-Chief Hal-leck wrote Grant: "It will require 60,000 men three months to take Charleston." Halleck went on: "I am satisfied that Admiral Dahlgren's letter was intended simply as an excuse in advance for the inability of the ironclads to accomplish anything against Charleston." [103] With the harbor heavily mined, it is doubtful whether any ironclad could have entered without being blown up, not to mention the fact that dozens of heavy guns were ready to fire on the channel which they had to use. General Schimmelfen-nig, stationed on Folly Island, was ordered to keep the Confeder-ate forces on James Island as actively engaged as possible so that none could be withdrawn and sent to Virginia. From deserters Schimmelfennig gained an accurate report of what troop move-ments were taking place as well as what changes were being made in the defenses. [104]

At the end of April, 1864, General Schimmelfennig was the commanding officer on Folly Island. With him were Col. Leopold von Gilsa, Col. Eugene A. Kozlay, Col. Adolph von Hartung, and Col. William Heine. When Gillmore learned that he was going to command the troops that were being sent to Fortress Monroe, he took nearly 20,000 of his best troops. Even with such a large withdrawal, Schimmelfennig had 6,000 troops on Morris and Folly islands, backed up by another 8,000 at Port Royal and Hilton Head. Ripley had, at the same time, less than 2,000 troops with which to defend Charleston. In the meantime, Gen. Samuel Jones, having sent off his last infantry brigade to Virginia, wrote to Commodore D. N. Ingraham, commander of the naval forces in Charleston, asking him to muster into service all of the employ-ees and detailed men that were in the navy department. He said that he had requested the mayor to organize the fire department into companies for service, as well as the employees of the rail-road companies. The manpower shortage had reached a desperate state. [105]

As soon as the members of the fire department were organized as the Fire Battalion, as many as could be spared from their duties were sent to the defenses on James Island. The situation had become so critical that General Jones did not have enough troops to man the guns. A little later, Flag Officer John Randolph Tucker, who had succeeded Commodore Ingraham, organized the Charleston Naval Battalion, composed of sailors on the inactive Confederate ironclads, which had been lying in the harbor for months. Jones accepted the battalion and tried to arm the sailors as well as he could. Desperately in need of reinforcements, he wrote to the adjutant general in Richmond, but he received a laconic reply from Bragg: "For the present General Jones' only reliance for assistance must be on the reserves." There were no troops left in the Confederacy to send to Jones.[106]

By the end of May, 21 ships were anchored at the mouth of the harbor; 24 others were anchored in nearby inlets. Jones had every reason to be apprehensive of an attack. When Union forces landed on James Island, which turned out to be a feint, Jones wired Brigadier General Robertson to "send every available man by the most expeditious route." But there were few available men to send.[107]

By the middle of June, with 13 warships and 46 transports anchored in Port Royal Sound and additional troops being landed on Folly Island, it was obvious to General Jones that a major attack was about to take place. Espionage was not needed by the Union forces. All they had to do was read the Charleston newspapers to find out that the Second Regiment, South Carolina's artillery, was no longer in Charleston; that two companies of the German Light Artillery had been disbanded; that General Jones was calling for the reserves to report to the Charleston District on July 5; and that there had been no telegraphic communication between Charleston and Virginia for over a week.[108]

At the end of June, every available Union soldier was being brought from Florida, Beaufort, and the Northern District and assembled for another assault on Charleston under the command of Brig. Gen. John P. Hatch. Major General Foster was to accompany the expeditions, "but only to give advice and assistance." The transports and men-of-war sailed under sealed orders, which were given to the commanding officer of each transport and clearly marked on the outside: "To be opened after leaving the harbor _____ miles, and after steering southerly in a _____ direction. After which the lights of every boat in the expedition must be extinguished." [109] General Jones was trying to get every man in position to meet the attack, but where would it come? He did not have long to wait for an answer, but instead of a single assault on a given place, it was a five-pronged attack.

5

"To capture Richmond would be grand, but to capture Charleston would be glorious." [110] Maj. Gen. John G. Foster had assumed command of the Department of the South when General Gillmore was transferred. General Foster was thoroughly familiar with the area; he had been engineer officer on Fort Sumter and was with Major Anderson when he capitulated on April 13, 1861. Apparently he was the only officer with Anderson who received a brevet for the part he played at Sumter, and according to Anderson he was the least deserving. [111] He had wanted to return to the Charleston area, but, since he was unacceptable to General Gillmore, he had spent most of the war on the North Carolina coast. In relinquishing command, General Gillmore had turned over between 18,000 and 19,000 well-equipped troops. [112] The Confederate forces in the Charleston area, on the other hand, had been depleted more and more in order to bolster the armies of Northern Virginia. The situation had become so desperate that the Charleston fire companies at times had to act as firemen and soldiers; even the Citadel cadets were kept on a stand-by basis. [113] A Confederate deserter said: "They have taken away nearly all the troops from James Island." General Foster was aware of the conditions in Charleston, and of the manpower shortage. He decided, therefore, to see if he could not be the conqueror of the "Cradle of Secession."

Foster wrote General-in-Chief Halleck on June 15, 1864, that Fort Sumter could be taken with 5,000 men provided with scaling ladders.[114] With that number of men he would be doubly sure of success, for the garrison at that time consisted of not more than 300 troops. Halleck replied that he could not see the object of capturing the fort unless the fleet advanced and captured Charleston. He went on to reveal his feeling about the navy: "I think it is now pretty well demonstrated that they will do nothing of the kind." [115] Furthermore, he declared, Sumter, if captured, could only be held at great sacrifice of life. In light of the fact that the Confederate forces had held the fort under intense bombardments for over three years with comparatively light losses, this seems a rather strange remark. General Halleck said that, since the Southern coast had been stripped of Confederate troops, General Grant wanted Foster to make raids and attacks in order to tie up as many of the remaining troops as possible.

General Foster's first plan of attack differed somewhat from that of his predecessor; he wanted to land troops on the mainland by coming through Dewee's Inlet or Price's Inlet to the north of Charleston and take Mt. Pleasant and Sullivan's Island from the rear.[116] Admiral Dahlgren thought this was a good idea, but when he was asked if he would run his fleet over the mine fields and by the fortifications into the inner harbor and up the Wando River to protect the army's flank, he refused; consequently, the plan was dropped.[117]

General Foster then devised another plan which varied from that of General Gillmore in one respect only—that he would attempt another landing on the southern tip of James Island. In addition, he would try an amphibious assault on Fort Johnson, an attack on Johns Island, and a heavy bombardment by the fleet in the Stono River on Battery Pringle. He also planned to ascend the North Edisto River, cut the Charleston and Savannah Railroad at Adams Run, and, if possible, destroy the railroad bridge at Jacksonboro. General Foster's plan required that five attacks take place almost simultaneously.

By the middle of June, the Confederate command was aware that an attack was in the making; they received information that 13 warships and 46 transports were anchored in Port Royal

Sound.[118] General McLaws in Savannah was alerted, as it could not be determined where the attacking force would strike. However, on July 1, the gunboat *Dia Ching* was ordered to drag for mines at the mouth of the Stono River. When this occurred, Gen. Samuel Jones was convinced that one of the attacks would be launched on the lower end of James Island, as in 1862 and 1863; he was correct in his surmise.[119]

On the morning of July 2, 1864, the Union forces landed several regiments, about 2,500 men, on the southern end of James Island under cover of heavy fire from two monitors and several gunboats. Maj. Edward Manigault made an obstinate stand at River's Causeway, but his small force, with two field pieces, was outflanked before reinforcements arrived and both guns were captured.[120] These were the guns that had been jettisoned when the Union tug *General Milton* had hung up on the piling at Willtown Bluff and was subsequently abandoned and burned. This incident had occurred the previous July at the time of the diversionary attack up the South Edisto River when the Union forces attempted to destroy the bridge of the Charleston and Savannah Railroad at Jacksonboro. Confederate forces had succeeded in raising the guns from the bottom of the river.[121]

Pushing forward, the Union forces firmly entrenched themselves. During the fighting on July 2, Col. Wilhelm Heine of the 103d New York, who was in command of some of the attacking force, made himself conspicuous by wearing white clothes; he was noticeable throughout the day for his gallantry.[122] Every Confederate soldier took a shot at the conspicuous figure, but, since they were outfitted with obsolete Belgian guns that were unreliable even at short range, Colonel Heine was not injured.[123]

With Confederate forces so weak on the island, Brigadier General Taliaferro could not counterattack until he had enough troops to insure some measure of success. He tried to get men wherever he could. One source was Fort Johnson, from which Taliaferro diverted 100 men, leaving only a skeleton crew to man the guns in the fort. This was just what General Foster wanted;

when he made his amphibious assault on the fort, there would be little resistance.

On the night of July 2–3, 1864, the troops who were going to make the amphibious assault assembled at Paine's Wharf on Morris Island. They consisted of the 52d Pennsylvania Volunteer Infantry and the 127th New York Volunteer Infantry along with 60 men from the Third Rhode Island Artillery, a total of 1,000 men.[124] Because of the low tide, some of the assaulting craft ran aground. The plan was for each boat to cross the harbor until it was opposite the beach (which no longer exists) between Battery Simkins and Fort Johnson, turn left, pull hard for shore, and make attack with bayonets. They did not get under way until 2 A.M. on July 3. The pilot lost his way in the tortuous channel, and the boats were rowed by landlubbers, and confusion soon prevailed. Finally Colonel Hoyt of the Pennsylvania troops succeeded in finding a narrow channel leading to the beach, but by this time they had been discovered by the Confederate forces, who opened up on them. However, because they could not depress their guns sufficiently, most of the fire passed harmlessly overhead. Colonel Hoyt and some of his men landed and pushed toward Fort Johnson. In the meantime, the remaining boats began to retreat, though no order had been given, leaving Colonel Hoyt and his men isolated in front of the fort.[125]

While this was going on Lt. Col. Joseph A. Yates was at Fort Johnson with nearly half of his garrison withdrawn to meet the threat on the lower end of James Island. Fortunately for him, a picket of 30 men, under the command of Lieutenant Lowndes, fired from nearby Battery Simkins on the rear of the assaulting troops.[126] Realizing that he was receiving no reinforcements and that resistance was useless, Colonel Hoyt and 139 men surrendered, the only thing he could have done under the circumstances.

Of the troops in the boats, 119 were killed or wounded. Only darkness saved the expedition from destruction.[127]

Colonel Yates had more prisoners than he had troops with

which to guard them. He therefore ordered the prisoners into the bombproof until he could get enough men to prevent their escape. With the arrival of the Citadel cadets, the prisoners were taken to the city for safekeeping.

The Federal plan of attack was well conceived, but it ended in failure. If successful, the amphibious assault on Fort Johnson would have been disastrous to the defenders, especially if the Union forces on the southern part of James Island had completed a pincer movement and joined the amphibious troops, which would have given them the entire eastern side of the island. With this foothold, it is doubtful if enough Confederate troops would have been available to hold the entire island. And, as General Beauregard had always said, James Island was the key to Charleston.

An inquiry was instituted to ascertain the cause of the failure of the amphibious assault. The blame was placed on the commanding officer, Colonel Gurney of the 127th New York, who, instead of accompanying the assault, remained at Paine's Wharf, the point of embarkation. Mention was also made of the "want of dash, energy, and authority on the part of the subordinate officers." The report cited the expedition as a "highly important one" and praised Colonel Hoyt and the men who landed with him for their bravery.[128]

On the same day General Jones wrote a letter to Colonel Yates thanking him and his command "for the gallant and complete repulse of the enemy this morning." During the attack Colonel Yates received a slight wound in the hand.[129]

Meanwhile General Taliaferro, who was in command of the defenses of James Island, was in desperate need of troops. The Naval Battalion, consisting of seamen from the gunboats and some Georgia troops, had been sent to him, 375 men in all. But he wanted to know what had happened to the Fire Brigade and if the Citadel cadets could be sent to him.[130] On July 3—the assault on Johnson was made before daylight that same day—another skirmish took place on James Island. The Confederate forces re-established their lines, which brought them within range of the guns of the monitors and gunboats in the Stono River. The Union lines were also within range of the heavy guns of the Confederate works, but when their ammunition ran low, they had to stop firing.[131]

With so many attacks taking place, and with the Confederate manpower shortage so desperate, General Jones wrote to Brig. Gen. James Chesnut, Jr., in Columbia, asking him if there was a regiment of clerks, detailed men, and employees which could be sent immediately to the defense of Charleston. He asked for them again the next day. Somehow General Chesnut gathered together enough men to send 13 companies to General Jones. Most of them had probably had no previous military experience.[132]

On the same day some of the Union fleet had gone farther up the Stono River and were furiously bombarding Battery Pringle, located at the extreme right of the works built across the island.

The previous day, a force of about 4,000 men had landed on Seabrook's Island under the command of Brig. Gen. John P. Hatch. They had orders to go to John's Island, push forward to the upper end, and then cross to the mainland and cut the Charleston and Savannah Railroad. If that was not possible, they were to destroy the railroad bridge over Rantowles Creek with artillery. The landing at Seabrook's Island was not completed until the next day, July 3.[133]

Simultaneously, Brig. Gen. William Birney continued up the North Edisto River with 1,200 infantry and two pieces of artillery. He had orders to place torpedoes under the tracks at Adam's Run and destroy the railroad bridge at Jacksonboro. General Foster accompanied General Birney's expedition.

General Jones asked that troops be sent to him from every available source. A regiment on Sullivan's Island was sent to James Island, and troops were even diverted from General Johnston's hard-pressed forces near Atlanta to help repel these attacks. In addition, troops were being rushed over from Savannah.[134]

General Birney's expedition continued up the North Edisto River, accompanied by the gunboats *Dia Ching*, *Wamsetta*, and *Geranium*. They landed almost unopposed at White Point, on the lower end of Slann's Island, and moved slowly up the island until they ran into a Confederate battery on the other side of King's (McLeod) Creek. In the meantime, the three gunboats had come up the Dawhoo River, taken positions in one of the upper reaches, and proceeded to shell the battery from the distance of a mile. At first their shells fell within the lines of their own advancing troops, but this situation was corrected by lengthening the fuses. The superior gunfire of the navy, in addition to the two guns with the 1,200 troops, should have silenced the Confederate battery, making the crossing easy.[135]

In his report, General Foster stated that "General Birney, however, did not move forward with enough alacrity." He went on to say: "at the intersection of the road by a creek, he found a small force of the enemy posted with a few pieces of artillery. I ordered General Birney to cross the creek with a boat (which I furnished him, on wheels, for emergencies like this), while I went up Dawhoo Creek with two small gunboats . . . and shelled the battery on the flank. General Birney, however, soon reported his incapability to carry out my order, and asked to withdraw, which I was forced to allow him to do." The fighting at King's Creek lasted only two hours. Why General Birney did not push forward and cut the railroad at Adam's Run will probably never be known. Had he done so, it would probably have prevented or at least greatly delayed the reinforcements being sent from Savannah and from General Johnston's army. General Foster was disgusted with General Birney's attitude; he ordered his 1,200 troops to James Island to reinforce General Schimmelfennig's forces and sent General Birney back to Florida.[136]

A naval battery, manned by marines from the fleet, accompanied General Birney's troops. When the order for retreat was given, they did not receive word. Consequently, the marines constituted a rear guard and had to haul their guns by hand over two miles. They eventually embarked in safety.[137]

Back at James Island on the night of July 4–5, the monitors and gunboats threw shells at the Confederate lines at five-minute

intervals. The Stono River was full of ships, and General Taliaferro begged for a torpedo boat to be sent down to attack some
of them. One of his later reports read: "The torpedo-boat did not
come down." [138] No reason was given; a night attack might have
caused at least a temporary withdrawal of the Union ships and
enabled General Taliaferro to extend his lines. On July 4, General Birney's 1,200 troops, which had been withdrawn from
Slann's Island in the North Edisto River, landed on James Island
and joined those of General Schimmelfennig. This gave him
numerical superiority over the Confederate troops there.[139]

On July 5, things were moderately quiet on James Island. In
the morning the Federal forces formed two lines of battle, but
there was no concerted forward movement. The next two days
were similar; skirmishes took place along the entire Confederate
line across the island, and there was one heavy bombardment
from the Union batteries on Morris Island and the fleet.[140]

On July 8, the monitors *Lehigh* and *Montauk*, with the *Pawnee*, *MacDonough*, *Racer*, and *Para*, shelled Battery Pringle, on
the Stono River side of James Island, from a distance of 3,200 to
4,400 yards. Several guns at Battery Pringle were disabled, and
the gunners at times had to take to their bombproofs. The only
gun that could reach the monitors was a ten-inch Columbiad. The
report of the Captain of the monitor *Montauk* stated: "The accuracy of the rebel fire was also considerable." [141]

The official reports state that 347 shots of all caliber were fired
at Battery Pringle and that 298 were effective. The shooting was
remarkably accurate, considering the size of the target and the
range. The ships farther down the river were shooting unopposed
into the Confederate lines on James Island.[142]

The following day the ships again opened up on Battery Pringle, but during the night the Confederate forces had erected a
seven-inch Brooke gun. This was fired with such accuracy that it
drove the wooden vessels in the fleet out of range and even kept
the monitors at a distance. That night, with the flood tide, the
Federal forces set adrift three fire rafts to burn the unfinished

bridge between James and John's islands. However, a naval detachment brought them ashore before they reached the bridge, and the bridge remained intact.[143]

On July 10, the Confederate commander noted troops embarking from Legareville on John's Island and movements among the troops on James Island. However, at 8 P.M. that night an amphibious assault was made on Battery Simkins, 1,100 yards in front of Fort Johnson. Prior to the assault, the battery received a heavy bombardment from the guns on Morris Island. Therefore, when the assault occurred and some boats effected a landing, the gunners were ready and immediately repulsed the attack. They were reinforced by a section of Louisiana light artillery and a company of marines who had been rushed there to strengthen the garrison.[144]

That night the lower part of James Island received a heavy shelling from the fleet anchored in the Stono River. After eight days and nights of unremitting bombardment, on July 11 the Federal forces sailed away to Hilton Head.

In the meantime, General Hatch with his 4,000 troops marched up John's Island. Because large numbers of his troops became exhausted from the intense heat, the marches were limited to only a few miles each day. Had he pushed forward before the Confederate forces could concentrate troops to meet him, he probably would have been able to occupy the entire island without opposition and to achieve his objective by crossing over to the mainland and destroying part of the Charleston and Savannah Railroad at Rantowles. But because he advanced so slowly, the Confederate troops were able to concentrate in sufficient numbers to hold him at "Bloody Bridge" and ultimately cause his withdrawal.

In addition to the 4,000 troops under his immediate command, General Hatch received 1,000 reinforcements, who landed at Legareville on John's Island and joined his troops as they moved up the island. This made an imposing force. By July 5 they had marched up the Stono River side of John's Island to a point opposite Battery Pringle and occupied a strong position on Burden's Causeway, with a marsh in front, the Stono River on the right, and an almost impenetrable jungle on the left. A small bridge on the main road up the island crossed the marsh; aside from that, the only access to this strong position was by an almost impossible flanking movement. Furthermore, the Federal position was above Battery Pringle on the opposite side of the Stono River on James Island; this gave General Hatch's artillery an excellent opportunity to enfilade the battery.

Troops from Savannah and from General Johnston were arriving. On July 7, General Saxton—General Hatch had temporarily relinquished his command to assume over-all command—advanced with his troops against the Confederate rifle pits and some artillery that was located on a slight rise of ground on the other side of the bridge on Waterloo plantation. But the Federal forces, consisting of only one regiment and one battery of artillery, were unsupported and therefore repulsed. General Hatch stated in his report of the action: "Had the advance been supported, the enemy's artillery would have been captured." [145] Why more Federal troops were not committed is not clear. The Federal forces maintained a position on the far side of this bridge.

The next day the heavy guns of Battery Pringle opened on the Union camp. The bursting shells made it uncomfortable for the troops, but General Hatch's laconic report stated "no casualties." Some time during the day he received more reinforcements, the Montgomery brigade of the ill-fated Edisto River venture, which gave him an overwhelming numerical superiority over the Confederate forces.

At 5:45 on the morning of July 9, a brigade of Georgia troops under the command of Col. George P. Harrison, Jr., who had been hurriedly brought to meet the threat, advanced against the Federal lines and were met by heavy fire. Their advance was bloodily contested, and they had over 100 casualties. The casualties would probably have been even heavier had it not been for the dense smoke arising from the Federal lines. Apparently there was no wind that morning to dispel it, and in some places it was so thick that it was impossible to see a man at five paces.[146]

When the Federal forces began to be pushed back, the reserves —also consisting of Georgia troops—were committed to action; this forced the Federal troops to fall back over the bridge to their strong entrenchments on the other side. Brigadier General Robertson, in order to hold down his casualties, ordered Colonel Harrison not to continue the assault, but to hold the ground already taken. During the action some of the Federal forces succeeded in turning the right flank of the Confederate line. This threat was met by a small company of only 21 men under the command of Capt. Tillman H. Clark of the Second South Carolina Cavalry, who fought dismounted. When it was over, only eight men remained; seven had been killed and six wounded. Capt. William B. Dean, with 13 men of the same regiment, charged the left flank of the Union lines, throwing it into confusion and stopping the movement.[147]

On July 9, Admiral Dahlgren went ashore on John's Island to confer with General Foster, whom he found in conversation with General Hatch. The two generals thought that the Confederate forces on John's Island consisted of between 3,000 and 4,000 men. The next day General Foster said that he did not think the Confederate forces were as strong as he first supposed. The general said "that he had done all he intended," and Admiral Dahlgren wrote in his diary, "I am utterly disgusted." [148]

The fight on John's Island was spoken of by the Confederate forces as "Waterloo" and by the Union Forces as "Bloody Bridge." [149]

The entire time the fighting was going on at these places along with the amphibious assaults, Fort Sumter was receiving a terrific pounding. Actually it was the beginning of the third major bombardment, and in order to keep the citizens of Charleston from becoming complacent, a heavy fire was kept up on the city.

The first 11 days of July were tense for the defenders of Charleston. A Northern source said: "The combined movements, admirably planned, against a weaker enemy came to naught, for want of concerted action and persistence in attack. At every point we largely outnumbered the enemy." Had General Hatch committed all of his troops, he might have overrun John's Island, "and the James Island lines thus flanked, Charleston would have fallen." [150]

Brig. Gen. Alexander Schimmelfennig, who was in command of the troops on James Island, was of Prussian birth and spoke English with a heavy accent. With typical Prussian thoroughness, he prepared a map of John's Island showing every road and creek. He sent out a reconnoitering party with the map and gave them orders to halt where the road turned to the right, as his map would show, and await further directions. But when they arrived at the designated point, they found that the road turned to the left. They sent a man back for further instructions and to explain their dilemma. The general replied, "The map is all right; but this country is all wrong." He even had his own peculiar way of dealing with the mosquitoes, "by smearing his face with kerosene oil, choosing to endure the odor rather than the loss of blood." [151]

8

The Third Great Bombardment of Sumter

AT THE FIRST SIGN OF DAY ON THE MORNING OF JULY 7, 1864, a shell was seen hurtling through the air. This was followed by a loud report from one of the heavy guns on Morris Island. The third great bombardment of Fort Sumter had begun. General Foster wrote to General Halleck in Washington that he thought Fort Sumter was being strengthened—which, indeed, it was—and that in his opinion it was necessary to demolish the walls that were still standing. Consequently, he had ordered a renewal of the bombardment, with all of his guns aiming at the remaining section of the wall that was still in a vertical position. As soon as it was flattened, he planned to float down and explode huge mines against it until the wall toppled over. Then he would make an amphibious assault and carry the fort by storm.[1]

At this time five simultaneous attacks were being made in and around Charleston. The violence of the bombardment was a sur-

296

prise to the garrison; for the past several months the firing on the fort had been somewhat desultory. The fire from the huge 300-pounder rifle guns on Morris Island was doing severe damage to the remaining part of the wall. The other heavy rifled guns were concentrating their fire along with this, and the crest of the wall was breached in three places. At one place the gap was only 20 feet above the water. Every evening at dusk the garrison would place wire fencing and other entanglements on the slope, and sharp-pointed wooden stakes were placed in the gap to pierce anyone who might try to jump down onto the parade ground.[2] The fort would have crumbled under the constant gunfire, but every night about 150 workmen repaired the damage done by the heavy shells. Darkness made it impossible to sight the big guns with any accuracy, so their firing stopped at nightfall, but then the mortars started up. The fuses were carefully timed, and it was no problem to shoot accurately with them. Consequently, the garrison was under bombardment both day and night. To alleviate some of the firing on Sumter, Confederate guns on Sullivan's Island, along with those on James Island, would attempt to silence the huge rifles on Morris Island. But soon, since their shelling was having little effect and ammunition was running low, the gunners were ordered to desist. By this time General Foster had brought up some 13-inch mortars, and the concussion of the heavy shells jarred the casemates deep below. At times the mortars from Morris Island were fired by volley.[3]

The transfer of troops and supplies could be made only at night. The vessels would leave Charleston after dark and tie up at Sumter dock. The mortars, which had the range precisely, would fire all during the night on the chance of hitting some vessel or barge unloading troops and supplies; it was not unusual for one to be sunk or badly damaged.

On the first day of the bombardment, the flagstaff was shot down three times and the flag torn to pieces, but each time it was replaced. At one point the Union forces started using incendiary shells, but they stopped when they realized that they were doing no harm in the rubble of the fort.[4] With the wall crumbling under the incessant fire from the heavy guns, and with no material available to make necessary repairs, Capt. John Johnson, the engineer at Sumter, requisitioned 1,000 bags of sand a night to be delivered to the fort. These had to be lightered over at night, and even then it was a hazardous undertaking to unload them undetected in order not to bring the fire of the mortars. All the while the workmen repairing the damage were under fire from the mortars, and several of them were killed or wounded.[5]

Sumter was now under the command of Capt. John C. Mitchel, an Irishman who had thrown in his lot with the Confederacy. After lunch on July 20, he climbed to the western angle of the gorge to scan the movements of the blockading vessels anchored offshore prior to writing his daily report. Standing just outside the sentry post, which was well sandbagged, he rested his spyglass on the parapet for a better look. The day was clear, and he could easily see the gunners busily loading and firing the heavy guns on Morris Island. While he was watching, one of the large mortar shells burst about 80 feet overhead, probably because its fuse was too short. The garrison was used to such things and thought little of it. Captain Mitchel did not even duck back into the protection of the sentry post, but continued to make his observations. One large fragment of the shell fell and struck him on the left hip. Getting him down the narrow staircase to the lower part of the fort was a difficult task. Though he was bleeding profusely, he remained in perfect control of his faculties; four hours later he died.[6] The following day Capt. Thomas A. Huguenin assumed command.

During the three weeks the fort had been under bombardment it had received an average of 392 shots a day, most of it fired by the huge 200- and 300-pounders and the 13-inch mortars. General Foster and Admiral Dahlgren went on the monitor *Lehigh* to see what effect the gunfire was having on the fort. After examining it carefully, the admiral wrote, "The northeast front still stands erect, and the work is nearly impregnable." [7]

Toward the end of July, while he was making a tour of inspection, Captain Johnson was severely wounded in the head by a fragment of mortar shell. He had been on continuous duty as engineer officer at the fort for eight months.[8]

With the incessant firing, the big guns on Morris Island either burst or otherwise became disabled. The 200-pounder Parrott in Fort Putnam burst on round 1300, a remarkable record.[9] One ten-inch Columbiad had 18 inches of its muzzle blown off by a premature explosion but continued firing anyway. Foster's chief of artillery was becoming worried about his guns, as he had very few in reserve. Finally he was compelled to call on the navy for replacements. Admiral Dahlgren quickly replied to his request by lending him six 11-inch guns, along with their crews and ammunition. In addition, the navy loaned some ammunition for the 200- and 300-pounder Parrott guns so that there would be no abatement in the rate of fire.[10]

On the evening of August 28, the garrison heard a large explosion near the wharf on the city side of the fort. Three nights later a similar explosion took place off the east angle of the fort. General Foster, aided by Admiral Dahlgren, was floating rafts loaded with powder into the harbor. They were towed into position by one of the monitors, and about 1,000 yards from the fort they were cut adrift; it was hoped that they would land under one of the walls. Because they exploded prematurely, however, no damage was done.[11]

General Schimmelfennig, commanding officer on Morris Island, had a better idea for breaching the wall. Calling in the colonel, he said, "Ze Rhode Island Artillery will bore ze hole in ze wall of Sumter about ze size of ze barrel, then you will take ze keg of powder in ze boat, place it in ze hole made by ze artillery, then ze fort and yourself will be blown to h——l; and your whole duty as a soldier will be done." The colonel asked for time to carry out the plan, but, since no one volunteered for the job, it was never put into effect. The gunners of the Third Rhode Island Artillery were experts, who could shoot down the flagstaff almost at will, but it is not quite clear how the man with the keg of powder was to row undetected from Morris Island and squeeze himself and the keg into the hole.[12]

General Foster came up with another idea, which apparently died aborning. He wrote to the chief of staff in Washington that he wanted to have two assaulting arks built, each capable of holding 1,000 men. They were to have 50 oars on each side and draw 26 inches of water when loaded. Sharpshooters would be elevated to pick off any men of the garrison who showed themselves; no mention was made of the garrison shooting the sharpshooters as the arks approached the fort. Assaulting ladders 51 feet long, operated by machinery, would enable the troops to land on the parapet. Since the garrison seldom exceeded 300 men, Foster, with 2,000 men, wanted to be sure of success.[13]

In spite of the incessant bombardment, which at times would slow down, the fort was being strengthened. It was actually stronger at the end of the bombardment than at the beginning.[14]

Officially the third great bombardment ended on September 8, 1864, after a period of 60 days and nights, during which 14,666 rounds were fired at the fort. The initial bombardment, which occurred when Major Anderson was in command, lasted about 34 hours. After a short lull, the last—and eighth—minor bombardment started; it ended eight days later on September 18.

The Union troops were working at Battery Gregg, a distance of 1,400 yards from the fort, but they were forced to take shelter from the sharpshooters on Sumter who were using Whitworth rifles armed with telescopic sights. From this time until Charleston was evacuated, four and a half months later, the fort received sporadic shots from the batteries on Morris Island.

At the end of the second great bombardment, General Gillmore spoke of the artillery arrayed against Sumter as "probably excelling any artillery ever brought on the field in siege operations."[15] The artillery used for the third great bombardment was even heavier, for it had more 300-pounder Parrott guns and 13-inch mortars.

At the end of the third great bombardment, Col. W. W. H. Davis of the 104th Pennsylvania wrote: "the tenacity with which the enemy held on to Sumter was wonderful."[16]

The five-pronged attack had failed. In spite of an overwhelming superiority of troops and equipment, in addition to the backing of a heavily armed fleet, the Charleston defenses had once more proven impregnable. Realizing the hopelessness of the situation, the authorities in Washington ordered Foster to send his best troops to Virginia. Foster wrote Admiral Dahlgren that "the land force now under my command is inadequate to make any aggressive movement." Writing to Halleck in reference to the withdrawal of troops, Foster said that it would leave him very weak "if the rebels attack us, which I consider out of the question." The last thing General Jones had in mind was an amphibious assault against Morris Island; consequently, both sides remained on the defensive.[17]

Firing on Fort Sumter continued day and night through the first week in September. Since Sumter was still defiant, the large guns opened on Charleston at 15-minute intervals, aiming so that their shells would fall in the upper part of the city. On September 1, General Schimmelfennig was invalided and sent home. When his transport passed through the fleet, he was given a salute, a token of the respect Admiral Dahlgren had for him. His successor was Brig. Gen. R. Saxton. As he was setting up headquarters on Morris Island, he wrote Foster that he had "no faith in the impregnability of Charleston" and came up with the idea of conquering the city. "With a sufficient number of Parrott, 30, 100, and 200 pounders, well sighted, with good iron carriages capable of firing an elevation of 40 degrees . . . Charleston is at your mercy." His idea was not exactly a novel one; furthermore, he seemed to have overlooked the fact that Charleston had been under bombardment for a year with no thought of surrendering. Because the guns were worn out and ammunition was scarce, his plan was not put into effect. Even after the majority of his troops were withdrawn, in October Saxton still had 5,500 men on Morris Island.[18]

Meanwhile, Admiral Farragut, in spite of the many obstructions, had entered Mobile Bay. Beauregard wired Jones from Petersburg, Virginia: "Renew rope obstructions near Sumter, and put down new ones near mouths of Ashley and Cooper

rivers, with proper piling. Farragut may soon pay you a visit."
Beauregard did not want Farragut to repeat his achievement at
Charleston.[19]

General Ripley was in trouble again. What had been generally
known, but somehow overlooked, finally came to light, and it was
so serious that some action had to be taken. When General Jones
was in Summerville, less than 30 miles from his headquarters,
Ripley took exception to an order issued by Major Lay. Lay,
Jones's senior assistant adjutant and inspector general, had authority to give orders when Jones was temporarily away from
headquarters. Ripley, writing to General Cooper in Richmond,
had to pass his correspondence through the chain of command.
Jones endorsed Lay's order and explained why he had given it.
He went on to say of Ripley: "he not only refused to receive and
obey them, but came in person to my headquarters, very much
excited, and in violent, rude and insulting manner and language,
accompanied with threats to Major Lay, refused to obey or receive orders from my headquarters." General Cooper thought
that Ripley was guilty of insubordination, but when his letter
reached Richmond, President Davis sent Beauregard to Charleston to investigate the case. Talking to some of the officers, Beauregard ascertained that on July 2, the day of the attack on James
Island, Ripley had been "indulging in the use of intoxicating
liquors" and was "in no condition properly to discharge his duties." Beauregard recommended that he be sent to active service
in the field, "where time, reflection, and a stricter discipline may
have their favorable influence over him." When the report
reached Cooper, he endorsed it with the recommendation that
Ripley be removed from "his command and no other assignment
be accorded to him." The signalmen on Morris Island had read a
Confederate message which inquired when Beauregard would be
there, and General Saxon, newly arrived on Morris Island, proposed to give him a salute with one of his 200-pounder Parrott
guns. Whether the salute was given is not mentioned.[20]

In seeking a replacement for Ripley, Beauregard recommended
that his chief engineer, Col. D. B. Harris, be promoted to Briga-

dier General. Harris had been in Charleston for months and was thoroughly familiar with its defenses. Unfortunately, just when Beauregard was making his recommendation, Colonel Harris was dying of yellow fever.[21]

Lt. Gen. William J. Hardee, one of Hood's corps commanders, was ordered by President Davis to assume command of the department of South Carolina, Georgia, and Florida. Hood had been highly critical of him for the way he had handled his corps at the Battle of Peachtree Creek, Georgia, and the two were barely on speaking terms.[22] On October 5, 1864, Hardee arrived in Charleston and assumed command.[23] A week later, Major General Jones was assigned "to the command of a district to be known as the District of South Carolina, which will comprise all of the state except the Third Military District. He will establish his headquarters for the present at Mount Pleasant." Learning that Harris was dead, Beauregard recommended that either Col. Alfred Rhett or Col. William Butler be promoted to replace Ripley. Instead, Maj. Gen. Robert Ransom was ordered to report to Hardee for assignment to the First Military District in South Carolina. Actually, Ransom was being sent to replace Jones, who was absent on sick leave. The First Military District really was the "Department of the Damned." [24]

In inspecting the troops, Hardee found that many of the men were "absolutely barefooted" and that, with blankets lacking and almost no quinine available, many were suffering from malaria. In addition, most of the men were raw militia, former office-workers, or firemen turned soldiers, and there was an acute shortage of ammunition.[25]

9

A City of Ashes

1

ATLANTA WAS IN FLAMES; SHERMAN WAS ON THE MARCH. BUT the big question was, in what direction? Atlanta is actually north of Charleston. When he started his famous "March to the Sea," probably Sherman and only one or two others knew his actual destination. The Confederate forces were certainly vague as to his intentions. Shortly after leaving Atlanta, Sherman could have (1) turned east towards Augusta, seized the railroad, and coming via Branchville, South Carolina, attacked Charleston from the rear; (2) turned south, taken Macon, and then turned toward Montgomery, Alabama, or even Mobile; (3) continued in a southeasterly direction, crossing the middle of Georgia, with Savannah as his goal. He chose the latter.[1] While the "Georgia Campaign" did not directly affect the siege of Charleston, it had an indirect effect upon it. Defenses had to be strengthened to meet the attack from the rear; troops had to be stripped from Charles-

304

ton's meager garrison to meet the threat; and generals were shifted around.

Sherman started off with over 70,000 battle-seasoned veteran troops, consisting of four corps in addition to Kilpatrick's cavalry. Opposing this large force was a comparatively small group of militia and reserves under Gen. Howell Cobb and Wheeler's cavalry. The cavalry did an excellent job of harassing the large army on its front and flanks, but in no way impeded its advance. Hood and his army were no longer a threat to Sherman's rear guard, as he was marching in the opposite direction toward Tennessee. Opposing armies were turned back to back marching away from each other.[2]

Immediately after Sherman left Atlanta in the middle of November, 1864, Lieutenant General Hardee, whose headquarters were in Charleston, was ordered by the secretary of war to send the Fifth Georgia Regiment, then in South Carolina, to General Cobb to defend Macon. Hardee's command was extended immediately to embrace all of that "part of Georgia, south of the Chattahoochee River," and he was instructed by the authorities in Richmond to obtain "an adequate force by concentrating detachments from garrisons, convalescents from hospitals, reserves, militia, and volunteers." Brig. Gen. James Chesnut, Jr., commanding the South Carolina Reserves, volunteered to go to Georgia with his reserves, provided he retained his rank. His request was granted by President Davis. Hardee, who had gone to Macon to meet the threat, telegraphed General Cooper in Richmond. "Believing the enemy has gone to Augusta, I have ordered all the disposable forces from this place to that point."[3] Sherman still had the Confederates guessing. Even General Halleck in Washington was unaware of his destination.[4]

With Hardee in Georgia, on November 21, 1864, Maj. Gen. Robert Ransom was ordered to Charleston to assume command of the Charleston area. General Jones, who was still in Charleston, but junior to Ransom, wrote to Flag Officer J. R. Tucker asking that James H. Tomb, formerly a member of the crew of the *David*, be sent to Georgia to lay land mines on the roads used by the advancing army. With the manpower shortage so desperate, every means had to be used to stop the advance of Sherman's mighty force.[5]

The situation was critical. President Davis created a new command for General Beauregard—"one of vast territory, cruel responsibilities, small resources and slight power."[6] The area stretched from the coast of Carolina and Georgia to the Mississippi River; it was a huge department, but there were few troops, the largest body being under the command of Hood and subject only to a certain vague supervision by Beauregard. Hardee's command was extended to include "Southern Georgia." Bragg, who had been cooling his heels in Wilmington, was sent by Davis to see what was going on and report back to him. He left Wilmington for Augusta with "but few troops, most of these being reserves which cannot be taken from the State." In the states' rights tradition, it was necessary to get special permission from the governor for any local troops, other than those in the Confederate service, to cross a state line.[7]

A week after Sherman had started on his march, General Jones in Charleston wired General Cooper in Richmond that he thought Sherman's destination was Charleston and that he did not have a sufficient number of troops to defend the city. By this time Jones was becoming extremely nervous; the following day he wired Cooper that he was in "daily expectation of an attack by water" and that reinforcements were absolutely essential.[8]

Beauregard, upon his arrival in Macon, wired Davis that he thought Sherman was headed for Port Royal, South Carolina; while Hardee, who was in Millen, Georgia, was under the impression that Sherman was going either to Augusta or to Savannah. Apparently every Confederate general had a different opinion as to his ultimate destination. With conditions becoming chaotic, the secretary of war enlarged Beauregard's command to be "extended to the coast and embrace all combinations against the present movements of the enemy." This was a somewhat nebulous area, with almost no troops, and Beauregard had only a nominal command.[9]

By the end of November, Jones was still requesting reinforcements from Richmond. Cooper sent back a telegram to the effect that Jones "must be as fully aware as the authorities here that there are no reinforcements that can be sent to you." Two days later General Bragg in Augusta sent a peremptory wire to Jones, telling him that he must hold the Savannah Railroad. In spite of the fact that Beauregard was in command of the entire area, and that Hardee was specifically in command of the district that included the Charleston and Savannah Railroad, Bragg had to enter the picture and add to the confusion.[10]

On November 30, 1864, a Union force of 5,000 troops, plus a naval brigade consisting of 500 sailors and marines under the command of Brigadier General Hatch, landed at Boyd's Neck and started for Grahamville, South Carolina, a few miles away, with the object of cutting the Charleston and Savannah Railroad. The commanding officer of the district, Col. Charles J. Colcock, had few troops available and, realizing that this was more than a demonstration, immediately called for help. In Savannah there were two brigades of Georgia militia under the command of Maj. Gen. Gustavus W. Smith, C.S.A. On receiving the news of the landing, Hardee ordered Smith and his militia to go to the support of Colcock. Because of the seriousness of the situation, Smith took his militia, "which was in direct violation of the statute organizing and calling them into service"—they could not leave the state of Georgia—and arrived at Grahamville at 8 A.M. on the morning of November 30. The militia, along with the few troops under the command of Colcock, met the advancing Union forces at Honey Hill, a short distance away. Along with five guns served by some South Carolina artillerymen they held off the advancing force. Later in the day they were reinforced by the 47th Georgia regiment, which was in Confederate service. Even with reinforcements the total number came to only 1,400. After fighting all day and sustaining 764 casualties, the Union forces withdrew at nightfall. The Confederate forces, who had been fighting from behind low breastworks and rifle pits, had only 50 casualties. Other reinforcements arrived too late to participate in the fighting. The day was saved by the courage and fighting ability of the Georgia militia. The next day they were relieved and returned to their native state.[11]

Instead of waiting to let Hardee, Smith's commanding officer, report his victory directly to General Cooper in Richmond, Bragg rushed off a telegram from Augusta, with instructions that copies be sent to President Davis and the secretary of war. The same day, General Hardee sent a restrained wire to Cooper telling him that the enemy "were met and repulsed." [12]

By early December it was apparent that Sherman was headed for Savannah. To meet the threat, 1,300 militia under Colonel DeSaussure were sent from Augusta to Savannah by way of Charleston. Jones was instructed by Hardee not to stop them, but to make sure that they reached their destination. Actually, the militia under DeSaussure was to have gone to Grahamville, but instead the cadets in Charleston were rushed there to join the militia. With the Union forces landing additional troops at Boyd's Neck, and knowing that the railroad again was their objective, Hardee ordered Jones to make his headquarters at Pocotaligo and "take immediate charge of the forces for the defense" of the railroad.[13]

With Hood moving in a westerly direction, opening the gap between his army and Sherman's, Beauregard, in Augusta, decided that Charleston would be the best place to set up his headquarters. He ordered Jones to overflow the rice lands, obstruct the roads with trees and plant land mines in them, and do everything possible to impede the advance of Sherman's troops. Beauregard told Hardee that no relief could be sent him; he also said that if he had to choose between the safe withdrawal of his troops and the safety of Savannah, he was to sacrifice the latter. It was soon apparent that the fall of Savannah was inevitable.[14]

Governor Bonham of South Carolina begged President Davis to send troops from Lee's army in Virginia to resist Sherman. Davis replied that he had corresponded with General Lee on the subject, but that because of Grant's recent operations it was impossible to do so. General Lee wrote Davis "that if troops were removed from his command, and sent south it will necessitate the abandonment of Richmond." [15]

Davis suggested to Beauregard that the gunboats in Charleston Harbor assume the offensive and sally out of the harbor, "perhaps to destroy his [the Union] depot at Port Royal." However, one gunboat had no motive power, and the others were unseaworthy and underpowered; if they had encountered heavy weather, they would have foundered before reaching Port Royal.[16]

On December 15, 1864, General Bragg wired from Charleston to Col. John B. Sale, military secretary to Davis, that "my services not being longer needed in this department, I shall leave this evening for Wilmington and resume my command." Two days later Bragg had a talk with Beauregard in Charleston and wired Davis that "after a conference with General Beauregard, I determined, as he had no duty to assign me, to return to Wilmington." With Bragg leaving Charleston, Davis ordered his aide-de-camp, Col. J. C. Ives, to proceed to Charleston and "keep me advised from there, either by telegraph or mail, of what is transpiring in that quarter." With such instructions, Ives did not have to go through official channels in reporting to Davis.[17]

With Savannah about to fall, General Cooper wired Beauregard that he "hoped Savannah may be successfully defended, but the defense should not be too protracted to the sacrifice of the garrison. The same remark is applicable to Charleston." Both cities could fall, but the garrison must be saved. Davis then wrote Beauregard that, if Savannah and Charleston were evacuated, he would "postpone such action as long as the safety of the army will permit." On December 21, 1864, Hardee evacuated Savannah, bringing out his troops, his light artillery, and most of his supplies. The heavy guns were spiked or otherwise disabled. The following day General Sherman wired President Lincoln: "I beg to present you, as a Christmas gift, the City of Savannah, with 150 heavy guns and plenty of ammunition, and also about 25,000 bales of cotton." [18]

In the immediate vicinity of Charleston, the situation was tense during the six weeks of Sherman's "March to the Sea," but little fighting took place. The defenses were stripped of the few troops that were available, and the rest were standing by, ready to leave at a moment's notice. The bombardment of Sumter dwindled to almost nothing. General Hatch, on Morris Island, stated in his report: "The battering of Sumter is, in my opinion, an idle waste of material, and the guns would be useless in an attack on Charleston." After two and a half years of almost incessant bombardment, with some of the heaviest guns then known, Sumter was still impregnable. Shortly afterward General Halleck informed Foster that Lieutenant General Grant wanted the expenditure of ammunition upon Charleston and Fort Sumter discontinued. Even Grant realized the hopelessness of the situation.[19]

In spite of the feeling that existed between the opposing forces, a spirit of chivalry prevailed. The war was still to be fought under certain rules, and the amenities of gentlemen were to be observed. During an exchange of prisoners under a flag of truce, Capt. Thomas Huguenin, then commanding officer of Fort Sumter, who had not been notified of the exchange, had his sharpshooter—he had no guns—fire on the batteries on the upper end of Morris Island. When he found out that he was firing while a truce was in force, he wrote the following note: *"Officer Commanding U.S. Forces on Morris Island: Sir:* Having just been informed by the authorities of the continuance of the truce which commenced yesterday, I beg leave to offer an apology for having fired upon batteries on the northern end of Morris Island this morning with sharpshooters. I have the honor to be, very respectfully, your obedient servant, *T. A. Huguenin, Captain, Commanding*." Equally courteously, Colonel Hallowell replied: "Your communication of this A.M., in explanation of the firing from Fort Sumter is received. The explanation is satisfactory. The firing from the batteries on this island will be discontinued. I have the honor to be, very respectfully, your obedient servant, *E. N. Hallowell*, Colonel Command."

Brig. Gen. Augustus Schimmelfennig, who had been on sick leave for two months, returned as commanding officer on Morris

Island.[20] Maj. Gen. Daniel Harvey Hill was ordered to "report without delay" to General Beauregard for duty at or near Charleston. Hill, who held the temporary rank of lieutenant general while under Bragg's command at Chattanooga, but who had dared to criticize Bragg's tactics, was relieved of command along with several other generals. Consequently, President Davis refused to present confirmation of his rank as lieutenant general to the senate; therefore he reverted to his former rank of major general.[21]

The Charleston and Savannah Railroad was the vital link between the two cities. Once Savannah was evacuated, it was essential that the rail line be held open so that Hardee could withdraw his troops. The Union forces naturally wanted to obstruct the passage of the trains carrying the retreating Confederate troops, but they also wanted to maintain the line in case Sherman decided to make a direct advance on Charleston. Hardee, having returned to Charleston, ordered McLaws, who had been in Savannah, to take immediate command of the railroad from Hardeeville and Pocotaligo. Awaiting Sherman's 60,000 battle-seasoned veterans were 7,000 Confederate troops stationed between Grahamville and the Combahee River. Fortunately for them, Sherman and his troops turned inland to continue their march across the Carolinas.[22]

It was only a question of time before Charleston would have to be evacuated. Beauregard, therefore, asked General Cooper in Richmond if the base of his operations should be toward North Carolina or Georgia. The following day instructions were sent to Hardee to make, "silently and cautiously, all necessary preparation for the evacuation of Charleston, should it become necessary, taking at the same time, the proper steps to save the garrison." [23]

Sherman, writing from Ossabaw Sound, Georgia, to Halleck in Washington, gave a report of his activities during the last month in which he stated: "The whole army is crazy to be turned loose in Carolina; and with the experience of the past thirty days, I judge that a month's sojourn in South Carolina would make her less bellicose." [24]

Things were singularly quiet in Charleston in the middle of December; not a shot had been fired by either side for over a week. Strangely enough, the forces on Morris Island were apprehensive of an amphibious assault by the Confederates. Dry brush was piled outside the forts and batteries so that it could be ignited to silhouette the advancing troops.[25]

On the last day of the year Sherman wrote to Adm. David Dixon Porter, the commanding officer of the North Atlantic Blockading Squadron, that he proposed to march through South Carolina, "tearing up railroads and smashing things generally, feign on Charleston, and rapidly come down upon Wilmington from the rear, taking all their works in reverse." Sherman had a mania for tearing up railroads.[26]

In spite of the seriousness of the situation in South Carolina, when Beauregard heard of Hood's crushing defeat by Thomas near Nashville, Tennessee, he requested to be relieved of the general command of the department of South Carolina, Georgia and Florida, as he felt his presence was absolutely required at Montgomery with the Army of Tennessee. What was left of Hood's army was in bad shape. Beauregard, writing final instructions to Hardee, told him that he had no reason to expect succor from an army of relief and that he must save his troops for the defense of South Carolina and Georgia.[27] The year 1864 ended with the Confederacy split in half. It was the beginning of the end.

2

"Should you capture Charleston, I hope that by some accident the place may be destroyed, and if a little salt should be sown upon its site it may prevent the growth of future crops of nullification and secession." These words were written from Washington by General Halleck, chief of staff, to General Sherman.[28] Sherman replied: "I will bear in mind your hint as to Charleston and don't think salt will be necessary. When I move the Fifteenth Corps will be on the right of the Right Wing, and their position will bring them naturally, into Charleston first; and if you have watched the history of that corps you will have remarked that they generally do their work up pretty well. The truth is the whole army is burning with insatiable desire to wreak vengeance upon South Carolina. I almost tremble at her fate." [29] The 15th Corps had made a name for itself by pillaging and burning everything between Atlanta and Savannah. Sherman's reply was written from Savannah while he was regrouping and reorganizing his army for the campaign of the Carolinas, which was to end in Greensboro, North Carolina, with the surrender of Gen. Joseph E. Johnston and what was left of his army. After nearly four years, the combined might of the Federal army and navy had been unable to capture Charleston; for this reason Sherman decided to bypass the city. He wrote to General Foster: "I regard any attempt to enter Charleston Harbor by its direct channel or to carry it by storm of James Island as too hazardous to warrant the attempt." [30] In spite of the fact that the garrison had been stripped of most of its troops, Sherman had a healthy respect for its fighting ability. In order to prevent any more troops being withdrawn from its defense, he asked Admiral Dahlgren to have his gunboats make demonstrations up the Edisto and Stono rivers. Writing to General Halleck, he said: "Of course, I shall keep up the delusion of an attack on Charleston always and have instructed General Foster to watch the harbor close from Morris Island . . . and to make a landing at Bull's Bay. . . . Admiral Dahlgren will also keep up the demonstration on Charleston." This was sound military strategy; the series of demonstrations tied down every available soldier, and none could be spared to oppose Sherman. [31]

Admiral Dahlgren, complying with Sherman's request, would send in picket boats and at times monitors to test the obstructions that guarded the harbor. On the night of January 15, 1865, the monitor *Patapsco* hit a mine when she was searching for obstructions. She sank in less than a minute; 62 members of her crew went down with her, and 43 were saved. The *Patapsco* sank 800 yards off Sumter, and only the tip of her stack showed above the water. The mine which she struck had recently been placed there by Capt. John A. Simon of the Confederate torpedo service.[32] After the loss of the *Patapsco*, Dahlgren called his captains together for a conference and advised them that they would be called upon to make an effort to take Charleston. He suggested an attack on Sullivan's Island, a run by Sumter and an attack on Fort Johnson, and a run all the way in the harbor and an attack on the city. His captains approved of the attack on Sullivan's Island but thought the other suggestions much too risky.[33] The admiral then went to Hilton Head to confer with General Foster, who approved of the attempt on Sullivan's Island. However, when the plan was submitted to General Sherman, he vetoed it; he wanted to stay with his original plan of effecting a landing at Bull's Bay, about 20 miles north of Charleston, and invading Charleston from the rear.

On January 30, 1865, Maj. Gen. Q. A. Gillmore was ordered to relieve Major General Foster as commander of the Department of the South, with headquarters at Hilton Head.[34] The war was nearing its end, and in order to save face Foster said that he was going on a leave of absence because of wounds received in the Mexican War, nearly 20 years previously. Admiral Dahlgren wrote in his diary, "I have an entire contempt for Gillmore because of his conduct last year. . . . So I briefly wrote to the Department [Navy] stating that with his [Gillmore's] arrival to take command, and asking to be relieved . . . I shall lose some prize money, too, but I will keep my self-respect which is better." [35] A week later Sherman's plan to bypass Charleston caused him to recall his request in order to fight it out "with the Rebels in front and Gillmore in the rear." Even Grant, in a letter to Halleck, expressed chagrin at the appointment of Gillmore.[36]

At the end of January the garrison of Fort Sumter consisted of about 300 men, composed of the 32d Georgia Volunteers and two companies of the First South Carolina Artillery. Improvements were being made daily, everything was in good order, and the fort was more impregnable than ever.[37] Her three guns on the northeast face still dominated the entrance of the harbor. These, along with the guns on Sullivan's Island and the recently laid mines, made it extremely perilous for any ship to enter.

In spite of the gravity of the situation, the Confederate officers, who had become bored, used the military signal to invite each other to cock fights. By this time all signals were being read easily by the Federal signalmen.[38]

As late as February 11, both Jefferson Davis and General Beauregard thought that Sherman had Charleston as his objective.[39] They had some reason for thinking so; that night an amphibious assault was made on Battery Simkins near Fort Johnson, and a landing had been made the previous day on the southernmost end of James Island. The amphibious assault on Simkins came to little. As soon as the barges were seen, they were met by artillery fire from Sullivan's Island and Simkins and withdrew without attempting to land.[40] The landing on James Island was much more serious. It was effected under the heavy fire of the monitors *Lehigh* and *Wissahicken* and a mortar schooner, and the Confederate pickets were driven back. While the landing was being made, the gunboat *MacDonough*, formerly a New York ferryboat, and a mortar schooner ascended the Folly River and opened fire on Secessionville by way of diversion.[41] Two regiments with field guns and two companies of skirmishers came ashore. Advancing under the protective fire of the gunboats, they got as far as the rifle pits that were being held by 131 men of the Palmetto Battalion under the command of Maj. Edward Manigault. With orders to hold the line to the last extremity, this small group made a heroic and stubborn resistance until overcome by sheer numbers, after sustaining casualties of 33 percent. Major Manigault was severely wounded and taken prisoner, and the rifle pits were carried by a front and flanking attack.[42]

The Union forces did not push the success forward; later that evening they fell back to Cole's Island under cover of the guns of the monitors. General Hardee thought the attack was merely a demonstration. However, to keep him off balance, the naval gunfire was continued for the next few days and nights, and the small number of troops remaining on James Island had to be on a constant alert. By this time most of the soldiers had been withdrawn and were heading towards North Carolina.[43]

In the meantime, General Hardee was alerted that another attack was about to take place by the sight of 18 vessels lying off the bar. On February 13, 13 of these vessels arrived off Bull's Bay.[44] The bay was extremely shallow, and all of the vessels except those of exceptionally light draft had difficulty getting close to shore; several ran aground in the attempt. Soon after their arrival, a gale began to blow from the northeast; that, along with the shallow water, made the bay utterly impassable, and, to make matters worse, it was impossible for the heavier gunboats to get within three miles of the shore, which deprived the assaulting troops and the lighter boats of any supporting naval gunfire. The next day an attempt was made to land in Sewee Bay, actually a part of Bull's Bay, with launches and small boats, but again they grounded in the shallow water and had to turn back. The entire time they were under fire from two guns on the shore, but apparently a moving boat was too small and elusive a target; only one hit was registered, which disabled a boat howitzer.[45] The following day the gale continued, making a landing impossible. Because of the crowded conditions on the transports, the troops were landed on Bull's Island. For two more days landings were attempted, but each ended in failure. Finally, on the morning of February 17 (Charleston was evacuated that night), troops went ashore at Graham's Creek near Buck Hall Plantation, where there were some Confederate guns. Seeing that the troops had finally effected a landing, the few remaining Confederate soldiers withdrew. Most had already been recalled in preparation for the evacuation.[46]

The assault on Bull's Bay accomplished nothing but preventing any Confederate troops from marching to Georgetown and then inland. The Confederate troops in Christ Church Parish, where the landing took place, were evacuated by steamer to Strawberry Ferry by way of Cordesville and then to St. Stephen's.[47]

While these demonstrations were going on, the guns on Morris

Island increased their rate of fire on the city. More shells were fired during the night, probably to prevent anyone from sleeping. By this time the range of the guns had increased to such a degree that shells were exploding in houses well above Calhoun Street.[48]

On February 14, General Beauregard sent instructions for the evacuation of Charleston. Most of the troops were to meet at St. Stephen's, located on the Northeastern Railroad (now the Seaboard Coast Line), then by train to join the troops retreating from Columbia, and eventually to move to North Carolina. Beauregard ended by saying: "It's [Charleston's] loss does not jeopardize the safety of the State of South Carolina, but the loss of its garrison would greatly contribute to that end." Rumors were spreading in Charleston that the city was to be evacuated, everyone was demoralized, and many tried to leave by any means available. Food by this time was extremely scarce, with flour bringing $1,200 a barrel (Confederate currency).[49] On February 15, most of the troops received word to be ready for evacuation. Detailed instructions were sent to Brig. Gen. Stephen Elliott on exactly how it was to be done; he was to spike his guns and destroy his gun carriages, but he was not to attempt to burst his guns or blow up his magazine so that the Federal forces would not know his intentions.[50]

General Beauregard had been urging Lieutenant General Hardee to hurry the evacuation so that there would be no danger of his troops being cut off on their way to North Carolina. When it was learned that Hardee was ill, with a threat of typhoid, Maj. Gen. Lafayette McLaws was rushed to Charleston to assume command.[51]

Union signalmen, who were reading all of the Confederate dispatches that were being sent between the city and the forts, were fully aware that the evacuation was about to take place, but they were not sure of the exact date. However, on the afternoon of February 17, a signal was sent from Charleston to Sullivan's Island: "Burn all papers before you leave." It was read by the Union signalmen on Morris Island. The evacuation was about to begin.[52]

On the night of February 17–18, 1865, the evacuation took place, with troops coming in from the outlying positions as well as from Fort Sumter. The men from the fort said that they would rather die in the ruins of Sumter, which they had defended for four years, than turn it over to the Federal forces. New flags were left flying over Fort Sumter, Fort Moultrie, and Castle Pinckney, which the troops hoped would lead the Federal forces to think that they were still occupied.[53] Before daylight on February 18, the last troops left Sullivan's Island, a picket of 30 mounted men who started over the bridge leading from the island to Mt. Pleasant. Sixteen mortars on Morris Island started firing at the bridge, hoping to destroy it. The picket started out at a walk in order to keep the bridge from shaking to pieces, but, as the fire increased, they began to gallop. The wooden bridge did not collapse. It was said that the noise of the galloping horses could be heard in Charleston.[54]

Most of the troops left the city that night, though one company did not get off until early on the morning of February 18. Shortly after the galloping pickets left Sullivan's Island, the magazine at Battery Bee blew up, and "it seemed as if the whole upper part of Sullivan's Island was lifted into the air." The force of the explosion was so great that it shook Morris Island.[55] Also on that morning the monitors started feeling their way into the harbor. With the sinking of the *Patapsco* fresh in mind, they were wary of the newly laid mines and other obstructions. When opposite Fort Moultrie, over which the flag was still flying, the monitor *Canonicus* fired two shots into the fort. As there was no reply and the fort looked deserted, the crew rightly assumed that it had been evacuated. These were the last shots fired in Charleston after nearly three years of almost continuous bombardment.[56]

About the time the *Canonicus* was coming into the harbor, a small boat left from Cummings Point carrying Capt. Samuel Cuskaden of the 52d Pennsylvania Infantry and a crew from the Third Rhode Island Artillery. On their way to Sullivan's Island, as they neared Fort Sumter, they saw a boat bearing a white flag. This boat was found to contain some musicians who had not joined the troops leaving for North Carolina. In the meantime, another boat carrying Maj. John A. Hennessy of the 52d Pennsylvania started for Fort Sumter. He had been told that the fort was heavily mined, but he and his crew scaled the parapet and hoisted the regimental flag, the first United States flag that had flown from the fort since April 13, 1861. The crews of the *Canonicus* and *Mahopac* gave "nine rousing cheers" when they saw the flag. Both boats started off for Fort Ripley; however, when he saw that Hennessy's boat was leading, Cuskaden, who by this time had picked up Lieutenant Colonel Bennett of the 21st U.S. Colored Troops, headed for Castle Pinckney. By now a navy cutter had joined in the race, and apparently won it; acting Ensign Broughton, in his official report to Admiral Dahlgren, said, "One of my boats landed at Castle Pinckney [and] hoisted the Stars and Stripes." [57] Hennessy's men had also joined in, and they too landed at Castle Pinckney, where there was a struggle to see who would be the first to raise the Stars and Stripes. After the flag was raised, everyone started off to see who would be the first to reach the city. This time Hennessy's boat won by about 50 yards. At some point Colonel Bennett had transferred into Hennessy's boat, and they landed at 10 A.M. at Mills (Atlantic) Wharf on the Cooper River near the foot of Broad Street.[58] Colonel Bennett, who had only 25 men with him, proceeded cautiously into the city, since he was not sure whether all of the Confederate forces had left. As they entered the city, a man approached them carrying a white flag. It was George W. Williams, a city alderman, "who by order of the mayor of the city was on his way to meet the U.S. authorities and tender the surrender of Charleston." [59] He bore a note from Mayor Macbeth which read: "The military authorities of the Confederate States have evacuated the city. I have remained to enforce law and preserve order until you take such steps as you may think best." [60]

By this time two companies of the 52d Pennsylvania Regiment had arrived, with about 30 men of the Third Rhode Island Artillery, who marched to The Citadel [Marion Square], where Colonel Bennett established his headquarters. A guard was also sent to the Arsenal. In the meantime, efforts were made to extinguish about 20 fires that were burning throughout the city. Every available man was impressed to accomplish this task. At 5 P.M. the 21st U.S. Colored Troops arrived.[61]

Admiral Dahlgren sent a dispatch to the secretary of the navy: "Charleston has been abandoned this morning by the rebels." General Gillmore also sent off a message about the evacuation, and an item in a Richmond newspaper said: "The city itself was little better than a deserted ruin." [62]

Writing of his entrance into the city, Admiral Dahlgren stated: "We passed Sumter, then Wagner, and all of the familiar scenery of the last two years; and so ends a command of two years of one of the largest fleets ever assembled under American Colors. There were at one time as many as ninety-six vessels." [63] One of his officers, who had been with him for months in the blockading squadron, said: "And thus, after a siege which will rank among the most famous in history, Charleston becomes ours." [64]

3

The night of February 17–18 was one of horror and chaos, undoubtedly the worst ever experienced in the history of the city. There were more women in the city than usual, as those from the outlying plantations were sent in to get them out of the way of Sherman's marauders.[65] For some days before the evacuation, cotton had been piled high in the public squares ready to be burned so that it would not fall into the hands of the Union troops. Now, with the evacuation a certainty, it was set on fire, along with thousands of bushels of rice, casting an eerie glow over the entire city. The enormous Blakely gun located at the corner of East Battery and South Battery was blown up with a tremendous charge of powder. The explosion was of such force that it badly damaged the piazzas of the house on the corner, and a 500-pound section of the gun landed on the roof of a residence about 100 yards away, where it remains in the attic to this day.

As dark approached, conditions became worse. No one dared to go to bed. Fires were breaking out all over the city, and since the white firemen, who acted in the dual capacity of militiamen, were gone, only Negro companies were left to fight them. The bridge across the Ashley River had also been set on fire. Along with the numerous other blazes, this made the city a raging inferno.

Early in the morning, as the last of the troops were leaving, the city was shaken by another tremendous explosion caused by the blowing up of the magazine on Sullivan's Island. Later in the morning another blast shook the city, the result of the explosion of the Northeastern Railroad depot in the upper part of the city. It was filled with food and other commodities that had to be left behind, together with a large amount of damaged gunpowder. People from the surrounding area rushed in to help themselves. Nearby some cotton was burning, which was to cause their doom. Some small boys, who found that black powder would make a blaze with lots of smoke when thrown on the fire, amused themselves by carrying handfuls of it from the depot, where it was stored, to the cotton. Some of the powder trickled through their fingers when they were carrying it, leaving a trail back to the depot. Somehow it was ignited, and before anyone could extinguish the fire the entire depot was blown up, along with about 150 people. Probably about an equal number were burned. The injured crawled away the best they could.[66] Houses near the depot caught fire, adding to the chaos. By this time some of the buildings in the western part of the city had caught on fire from the burning bridge. The city was on fire from river to river.

Another explosion was caused by the blowing up of the gunboat *Palmetto State* at her wharf. This was the gunboat that the women of the state had financed by selling their jewelry. Those who saw it said that the smoke from the explosion formed a perfect palmetto tree. In a few moments it wavered, gradually fell apart, and drifted away, almost as a symbol of what was happening to the state.[67] Shortly afterwards there was another explosion; this time it was the *Chicora*. Actually, she was only a floating battery—her boilers had given out the previous year. Finally there was an enormous explosion which was not only heard but felt over the entire city; 20 tons of powder had been ignited and had blown the gunboat *Charleston* to pieces. Fragments from her fell on the nearby wharves and quickly set them on fire.

It was rumored that the Arsenal (at Ashley and Bee streets), where a large quantity of powder was stored, was to be blown up and that a slow fuse had already been lighted. The women and children in the nearby houses fled for their lives. Either the fuse was never lighted or it went out, because there was no explosion. It was also rumored that unoccupied houses would be taken over by the Union troops, at which news the women and children rushed back and barricaded themselves in their homes.[68] The rest of the day was relatively quiet, though the fires burned on. Sunday, February 19, was a different story. The soldiers of the 21st U.S. Colored Troops, who were in possession of the city, started on a tour of liberation—anything that was not nailed down was taken. They went everywhere breaking into homes and helping themselves to whatever they wanted, cursing and raving at the inhabitants all the while.[69]

To stop some of the looting, a special order was issued the next day forbidding any soldier to enter the city without a pass from his commanding officer, with the exception of soldiers of the 21st U.S. Colored Troops. Any soldier who disobeyed the order would be arrested immediately and turned over to the provost guard.[70] A few days later the 127th New York Volunteers and the 21st U.S. Colored Troops were made the permanent garrison of Charleston under the command of Brigadier General Schimmelfennig. Their headquarters were at 27 King St. (Miles Brewton House).[71]

Since there was no communication with the interior of the state, General Sherman, ten days after the evacuation of the city, had not heard the news. He wrote to General Kilpatrick: "There is little doubt our troops are in Charleston." [72]

On February 28, General Order Number Eight was issued calling on the citizens of Charleston to take the oath of allegiance to the United States and providing that no passes or favors would be given to those who refused to take it. The order also stated that no guards would be placed over the houses of citizens for the

protection of private property, but that any person fearing molestation should display the United States flag in a conspicuous
position and that any person doing any damage to such a house
would be punished.[73] Nothing was said about what would happen
to a person who plundered a house not flying the United States
flag. Apparently the order was ignored, and plundering continued
unrestrained, for General Gillmore wrote from Hilton Head to
General Hatch in Charleston: "I hear on all sides very discouraging accounts of the state of affairs in Charleston; that no restraint
is put upon the soldiers; that they pilfer and rob houses at pleasure; that large quantities of valuable furniture, pictures, statuary, mirrors, etc., have mysteriously disappeared—no one knows
whither or by what agency; and that matters generally are at
sixes and sevens." Things must have gotten completely out of
hand if Gillmore found it necessary to write to one of his generals.[74] A month later Gillmore issued another order instructing the
officers stationed in Charleston to return the silver, pianos, organs, pictures, and works of art that they had stolen.[75] It would
appear that, with the officers looting and nothing being done
about it, it was perfectly all right for the soldiers to help themselves. It is not recorded whether any of the material was returned, for the simple reason that none of it was. Three weeks
later Gillmore wrote to Admiral Dahlgren asking him to help
stop the destruction of public and private property.[76] In early
March, one officer wrote that the soldiers near the entrenchments
(in the vicinity of Magnolia Cemetery, north of the city) were
continually plundering the property of citizens living near there
and that, with the troops under his command, he was powerless to
prevent these acts.[77]

That a single piece of furniture or silver survived is a miracle.
The silver could be buried, and most of it was, but nothing could
be done about the furniture. Some paintings were rolled up and
hidden in attics; most of the others usually had a bayonet thrust
through the throat if it was a man, or through the heart if it was a
woman. Holes were shot through the furniture. The buried silver
was usually located by the method of putting a rope around the

neck of the person who knew where it was and gently raising him off the ground, then easing him back so that his feet barely touched. After the second time, he usually gave the desired information.

Col. W. W. H. Davis of the 104th Pennsylvania was appalled at the wanton looting and burning of the outlying plantations. He wrote: "The plunder was not all obtained by soldiers, but officers received a fair share. Their conduct in this particular was disgraceful, and should have cost the offending ones their commissions. Some of them sent north pianos, elegant furniture, silverware, books, pictures, etc. to adorn their New England dwellings."

The soldiers entered one house that contained six family portraits. One, a full-length portrait painted by Romney, was cut out of the frame and the canvas thrown in the back yard, where it completely disintegrated. The other five portraits were stolen, together with many other articles. Years later the portraits turned up in a grocery store in Greenville, South Carolina. How or when they got there is not known. The only explanation is that the owner of the store, realizing they were of value, took them in by trade. The portraits were eventually acquired by members of the family from whom they were stolen.[78]

Sherman wrote to Gillmore in mid-March from near Fayetteville and asked that 2,500 troops be sent to him. He suggested that, if Gillmore could not spare the necessary men from garrison duty, he would not hesitate to burn Charleston "if the garrison were needed." [79] Actually, by that time there was not much of Charleston left to burn; most of the city had already been consumed in the "great conflagration" and the fires that had occurred during the bombardment and evacuation. It was a city of ashes.

In early May, General Sherman stopped by Charleston, his first visit there since his tour of duty at Fort Moultrie many years before. After looking over the ruins of the city he wrote: "Any one who is not satisfied with war should go and see Charleston, and he will pray louder and deeper than ever that the country may in the long future be spared any more war." [80]

Possibly William Howard Russell, the war correspondent for the London *Times*, best expressed the feeling of hatred that existed in the North when he wrote: "The war which was made to develop and maintain Union sentiment in the South, and to enable the people to rise against a desperate faction which had enthralled them, is now to be made a crusade against slave holders, and a war of subjugation—if need be, of extermination." Charleston to all intents and purposes was exterminated.[81] Russell landed in New York in the early part of the war, spent some time in Washington, then passed through the lines and traveled extensively through the South before returning to New York to sail for England. The book containing this statement was published in Boston in 1863.

In 1865, Charleston was as good as dead. No federal aid to rebuild the once great city was to be expected, and for a long time none came. There was only one reason for hope: the city's location. At the tip of the peninsula where, as Charlestonians say, "the Ashley and the Cooper meet and form the Atlantic Ocean," the city was and still is the natural port for a large area of the South and Midwest. Very slowly, commerce was revived.

And the city's poverty eventually became her greatest blessing. In the early twentieth century, Charlestonians could not afford to pull down their old buildings and put up new ones. As a result, when World War II finally brought prosperity again, those buildings that had survived the holocaust of the Civil War were refurbished and still stand today. They are lived in and worked in, and there has been no synthetic restoration.

BIBLIOGRAPHY

1. PUBLISHED RECORDS

Ammen, Daniel, *The Navy in the Civil War, The Atlantic Coast.* New York, 1905.

Anonymous, "Battle of Secessionville," *Confederate Veteran,* XXX (1922), 368–70.

———, "Submarine, History of," *Confederate Veteran,* XXXII (1924), 140.

Ashe, S. A., "Life at Fort Wagner," *Confederate Veteran,* XXXV (1927), 254–56.

Barnes, Frank, *Fort Sumter.* National Park Service Historical Handbook Series No. 12. Washington, D.C., 1952.

Beauregard, G. T., *Torpedo Service in the Harbor and Water Defences of Charleston,* Southern Historical Society Papers, V, No. 4 (April, 1878).

Boatner, Mark Mayo, III, *The Civil War Dictionary.* New York, 1959.

Bonham, Milledge L., Jr., *The British Consuls in the Confederacy.* Columbia University, XLII, No. 3 (1911).

Bradlee, Francis B. C., *A Forgotten Chapter in Our Naval History.* Salem, Mass., 1923.

Bridges, Hal, *Lee's Maverick General, Daniel Harvey Hill.* New York, 1961.

Capers, Walter B., *The Soldier-Bishop, Ellison Capers.* New York, 1912.

Cardoza, J. N., *Reminiscences of Charleston.* Charleston, 1866.

Carse, Robert, *Department of the South.* Columbia, 1961.

Cauthen, Charles E., *South Carolina Goes to War, 1860–1865.* Chapel Hill, N.C., 1950.

Chapman, John A., *History of Edgefield County.* Newberry, S.C., 1897.

Chesnut, Mary Boykin, *A Diary from Dixie.* New York, 1905.

Clarkson, H. M., *Confederate Veteran*, XXI (May, 1913).

Cochran, Hamilton, *Blockade Runners of the Confederacy.* Indianapolis and New York, 1958.

Courtney, William A., "Charleston in the War," *Year Book, 1883*, pp. 541–63. City of Charleston.

Cowley, Charles, *Leaves from a Lawyer's Life Afloat and Ashore.* Lowell, Mass., 1879.

Crawford, Samuel Wylie, *The Genesis of the Civil War, The Story of Sumter, 1860–1861.* New York, 1887.

Dahlgren, Madeleine Vinton, *Memoir of John A. Dahlgren, Rear-Admiral United States Navy.* Boston, 1882.

Davis, Jefferson, *The Rise and Fall of the Confederate Government*, II. New York, 1881.

Davis, W. W. H., *History of the One Hundred Fourth Pennsylvania Regiment.* Philadelphia, 1866.

Dennison, Frederic, *Shot and Shell, The Third Rhode Island Heavy Artillery Regiment, 1861–1865.* Providence, 1879.

Doubleday, Abner, *Reminiscences of Forts Sumter and Moultrie in 1860–61.* New York, 1876.

Du Pont, Henry A., *Rear-Admiral Samuel Francis Du Pont, U.S.N.* New York, 1926.

Easterby, J. H., *A History of the College of Charleston.* 1935.

———, *The South Carolina Rice Plantation as Revealed in the Papers of Robert F. W. Allston.* Chicago, 1945.

Eldredge, D., *The Third New Hampshire Regiment.* Boston, 1893.

Emilo, Luis F., *History of the Fifty-Fourth Regiment of Massachusetts Volunteer Infantry.* Boston, 1891.

Estvan, B., *War Pictures from the South.* New York, 1863.

Evans, Clement A., *A Confederate Military History*, V. Atlanta, 1899.

Ford, Arthur P., *Life in the Confederate Army, Being Personal Experiences of a Private Soldier in the Confederate Army*. New York and Washington, 1905.

Fort Sumter, Battle of, and the First Victory of the Southern Troops, Compiled chiefly from the detailed reports of the Charleston Press. Charleston, 1861.

Fort Sumter, "Corrected Roll of the Commander of that Military Post," *Year Book, 1884*, p. 403. City of Charleston.

Fort, W. R., "First Submarine in the Confederate Navy," *Confederate Veteran* (Oct., 1918), p. 459.

Freeman, Douglas Southall, *R. E. Lee*, I. New York, 1934.

Freemantle, James Arthur Lyon, *Three Months in Southern States April–June 1863*. New York, 1864.

Gilchrist, Robert C., "Confederate Defense of Morris Island," *Year Book, 1884*, pp. 350–402. City of Charleston.

Gillmore, Q. A., *Engineer and Artillery Operations Against the Defenses of Charleston Harbor in 1863*. New York, 1865.

———, *Supplementary Report to Engineer and Artillery Operations Against the Defenses of Charleston Harbor*. New York, 1868.

Gilman, Caroline Howard, "Letters of a Confederate Mother," *Atlantic*, CXXXVII (1926), 503–15.

Glassel, William T., *Reminiscences of Torpedo Service in Charleston Harbor*, Southern Historical Society Papers, IV (1877), 225–35.

Greeley, Horace, *The American Conflict*, II. Hartford, 1866.

Hagood, Johnson, *Memoirs of the War of Secession*. Edited by U. R. Brooks. Columbia, S.C., 1910.

Harris, W. A., comp., *The Record of Fort Sumter from its Occupation by Major Anderson to its Reduction by South Carolina Troops*. Columbia, S.C., 1862.

Hayes, John D., "The Battle of Port Royal, From the Journal of John Sanford Barnes," *New-York Historical Society Quarterly*, October, 1961.

Henry, Ralph Selph, *The Story of The Confederacy*. New York, 1943.

Higginson, Thomas Wentworth, *Army Life in a Black Regiment.* Ann Arbor, 1960.

Holmes, Charlotte R. (copyright by), *The Burckmyer Letters, March, 1863–June, 1865.* Columbia, S.C., 1926.

Horn, Stanley F., *The Army of Tennessee.* Norman, Oklahoma, 1955.

Inglesby, Charles, *Historical Sketch of the First Regiment of South Carolina Artillery (Regulars).* Charleston, n.d.

Johnson, John, *The Defense of Charleston Harbor.* Charleston, 1890.

Jones, Katherine M., *Heroines of Dixie.* Indianapolis and New York, 1955.

Jones, Samuel, *The Siege of Charleston.* New York, 1911.

Journal of the Convention of the People of South Carolina. Columbia, S.C., 1862.

Journal of the South Carolina Executive Councils of 1861 and 1862. South Carolina Archives Department, Columbia, S.C., 1956.

Kershaw, John, *History of the Parish and Church of Saint Michael, Charleston.* Charleston, 1915.

King, W. R., *Torpedoes: Their Invention and Use.* Washington, 1866.

Lawton, Eba Anderson, *Major Robert Anderson and Fort Sumter 1861.* New York, 1911.

La Bree, Ben, ed., *The Confederate Soldier in the Civil War.* Louisville, 1895.

Lawrence, R. DeT., "Battle of Secessionville," *Confederate Veteran*, XXX (1922), 410.

Lebby, Robert, "The First Shot on Fort Sumter," *South Carolina Historical and Genealogical Magazine*, XII, No. 3 (July, 1911), 141–45.

Maine Regiment, The Story of the Eleventh. New York, 1896.

Miller, F. T., ed., *The Photographic History of the Civil War.* 10 vols. New York, 1911.

Morgan, James Morris, *Recollections of a Rebel Reefer.* Boston, 1917.

Neuffer, Claude H., ed., *The Christopher Happoldt Journal.* Charleston, 1960.

News and Courier, "Our Women in the War, The Lives They Lived; The Deaths They Died," from the *Weekly News and Courier*, Charleston, 1885.

Official Records of the Union and Confederate Armies in the War of the Rebellion. Washington, D.C., 1880–1901.

Official Records of the Union and Confederate Navies in the War of the Rebellion. Washington, D.C., 1894–1922.

Olmstead, Charles H., *Reminiscences of Service with the First Volunteer Regiment of Georgia Charleston Harbor in 1863.* Savannah, 1879.

Orvin, Maxwell Clayton, *In South Carolina Waters 1861–1865.* Charleston, 1961.

Palmer, Abraham J., *The History of the Forty-Eighth Regiment of New York Volunteers.* Brooklyn, 1885.

Parker, William Harwar, *Recollection of a Naval Officer 1841–1865.* New York, 1883.

Perry, Milton F., *Infernal Machines.* Baton Rouge, 1965.

Porter, Anthony Toomer, *Led On! Step by Step.* New York and London, 1898.

Price, Isaiah, *History of the Ninety-Seventh Regiment Pennsylvania Volunteer Infantry 1861–65.* Philadelphia, 1875.

Price, Marcus W., "Ships That Tested the Blockade of the Carolina Ports 1861–1865," *American Neptune*, July, 1948, pp. 196–241.

Ravenel, Mrs. St. Julien, *Charleston, the Place and the People.* New York, 1916.

Reid, Whitelaw, *Ohio in the War: Her Statesmen, Her Generals, and Soldiers*, 2 vols. Columbus, Ohio, 1893.

Ripley, R. S., "Charleston and Its Defences," *Year Book, 1885*, pp. 347–58. City of Charleston.

———, *Correspondence Relating to Fortifications of Morris Island.* New York, 1878.

Robertson, John, comp., *Michigan in the War.* Lansing, 1880.

Roman, Alfred, *The Military Operations of General Beauregard*, I and II. New York, 1884.

Russell, William Howard, *My Diary, North and South*. Boston, 1863.

Salley, A. S., *The Flag of the State of South Carolina*. South Carolina Historical Commission Bulletin, No. 2, 1915.

Sass, Herbert Ravenel, "The Story of the Little David," *Harper's* (May, 1943).

Scharf, J. Thomas, *History of the Confederate States Navy*. New York, 1887.

Smythe, Augustine T., Jr., "Torpedo and Submarine Attacks on the Federal Blockading Fleet off Charleston During the War of Secession," *Year Book, 1907*, pp. 53–64. City of Charleston.

Smythe, Mrs. A. T., Miss M. B. Poppentheim, and Mrs. Thomas Taylor, *South Carolina Women in the Confederacy*. Columbia, S.C., 1903.

Snowden, Yates, "Charleston in War-Time," *Year Book, 1908*. City of Charleston.

Snowden, Yates, and H. G. Cutler, *History of South Carolina*, II. Chicago and New York, 1920.

Soley, James Russel, *The Navy in the Civil War: The Blockade and the Cruisers*. London, 1898.

Spaulding, Oliver Lyman, Jr., "The Bombardment of Fort Sumter," *Annual Report of the American Historical Association for the Year 1913*, pp. 177–203.

Stanton, C. L., "Submarines and Torpedo Boats," *Confederate Veteran*, XXII, No. 9 (September, 1914).

Stern, Philip Van Doren, *When the Guns Roared*. New York, 1965.

Swanberg, W. A., *First Blood*. New York, 1957.

Thomas, John P., *Historical Sketch, South Carolina Military Academy*. Charleston, 1879.

Todd, William, *The Seventy-ninth Highlanders New York Volunteers in the War of the Rebellion 1861–1864*. Albany, 1886.

Tomb, James H., "The Last Obstructions in Charleston Harbor, 1863," *Confederate Veteran*, XXXII (1924), 98–99.

Vizetelly, Frank, "When Charleston was Under Fire," *New Age Magazine*, XV, No. 3 (Sept., 1911).

Wallace, Duncan D., *A Short History of South Carolina*. Chapel Hill, N.C., 1951.

Wells, Edward L., *A Sketch of the Charleston Light Dragoons*. Charleston, 1886.

Within Fort Sumter, or a View of Major Anderson's Garrison Family for One Hundred and Ten Days, By one of the Company. New York, 1861.

Withington, Sidney, *Two Dramatic Episodes of New England Whaling*. The Marine Historical Association, Mystic, Conn., July, 1958.

Woodman, John E., Jr., "The Stone Fleet," *American Neptune* (October, 1961).

2. MANUSCRIPT SOURCES

Bacot, Richard H., Letters of, in South Caroliniana Library. Bacot was an officer on the gunboat *Charleston*.

Baker, Henry Hyrne, Letter dated April 19, 1861, owned by James Snowden, Esq. Tells of preparations for and attack on Fort Sumter.

Barnwell, Edward W., Letters of, in South Caroliniana Library. Letters to his wife commenting on the bombardment of Charleston and blockade-running.

Bisbee, Ira W., Letter of, in South Caroliniana Library, dated November 10, 1861. Describes the Battle of Port Royal and tells of conditions of forts after the bombardment.

Calhoun, John A., Letter of, in South Caroliniana Library, dated January 6, 1862. States that Beauregard ordered the construction of the forts at Port Royal only after pressure from the governor and leading citizens.

Capers, Ellison, Letter of, in Hinson Collection, Charleston Library Society, dated June 17, 1862. Tells of the Battle of Secessionville.

Cheves Collection, Letters in the South Carolina Historical Society. Many tell of the harbor defenses and the amphibious assault on Morris Island.

Clark, W. A., Letter in Hinson Collection, Charleston Library Society. From Clark to Hinson in reference to the number of sinkings of the *Hunley*.

Crawford, Samuel W., Diary of, in Library of Congress. Kept while Crawford was with Major Anderson in Fort Sumter.

DeSaussure, Wilmot G., Letters of, in Charleston Library Society. Pertaining to defenses in the city.

Dickson, B. E., Three manuscript volumes in South Caroliniana Library. Records of the first and second regiments of Artillery, South Carolina Volunteers.

Dixon, George E., Letter of, in Department of Naval History, Washington, D.C., dated February 5, 1864. Tells of training the crew of the *Hunley*.

Douglass, John, Letter of, in South Caroliniana Library. Addressed to Dr. Robert Lebby, requesting information as to who fired the "first shot."

Engineers, Department of, manuscripts in South Caroliniana Library. Sixty-eight reports pertaining to the defenses of Charleston Harbor.

Health Department Records, Charleston County. Record of burial place of Sgt. James Edward Galway, who was killed by explosion of gun at Fort Sumter at time of evacuation.

Hinson, William G., Collection of, in Charleston Library Society. This collection contains a wealth of material pertaining to the war, consisting of letters, orders, and newspaper clippings.

Honour, Theodore A., Letters of, in South Caroliniana Library. Description of the *Hunley* at time of sinking at Fort Johnson, as well as of bombardment of Charleston.

Jones, Lt. C.S.A., Corps of Engineers, Letter of, in Hinson

Collection, Charleston Library Society. Tells of evacuation of Federal forces after the Battle of Secessionville.

Keitt, Ellison, manuscript in South Caroliniana Library. Tells of conditions in and around Charleston during the closing period of the war.

Keller, Edward Henry, Diary of, in South Caroliniana Library. Tells of conditions just before the evacuation of Charleston.

Marple, Alfred, Diary of, in South Caroliniana Library. Captain in the 104th Pennsylvania Regiment stationed on Morris Island.

Military Affairs 1860–65. In South Carolina Archives Department. Letters and military material.

Palmer, Alden D., Letter of, owned by Mrs. John F. Culhane, Minneapolis, Minn. A member of the Ninth Maine Regiment. Letter written from Morris Island.

Parker, Francis L., typewritten copy, owned by Edward F. Parker, M.D., of a letter written at the Battle of Fort Sumter (April, 1861) as seen from Morris Island.

Petrel, H. M. S., Log of, in the Public Records Office, Ashbridge Park Berkhamstead, Herts, England. Record Volume Adm. Class 53, Piece Number 8312.

Schimmelfennig, Augustus, Letters of, in South Caroliniana Library. Description of amphibious assault on Fort Johnson and fighting on John's Island.

Schirmer, Jacob, Diary of, in South Carolina Historical Society. Kept by Schirmer for almost the entire war.

Sheppard, John L., and Benjamin, Letters of, in South Caroliniana Library. Describe the Battle of Secessionville.

Thompson, John, Letters of, in Public Record Office, Belfast, North Ireland. Thompson was a private at Fort Sumter with Anderson. Gives an excellent description of Wigfall asking for the surrender of the fort.

Welsh, Stephen, manuscript in Hinson Collection in Charleston Library Society. Excellent description of the firing on the *Star of the West*.

Yates, William B., Diary of, owned by Judge William Henry
Simmons. Tells of burying the private killed at Fort Sumter
at time of evacuation.

NEWSPAPERS

Throughout the war, both the Charleston *Courier* and the
Charleston *Mercury* continued publishing. In time, with the
scarcity of newsprint, the size of the newspapers was reduced, but
all important activities throughout the Confederacy appeared in
some detail. All of the news from Northern sources was listed
under "foreign news."

Any engagement that took place in and around Charleston
naturally appeared in both newspapers, and the reports in both
were quite similar. The *Courier*, which has been put on micro-
film, was consulted much more frequently than the *Mercury*, not
only because of its convenience, but to avoid damage to the latter
by excessive use. The files of both newspapers are in the Charleston Library Society.

The New York *Times* and the New York *Herald* have been
consulted for articles pertaining to Charleston. These files (mi-
crofilm) are in the New York Public Library. In the South
Caroliniana Library (Columbia, South Carolina), there is an
excellent collection of newspapers of several cities and towns
throughout the state. To some extent, these have been consulted,
but it was found that articles pertaining to activities around
Charleston were rewrites or, in most cases, direct quotations from
one of the Charleston papers.

NOTES

History cannot be changed, but to some extent it can be recon-
structed. In the heat of the battle, with men's emotions so involved, no two can give an accurate report of what takes place at

any precise moment. However, when various reports are put together, not only those of men fighting side by side, but those of opposing participants, a clear, and in most cases accurate, picture evolves.

In this work, the *Official Records of the War*, both army and navy, published over a period of 42 years by the United States government, have been relied on most heavily. It contains the correspondence, orders, and other communications of both the Confederate and Union forces. Naturally they are not complete; many records of the Confederacy were lost or destroyed during the closing days of the conflict, and doubtless much material containing pertinent data was captured by both sides and ultimately lost. Even in the *Official Records* discrepancies occur, but again, a clear picture usually emerges.

Much has been written about the siege of Charleston. However, most of these works do not cover the entire period from the signing of the Ordinance of Secession until the time of the evacuation of the city over four years later. Maj. John Johnson, in his monumental work *The Defense of Charleston Harbor*, covers the 1863–65 period. Johnson was engineer officer on Fort Sumter for 15 months, during which time some of the most intense fighting took place. This meticulously detailed book is invaluable to any student of the siege.

Alfred Roman, in his two-volume *Military Operations* (actually a military biography of General Beauregard), covers in some detail the period that Beauregard spent in Charleston, but most of this work is devoted to his activities elsewhere.

Engineer and Artillery Operations Against the Defenses of Charleston in 1863, by Maj. Gen. Q. A. Gillmore, U.S.A., is most useful, but almost everything in this work can be found in one of the many volumes of the *Official Records*.

The Siege of Charleston by Maj. Gen. Samuel Jones, C.S.A., is excellent on the period involved. Unfortunately, General Jones did not live to complete the work, and, as his daughter states in the introduction, "the following brief historical study is a fragment of a work which was intended to cover the operations

against Charleston from the beginning to their consummation."
Many others have written competently about various aspects of
the siege.

No attempt has been made to give the number and sizes of
guns at any particular place or at any given time. Guns were
moved whenever the occasion required. Fort Sumter started off
with a heavy armament, but after several bombardments it had at
one time only a single 32-pounder that was used as a sunrise and
sunset gun. Almost the same thing applies to the various military
units, for they were continually changing, especially if in the
state or Confederate service. The Federal units in the area were
generally stable. Some of the troops in state service enlisted for a
six-month period, others for twelve months. After the expiration
of their terms, they frequently re-enlisted in some other unit.
Beauregard said: "There are no less than three First Regiments
of South Carolina troops in sight of Charleston, all on artillery
duty . . . the result being much confusion. Moreover, there is
another First Regiment (Gregg's old regiment) in Virginia."

The rank of an officer is generally given as what it was at the
time the action took place. Specifically, Maj. Stephen Elliott at
one time was in command at Fort Sumter, later was transferred
to Virginia, and subsequently attained the rank of Brigadier
General.

The War of the Rebellion: A Compilation of the Official Records of the Union and Confederate Armies, published by the
United States government, is cited as *O.R.* Unless otherwise
noted, it refers to Series One of the Army records. Navy records
are cited as *O.R., Navy*, followed by the volume number, also
Series One unless otherwise noted. Volume XIV of both the army
and navy records covers incidents that took place in and around
Charleston.

NOTES

CHAPTER 1

1 *Journal of Convention*, 37 ff.; Cauthen, 70, 139.
2 *Mercury*, Dec. 21, 1860; Cauthen, 71.
3 *Courier*, Dec. 22, 1860.
4 *Ibid.*
5 Evans, V, 4; Snowden and Cutler, II, 666; Porter, 122; Cauthen, 68, 133; Swanberg, 71.
6 *Courier*, Dec. 20, 1860; Swanberg, 10.
7 *O.R.*, I, 88, 95; Crawford, 62; *Courier*, Apr. 11–12, 1961 [*sic*]; Swanberg, 7.
8 *S.C. Hist. Mag.*, Jan. 1938, 7.
9 Crawford, 7; Cauthen, 92; Swanberg, 2.
10 *Battle and Leaders* (*B & L*) I, 40; Spaulding, 179; Swanberg, 34.
11 *O.R.*, I, 75–76; Swanberg, 41.
12 *Ibid.*, 82, 87.
13 *B&L*, I, 41; Cauthen, 98; *O.R.*, I, 72.
14 *Ibid.*, 103.
15 *Ibid.*, 88, 93, 98, 96; Cauthen, 93; Swanberg, 47.
16 *Journal House of Representatives*, 1861, Message 1, 31; Cauthen, 80, 98; Crawford, 88.
17 Spaulding, 181; Doubleday, 43, 47.
18 *O.R.*, I, 105, 87; Spaulding, 182; *Within Fort Sumter*, 8. Crawford, 103, 129, states that they were lighters.
19 *O.R.*, I, 2; *S.C. Hist. Soc. Mag.*, July 1961, 149; Crawford, 107; *B&L*, I, 45; Doubleday, 65; *Courier*, April 11–12, 1961 [*sic*].
20 Crawford, 107; *O.R.*, I, 91.
21 Porter, 121.
22 *Mercury*, Dec. 28, 1860; Crawford, 108.
23 *O.R.*, I, 112; LIII, 62; Cauthen, 98; Crawford, 119; Swanberg, 131.
24 *O.R.*, I, 3; Crawford, 111; Doubleday, 79; Cauthen, 98–99; Swanberg, 104.
25 *Journal of Convention*, 107; *Courier*, April 11–12, 1961 [*sic*].
26 *O.R.*, I, 109; *Mercury*, Dec. 28, 1860; Capers, 46; Wallace, 531; *Courier*, April 11–12, 1961; Swanberg, 107.

27 *Mercury*, Dec. 28, 1860; *O.R.*, I, 4; Crawford, 116; Swanberg, 108.
28 Easterby, *College of Charleston*, 145.
29 *Mercury*, Dec. 29, 1860.
30 Gilman, 504; Cauthen, 93.
31 *O.R.*, I, 72, 6, 130, 129; Cauthen, 115.
32 *Journal House of Representatives*, 1861, 175; Thomas, 37; Roman, I, 29; *Mercury*, Jan. 10, 1861; *Journal of Executive Councils*, 37.
33 *Journal of Executive Councils*, 6.
34 *O.R.*, I, 130–31, 121; Swanberg, 127.
35 *Journal of Executive Councils*, 8.
36 *Courier*, Jan. 15, 1861; *O.R.*, I, 9; *Journal of Executive Councils*, 12.
37 Welsh, ms, Hinson Collection, Charleston Library Society.
38 Crawford, 183–84; *Journal of Executive Councils*, 26; Clarkson, 234; Doubleday, 103; *Courier*, Jan. 10, 1861; *O.R.*, I, 10.
39 Crawford, 133, 186; Doubleday, 101; *O.R.*, I, 132, 134; *S. C. Hist. Soc. Mag.*, July, 1961, 148; *Within Fort Sumter*, 15; Cauthen, 102.
41 *O.R.*, I, 136.
42 Smythe, 9; Swanberg, 146.
43 Salley, No. 2.
44 *O.R.*, I, 134; *Journal of Executive Councils*, 12; Crawford, 189; Cauthen, 103; Swanberg, 90.
45 *O.R.*, I, 135; *Ibid.*, LIII, 117; *Journal of Executive Councils*, 13; Crawford, 191.
46 *O.R.*, LIII, 126; *Journal of Executive Councils*, 15.
47 *Journal of Executive Councils*, 13–14, 22; Doubleday, 124.
48 *Journal of Executive Councils*, 21, 23; Spaulding, 202.
49 Military Affairs 1860–65 (letter) in South Carolina Archives.
50 *O.R.*, I, 144; Crawford, 202; Cauthen, 124.
51 *Journal of Executive Councils*, 35; *O.R.*, I, 143.
52 *Journal of Executive Councils*, 34, 17; Crawford, 193; Cauthen, 103, 118; Swanberg, 157.
53 Salley, No. 2.
54 *Journal of Executive Councils*, 36, 42.
55 *O.R.*, I, 170, 175; Doubleday, 113; Swanberg, 155, 177; Cauthen, 119.
56 *O.R.*, I, 162, 159; *Courier*, Jan. 9, 1861; Doubleday, 117; *Journal of Executive Councils*, 26.
57 Doubleday, 112.
58 *Journal of Executive Councils*, 39, 40, 42, 45–46.
59 *Ibid.*, 48, 54, 60.
60 *O.R.*, I, 181.
61 *Journal of Executive Councils*, 62, 64–67; Cauthen, 109.
62 *O.R.*, I, 260, 272.
63 Doubleday, 129, 130; *O.R.*, I, 192, 273; Evans, V, 621; Smythe, 159.

64 *O.R.*, I, 195; Cauthen, 120–21; Swanberg, 244.
65 *O.R.*, I, 276.
66 Doubleday, 122.
67 *O.R.*, I, 211, 157, 195; Easterby, *South Carolina Rice Plantation*, 172; Crawford, 372; Cauthen, 126; Swanberg, 242.
68 *O.R.*, I, 218.
69 *O.R.*, I, 282, 300.
70 Gilman, 503; *O.R.*, I, 281.
71 *B&L*, I, 82; *O.R.*, I, 223, 226.
72 *O.R.*, I, 222, 283.
73 *Ibid.*, I, 230, 285, 232, 283; Swanberg, 272.
74 *O.R.*, I, 291.
75 *Ibid.*, I, 226, 235; *O.R.*, *Navy*, IV, 228; Cauthen, 126; *O.R.*, *Navy*, I, 232; Swanberg, 255.
76 *O.R.*, I, 235, 241.
77 Crawford, 382; *O.R.*, I, 248n, 294; Roman, I, 34; Swanberg, 281.
78 *O.R.*, I, 251; Cauthen, 127.
79 *O.R.*, I, 228; Cauthen, 126–27; Swanberg, 255, 260.
80 *O.R.*, I, 246–47.
81 *Ibid.*, 247.
82 Crawford, 398, 400.
83 *O.R.*, I, 249.
84 *Ibid.*, 17.
85 *Ibid.*, 292–93.
86 *Ibid.*, 17.
87 *Ibid.;* Doubleday, 115.
88 *O.R.*, I, 13, 59.
89 Crawford Diary; Swanberg, 292.
90 *O.R.*, I, 13.
91 *B&L*, I, 75, 82; Crawford, 424; *O.R.*, I, 59.
92 *O.R.*, I, 301.
93 Crawford Diary.
94 Doubleday, 140, 165; Crawford, 445.
95 Spaulding, 202.
96 *O.R.*, LIII, 142; *Ibid.*, I, 14.
97 Crawford, 425.
98 *O.R.*, I, 60; *B&L*, I, 76.
99 Letter of John Thompson, dated April 28, 1861. Public Record Office, Belfast, North Ireland.
100 Hinson Collection, Charleston Library Society.
101 Doubleday in *Courier*, April 22, 1861; *Within Fort Sumter*, 41, 43; *O.R.*, I, 37.
102 *Ibid.*, 39, 40, 50, 51.
103 *Battle of Fort Sumter*, 13; Surgeon Edward Parker's statement.
104 Roman, I, 432; *O.R.*, I, 44, 54; *Courier*, April 13–15, 1861.
105 *B&L*, I, 66.
106 Roman, I, 43; Doubleday, 145–46.

107 *O.R.*, I, 18; Crawford, 431.
108 Katherine M. Jones, 18.
109 *Battle of Fort Sumter*, 5, 7; *O.R.*, I, 21.
110 Crawford, 431; *B&L*, I, 55, 69, 70; *O.R.*, I, 20.
111 Doubleday, 147; Crawford Diary; *O.R.*, I, 40, 20, 19.
112 *O.R.*, I, 19.
113 *Ibid.*, 11; Doubleday, 153; *B&L*, I, 68.
114 *Battle of Fort Sumter*, 17; Crawford, 434.
115 Crawford, 432.
116 *Courier*, April 16, 1861; Crawford, 434; Roman, I, 46.
117 *Battle of Fort Sumter*, 18.
118 Doubleday, 156; *B&L.*, I, 72; *O.R.*, I, 22.
119 Easterby, *South Carolina Rice Plantation*, 174.
120 *O.R.*, I, 23; Katherine M. Jones, 20.
121 *O.R.*, I, 32; Roman, I, 46.
122 *B&L*, I, 54.
123 *O.R.*, I, 22–23, 32; Crawford, 438; Doubleday, 159; *Within Fort Sumter*, 55; Chestnut, 43.
124 *O.R.*, I, 38, 57, 32; Barnes, 18; *Courier*, April 13–15, 1861; Thompson letter in Public Record Office, Belfast, North Ireland.
125 *O.R.*, I, 23; Crawford, 440; *Within Fort Sumter*, 57.
126 Barnes, 20; *O.R.*, I, 23, 37–39; Crawford, 439–41; Doubleday, 162–63; *Within Fort Sumter*, 47–59; Crawford Diary; Cauthen, 132.
127 *O.R.*, I, 38, 63.
128 Crawford, 441; *B&L*, I, 73; *O.R.*, I, 64.
129 Crawford, 442; Doubleday, 170; Swanberg, 321.
130 Crawford, 441; *Courier*, April 11–12, 1861.
131 Philadelphia *Inquirer*, April 15, 1861.
132 *O.R.*, I, 32–33.
133 *Battle of Fort Sumter*, 22; Crawford, 446.
134 Spaulding, 202.
135 *O.R.*, I, 65.
136 *Battle of Fort Sumter*, 28; *Courier*, April 13–15, 1861; Philadelphia *Inquirer*, April, 15, 1861; Schirmer Diary.
137 Roman, I, 48, 52.
138 *Battle of Fort Sumter*, 11–12, 24; Parker ms in Hinson Collection, Charleston Library Society.
139 Doubleday, 162.
140 *Mercury*, April 15, 1861.
141 *O.R.*, I, 56; *Battle of Fort Sumter*, 13.
142 Samuel Jones, 45; *O.R.*, I, 28.
143 Samuel Jones, 17.
144 Barnes, 18.
145 *O.R.*, I, 11; *O.R.*, *Navy*, IV, 249.
146 *Courier*, April 13–15, 1861; Roman, I, 45.
147 *O.R.*, I, 11.

148 *Ibid.*, 56.
149 Health Department Records; *O.R.*, LIII, 175.
150 *O.R.*, I, 12; Swanberg, 332; Boatner, 15.
151 Cauthen, 133; Wallace, 528.
152 *O.R.*, LIII, 148.
153 *Ibid.*, 151.
154 *Ibid.*, 153.
155 *Ibid.*, 160.
156 *Ibid.*, 167, 171, 172.
157 *O.R.*, VI, 85, 329.
158 Boatner, 14; *O.R.* Series Four, I, 414; *Ibid.*, LIII, 176.
159 *Ibid.*, VI, 1.
160 *Ibid.*, LIII, 179.
161 Freeman, 631.
162 Cauthen, 138.
163 *O.R.*, VI, 321.
164 *Ibid.*, 168.

CHAPTER 2

 1 Hayes, 365.
 2 *O.R.*, LIII, 168.
 3 *Ibid.*, VI, 6; *O.R.*, Series Four, I, 414.
 4 *Ibid.*, VI, 19.
 5 *Ibid.*, VI, 16; *O.R.*, LIII, 179; Roman, I, 51; Snowden, II, 692; Happoldt Journal, 105.
 6 *O.R.*, *Navy*, XII, 208; Snowden, II, 694; *B&L*, I, 674; Russell, 546.
 7 Hayes, 376.
 8 *Ibid.*, 378.
 9 *O.R.*, *Navy*, XII, 259; *O.R.*, VI, 185.
10 Hayes, 383; *O.R.*, VI, 24, 27; *B&L*, I, 691, 678.
11 *B&L*, I, 680; Du Pont, 124.
12 Hayes, 384.
13 *B&L*, I, 681; *O.R.*, *Navy*, XII, 268; *Harper's Weekly*, Nov. 30, 1861, p. 762; Carse, 12.
14 *O.R.*, VI, 17; Hayes, 393; Freeman, 608.
15 Snowden and Cutler, II, 696; *O.R.*, VI, 10, 12, 15–16, 25, 30–31.
16 Hayes, 392.
17 Du Pont, 132; Hayes, 393.
18 *O.R.*, *Navy*, XII, 264; *B&L*, I, 686, 689; Freeman, 609.
19 Hayes, 365.
20 Letter dated Jan. 9, 1862, from Beauregard to John A. Calhoun, in South Caroliniana Library, Columbia, S.C.; *O.R.*, Series Four, I, 414.
21 *1898 Year Book*, 353; Cardoza, 83; *Journal House of Representatives*, 1861, p. 143; *Harper's Weekly*, Nov. 30, 1861, p. 762.

22 Cauthen, 137; Schirmer Diary.
23 *O.R.*, VI, 313, 318.
24 *O.R.*, VI, 309.
25 Freeman, 608.
26 *O.R.*, VI, 312.
27 *Ibid.*, 313, 314.
28 *O.R.*, LIII, 186, 191.
29 Freeman, 622; *O.R.*, VI, 329.
30 *Ibid.*, LIII, 193–94.
31 *Ibid.*, VI, 367.
32 *Ibid.*, 390, 394.
33 *Ibid.*, 31.
34 *Ibid.*, 335.
35 Smythe, 173.
36 Schirmer Diary.
37 *Ibid.*
38 *1880 Year Book*, 307.
39 *Courier*, May 13, 1861.
40 *O.R.*, *Navy*, XII, 207, 416.
41 Withington, 49.
42 *O.R.*, *Navy*, XII, 417.
43 Withington, 51.
44 *Ibid.*
45 *O.R.*, *Navy*, XII, 422.
46 *Ibid.*, 421.
47 *O.R.*, VI, 42; Freeman, 618.
48 *Mercury*, December 21, 1861, 2/1.
49 Withington, 45, 61; Woodman, 233.
50 *Ibid.*, 63.
51 *O.R.*, *Navy*, XII, 551.
52 *O.R.*, VI, 346, 353.
53 Freeman, 629.
54 Perry, 30; *O.R.*, *Navy*, XII, 502–504.
55 *O.R.*, VI, 103, 327, 329.
56 *Ibid.*, 400.
57 *Ibid.*, 334, 402, 407.
58 *Ibid.*, 395, 337.
59 *Ibid.*, 407.
60 *Ibid.*, 417.
61 *Ibid.*, 419.
62 *Ibid.*, 420, 423.
63 *Ibid.*, 424; Grayson Diary in *South Carolina Historical Magazine*, June, 1962, p. 139.
64 *O.R.*, VI, 504, 521.
65 *Ibid.*, 509.
66 *Ibid.*, 503.
67 *Mercury*, Sept. 30, 1862.

68 *O.R.*, XIV, 15; *O.R.*, *Navy*, XII, 820, 822; *Mercury*, May 14, 1862 and Sept. 30, 1862.
69 *O.R.*, *Navy*, XIII, 5, 6; *Ibid.*, XII, 807, 821, 825.
70 *Courier*, May 14, 1862; *News and Courier*, Oct. 12, 1885 [*sic*]; Schirmer Diary, May 13, 1862; *O.R.*, XIV, 506, 509.
71 *Mercury*, Aug. 1, 1862.
72 Appletons Encyclopedia, 224.
73 *O.R.*, XIV, 985.
74 *Ibid.*, 470, 480, 482.
75 *Ibid.*, 510.
76 *Ibid.*, 496.
77 *Ibid.*, 540.
78 *Ibid.*, 517.
79 *O.R.*, XIV, 524.
80 Hagood, 96; Cowley, 63.
81 Information from Warren Ripley.
82 *O.R.*, XXVIII, Pt. 1, p. 69; *Ibid.*, XIV, 1001.
83 *Ibid.*, 353.
84 *Ibid.*, 40.
85 *Ibid.*, 534–35.
86 Eldredge, 166.
87 Hagood, 92; Price, 114.
88 *O.R.*, XIV, 567, 566, 556, 554.
89 *Ibid.*, 567.
90 Eldredge.
91 *O.R.*, XIV, 558.
92 *Ibid.*, 27, 36; Hagood, 86, 91.
93 Eldredge, 169.
94 *Ibid.*, 168; *O.R.*, XIV, 555.
95 Hagood, 91; Price, 117; *O.R.*, XIV, 35.
96 Hagood, 93.
97 Samuel Jones, 112; *O.R.*, XIV, 94; Hagood, 94.
98 *O.R.*, XIV, 52, 62, 63, 96.
99 *Ibid.*, 70, 87.
100 *Ibid.*, 63, 96.
101 *Ibid.*, 72; Robertson, 115.
102 *O.R.*, XIV, 75–76, 94.
103 *Ibid.*, 55; Letter dated June 17, 1862, from Ellison Capers, in Hinson Collection, Charleston Library Society.
104 *Mercury*, June 21, 1862; *O.R.*, XIV, 99.
105 *Ibid.*, 89, 1014, 1015; Hagood, 95.
106 Eldredge, 172; Price, 127; *O.R.*, XIV, 75.
107 *Mercury*, June 17, 1862; *O.R.*, XIV, 87, 94.
108 *Ibid.*, 71.
109 *Ibid.*, 51, 90.
110 Price, 115; *O.R.*, XIV, 70.
111 Eldredge, 174.

112 *O.R.*, LIII, 308.
113 Schirmer Diary, June 16, 1862.
114 Ravenel, 408.
115 Eldredge, 180.
116 *O.R.*, XIV, 43.
117 *Ibid.*, 46.
118 *Ibid.*, 359.
119 *Ibid.*, 43, 583; Letter from Lieutenant Jones, Corps of Engineers, in Hinson Collection, Charleston Library Society.
120 Samuel Jones, 111; Cowley, 62.
121 Boatner, 631.
122 *O.R.*, XIV, 353–54, 1013.
123 *Ibid.*, 43, 979, 991; Boatner, 58.
124 *O.R.*, XIV, 568–69; LIII, 256.
125 *O.R.*, XIV, 570.
126 *Ibid.*, 573, 579, 583–85, 597.
127 *Ibid.*, 586, 594, 597.
128 *Ibid.*, 601, 600, 603, 605–608.
129 *Ibid.*, 613.
130 *Ibid.*, 614–16.
131 *Ibid.*, XIV, 617, 629.
132 *Ibid.*, 642.
133 *Ibid.*, 668.
134 *Ibid.*, 666.
135 LIII, 264.
136 *O.R.*, XIV, 620.
137 *Ibid.*, 700, 706.
138 *Ibid.*, 695.
139 *Ibid.*, 692.

CHAPTER 3

1 Hayes, 379.
2 *Ibid.*, 390; *B&L*, I, 674, 676, 679; *O.R., Navy*, XII, 247.
3 Snowden and Cutler, II, 755.
4 *O.R.*, XIV, 201; Johnson, 28; *O.R., Navy*, XIII, 563.
5 *O.R.*, XIV, 756.
6 Snowden and Cutler, II, 756; *O.R., Navy*, XIV, 219; Schirmer Diary.
7 *O.R. Navy*, XIV, 494; Price, 230; Johnson, 34; *O.R., Navy*, Series Two, I, 267.
8 *Journal of Executive Councils*, 91.
9 *Courier*, Feb. 27, Mar. 12, and Mar. 13, 1862.
10 *Courier*, Mar. 11, Mar. 13, and May 12, 1862.
11 *Journal of Executive Councils*, 123.

12 *Journal of Executive Councils*, 157, 211, 245, 252–53, 258; *Journal of Convention*, 613; *1883 Year Book*, 551.
13 *Courier*, Aug. 23, 1862; Schirmer Diary, Oct. 11, 1862; *Mercury*, Oct. 13, 1862.
14 Parker, 292.
15 Samuel Jones, 145.
16 *O.R., Navy*, XIII, 579, 580; Samuel Jones, 146; Scharf, 676.
17 *O.R., Navy*, XIII, 593.
18 *Ibid.*, 582, 584.
19 *Ibid.*, 620.
20 Schirmer Diary, Jan. 31, 1863.
21 *O.R., Navy*, XIII, 577–78, 587.
22 Samuel Jones, 152; *Civil War Centennial Commission*, VI, No. 1 (January, 1963).
23 Bonham, 119; *O.R., Navy*, Series Two, III, 678.
24 Samuel Jones, 154; *O.R., Navy*, XIV, 231.
25 *Ibid.*, XIII, 588, 590, 597; Samuel Jones, 154.
26 Scharf, 680; Parker, 297.
27 Information from John G. Leland, Esq.
28 *O.R.*, XIV, 749.
29 *Ibid.*, 755, 757, 759, 765, 773, 781, 782, 799.
30 *O.R.*, LIII, 291.
31 Du Pont, 174; *O.R.*, XIV, 425; Dahlgren, 520.
32 *O.R.*, XIV, 769–70; *Southern Historical Society Papers*, IV, (1877), 147; Roman, II, 74, 478; Greeley, II, 470; Letter dated Apr. 15, 1863, from Captain Charles Haskell to his sister Sophy (Cheves Collection in South Carolina Historical Society); *Harper's Weekly*, Apr. 25, 1863, p. 258. *Illustrated London News*, June 15, 1963 [*sic*], 924.
33 *Mercury*, Apr. 11, 1863; Vizetelly, 222.
34 *O.R., Navy*, XIV, 5, 9; Du Pont, 189.
35 *O.R.*, XIV, 241, 269.
36 Vizetelly, 224.
37 Du Pont, 192; Snowden and Cutler, II, 759; Eldredge, 405; *O.R., Navy*, XIV, 9, 11, 21; *Leslie's*, May 2, 1863.
38 *O.R., Navy*, XIV, 3, 25, 111; *Ibid.*, Series Two, I, 159.
39 *Ibid.*, XIV, 23.
40 *O.R.*, XIV, 242.
41 *Ibid.*, 269, 273.
42 *Ibid.*, 276.
43 *Ibid.*, 241–42.
44 Inglesby, 9.
45 Vizetelly, 225; Johnson, 77.
46 *O.R.*, XXVIII, Pt. 1, p. 39.
47 *Ibid.*, XIV, 442.
48 *Ibid.*, 437.
49 *Ibid.*, 437, 897.

50 *Ibid.*, 440–41.
51 Davis, 196; Johnson, 43; *O.R., Navy*, XIV, 45, 52, 58; Roman, II, 76; *O.R., Navy*, XIII, 699; *Leslie's*, March 21, 1963. *Petrel, H.M.S.* log of, Public Records Office, Ashbridge Park, Berkhamstead, Herts, England. Record volumn Adm. Class 53, Piece Number 8312.
52 Johnson, lxiv.
53 *O.R., Navy*, XIV, 230.
54 Davis, 200; *O.R., Navy*, XIV, 33, 456; *O.R.*, XIV, 424, 469.
55 *Ibid.*, 1015, 1017.
56 Johnson, 77.
57 W. W. H. Davis, 198.
58 *O.R., Navy*, XIV, 112.
59 *Ibid.*, 25.
60 *Ibid.*, 257, 277, 438.
61 Johnson, 65.
62 *O.R.*, XIV, 902.
63 Johnson, 66.
64 *O.R.*, XIV, 926.
65 *O.R., Navy*, XIV, 300.
66 *O.R.*, XIV, 891.
67 *Ibid.*, 900–901, 451.
68 *Ibid.*, 917.
69 *Ibid.*, 923, 931.
70 *Ibid.*, 446.
71 *Ibid.*, 961.
72 *Ibid.*, 971.

CHAPTER 4

1 Eldredge, 247.
2 Price, 87.
3 *O.R.*, VI, 420.
4 *Ibid.*, LIII, 152; *Ibid.*, XIV, 881.
5 *Ibid.*, 610.
6 Gilchrist, 355; Johnson, 22.
7 *O.R.*, XIV, 975.
8 *Ibid.*, XXVIII, Pt. 1, p. 6.
9 *Ibid.*, XXVIII, Pt. 2, p. 6 [*sic*]; Gillmore, 22.
10 Palmer, 73; Gillmore, 22; *O.R.*, XXVIII, Pt. 1, p. 8.
11 *Ibid.*, 65.
12 *Ibid.*, 11; Gillmore, 26.
13 *O.R.*, XXVIII, Pt. 1, p. 71; Letter dated July 11, 1863, from Lt. Moultrie Horlbeck to Charles Haskell, Cheves Collection in South Carolina Historical Society.
14 *O.R.*, XXVIII, Pt. 2, p. 537; *Ibid.*, Pt. 1, p. 71; Dahlgren, 398.

15 Palmer, 84.
16 *O.R.*, XXVIII, Pt. 1, p. 12, 370; Dahlgren, 399.
17 Eldredge, 230.
18 Palmer, 86; Dahlgren, 399.
19 Johnson, 17; Eldredge, 305.
20 *Courier*, July 16, 1863.
21 *O.R.*, XXVIII, Pt. 2, p. 184.
22 *Ibid.*, Pt. 1, p. 415.
23 *Ibid.*, 210, 360.
24 *Ibid.*, 356.
25 Eldredge, 307.
26 *Courier*, July 13, 1863.
27 Price, 158; Emilo, 52; *O.R.*, XXVIII, Pt. 1, p. 11, 75; *Ibid.*, Pt. 2, p. 65, 194; Johnson, 96; Hagood, 138.
28 *O.R.*, XXVIII, Pt. 1, p. 74.
29 *Ibid.*, Pt. 1, pp. 75, 541.
30 *O.R.*, XXVIII, Pt. 2, p. 230; *Courier*, July 16, 1863.
31 Dahlgren, 401; Gillmore, 37; *O.R.*, XXVIII, Pt. 2, p. 20.
32 Johnson, 101; Jones, S., 217; *O.R.*, XXVIII, Pt. 1, p. 417.
33 *Ibid.*, 76, 417, 572.
34 Gilchrist, 365; Johnson, 103.
35 Dahlgren, 403; estimate by C. C. Pinckney (1961) as to area.
36 Eldredge, 314; *O.R.*, XXVIII, Pt. 1, p. 418; Johnson, 106n.
37 Palmer, 99.
38 Johnson, 101.
39 *O.R.*, XXVIII, Pt. 1, p. 525.
40 Emilo, 78.
41 Palmer, 104.
42 *O.R.*, I, 77.
43 Eldredge, 320; Palmer, 111.
44 *O.R.*, XXVIII, Pt. 1, p. 357; Palmer, 114.
45 *O.R.*, XXVIII, Pt. 1, pp. 406, 550.
46 *Courier*, July 18, 1863.
47 Eldredge, 316.
48 Emilo, 87; Eldredge, 316.
49 *Courier*, July 21, 1863.
50 Gilchrist, 371; Samuel Jones, 243.
51 *Courier*, July 18, 1863.
52 *O.R.*, XXVIII, Pt. 2, p. 22.
53 *Ibid.*, Pt. 1, p. 202; *O.R.*, LIII, 13; Palmer, 112.
54 *O.R.*, XXVIII, Pt. 1, p. 348.
55 Eldredge, 320.
56 Emilo, 5, 12; *O.R.*, XXVIII, Pt. 1, p. 362.
57 Eldredge, 327; Davis, 247.
58 *O.R.*, XXVIII, Pt. 2, p. 29.
59 Gillmore, 36.
60 *O.R.*, XXVIII, Pt. 1, p. 77.

61 *Ibid.*, 431.
62 *O.R.*, XXVIII, Pt. 2, p. 261; *Ibid.*, Pt. 1, p. 479; Dahlgren, 407.
63 Gilchrist, 384.
64 Dahlgren, 409.
65 Wells, 24.
66 Price, 178.
67 Gilchrist, 382.
68 *Ibid.*, 377.
69 Eldredge, 311.
70 Gilchrist, 381.
71 Gillmore, 154; *The Story of the Eleventh Maine Regiment*, 154.
72 *O.R.*, XXVIII, Pt. 2, p. 340.
73 *Ibid.*, 41, 71.
74 Honour letter dated Sept. 7, 1863, in collection of South Caroliniana Library; Eldredge, 362; Davis, 267.
75 Hagood, 189, 190.
76 *O.R.*, XXVIII, Pt. 1, pp. 26, 89, 118; Dahlgren, 413.
77 *O.R.*, XXVIII, Pt. 1, pp. 91, 106; Davis, 275.
78 Eldredge, 367; *O.R.*, XXVIII, Pt. 2, p. 86.
79 *O.R.*, XXVIII, Pt. 1, p. 327.
80 *Ibid.*, 3; Palmer, 71, 120.
81 Wells, 27.
82 *O.R.*, XXVIII, Pt. 1, pp. 619, 691, 694.
83 *Ibid.*, 688, 694, 699.
84 *Ibid.*, 690, 699.
85 *Ibid.*, 698.
86 Copy of a letter dated June 6, 1901, from John N. Gregg, former sexton, St. Philip's Church.

CHAPTER 5

1 Gething, Peter, Major, Australian Army.
2 Johnson, 180–89, 112.
3 Gillmore, 57; *O.R.*, XXVIII, Pt. 1, p. 607.
4 *O.R.*, *Navy*, XIV, 453; Johnson, 120.
5 *O.R.*, XXVIII, Pt. 1, p. 598.
6 *Ibid.*, 23, 611; *O.R.*, XXVIII, Pt. 2, pp. 57, 59.
7 *O.R.*, *Navy*, XIV, 501; *O.R.*, XXVIII, Pt. 1, p. 87.
8 Johnson, 131.
9 *O.R.*, XXVIII, Pt. 1, pp. 23, 598.
10 *Ibid.*, LIII, 93.
11 *O.R.*, XXVIII, Pt. 1, p. 23.
12 Gillmore, 143.
13 *Ibid.*, 83, 328; *O.R.*, XXVIII, Pt. 2, p. 311; Johnson, 135.
14 Gillmore, 329; *O.R.*, *Navy*, XIV, 528, 531, 560.

15 *Courier*, Sept. 3, 1863.
16 Johnson, 143.
17 Roman, II, 152.
18 *O.R., Navy*, XIV, 549.
19 *Ibid.*, 550.
20 *O.R.*, XXVIII, Pt. 1, p. 715.
21 *Ibid.*, 717.
22 *Ibid.*, 718.
23 *Ibid.*, 718.
24 *Ibid.*, 124.
25 *Ibid.*, 722.
26 *Ibid.*, 716.
27 *Courier*, Sept. 9, 1863.
28 *O.R., Navy*, XIV, 552.
29 *Ibid.*, 554.
30 *Ibid.*, 549.
31 Davis, 282.
32 Johnson, 158.
33 *O.R.*, XXVIII, Pt. 2, p. 344.
34 *O.R., Navy*, XIV, 633; *Courier*, Sept. 1, 1863.
35 *O.R., Navy*, XIV, 608.
36 Gillmore, 77; *O.R.*, XXVIII, Pt. 2, p. 288.
37 *Ibid.*, 89.
38 Scharf, 700.
39 *O.R., Navy*, XIV, 608; Johnson, 147.
40 *O.R.*, XXVIII, Pt. 1, p. 727.
41 *O.R., Navy*, XIV, 68; *Mercury*, Sept. 12, 1863.
42 *O.R.*, XXVIII, Pt. 2, p. 354.
43 Gillmore, 77.
44 *O.R.*, XXVIII, Pt. 2, pp. 367–68.
45 *Ibid.*, 371; Perry, 21.
46 *O.R.*, XXVII, Pt. 2, p. 374.
47 *Ibid.*, 389.
48 *Ibid.*, 382, 388.
49 *Ibid.*, 102.
50 *Ibid.*, 100, 105, 108, 134.
51 *Ibid.*, 103, 111.
52 *Ibid.*, 390, 503.
53 *Ibid.*, 392, 397.
54 *Ibid.*, 398.
55 *Ibid.*, 438.
56 *O.R.*, XXVIII, Pt. 1, pp. 602, 630.
57 Dahlgren, 420.
58 *O.R.*, XXVIII, Pt. 2, p. 446.
59 *Ibid.*, Pt. 1, p. 630.
60 *Ibid.*, 632.
61 *Ibid.*, 604.

62 Dennison, 195, 197; *O.R.*, XXVIII, Pt. 1, p. 632.
63 Roman, II, 167.
64 Dennison, 201.
65 *Ibid.*, 196; Dahlgren, 421; Gillmore, 156.
66 Johnson, 171; Dahlgren, 423; *O.R.*, XXVIII, Pt. 1, p. 632.
67 Johnson, 173; *O.R.*, XXVIII, Pt. 1, pp. 604, 669.
68 *Ibid.*, Pt. 2, pp. 484, 487, 489.
69 *O.R.*, XXVIII, Pt. 1, p. 604.
70 *Ibid.*, Pt. 2, p. 500.
71 *O.R.*, XXVIII, Pt. 1, p. 637.
72 *Ibid.*, 740.
73 *Ibid.*, 605, 665, 742; Johnson, 175.
74 Dennison, 196.
75 Johnson, 180.
76 *O.R.*, XXVIII, Pt. 2, p. 124.
77 Gillmore, 149; Davis, 285.
78 Gillmore, 156; Johnson, 185–86.
79 *O.R.*, XXVIII, Pt. 1, p. 644.
80 *Ibid.*, Pt. 2, p. 522; *South Carolina Historical Magazine*, Oct., 1963, p. 217.
81 *O.R.*, XXVIII, Pt. 1, p. 648; *Ibid.*, Pt. 2, p. 546.
82 Johnson, 194.
83 Johnson, 190.
84 *O.R.*, XXVIII, Pt. 2, p. 546.
85 *South Carolina Historical Magazine*, Oct., 1963, p. 217; Holmes, 236.
86 *O.R.*, XXVIII, 130, 136.
87 *Ibid.*, 94.
88 Roman, II, 472.
89 *O.R.*, XXVIII, 583–90.

CHAPTER 6

1 Letter dated Apr. 15, 1960, from Capt. Kent Loomis, U.S.N. (Ret.), Assistant Director of Naval History.
2 *O.R.*, XIV, 648, 661.
3 *Ibid.*, 670, 1019; *Journal of Executive Councils*, 272.
4 *O.R.*, XIV, 820.
5 *Ibid.*, 837; Johnson, clx.
6 *O.R.*, XIV, 837.
7 *Ibid.*, 843.
8 *O.R.*, *Navy*, XIV, 14, 688, 729.
9 Scharf, 690.
10 *Ibid.*, 693; Parker, 319.
11 *O.R.*, XIV, 926.
12 *Ibid.*, 965.

13 *O.R.*, XXVIII, Pt. 2, p. 191; Scharf, 696; *O.R.*, XXXV, Pt. 2, p. 342.
14 *Ibid.*, XXVIII, Pt. 2, p. 280.
15 Tablet on White Point Gardens (Battery).
16 *O.R.*, XXVIII, Pt. 2, p. 252.
17 Johnson, xciv; *O.R., Navy*, XIV, 498.
18 *Ibid.*, 497; Johnson, xciv.
19 *O.R.*, XXVIII, Pt. 2, p. 322.
20 Letter dated May 26, 1961, from Dr. P. K. Lundeberg, Division of Naval History, Smithsonian Institute.
21 Information from Isaac Bryan, grandson of Theodore D. Stoney; Sass in *News and Courier*, Feb. 24, 1957.
22 *South Carolina Historical Magazine*, Jan., 1964, p. 42.
23 Sass in *Harper's Magazine*, 1943, 622.
24 *South Carolina Historical Magazine*, Jan., 1964, p. 42.
25 *Ibid.*, Jan., 1953, p. 33.
26 Sass.
27 Johnson, clxii.
28 *Ibid.*, clxiii.
29 Snowden in *Sunday News*, July 16, 1905; *O.R. Navy*, XV, 18.
30 Johnson, clxiii.
31 *Southern Historical Society*, IV, 1877, 233.
32 Eldredge, 400; letter from Surgeon Alden D. Palmer of the Ninth Maine (owned by Mrs. John F. Culhane of Minneapolis, Minn.).
33 Roman, II, 181.
34 *Ibid.*, 182.
35 Dahlgren, 426.
36 *O.R.*, XXXV, Pt. 1, pp. 532, 603.
37 *O.R., Navy*, XV, 358.
38 *Ibid.*, 358, 405.
39 *O.R.*, XXVIII, Pt. 2, p. 420.
40 *Ibid.*, 525.
41 *Ibid.*, 575.
42 *O.R.*, XXXV, Pt. 1, pp. 546, 548.
43 *O.R., Navy*, XV, 733; *O.R.*, XXXV, Pt. 2, pp. 402, 406, 408.
44 *Ibid.*, 396.
45 *O.R., Navy*, XV, 719, 733; *Civil War Naval Chronology, 1861–1865*, IV, 44.
46 *O.R.*, XLVII, Pt. 2, p. 1201.
47 *O.R., Navy*, XVI, 338.
48 *Sunday News*, article dated January 16, 1895.
49 *The Submarine in the United States Navy*, Navy Dept., 1960.
50 *O.R.*, XXVIII, Pt. 2, p. 265.
51 *O.R., Navy*, XXVI, 187.
52 *O.R.*, XXVIII, Pt. 2, p. 285.
53 *O.R., Navy*, XIV, 513.
54 *O.R.*, XXVIII, Pt. 1, p. 670.
55 Honour letter in South Caroliniana Library.

56 *O.R.*, XXVIII, Pt. 1, p. 551.
57 Letter dated May 3, 1915, from W. A. Clark to W. G. Hinson in Charleston Library Society; *Confederate Veteran*, Sept., 1914, p. 398.
58 Hasker in *Confederate Veteran*, Oct., 1918, p. 459.
59 *O.R., Navy*, XIV, 497.
60 *O.R.*, XXVIII, Pt. 2, p. 351.
61 *Ibid.*, 376.
62 *O.R.*, XXVIII, Pt. 1, 145; Hunley letter in Citizens' File in National Archives Record Group 109. War Dept. Collection of Confederate Records.
63 Alexander in *Southern Historical Society Papers*, XXX (1902), 164.
64 Information from Confederate Museum, Richmond, Va.
65 *O.R.*, XXVIII, Pt. 2, p. 553.
66 Roman, II, 183; Name on Monument in Bethany Cemetery, Charleston, S.C.
67 *O.R., Navy*, XV, 334.
68 *Ibid.*, XV, 227, 238.
69 *Ibid.*, XV, 226.
70 Letter dated Feb. 5, 1864, from Dixon to Captain Cothran of Mobile.
71 *O.R., Navy*, XV, 327; *Civil War Naval Chronology*, Pt. IV, 23.
72 *O.R.*, XXXV, Pt. 1, pp. 112–13.
73 *O.R., Navy*, XV, 334.
74 Von Kolnitz in *U.S. Naval Proceedings*, Oct., 1937, p. 1455.
75 Roman, II, 529.
76 Extracts from the *Annual Report of the Chief of Engineers to the Secretary of War*, Washington, D.C., Oct. 20, 1873.
77 In Charleston Museum.
78 *Annual Report of the Chief of Engineers, U.S. Army, 1909*, Pt. 2, p. 1316.
79 *Southern Historical Society Papers*, Apr., 1878, p. 153.
80 Roman, II, 529.
81 *O.R., Navy*, XXVI, 187.
82 *Confederate Veteran*, (1914), 398; *State* (Columbia, S.C.), Sept. 13, 1914.
83 Olmstead, 13.
84 *Courier*, May 13, 1861.
85 *O.R., Navy*, Series Two, I, 60.
86 *Courier*, May 13 and 14, 1861.
87 *O.R., Navy*, V, 629.
88 *Courier*, May 14, 1861; *1883 Year Book*, 557; Smythe, 363.
89 Morgan, 100.
90 Roman, II, 55.
91 *Journal of Executive Councils*, 137.
92 Scharf, 480; *1883 Year Book*, 560.
93 Holmes, 432.
94 Freemantle, 147; Scharf, 483.
95 Marcus W. Price, 204.

96 *South Carolina Historical Magazine*, Jan., 1962, p. 40.
97 *News and Courier*, "Our Women in the War," Weekly 1885.
98 Scharf, 471; Morgan, 101; says 60 trips.
99 Marcus W. Price, 213.
100 *1883 Year Book*, 562–63.
101 *Ibid.*, 560; Scharf, 488.
102 Marcus W. Price, 205.
103 *Ibid.*, 202; *O.R.*, XXXV, Pt. 1, p. 31; *ibid.*, Pt. 2, p. 40.
104 Dahlgren, 532, 608; Soley, 108.
105 Scharf, 490; *Courier*, Jan. 20, 1865.
106 *O.R.*, XLVII, Pt. 1, p. 1015; Holmes, 465.
107 *1883 Year Book*, 561.
108 *O.R.*, LIII, Pt. 1, p. 1021; Scharf, 490.
109 Marcus W. Price, 237.
110 Scharf, 469.

CHAPTER 7

1 *O.R.*, XXVIII, Pt. 2, p. 511.
2 *Ibid.*, 57.
3 *Ibid.*, 58.
4 *Ibid.*, 59.
5 Vizetelly, 346.
6 *Ibid.*, 344.
7 *Courier*, Aug. 24, 1863; Holmes, 161.
8 *Courier*, Aug. 25 and Aug. 27, 1863.
9 Vizetelly, 344.
10 *O.R.*, XXVIII, Pt. 1, p. 30; *Courier*, Sept. 17, 1864.
11 *Ibid.*, Aug. 25, 1863.
12 *Story of the Eleventh Maine*, 139 ff.
13 Davis in Hinson Collection in Charleston Library Society.
14 *O.R.*, XXVIII, Pt. 1, p. 599.
15 *Ibid.*, 683.
16 *O.R.*, XXVIII, Pt. 2, pp. 509, 512; Kershaw, 32.
17 *O.R.*, LIII, 106.
18 *Ibid.*, XXVIII, Pt. 1, p. 185.
19 *Ibid.*, 685–86.
20 Honour Letter dated Dec. 26, 1863, in South Caroliniana Library, Columbia, S.C.
21 *O.R.*, XXXV, Pt. 1, p. 137.
22 Gillmore, 85, 157.
23 *1896 Year Book*, 359.
24 Ravenel, 503.
25 Schirmer Diary, May 13, 1864.
26 *Courier*, Jan. 18 and 25, 1864; *O.R.*, XXXV, Pt. 1, p. 467.

27 *O.R.*, XXXV, Pt. 1, p. 6.
28 *Ibid.*, 135.
29 *O.R.*, XLVII, Pt. 2, p. 58.
30 Ravenel, 505; Morgan, 198.
31 Holmes, 127.
32 Honour Letter dated Aug. 22, 1863, in South Caroliniana Library, Columbia, S.C.
33 Cowley, 120; Samuel Jones, 197.
34 Schirmer Diary, Nov. 30, 1861; Holmes, 165.
35 *News and Courier*, "Our Women in the War," 1885.
36 Gilman, 507.
37 *O.R.*, XIV, 257.
38 Smythe, 142; *South Carolina Historical Magazine*, Apr., 1962, p. 35.
39 *News and Courier*, "Our Women in the War," 1885.
40 Holmes, 170.
41 *News and Courier*, "Our Women in the War," 1885.
42 Smythe, 124, 155.
43 Holmes, 298; *Ohio History*, LXXI, No. 1 (Jan., 1962), 250.
44 Holmes, 240.
45 Smythe, 363.
46 *Ibid.*, 130.
47 *Ibid.*, 153; Holmes, 274.
48 *Ibid.*, 86; Smythe, 363.
49 DeSaussure to Bonham, Hinson Collection, Envelope No. 1, Charleston Library Society.
50 Keller Diary in South Caroliniana Library, Columbia, S.C.
51 Holmes, 459.
52 Keller Diary.
53 *New York Times*, Sept. 5, 1863.
54 *O.R.*, Series Four, I, 1021; Perry, 5–8.
55 Scharf, 753.
56 *O.R.*, XI, Pt. 3, p. 510.
57 Scharf, 753; *Civil War Naval Chronology*, IV (1865), 55.
58 *Journal of Executive Councils*, 214.
59 *Ibid.*, 272.
60 *Southern Historical Society Papers*, III, 1877, 256; *North American Review*, II (Sept.–Oct., 1878), 207.
61 Roman, II, 13.
62 *Southern Historical Society Papers*, IV (1877), 147–48; Roman, II, 74; *O.R., Navy*, XVI, 411.
63 *O.R.*, XIV, 735.
64 *Ibid.*, 700.
65 *Ibid.*, 700; Roman, II, 48.
66 *O.R.*, XIV, 765, 769–70.
67 Greeley, II, 470; Scharf, 752.
68 Snowden and Cutler, II, 759; Eldredge, 413; *O.R., Navy*, XIV, 11; *ibid.*, XVI, 431; *O.R.*, XIV, 1017.

69 Roman, II, 478.
70 *O.R.*, XXVIII, Pt. 2, p. 195.
71 *Ibid.*, 293, 300, 311, 323, 336; *O.R.*, *Navy*, XIV, 766.
72 *O.R.*, XXVIII, Pt. 2, p. 290, 380.
73 *Ibid.*, 293; *O.R.*, XXXV, Pt. 1, pp. 539, 594; *O.R.*, *Navy*, XIV, 445, 515.
74 *Southern Historical Society Papers*, IV (1877), 226.
75 *O.R.*, XIV, 951.
76 *Ibid.*, 952; Vizetelly, 220.
77 *O.R.*, XIV, 948.
78 *Ibid.*, XXVIII, Pt. 2, p. 323.
79 *O.R.*, XIV, 826, 830.
80 *O.R.*, *Navy*, XIV, 584.
81 *Ibid.*, XVI, 378.
82 *Ibid.*, 355, 376–77.
83 *Ibid.*, 295, 375, 385.
84 *Ibid.*, 379, 386.
85 *Ibid.*, 380, 386.
86 *Ibid.*, 384; *O.R.*, *Navy*, XIV, 735.
87 *Confederate Veteran*, XXXII (1924), 98.
88 *Southern Historical Society Papers*, III (1877), 256; *Ibid.*, V, 155; Jefferson Davis, II, 208.
89 *O.R.*, XXXV, Pt. 1, pp. 109, 129.
90 *Ibid.*, 31, 111, 468, 602.
91 *Ibid.*, 466.
92 *Ibid.*, 598, 621, 113.
93 *Ibid.*, 545, 642, 369.
94 Henry, 315.
95 *O.R.*, XXXV, Pt. 2, pp. 361, 370.
96 *Ibid.*, 364.
97 *Ibid.*, 372.
98 *Ibid.*, 398, 423.
99 *Ibid.*, 404, 426.
100 *Ibid.*, 427, 434, 443–44; Bridge, 255–62.
101 *O.R.*, XXXV, Pt. 2, pp. 453, 490, 491, 513.
102 *Ibid.*, 34, 55, 59.
103 *Ibid.*, 428, 434, 440, 68.
104 *Ibid.*, 70, 72, 101.
105 *Ibid.*, 78, 92, 470, 471.
106 *Ibid.*, 489, 534, 493.
107 *Ibid.*, 495.
108 *Ibid.*, 532, 538, 153.
109 *Ibid.*, 154.
110 *Story of the Eleventh Maine*, 109.
111 Crawford, 471.
112 *O.R.*, XXXV, Pt. 2, p. 73.
113 *Ibid.*, 505.

114 *Ibid.*, 144.
115 *Ibid.*, 155.
116 *Ibid.*, 130.
117 *Ibid.*, 146.
118 *Ibid.*, 532.
119 *O.R., Navy*, XV, 551; *O.R.*, XXXV, Pt. 1, p. 2.
120 *O.R.*, XXXV, Pt. 1, p. 14; W. W. H. Davis, 314; Dennison, 259.
121 Higginson, 138.
122 Emilo, 204.
123 Ford, 36.
124 *O.R.*, XXXV, Pt. 1, p. 15.
125 *Ibid.*, 40.
126 Johnson, 218.
127 Dennison, 258.
128 *O.R.*, XXXV, Pt. 1, p. 41.
129 *Ibid.*, 261; *Courier*, July 4, 1864.
130 *O.R.*, XXXV, Pt. 2, p. 534; *Ibid.*, Pt. 1, p. 158.
131 *Ibid.*, 159.
132 *O.R.*, LIII, 361, 365.
133 *Ibid.*, XXXV, Pt. 1, pp. 14, 84.
134 *Ibid.*, Pt. 2, p. 570.
135 *O.R., Navy*, XV, 554; *O.R.*, XXXV, Pt. 1, p. 51.
136 *Ibid.*, 14, 52; Emilo, 212; *O.R.*, XXXV, Pt. 2, p. 553.
137 W. W. H. Davis, 326.
138 *O.R.*, XXXV, Pt. 1, p. 160.
139 *Ibid.*, 51.
140 *Ibid.*, 162.
141 *Ibid.*, 169; *O.R., Navy*, XV, 558.
142 *Ibid.*, XV, 558; *O.R.*, XXXV, Pt. 1, p. 164.
143 *Ibid.*, 164, 169.
144 Johnson, 217; *O.R.*, XXXV, Pt. 1, p. 169.
145 *Ibid.*, 85.
146 *Ibid.*, 255.
147 *Ibid.*, 267.
148 Dahlgren, 467.
149 Emilo, 214.
150 *Ibid.*, 215.
151 Dennison, 255.

CHAPTER 8

1 *O.R.*, XXXV, Pt. 1, p. 15.
2 Johnson, 225.
3 *O.R.*, XXXV, Pt. 1, p. 219.
4 *Ibid.*, 223.

5 *Ibid.*, 227; Johnson, 225.
6 Johnson, 227.
7 *Ibid.*, 228; *O.R.*, XXXV, Pt. 1, p. 232.
8 *Ibid.*, 230; Johnson, 231.
9 *O.R.*, XXXV, Pt. 2, pp. 191, 207.
10 *Ibid.*, 216.
11 *O.R.*, Pt. 1, pp. 238, 240.
12 Dennison, 255.
13 *O.R.*, XXXV, Pt. 1, p. 21.
14 Johnson, 234.
15 Gillmore, 149.
16 Davis, 302.
17 *O.R.*, XXXV, Pt. 2, pp. 241, 247, 23.
18 *Ibid.*, 284, 264, 276, 295, 320.
19 *Ibid.*, 617.
20 *Ibid.*, 629, 630, 632, 304.
21 *Ibid.*, 633.
22 Horn, 373; Henry, 392.
23 *O.R.*, XXXV, Pt. 2, pp. 635, 637.
24 *Ibid.*, 646, 649.
25 *Ibid.*, 636, 640.

CHAPTER 9

1 *O.R.*, XLIV, 875, 859.
2 Henry, 425.
3 *O.R.*, XLIV, 864, 869, 872, 877.
4 *Ibid.*, XXXV, Pt. 2, p. 328.
5 *O.R.*, XLIV, 877, 880, 885.
6 Henry, 421.
7 *O.R.*, XLIV, 880, 881.
8 *Ibid.*, 885, 889.
9 *Ibid.*, 890, 899, 901.
10 *Ibid.*, 903, 913, 911.
11 *Ibid.*, 416, 425.
12 *Ibid.*, 919.
13 *Ibid.*, 923, 927.
14 *Ibid.*, 933, 937, 940–41.
15 *Ibid.*, 952, 966.
16 *Ibid.*, 954.
17 *Ibid.*, 958, 963.
18 *Ibid.*, 963, 969, 974.
19 *Ibid.*, 506, 535.
20 *Ibid.*, 648, 657.
21 **Ibid.**, 985.

22 *Ibid.*, 991, 1000.
23 *Ibid.*, 993, 994.
24 *Ibid.*, 702.
25 *Ibid.*, 759, 819.
26 *Ibid.*, 843.
27 *Ibid.*, 1009.
28 *O.R.*, XLIV, 741.
29 *Ibid.*, 799.
30 *O.R.*, XLVII, Pt. 2, p. 97.
31 *Ibid.*, 122, 136.
32 *O.R.*, XLVII, Pt. 1, p. 1135.
33 Dahlgren, 492.
34 *O.R.*, XLVII, Pt. 2, p. 179.
35 Dahlgren, 495.
36 *O.R.*, XLVII, Pt. 2, p. 582.
37 Keller Diary; Johnson, 257.
38 *O.R.*, XLVII, Pt. 1, p. 1015.
39 *O.R.*, XLVII, Pt. 2, p. 1157.
40 *Ibid.*, Pt. 1, p. 1017; *O.R.*, XLVII, Pt. 2, p. 1159.
41 Dahlgren, 496.
42 *Courier*, Feb. 11, 1865; Johnson, 249.
43 *O.R.*, XLVII, Pt. 1, p. 1017.
44 *Ibid.*, Pt. 2, pp. 417, 1169.
45 Johnson, 251.
46 *O.R.*, XLVII, Pt. 1, p. 1023.
47 *Ibid.*, Pt. 2, 1179.
48 *Ibid.*, 403.
49 Keller Diary.
50 *O.R.*, XLVII, Pt. 2, p. 1195.
51 *Ibid.*, 1202, 1205.
52 Dennison, 295.
53 Smythe, 165; Johnson, 256.
54 Keitt ms in South Caroliniana Library, Columbia, S.C.
55 Dennison, 296.
56 *O.R.*, *Navy*, XVI, 258; Cowley, 163.
57 *O.R.*, *Navy*, XVI, 252; *Courier*, Feb. 20, 1865.
58 *Ibid.*, Feb. 20, 1865; 1859 *City Directory*.
59 Emilo, 283; *Courier*, Feb. 20, 1865.
60 *O.R.*, LIII, 61.
61 *Ibid.*, XLVII, Pt. 1, p. 1018; *Ibid.*, LIII, 60; Cowley, 169.
62 *O.R.*, XLVII, Pt. 2, pp. 473, 511.
63 Dahlgren, 514.
64 Cowley, 167.
65 Smythe, 164.
66 *O.R.*, XLVII, Pt. 2, p. 659; *Courier*, Feb. 20, 1865; Greeley, II, 702.
67 *Courier*, Feb. 20, 1865; Cowley, 172.
68 Smythe, 166; *Civil War Naval Chronology*, IV, 15.

69 *O.R.*, XLVII, Pt. 2, p. 491; Smythe, 166.
70 *O.R.*, XLVII, Pt. 2, p. 508.
71 *Ibid.*, 593.
72 *Ibid.*, 603.
73 *Ibid.*, 616.
74 *Ibid.*, 641.
75 *O.R.*, XLVII, Pt. 3, p. 72.
76 *Ibid.*, 272–73.
77 *O.R.*, XLVII, Pt. 2, p. 726.
78 Information from Mrs. Harriott Rutledge Seabrook (1963).
79 *O.R.*, XLVII, Pt. 2, p. 856.
80 *Ibid.*, Pt. 1, p. 38.
81 Russell, 584.

INDEX

A and A (bark), 242
Abbot, Trevett, Lt. Comdr., 127
Adams, Charles Francis, 246
Adams, John H., 1
Adams Run, S.C., 157, 285, 289
A. H. Thompson (schooner), 64, 68
Aid (guard boat), 22
Aiken, William, Ex-Gov., 202
Aimar, M. L., Capt., 82
Alexander, W. A., 228, 233
"Alligators," 270
Allston, Charles, Col., 14
"American Diver," 236
Amphibious assault, 38, 144, 155, 287, 292, 294, 315
Anderson, Richard H., Col., 64
Anderson, Robert, Maj., 6, 18, 36, 39, 55, 58, 61
Apprentices' Library, 82
Arsenal, Federal, 5, 8, 15, 320, 322
Assaulting arks, 300
Atlanta, Ga., 304
Atlantic Wharf, 219, 319
Augusta, Ga., 3, 91, 304
Augusta, U.S.S., 129

Bache, A. D., Prof., 84
Bachman, John, Rev., 2
Badger, Oscar C., Fleet Capt., 189
Baggott, James M., Sgt., 105
Balch, G. B., Capt., 88
Baltic (steamer), 48, 58
Baltimore American, 142
Baltimore, recruits from, 31
Barnes, John S., Act. Lt., 74
Barton, William B., Col., 165
Barton (steamer), 212

Bath House, 257
Battery Beauregard, 68, 70, 137
Battery Bee, 137, 318
Battery Brown, 185
Battery Gregg, 137, 164, 173
Battery Island, 63, 93, 115
Battery Lamar, 109
Battery Marshall, 235, 237
Battery Pringle, 285, 289, 291
Battery Reed, 107
Battery Simkins, 191, 287, 292, 315
Battery, The. *See* White Point Gardens
Battery Wagner, 118, 137, 155, 161, 216; evacuation of, 179; first assault on, 157; naval bombardment, 173; second assault, 163
Bay Point, S.C., 67
Beach Channel. *See* Maffitt's Channel
Beard, Henry, 233
Beaufort, S.C., 63, 66
Beauregard, A.N.T., Capt., 218, 223
Beauregard, P.G.T., Gen., 36, 55, 57, 75, 134, 144, 146, 149, 153, 157, 168, 172, 179, 199, 229, 232, 237, 279, 302, 306, 311; assumes command, 28, 116; leaves command, 64, 281
Bee's Ferry, 133
Belgium rifles, 286
Benham, Henry N., Brig. Gen., 108, 111, 113, 143
Benjamin, Judah P., (Confederate) Sec. of State, 77, 79, 87, 130
Bennett, Augustus G., Lt. Col., 319

363

Bibb, U.S.S., 275
Bier, George H., Lt., 128
Birney, William, Brig. Gen., 289, 290
Black, George S., Commodore, 226
Black Island, 256, 277
Blakely gun, 198, 320
Blockade, 84, 241, 248, 261
Blockade-runners, 65, 84, 88, 149, 216, 261
Blockade Strategy Board, 67
Block Island. *See* Black Island
"Bloody Bridge," 292
Bonham, Milledge L., Gov., 119, 265, 308
Bonneau, F. W., 244
Booms, channel, 97, 118, 135, 144, 274
Boyd's Neck, S.C., 307
Boyleston, S. Cordes, Lt., 146
Braddocks Point, S.C., 80
Bragg, Braxton, Gen., 198, 279, 306, 309, 311
Breach Inlet, 235, 243
Breaman, J. D., 240
British consul, 130, 253
Broad River, S.C., 91
Brockbank, Robert, 233
Broughton, Ensign, 319
Brown, J. E., Gov. (Ga.), 91
Buchanan, James, Pres., 8, 12
Buck Hall Plantation, 316
Buell, Don Carlos, Maj., 7
Bullock, James D., Comdr., 226
Bull's Bay, 209, 313, 316
Bunch, Robert, 130, 253
Burdens' Causeway, 293
"Burnt District," 258
Burt, Armisted, 61
Bushnell, David, 227
Butler, Benjamin F., Maj. Gen. ("Beast"), 107, 254
Butler, William, Col., 181, 303

Cairo, U.S.S., 271
Calhoun, John A., 75
Calhoun, John C., 182
Calibogue Sound, S.C., 80
Cameron & Co., 212
Cameron, Simon, Sec. of War, 31, 33, 61
Canadaigua, U.S.S., 237

Cane, Michael, 231
Cannon, J. Walker, 220
Canonicus, U.S.S., 318
Cape Fear River, N.C., 248
Cape Hatteras, N.C., 69
Capers, Ellison, Maj., 12, 107
Carlin, James, Capt. (civilian), 217, 226, 244
Carlson, C. F., Cpl., 235
Carmody, John, Sgt., 46
Carolina Art Association, 82
Castle Pinckney, 4, 13, 132, 318
Cathedral of St. John and St. Finbar, 82
Cat Island (Wando River), 275
Catskill, U.S.S., 138, 155
Champliss, Nathaniel R., Maj., 224
Chapman, Conrad Wise, 228, 234
Charleston and Savannah Railroad, 77, 92, 99, 117, 119, 133, 149, 285, 289, 307, 311
Charleston, C.S.S., 322
Charleston Daily Courier. See Courier
Charleston evacuated, 318
Charleston Hotel, 3, 252
Charleston Mercury, 2, 15, 20, 61, 87, 254
Chaulk, John, 219
Chesnut, James, Brig. Gen., 38, 289, 305
Chesterfield (steamer), 180, 273
Chester, James, Sgt., 46
Cheves, John R., Dr., 97, 118, 269
Cheves, Langdon, 138
Chew, Robert L., 35
Chicora (blockade-runner), 249
Chicora, C.S.S., 125, 146, 195, 212, 231, 268, 321
Chisolm, A. R., Lt. Col., 31, 38
Chisolm, J. J., Dr., 60
Christ Church Parish, 132, 316
Church Flats, 222
Churchill, W. L., 237
Circular Congregational Church, 82
Citadel Academy, 16
Citadel cadets, 16, 18, 56, 284, 288, 308
Clark, Tillman H., Capt., 294
Clingman, Thomas L., Brig. Gen., 230
Clyde Bank (Scotland), 246

Cobb, Howell, Maj. Gen., 305
Colcock, Charles J., Col., 307
Cole's Island, S.C., 63, 92, 100,
    115, 148, 315
Colhoun, Edmund R., Comdr., 191
Colt, A. H., Capt., 4
Columbia, S.C., 3
Commodore MacDonough, *U.S.S.*,
    123, 291, 315
Confederate Congress, 110
Confederate Torpedo Service, 275,
    276
Conflagration (Dec., 1861), 80
Connecticut troops
    6th Connecticut Infantry, 155,
        164
    7th Connecticut Infantry, 105,
        155
Conover, F. S., Act. Lt., 123
Cooper River, 271, 273
Cooper, Samuel, Adj. Gen., 7, 79,
    114, 311
Coosawhatchie, S.C., 76, 89
Cordesville, S.C., 316
Cotton Press, 257
Cotton restrictions, 244
Courier, 124, 126, 156, 159, 161,
    167, 168, 193, 231, 233
Cove Inlet, 37
Coxetter, Louis M., 244
"Cradle of Secession," 84, 97, 284
Crawford, Samuel Wylie, Surgeon,
    10, 39, 44
Cummings Point, 37, 43, 179
Cunningham, John, Col., 16
Cuskaden, Samuel, Capt., 318
Cuthbert, G. B., Capt., 44

Dahlgren, John A., Rear Adm.,
    155, 161, 172, 188, 194, 230,
    274, 282, 294, 320, 323
Dandelion (tug), 145
Dandy, George B., Col., 165
Dantzler, O. M., Lt. Col., 181, 237
David, *C.S.S.*, 198, 199, 219, 223,
    225
Davis, Charles Henry, Capt., 86
Davis, Jefferson C., Lt., 10, 19, 38,
    44
Davis, Jefferson, Pres., 26, 27, 38,
    56, 91, 134, 202, 226, 244, 266,
    279, 302, 306

Davis, Nicholas, 231
Davis, W. W. H., Col., 145, 180,
    248, 278, 300, 324
Dawhoo River, 270, 290
Dean, William B., Capt., 294
DeCamp, John, Capt., 223
DeSaussure, Wilmot G., Brig. Gen.,
    14, 200, 265, 308
Dewee's Inlet, 285
Dia Ching, *U.S.S.*, 286, 289
"Diver," 235
"Dixie," 208
Dixon, George E., Lt., 234, 236
Doubleday, Abner, Capt., 10, 24,
    44
Doyle, Frank, 231
Dozier, Wm. G., Lt., 214–215
Drayton, Percival, Capt., 75, 137
Drayton, Thomas, Brig. Gen., 75,
    90
Drummond lights, 22, 31
Drunken Dick Shoals, 213
Dunovant, John, Brig. Gen., 24, 26
DuPont, Samuel Francis, Rear
    Adm., 69, 84, 95, 117, 120,
    130, 135, 141
Duqucron, Augustus, Capt., 225

Eason, J. M., 125
Easterby, Samuel, 219
Ebaugh, D. C., 219
E. B. Hale, *U.S.S.*, 108
Echols, William H., Maj., 115
Edisto Island, 63, 100
"Edith" (Columbiad), 19
Ella Warley (blockade-runner),
    216
Ella and Annie (blockade-runner),
    243
Ellen, *U.S.S.*, 108
Elliott's Cut, 93
Elliott, Stephen, Maj., 189, 191,
    195, 202, 208, 317
Emery, Sabine, Col., 165
Enfilading Battery, 45
Ericsson, John, Capt., 271
Etiwan (steamer), 231
Evacuation of Charleston, 318
Evans' Brigade, 149
Evans, N. G., Brig. Gen., 91, 101,
    104, 110, 210, 279
Executive Council, 25, 27, 91, 97

Federal Arsenal. *See* Arsenal
Fernandina, Fla., 73, 254
Fickling, E. S., Lt., 217
Fielding, George, Pvt., 60
Fire barges, 48
Fire Brigade (Battalion), 282, 288
Fire companies, 284
Fire rafts, 31, 291
First Military District, 92, 279, 303
"Fishboat," 232, 239
Fishing Rip Shoals, 71
"Fish torpedo-boat." *See* "Fishboat"
Fitter, Sgt., 256
Flag, U.S.S., 129
Floating battery, 23, 37, 40, 64, 67
"Florida expedition," 278
Flynn, John, Pvt., 163
Folly Island, 99, 148, 149, 282
Folly Island Channel, 271
Forsyth, John, Col., 149
Fort Beauregard. *See* Battery
　Beauregard
Fort Elliott, 63
Fort Fisher, 248
Fort Hamilton, 25
Fort Johnson, 9, 11, 24, 43, 98,
　139, 191, 230, 285, 286, 287
Fort Lafayette, 221
Fort McAllister, 133
Fort Morris, 16, 20
Fort Moultrie, 4, 14, 19, 24, 137,
　191, 204, 318
Fort Palmetto, 63
Fort Pemberton, 98, 121
Fort Pickens, Fla., 35
Fort Pickens, S.C., 63
Fort Pulaski, Ga., 152, 164, 184
Fort Putnam, 200, 208, 299
Fort Ripley, 94, 132, 319
Fort Schnierle, 63
Fort Strong, 200, 206
Fort Sumter: 4, 35, 94, 140, 318;
　amphibious assault on, 195; eighth
　minor bombardment, 300; explo-
　sion in, 207; first great bombard-
　ment, 185, 187, 189; initial bom-
　bardment, 42; second great bom-
　bardment, 200, 206; third great
　bombardment, 296, 300; Union
　occupation of, 9, 11, 319
Fort Wagner. *See* Battery Wagner
Fort Walker, 68, 71, 121

Fort Warren, 221
Foster, J. G., Maj. Gen., 8, 20, 29,
　32, 187, 260, 283, 286, 294,
　314
Fox (blockade-runner), 249
Fox, Gustavus V., 30, 33, 58, 61,
　84
"Frame torpedo," 132, 274
Fraser, John, & Co., 216, 223, 229,
　244
Fraser, Trenholm & Co., 244
Freemantle, J. A. L., Lt. Col., 244
French, Rodney, Capt., 85
Frost, Edward D., Capt., 207
Fulton, Robert, 228

Gaillard, P. C., Lt. Col., 106, 108,
　162
Gallipoli, 183
Galway, James Edward, Pvt., 60
Garden's Corner, S.C., 77
Gardner, J. L., Col., 6
Garrison flag, 42, 51, 57, 196
Gas Works, 82
General Clinch (guard boat), 14,
　16, 22
General Milton (tug), 286
General Parkhill (ship), 243
Georgetown, S.C., 92, 316
Georgia troops
　Anderson's Brigade, 197, 199
　Georgia Battalion, 201
　Georgia Brigade, 293
　Georgia Militia, 307
　1st Georgia Infantry, 240, 305
　23rd Georgia Infantry, 180
　32nd Georgia Infantry, 166, 314
　47th Georgia Infantry, 104, 307
　63rd Georgia Infantry, 163
Geranium, U.S.S., 289
Germans' Turners Hall, 257
Gettysburg, 151
Gettysburg, U.S.S., 247
Gibbes, Lewis R., Prof., 31
Gibbes, R. W., Surgeon, 55
Gillmore, Quincy A., Maj. Gen.,
　80, 140, 153, 161, 194, 200,
　251, 254, 274, 282, 284, 314,
　320, 323
Gilmer, Jeremy F., Maj. Gen., 199,
　216, 280
Gist, S. R., Brig. Gen., 92, 101

Gist, William H., Ex-Gov., 12, 62
Glassell, W. T., Lt., 145, 213, 219
Gordon (steamer), 243
Gorgas, Josiah, Col., 198, 280
Gourdin, Robert N., 182
Governor (transport), 120
Graham, Robert F., Col., 155
Graham's Creek, 316
Grahamville, S.C., 307
"Grand drunk," 248
Grant, U.S., Gen., 282, 310
Gray, M. M., Capt., 272, 275
Greek fire, 255, 260
Gregg, Maxcy, Col., 25
Grey, Sylvester H., Capt., 158
Grimball's Plantation, 111
Grimball, Thomas, 102
Guard boat, 10
Gurney, William, Col., 288

Hagood, Johnson, Brig. Gen., 99,
    101, 107, 157, 166
Hale, T. S., Capt., 257
Halleck, Henry W., Maj. Gen., 153,
    171, 199, 282
Hall, Norman J., Lt., 9, 21, 51
Hallowell, E. N., Col., 310
Halsey, E. Lindsley, 29
Halsted, O. S., Jr., 260
Hamilton, D. H., 62
Hamilton, John, Capt., 22
Hammond, James H., 61
Hammond, Samuel Leroy, Capt.,
    172
Hampton Roads, Va., 69
Hand grenades, 158, 195
Harbor obstructions, 266
Hardeeville, S.C., 90, 311
Hardee, William J., Lt. Gen., 303,
    305, 317
Harriett Lane, U.S.S., 48, 58
Harris, D. B., Col., 118, 146, 184,
    224, 274, 302
Harrison, George P., Jr., Col., 293
Hart, Peter, 51
Hartstene, Henry J., Capt., 30, 55,
    77, 123
Harvey, James E., 36
Haskell, Charles T., Jr., Capt., 154
Hasker, Charles H., Lt., 231
Hatch, John P., Brig. Gen., 259,
    283, 289, 292, 294, 310, 323

Hatch, L. M., Col., 63
Hats, 265
Hattie (blockade-runner), 249
Hayne, Isaac W., 91
Haynesworth, George Edward, Ca-
    det, 18
Heine, William, Col., 282, 286
Henerey, W. S., 224
Hennessy, John A., Maj., 319
Herald (blockade-runner), 245
Hero (blockade-runner), 117
Heylinger, L., Maj., 215
Hibernian Hall, 83, 124
Higginson, Thomas W., Col., 154
"Highlanders." *See* New York
    troops
Hill, Daniel Harvey, Maj. Gen.,
    279, 311
Hill's House, 108
Hilton Head, S.C., 67, 100, 113,
    314
Hog Island Channel, 271
Honey Hill, S.C., 307
Honour, Theodore A., 230
Hospitals, 169, 265
"Hot shot," 47, 49
Hough, Daniel, Pvt., 56, 60
Housatonic, U.S.S., 129, 227, 229,
    236
Howard, O. H., Lt., 102
Hoyt, Henry M., Col., 287
Huger, Arthur M., Maj., 73
Huger, Benjamin, Maj. Gen., 7, 15,
    114
Huger, C. K., Lt. Col., 97
Huguenin, Thomas, Capt., 298,
    310
Humphreys, F. C. (military store-
    keeper), 15
Hunley, Horace Lawson, 232
Hunley (submarine), 227, 234
Hunter, David, Maj. Gen., 100,
    111, 135, 141, 143

Illustrated London News, 136, 254
Indian Chief (receiving ship), 233,
    234
Inglesby, Charles, Capt., 140
Ingraham, D. C., Commodore, 125,
    129, 213, 239, 282
Iron Battery, 44, 47

Isaac P. Smith, U.S.S., 70, 120, 222
Isabel (blockade-runner), 245
Isabel (steamer), 56, 58
Isle of Palms, 235
Ives, J. C., Col., 309

Jacksonboro, S.C., 285, 289
James, George S., Capt., 42
James Island, 91, 99, 111, 160, 282, 285, 286, 290, 315
Jamison, David F., 2, 23
Jeter, B. A., Lt., 107
Jockey Club, 263
Johns Island, 100, 285, 289, 292
Johnson, John A., Capt., 184, 208, 298
Johnston, Joseph E., Gen., 281, 289, 293, 313
John Street, 260
Jones, F. M., 212
Jones, Samuel, Maj. Gen., 58, 112, 280, 282, 289, 302
Jonquil (tug), 275
Jordon, Thomas, Brig. Gen., 212, 229

Kate (blockade-runner), 245
Keenan, Edward J., Lt., 102
Keitt, L. M., Col., 178
Kelly, John, 231
Keokuk, U.S.S., 138, 140, 145
Keystone State, U.S.S., 128
Kiawah Island, 198
Kilpatrick, H. J., Maj. Gen., 305, 322
King, Gadsden, Capt., 44
King's Creek, 290
Kitching, J. B., Lt., 107
Knight, Charles R., Lt. Col., 162
Kozlay, Eugene A., Col., 282

LaCoste, Adolphus W., 146
LaCoste, James, 146
Lady Davis, C.S.S., 81
Lamar, Thomas G., Col., 104, 108
Lamon, Ward H., 32
Land mines, 176, 197, 308
Lawton, Alexander R., Maj. Gen., 90
Lay, J. F., Maj., 302
Lead, 264

Lebby, H. S., 244, 249
Lee, Francis D., Capt., 63, 211, 223, 268, 272
Lee, Robert E., Gen., 76, 77, 87, 89, 91, 98, 154, 265
Lee, Stephen D., Capt., 38, 53
Legare Point, 122, 230
Legareville, 100, 292
Lehigh, U.S.S., 189, 200, 203, 291, 298, 315
Leopard (blockade-runner), 117
"Liberty Pole," 3
Lighthouse Inlet, 99, 154, 243, 272
Lincoln, Abraham, Pres., 31, 33, 59, 67, 68, 84, 114, 142, 241
"Little David." *See David, C.S.S.*
Little, Edward H., Capt., 165
Little Folly Island, 150, 153
Live Yankee (steamer), 217, 227
Lockwood, Robert W., 244
Lockwood, Thomas J., 244
Lodebar (school ship), 82
London Times, 60, 88, 325
Longstreet, James, Lt. Gen., 114
Looting, 322, 324
Louisiana troops
    Light Artillery, 292
    4th Louisiana Infantry, 103, 107
Lowndes, Edward, Lt., 287
Lyons, Benjamin, Lt., 105
Lyons, Lord, 89

Macbeth, Charles, Mayor, 3, 11, 157, 319
McClintock, James, 230
McCrady, John, Prof. (Capt.), 14, 90
MacDonough, U.S.S. See Commodore MacDonough, U.S.S.
McEnery, J., Lt. Col., 107
McHugh, Charles, 233
Mackay, E. R., Capt., 225
McKethan, H., Col., 162
McLaws, Lafayette, Maj. Gen., 281, 286, 317
McLeod Creek. *See* King's Creek
Maffitt's Channel, 22, 87, 88, 129
Magnolia Cemetery, 323
Magrath, A. G., Judge, 24, 36, 57
Magrath, W. J., 102
Magruder, J. B., Maj. Gen., 114
Mahopac, U.S.S., 319

Maillefert, Benjamin, 238
Main Channel, 86
Maine troops
  9th Maine Infantry, 155, 164
  11th Maine Infantry, 131, 254
Manigault, Arthur M., Col., 92
Manigault, Edward, Maj., 286, 315
Marblehead, U.S.S., 222
Margaret and Jessie (blockade-runner), 247
Margaret Scott (ship), 87
Marine Hospital, 82
Mariner's Church, 82
Marion (guard boat), 22, 25
Marion Square, 76, 319
Marshall, John, 233
Marsh & Son, 124
Marsh Battery, 177, 186, 254, 256
Mary Haley (schooner), 242
Maryland Historical Society, 219
Mason, James, Commissioner, 130
Massachusetts troops
  28th Massachusetts Infantry, 105
  54th Massachusetts Infantry, 164, 171
Massachusetts, U.S.S., 275
Maury, Matthew Fontaine, 266
Maynard Arms Co., 4
Meade, R. K., Lt., 11, 13, 19, 24, 38, 48, 60
Memminger, Christopher Gustavus, 26
Memphis (blockade-runner), 117
Memphis, U.S.S., 129, 222
Mercedita, U.S.S., 127
Mercer, Hugh W., Brig. Gen., 102, 133
Michigan troops
  8th Michigan Infantry, 105, 108
Middle Ground Battery. *See* Fort Ripley
Miles, William Porcher, 26, 53, 134, 212
Mills House, 4, 81, 82
Mills Wharf. *See* Atlantic Wharf
Mines, contact, 90, 135, 137, 200, 275
Mines, electrically controlled, 138, 273
Minho (blockade-runner), 247, 250
Minnesota, U.S.S., 267

Missroon, J. S., Commodore, 85
Mitchel, John, Capt., 149, 153, 192, 298
Mobile, Ala., 3
Monitor, U.S.S., 271
Montauk, U.S.S., 133, 155, 163, 271, 291
Montgomery, Ala., 26
Morgan, Guy D., 84
Morris Island, 16, 29, 38, 99, 151, 186, 251, 282; amphibious assault, 155; evacuation of, 179, 190; first assault on Wagner, 157; Neck Battery, 118, 152; second assault on Wagner, 161, 162
Morris Island Lighthouse, 85, 86
Morrison, David, Lt. Col., 109
Mortar batteries, 43
Mounted couriers, 173
Mt. Pleasant, 37, 236, 285, 318

Nahant, U.S.S., 138, 155, 203
Nance, William F., Capt., 230
Nantucket, U.S.S., 138
Nassau, B.W.I., 215, 246
Nathan, M. H., Fire Chief, 55, 254
Naval Battalion, Charleston. *See* South Carolina troops
"Naval battery," 185
Neck Battery, 118, 152
Negro firemen, 252, 321
New Bedford, Mass., 85, 87
New Hampshire troops
  3rd New Hampshire Infantry, 101, 106, 155, 164, 179
  7th New Hampshire Infantry, 170
New Ironsides, U.S.S., 135, 163, 188, 199, 216, 220, 229
New London, Conn., 85
New Smyrna, Fla., 66
New York Herald, 87, 142
New York Times, 17, 113, 266
New York Tribune, 99
New York troops
  Engineers, 105
  46th New York Infantry, 106
  48th New York Infantry, 155, 164, 169
  79th New York Infantry (Highlanders), 105, 109

100th New York Infantry, 165
103rd New York Infantry, 286
127th New York Infantry, 287, 288, 322
Niagara, U.S.S., 84, 242
Nicholson, J. W. A., Lt., 121
Nina (guard boat), 11, 13, 22
North Carolina troops
    31st North Carolina Infantry, 162, 165, 166, 170
    51st North Carolina Infantry, 162
Northeastern Railroad Depot, 321

Olmstead, Charles H., Col., 230, 240
Olustee, Fla., Battle of, 281
Onward, U.S.S., 95
Ordinance of Secession, 1, 82
Ottowa, U.S.S., 96, 129, 194, 221

Packet boats, 245
Paine's Wharf, 287
Palmetto flag, 20, 57
Palmetto State, C.S.S., 125, 212, 231, 321
Para, U.S.S., 291
Parker, Foxhall A., Comdr., 185
Park, Thomas, 233
Passaic, U.S.S., 137, 140, 185, 189
Patapsco, U.S.S., 185, 200, 272, 276, 313
Patterson, Joseph, 233
Pawnee, U.S.S., 48, 58, 222, 272, 291
Payne, John, Lt., 230, 231
Pee Dee River shipyard, 225
Pemberton, John C., Lt. Gen., 91, 96, 154
Pembina, U.S.S., 96
Pennsylvania troops
    52nd Pennsylvania Infantry, 287, 318
    76th Pennsylvania Infantry, 155, 164
    100th Pennsylvania Infantry (Roundheads), 105
    104th Pennsylvania Infantry, 248, 324
Petrel, H.M.S., 130, 142
Pettigrew, J. Johnston, Col., 12
Phoenix Fire Company, 259

Pickens, Francis W., Gov., 2, 8, 12, 16, 27, 62, 75, 77, 92, 98, 101
Pickering, Charles W., Capt., 237
Pikes, 97
Pilings, 63, 133
Pilot boat, 21
Pilot fees, 246
Pinckney, C. C., Capt., 181
Pinckney Mansion, 81
Pinckney, Mrs., 81
Pinckney, R. S., Lt., 266
Pinckney Street, 252
Planter (steamer), 75, 93
Pocahontas, U.S.S., 58, 75
Pocotaligo, S. C., 91, 157, 308
Pon Pon River, 270
"Poor Man's Hole," 273
Porter, Benjamin H., Ensign, 196
Porter, David Dixon, Rear Adm., 269, 312
Port Royal, 64, 66, 76, 86, 100, 282, 285
Poulnot, W. P., 226
Powder rafts, 299
Powhatan, U.S.S., 58, 213
Presto (blockade-runner), 247
Preston, William, Lt., 51
Price's Inlet, 285
Prices of commodities, 263, 317
Pringle, Robert, Capt., 173
Prioleau, Charles K., 40
Pryor, Roger, 41, 53, 54, 57
Putnam, H. S., Col., 163, 170

Quaker City, U.S.S., 128
Quinine, 247

Racer, U.S.S., 291
Railroads. *See* Charleston and Savannah Railroad
Raines torpedoes, 133, 149
Rains, G. J., Brig. Gen., 197, 267, 276
Ramsay, David, Maj., 163
Randlett, James F., Capt., 179
Randolph, George W., Sec., 102, 267
Ransom, Robert, Maj. Gen., 303, 305
Rantowles Creek, 289
"Rat holes," 88, 161, 172
Rattle Snake Shoal, 88

Ravenel, St. Julian, Dr., 219
Readick, W. E., Lt., 163
Rhett, Alfred, Col., 144, 185, 189, 257, 303
Rhett, Robert Barnwell, 17, 87, 254
Rhind, A. C., Comdr., 139, 145
Rhode Island troops
    3rd Rhode Island (Heavy) Artillery, 106, 205, 287, 318
Riley, James R., Capt. (civilian), 181
Rion, James H., Maj., 161
Ripley, Roswell S., Brig. Gen., 19, 43, 57, 64, 77, 89, 117, 144, 172, 209, 232, 276, 280, 302
River's Causeway, 286
Rives, A. L., Lt. Col., 224
Roanoke, U.S.S., 267
Robertson, Beverly H., Brig. Gen., 283, 294
Robie, Chief Engineer, 148
Robin Hood (ship), 87
Rogers, C. R. P., Comdr., 74
Rogers, John, Comdr., 74
Roman Catholic Bishop, 83
Roman Catholic Orphan House, 82
Roper Hospital, 82
Rover (pilot boat), 243
Rowan, Stephen C., Capt., 59, 218, 222
Ruffin, Edmund, 44
Russell, Earl, 89, 130
Russell, H. P., sash and blind factory of, 81
Russell, William Howard, 60, 68, 325
Rutledge, John, Capt., 81, 127
Ryan, William H., Capt., 16, 166

Sabine, U.S.S., 121
St. Andrews Hall, 1, 83
St. Cecilia Society, 263
St. Michael's Alley, 257
St. Michael's Church, 2, 81, 254, 257
St. Paul's Church, 259
St. Philip's Church, 2, 129, 258
St. Stephens, S. C., 316
Sale, John B., Col., 309
Sales (of merchandise), 261
Salt, 264

Sandbags, 262
Sass, J. K., 268
Savannah, Ga., 22, 86, 265, 289, 308, 309
Savannah River, 90
Saxton, Rufus, Brig. Gen., 293, 301
Schimmelfennig, Alexander, Brig. Gen., 278, 282, 291, 295, 299, 310, 322
Schnierle, John, Maj. Gen., 16
Scotch gingham, 262
Scotia (blockade-runner), 118
Seabrooks Island, 148, 289
Secessionville, Battle of, 97, 98, 105, 111, 112
Second Presbyterian Church, 259
Sellmer, Charles, Lt., 254
Seneca, U.S.S., 90
Serrell, Edward W., Col., 255
Seward, William H., Sec. of State, 89, 144, 242
Sewee Bay, 316
Seymour, Truman, Brig. Gen., 144, 149, 163, 165
Shaw, Robert Gould, Col., 165, 171
Sheliha, Victor Von, Lt. Col., 225
Shell Point, 192
Shelton, William, Sgt., 163
Sherman, Thomas W., Brig. Gen., 65, 69, 76, 80
Sherman, William Tecumseh, Maj. Gen., 304, 313, 324
Shoes, 263
Signal corps, Confederate, 164
Silver, 263, 323
Simkins, W. S., Cadet, 18
Simon, John A., Capt., 314
Simons, James, Brig. Gen., 43, 51
Skull Creek, S.C., 70
Slann's Island, 291
Slidell, John, Commissioner, 130
Smalls, Robert, 94
Smith, A. D., Lt. Col., 106
Smith, Gustavus W., Maj. Gen., 115, 307
Smith, Mr. (diver), 233
Smith, W. D., Brig. Gen., 103
Snyder, G. W., Lt., 51, 55
Soldier Relief Association, 262

South Carolina Executive Council, 23, 124, 212
South Carolina Institute Hall, 2, 82
South Carolina Railroad, 91
South Carolina Society Hall, 257
South Carolina troops
  Carolina Light Infantry, 13
  Charleston Battalion, 106, 162, 195
  Charleston Naval Battalion, 283, 288
  Citadel Cadets, 16, 18, 56, 284, 288, 308
  Fire Brigade, 282, 284, 288
  Fourth Brigade, 16
  German Artillery, 14, 76, 199, 283
  Irish Volunteers, 16
  LaFayette Artillery, 14
  Marion Artillery, 14
  Meagher Guards, 13
  Palmetto Battalion, 315
  Palmetto Guards, 44, 57
  Pee Dee Battalion, 106
  South Carolina Reserves, 305
  Washington Artillery, 14
  Washington Light Infantry, 13, 201
  1st South Carolina Artillery, 139, 257, 314
  1st South Carolina Infantry, 103
  2nd South Carolina Artillery, 283
  2nd South Carolina Cavalry, 294
  17th South Carolina Infantry, 16
  20th South Carolina Infantry, 180
  21st South Carolina Infantry, 155
  25th South Carolina Infantry, 172
  27th South Carolina Infantry, 205
South Edisto River, 270
Southern Torpedo Co., 224
Southern Wharf, 94
Spar torpedo, 212, 213, 214
Sprague, Charles, 233
Stanton, C. L., Lt., 231, 240
Stanton, Edwin, Sec. of War, 100, 113, 177
Star of the West (steamer), 17, 20, 35

"State" (gunboat), 125
State flag, 20
State legislature, 9, 244
State Marine Battery (Mine) Commission, 268
Stellin, U.S.S., 129
Stephens, Alexander, (Confederate) Vice-Pres., 26
Stevens, Isaac I., Brig. Gen., 74, 105
Stevenson, T. G., Brig. Gen., 164
Stevens, Peter F., Maj., 16, 18, 28, 44, 56
Stevens, T. H., Comdr., 194
Stillwagon, H. L., Capt., 127
Stone Fleet, 85, 88, 89
Stoney, Theodore D., 219, 224
Stono Inlet, 63, 96, 198
Stono River, 63, 92, 98, 99, 111, 285, 286, 291
Stono (steamer), 123
Stony Landing, 219
Strawberry Ferry, 316
Stringham, Silas, Commodore, 36
Strong, G. C., Brig. Gen., 155, 165
Stuart, James, 220
Submarine batteries (mines), 97, 212, 267, 272
Sullivan's Island, 37, 43, 236, 285, 314, 318
Sullivan's Island Channel, 88
Sumter County, S.C., 18
Sumter (steamer), 123, 180
Sunday News, 239
Susan G. Owens (ship), 243
Susquehanna, U.S.S., 72, 90
"Swamp Angel," 186, 255, 256
Swash Channel, 95

Talbot, Theodore, Lt., 24, 35
Taliaferro, William B., Brig. Gen., 160, 162, 286, 291
Tatnall, Josiah, Commodore, 70
Taylor and Goodyear, 266
Te Deum, 129
Terry, Alfred H., Brig. Gen., 154, 157
Thompson, John, Pvt., 52
Thompson (schooner), 64
Tomb, James H., Engineer, 219, 276, 305
Torch (ram), 211, 217, 226

Torpedo boats (rams), 216, 218, 226
Torpedo Bureau, 197, 267
Torpedoes (mines), 90, 92, 118, 142, 267, 271
Torpedo station, 267
Totten, Joseph G., Maj. Gen., 29
Tower Battery, 109
Townsend, J., 63
Trapier, James H., Brig. Gen., 23, 64, 76
Trenholm, George S., 246
Trenton, N.J., 256
Trezevant, J. T., Maj., 280
Tucker, John Randolph, Capt., 128, 203, 270, 283, 305
Tupper, James, Jr., Pvt., 205
Turner, J. N., Col., 187, 206
Turners Hall. *See* Germans' Turners Hall
Tyler, John, Ex-Pres., 26

Unadilla, *U.S.S.*, 96, 102
United States Coast Survey, 84
United States troops
9th Infantry, 17
21st Colored Infantry, 319, 322

Vandalia, *U.S.S.*, 121
Varing (revenue cutter), 85
Vicksburg, 112, 117
Vincent, Hugh E., 20
Virden, William H., 239
Virginia troops
Wise's Brigade, 197, 278
Von Gilsa, Leopold, Col., 282
Von Hartung, Adolph, Col., 282

Wabash, *U.S.S.*, 69, 71, 216, 223, 229
Wadmalaw Sound, 270
Wagener, John A., Col., 73, 76
Wages, 264
Wagner, Battery (Fort). *See* Battery Wagner
Wagner, Theodore D., 216
Wagner, T. M., Lt. Col., 108, 152
Walker, L. P., (Confederate) Sec. of War, 28, 33, 38, 40

Walker, W. S., Brig. Gen., 278
Wamsetta, *U.S.S.*, 289
Wando River, 132, 275, 285
Wappoo Cut, 118, 121
Waterloo Plantation, 293
Watson, Baxter, 241
Watson, Capt. (Royal Navy), 130
Watson, Edwin, 146
Weehawken, *U.S.S.*, 136, 155, 188, 190, 238, 271
Welles, Gideon, Sec. of Navy, 68, 84, 135
Whiskey, 101, 207
White Point Gardens, 132, 148, 189, 198, 260
Whiting, W. D., Capt., 221
Whiting, W. H. C., Maj. Gen., 27, 50, 62, 119, 133, 225
Whitney, B. A., 229
"Whitney Submarine boat," 229
Whitworth rifles, 174, 184, 202
Wigfall, Louis T., Col., 51, 53
Wigg, W. H., Capt., 139
Williams, E. P., Lt., 196
Williams, George W., 319
Williams, G. W. M., Col., 104
Willtown Bluff, 159
Wilmington, N.C., 248
Winan, Ross, 218
Winan's model, 218, 219
Wise, Henry A., Brig. Gen., 225, 278
Wissahicken, *U.S.S.*, 315
Wooden shoes, 263
Woods, Charles R., Lt., 17
Wool, John E., Maj. Gen., 12
Wright, Horatio G., Brig. Gen., 74, 99, 104, 111
Wright's River, Ga., 90

"Yankee Sympathizers," 169
Yates, Joseph, Col., 121, 139, 287
Yates, W. B., Rev., 60
Yazoo River, 271
Yeadon, Richard, 125
Yellow fever, 265
Young, Gourdin, 51
Young, Henry C., 2